AF805320

Studies in Art, Heritage, Law and the Market

Volume 11

Series Editors

Rachel Pownall, School of Business and Economics, Maastricht University
Maastricht, The Netherlands

Ana Quintela Ribeiro Neves Ramalho, Faculty of Law, Maastricht University
Maastricht, The Netherlands

Editor-in-Chief

Christoph Rausch, Faculty of Science and Engineering, Maastricht University
Maastricht, The Netherlands

Hildegard Schneider, Faculty of Law, Maastricht University
Maastricht, The Netherlands

Vivian van Saaze, Faculty of Arts and Social Sciences, Maastricht University
Maastricht, The Netherlands

Renée van de Vall, Faculty of Arts and Social Sciences, Maastricht University
Maastricht, The Netherlands

Lars van Vliet, Faculty of Law, Maastricht University, Maastricht, The Netherlands

Donna Yates, Faculty of Law, Maastricht University, Maastricht, The Netherlands

Advisory Editors

Bert Demarsin, KU Leuven, Leuven, Belgium

Hester C. Dibbits, Department of History, Erasmus University Rotterdam
Rotterdam, The Netherlands

Patty Gerstenblith, DePaul University, Chicago, USA

Susan Legêne, VU Amsterdam, Amsterdam, The Netherlands

Peggy Levitt, Department of Sociology, Wellesley College, Wellesley, USA

Simon Mackenzie, Faculty of Humanities and Social Sciences, Victoria University of Wellington, Wellington, New Zealand

Claartje Rasterhoff, Faculty of Arts and Social Sciences, Maastricht University
Maastricht, The Netherlands

Olav J. M. Velthuis, Faculty of Social & Behavioural Sciences, University of Amsterdam, Amsterdam, The Netherlands

Andrea Wallace, Law School, University of Exeter, Exeter, UK

Matthias Weller, Department of Law, University of Bonn, Bonn, Germany

The book series *Studies in Art, Heritage, Law and the Market* provides an international and interdisciplinary forum for volumes that

- investigate legal, economic, and policy developments related to arts, heritage, and intellectual property;
- critically assess how and for whom art and heritage values come about;
- promote novel forms of user engagement, participatory presentations, and digitalization of arts and heritage;
- examine the processes that transform cultural objects and practices into arts and heritage; and
- highlight new approaches in preservation and conservation science.

The series addresses a need for research and practice in the fields of art, culture, conservation, and heritage including a focus on legal and economic aspects. It deals with complex issues such as questions of authenticity and provenance; forgery and falsification; the illicit trade, restitution, and return of cultural objects; the changing roles of museums; the roles of experts and expertise; and the ethics of the art market.

Emiline Smith • Summer Austin
Editors

Researching a Rigged Game: Digital Approaches to Tracing the Illicit Trade in Cultural Objects

Springer

Editors
Emiline Smith
Scottish Centre for Crime & Justice Research
University of Glasgow
Glasgow, UK

Summer Austin
Institute of Archaeology
University College London
London, UK

ISSN 2524-7425 ISSN 2524-7433 (electronic)
Studies in Art, Heritage, Law and the Market
ISBN 978-3-032-02013-0 ISBN 978-3-032-02014-7 (eBook)
https://doi.org/10.1007/978-3-032-02014-7

This work was supported by University College London.

© The Editor(s) (if applicable) and The Author(s) 2026. This book is an open access publication.

Open Access This book is licensed under the terms of the Creative Commons Attribution-NonCommercial-NoDerivatives 4.0 International License (http://creativecommons.org/licenses/by-nc-nd/4.0/), which permits any noncommercial use, sharing, distribution and reproduction in any medium or format, as long as you give appropriate credit to the original author(s) and the source, provide a link to the Creative Commons license and indicate if you modified the licensed material. You do not have permission under this license to share adapted material derived from this book or parts of it.
The images or other third party material in this book are included in the book's Creative Commons license, unless indicated otherwise in a credit line to the material. If material is not included in the book's Creative Commons license and your intended use is not permitted by statutory regulation or exceeds the permitted use, you will need to obtain permission directly from the copyright holder.
This work is subject to copyright. All commercial rights are reserved by the author(s), whether the whole or part of the material is concerned, specifically the rights of translation, reprinting, reuse of illustrations, recitation, broadcasting, reproduction on microfilms or in any other physical way, and transmission or information storage and retrieval, electronic adaptation, computer software, or by similar or dissimilar methodology now known or hereafter developed. Regarding these commercial rights a non-exclusive license has been granted to the publisher.
The use of general descriptive names, registered names, trademarks, service marks, etc. in this publication does not imply, even in the absence of a specific statement, that such names are exempt from the relevant protective laws and regulations and therefore free for general use.
The publisher, the authors and the editors are safe to assume that the advice and information in this book are believed to be true and accurate at the date of publication. Neither the publisher nor the authors or the editors give a warranty, expressed or implied, with respect to the material contained herein or for any errors or omissions that may have been made. The publisher remains neutral with regard to jurisdictional claims in published maps and institutional affiliations.

This Springer imprint is published by the registered company Springer Nature Switzerland AG
The registered company address is: Gewerbestrasse 11, 6330 Cham, Switzerland

If disposing of this product, please recycle the paper.

Contents

About the Editors and Contributors

About the Editors

Emiline Smith is a Lecturer in Criminology at the University of Glasgow in Scotland (UK). She is a Fellow at the Centre for Criminology at the University of Hong Kong, and a member of the Scottish Centre for Crime and Justice Research, UK Blue Shield, the Trafficking Culture Research Consortium, and the Global Initiative Against Transnational Organized Crime. Combining a background in art history, archaeology, and criminology, Emiline's research concerns the protection, securitisation, and repatriation of cultural and natural resources. She fosters ethical, equitable collaboration between stakeholders in the protection of cultural and natural heritage and has widely published on these topics. Emiline has extensive experience in the Asia-Pacific region.

Summer Austin is a PhD candidate at the University College London Institute of Archaeology. Her doctoral research *Tut on Tour: 30 years of Demand Creation through Blockbuster Exhibition* investigates the role of blockbuster museums exhibitions and how they influence the demand for cultural heritage on the market and the consequences for such demand. Summer holds an Art History MSc in Collecting and Provenance in an International Context from the University of Glasgow, and MSc in Archaeology from the University of Edinburgh. Her research interests include the art and antiquities market, looting and trafficking of cultural and natural resources, museums and the market, ethics of ownership, art crime and cultural heritage law.

Contributors

Summer Austin Institute of Archaeology, University College London, London, UK

Richard A. D. Bott Department of History and Archaeology, Levels 1 and 2, Arts Precinct 25B, Wally's Walk, Macquarie University, Macquarie Park, NSW, Australia

Neil Brodie, Brighton, UK

Michelle D. Fabiani Department of Criminal Justice, University of New Haven, Henry C. Lee College of Criminal Justice and Forensic Sciences, West Haven, CT, USA

Michela De Bernardin Italian Institute of Technology (IIT) - Centre for Cultural Heritage Technology, Venice, Italy

Sara Ferro Italian Institute of Technology (IIT) - Centre for Cultural Heritage Technology, Venice, Italy

Riccardo Giovanelli Italian Institute of Technology (IIT) - Centre for Cultural Heritage Technology, Venice, Italy

Madison Leeson Italian Institute of Technology (IIT) - Centre for Cultural Heritage Technology, Venice, Italy

Isobel MacDonald Department of Greece and Rome, British Museum, London, UK

Melissa Metzgar American University of Rome, Rome, Italy

Mathilde Mura UMR 7041 ArScAn VEPMO and Archaïos, Paris, France

Bureau 278 UMR7299 Centre Camille Jullian Maison méditerranéenne des sciences de l'homme, Aix-en-Provence Cedex 2, France

Valerio Scuro Independent Scholar, Rome, Italy

Petra Seitz Bartlett School of Architecture, University College London, London, UK

Emiline Smith Scottish Centre for Crime & Justice Research, University of Glasgow, Glasgow, UK

Arianna Traviglia Italian Institute of Technology (IIT) - Centre for Cultural Heritage Technology, Venice, Italy

Laurel Zuckerman, Bry-sur-Marne, France

Introduction

Emiline Smith and Summer Austin

The illicit trade in cultural heritage is a serious transnational crime that deprives communities of their history and identity, erodes public trust, and undermines public institutions. To respond to this multifaceted challenge, researchers must operate at the intersection of law, archaeology, art history, digital forensics, and data science. This has brought renewed attention to the value and complexity of digital approaches for mapping the illicit trade of cultural objects. Increasingly, digital data has proven a valuable resource in studying the physical and digital movement of objects, as well as the social networks underpinning them, and their potentially illicit and unethical entanglements. This volume foregrounds these digital approaches, including but not limited to open data, open-source intelligence (OSINT), open-access scholarship, computational forensics, and archival digitisation, as core tools in a growing, interdisciplinary effort to combat the illicit trade of cultural objects.

Drawing from a diverse group of researchers and practitioners, this volume explores methodological, ethical and disciplinary considerations in the use of digital data to research the trade and transfer of cultural objects. As such, it will serve as an instructional guide to anyone who is interested in doing research on these topics. However, the content of these diverse chapters extends far beyond comprehensive methodological instruction; they also provide critical insights into the strengths and weaknesses of proposed methodological approaches, and offer thoughtful, nuanced discussions about ethical considerations, researcher positionality and the role of privilege in conducting research on these topics and employing proposed

E. Smith (✉)
Scottish Centre for Crime and Justice Research, University of Glasgow, Glasgow, UK
e-mail: Emiline.Smith@glasgow.ac.uk

S. Austin
Institute of Archaeology, University College London, London, UK
e-mail: summer.austin.20@ucl.ac.uk

© The Author(s) 2026

E. Smith, S. Austin (eds.), *Researching a Rigged Game: Digital Approaches to Tracing the Illicit Trade in Cultural Objects*, Studies in Art, Heritage, Law and the Market 11, https://doi.org/10.1007/978-3-032-02014-7_1

methodologies. Each author contributes unique perspectives, expertise and methodologies, and each has access to different types of open data. This volume aims to bridge disciplinary gaps, emphasizing that disciplinary diversity creates a rich foundation of novel approaches and analytical frameworks to digital data in the study of (illicit) trade of cultural objects.

While digital approaches are often positioned as more efficient or expansive than traditional modes of inquiry, particularly when addressing the rigged nature of the market, they also raise pressing ethical, methodological, and disciplinary questions around access, safety, verification, bias, and collaboration. Digital tools enable researchers to identify, map, and verify the movement of objects across time and space. These digital approaches range from big-data applications to detect looting (e.g. Altaweel et al. 2023; Malinverni et al. 2024), employing satellite imagery to measure the scale of loss caused by looting (Casana and Laugier 2017; Lauricella et al. 2017; Vincent et al. 2024) and analysing social networks underpinning illicit trade (Fabiani and Marrone 2021), to more low tech approaches including the analysis of auction catalogues (Brodie 2014, 2019), public registries, and mainstream publications such as architectural magazines (see e.g. Cascone 2022; Whoriskey et al. 2022). For instance, the recent case of Douglas Latchford, a disgraced dealer of Asian cultural objects, illustrates how his digital footprint enabled researchers to trace several looted Cambodian statues featured in an architectural magazine (Woodman et al. 2022). Open access data may therefore include anything from information in public-facing archives to intelligence gleaned from deep, methodical online searches. However, as of now, there is no standardized methodology or set of moral and ethical guidelines for using digital approaches to investigate the illicit trade in cultural heritage. This is partly due to the lack of clear boundaries within the interdisciplinary field dedicated to studying these issues.

Digital approaches to investigating cultural heritage frequently encompass open data, open-source tools, open-access resources, and open-source intelligence (OSINT). While often used interchangeably, these terms carry distinct meanings that warrant further clarification. Open data refers to information freely available for use, reuse, and redistribution without technical or legal barriers. It reflects a commitment to democratizing access to knowledge (Janssen et al. 2012; Jati et al. 2022). However, the boundaries of openness are not always clear-cut. Online content, though publicly available, may include information obtained without consent through leaks, hacks, or third-party disclosures which raise significant ethical and legal concerns. While the open nature of these sources may invite a lack of constraint, researchers must still adhere to ethical and legal frameworks — particularly when engaging with platforms where users may have a reasonable expectation of privacy (UC Berkely 2022). In addition, some data, while technically accessible, may require specialized skills or tools to retrieve, rendering it effectively closed to the general public. Closed-source information, by contrast, includes data protected by legal or institutional restrictions but which may be obtained through formal mechanisms such as court orders or voluntary disclosures (UC Berkeley 2022).

Open source typically refers to software released under licenses that allow users to view, modify, and redistribute it with minimal restrictions. It promotes transparency, collaboration, and adaptability, enabling researchers to tailor tools to specific research needs or contexts. This is exemplified by the work of Yates and Graham (2024) who employed open-source approaches to investigate reputational laundering within museum databases.

Finally, open-source intelligence (OSINT) refers to the structured collection and analysis of publicly available data to produce actionable insights (Hassan and Hijazi 2018; Miller 2018). OSINT extends beyond data gathering and involves verification, contextualization, and ethical interpretation, making the distinction between raw data and derived intelligence essential for rigorous research. Triangulation of OSINT intelligence, particularly in contexts where such data might be used in scholarly, legal or policy proceedings, is vital (Murray et al. 2022; UC Berkeley 2022). For example, Fabiani (2019) deploys OSINT methods to examine the relationship between archaeological looting and various forms of conflict in Lower Egypt between 2015 and 2017.

While digital approaches offer new tools, they also bring new responsibilities. Digital investigations into illicit cultural heritage trafficking have undoubtedly gained prominence and influenced policy, but the rapid evolution of technology has created ethical challenges—related to e.g. privacy violations, consent, data security and unintended consequences—that require careful consideration. Digital does not mean equitable, nor ethical or even accurate, thus it is necessary for anyone employing digital information to consider the ethical, moral, and legal implications for digital data use and dissemination.

The ethical use of digital data depends not only on legality and public availability but also on contextual factors such as informed consent, cultural sensitivity, and researcher positionality. Researchers must constantly balance their investigative goals against individuals' right to privacy and potential risks to already vulnerable and underrepresented communities—particularly when researching sensitive or sacred cultural objects (González-Ruibal and Moshenska 2015). When researching these sensitive topics, we should be moving past the notion of 'do no harm' to the aspiration of 'do good' (Kersel 2023). In essence, we should adhere to a broader call for rethinking data care, ethical inclusivity, responsibility, and dignity (Koenig 2024), stressing the need to recognize existing inequalities while challenging online/offline exceptionalism, and slowing down to make more deliberate ethical choices (Guzman and Dyer 2020).

Furthermore, researchers must consider the asymmetries of access that shape digital knowledge production. Open access is not always synonymous with equitable access, particularly where bandwidth limitations, language barriers, and digital divides persist. At the basic level, access to these online collections is not universal or democratic. Varying levels of access (fully open-access, institutional, and paid subscriptions) present researchers with funding and accessibility hurdles that perpetuate the 'digital divide' (van Dijk 2006).

In addition, digital accessibility remains a critical yet often neglected aspect of collection interfaces, with many platforms lacking essential features for users with visual impairments including the absence of built-in magnification or text-to-speech tools, insufficient colour contrast options, and inadequate alternative text for images.

These shortcomings exclude a significant portion of potential users and should be addressed by institutions. As the field becomes more reliant on digital techniques, it must also remain vigilant about the assumptions, omissions, and power relations embedded in its data sources and analytical tools.

Finally, digital research is not without risk. Recent discussions around mental health in open data research have underscored the psychological toll such work can take on researchers, highlighting the need for clear coping strategies and institutional support (Dyer and Ivens 2020; Fenge et al. 2019). Resources such as the Dart Center for Journalism & Trauma offer guidance on managing these challenges (see also Fiorella 2022). In the context of cultural heritage, investigating the illicit trade in cultural objects can expose researchers to distressing material including graphic imagery of site destruction, detailed accounts of individual and collective harm, online harassment, and in some cases, potential exposure to criminal liability. As such, researchers are strongly encouraged to adopt precautionary measures to protect their digital and physical safety and overall wellbeing (Dubberley et al. 2020; Hassan and Hijazi 2018).

As digital approaches gain prominence in researching the (illicit) trade in cultural objects, this volume invites readers to reflect not only on the power of these tools but also on their responsibilities as researchers and stewards of cultural heritage. While such methods offer unprecedented accessibility, transparency, and potential to influence policy, the rapid evolution of technology has outpaced the development of consistent ethical frameworks. The chapters in this volume demonstrate how publicly available data—from street-level imagery and social media to auction records and museum databases—can, when rigorously verified, be used to investigate, quantify, and even prevent looting and trafficking across diverse contexts. Yet with these opportunities come significant challenges in data management, interpretation, and ethical use. This volume therefore aims to equip researchers and practitioners with the critical understanding and practical tools needed to apply digital methods both effectively and responsibly, in accordance with the legal and ethical standards of the communities and countries they engage with.

This volume emerged from a very successful online conference held on 14 and 15 September 2023, titled 'Researching a Rigged Game: Open-Source Data & the Trade of Cultural Objects'. We chose this title because the global trade in cultural objects can be considered 'rigged' in many ways: the lack of regulation and accountability within the trade makes it susceptible to manipulation, opacity, and other illegal and unethical practices. Moreover, this trade favours exclusivity and exploitation over inclusivity and equity, benefiting only those who know how to play this game well.

In curating this volume, we made a deliberate choice to spotlight the contributions of emerging scholars. Although research into the trade and transfer of cultural objects is growing, at its core are a limited number of established scholars, traditionally from the fields of law and archaeology. Yet as Rusbridger (2009, quoted in Cairns 2013) states, "it cannot be true that there are only a handful of people worth listening to in the world". This volume therefore presents multifaceted contributions from scholars at various career stages to stimulate novel methodological approaches.

However, we acknowledge the limitations of our perspectives and the need for greater inclusion of voices from origin communities in knowledge creation around cultural heritage. It is important that we hold space for such perspectives, and hope that this volume will serve as a valuable resource and catalyst for further discussion in this field.

Due to the interdisciplinary array of practitioners and academics who have contributed to this volume, we were particularly committed to equitable peer review which prioritized diverse perspectives and promoted transparency and fairness. We thus facilitated peer review amongst authors who were eager to do so, and promoted constructive, courteous and clear feedback in their peer review as well as our editorial review.

The following chapters provide a nuanced and thoughtful exploration of the exciting possibilities of digital research into the trade in cultural objects. Rather than adhering to strict categorical divisions, these chapters are interwoven by recurring themes. These unifying threads encompass novel technologies and methodological approaches, highlighting the extensive opportunities they present. Simultaneously, the chapters underscore the critical importance of data-driven approaches in examining the (illicit) trade in cultural objects. They place particular emphasis on the necessity of triangulating and contextualizing data to guarantee robust and dependable outcomes, which is especially important when researching sensitive topics like the trade in and transfer of cultural objects (see Fabiani and Smith 2025). Likewise, it is important to acknowledge the limitations of our sources and methodologies, including their inherent biases and the absence of data and voices. We should work to address these limitations and inequalities through collaboration and capacity building, attempting to bridge the digital divide. These interconnected themes showcase both the exciting possibilities, and the rigorous standards required in this field of study. It is our hope that the collective insights offered in this volume can chart a path forward: one that responsibly harnesses open-source resources to protect our shared cultural heritage and advance scholarly understanding of an often-opaque trade that operates for the benefit of a select few.

The volume starts off with a useful introduction of OSINT research by **Valerio Scuro**. Building on their extensive professional experience, Scuro outlines an array of OSINT tools, opportunities and considerations when employing OSINT methodologies as practitioner. They furthermore provide some helpful suggestions on how to apply these tools to open-source data research into the trade in cultural objects.

The following chapter, by **Michelle D. Fabiani**, expands on the foundations of the previous chapter by presenting an instructional account of one method of quantifying open-source data, basing this approach on the Berkeley Protocols on Digital Open-Source Investigations and their professional experience as a co-director of the Cultural Resilience Informatics and Analysis (CURIA) lab. The chapter provides a diligent, step-by-step introduction to the analysis of a spatiotemporal dataset, consisting of reports from the American Schools of Overseas Research Cultural Heritage Initiative (ASOR CHI), whilst applying it to analyse cultural violence in the Syrian Conflict. The chapter provides thorough insight into the opportunities and challenges of the proposed method, including legal, ethical and practical considerations.

The next chapter by **Mathilde Mura** provides a thought-provoking discussion of the possibilities of employing open-access spatial data to analyse looting pits. Mura analyses the looting pits as if they were archaeological objects or structures themselves, offering a novel approach to this type of analysis while building a typology of looting pits in the process. Building on three regional case studies in Syria, Iraq and Afghanistan, they highlight trends and patterns in looting practices and targets, which can contribute to more effective protection of archaeological sites at risk.

In their chapter, **Madison Leeson, Michela De Bernardin, Riccardo Giovanelli, Sara Ferro and Arianna Traviglia** provide an extensive description of the Research, Intelligence and Technology for Heritage and Market Security (RITHMS) project. They employ three case studies of public databases of stolen, missing, unprovenanced and protected cultural objects, i.e. the Federal Criminal Police Office of Germany's Securius database, the Association of Art Museum Directors (AAMD) Object Registry database, and several databases of WWII-looted cultural objects. The authors advocate for multifaceted methodologies, encompassing techniques such as social network analysis, natural language processing models and OSINT, to aggregate and interrelate data from various origins, ultimately leveraging this consolidated data to extract actionable insights into the trade and movement of cultural objects.

Shifting to institutional collections, **Laurel Zuckerman** presents a novel computational approach to detecting possible deceit within provenance text. Focusing on Nazi looted art, this chapter presents an accessible digital tool developed for counting words linked to unreliability, uncertainty or anonymity, which may indicate potentially deceptive language within institutional collections. Against a backdrop of personal loss, Zuckerman clearly articulates the need for both heightened scrutiny of provenance texts and calls for greater transparency on the behalf of institutional collections.

Further reflecting on institutional collections, **Isobel MacDonald** offers a thoughtful synthesis and comparative review of current data-driven scholarship engaged with diverse collection databases, before critically reflecting on both the value of yet inherent biases and limitations of institutional collections as a data source. Recognizing that these information assemblages are manufactured entities shaped by colonial legacies and biases, MacDonald argues that is vital that practitioners approach these sources critically and acknowledge the ethical challenges of data integrity and data absence. MacDonald calls on heritage institutions to prioritize cataloguing strategies that better represent the complex global histories, people, and communities to which the objects within collections belong.

Richard Bott examines the presentation of (in)authenticity of papyruses in institutional catalogues to better understand reliability of the information within collections. This study suggests the treatment of forgeries within collections is more nuanced than typically portrayed, although the reasons for presenting material as either authentic or inauthentic are frequently not transparent. The issue, then, is not that collections are unwilling to admit to owning forgeries, but that they do not record and share their reasonings material may be (in)authentic. As such, when forgeries are mistakenly presented as authentic, their legitimacy appears secure, and forgeries become harder to identify, damaging both the research corpus and confidence in the collection.

Petra Seitz's chapter offers an original contribution to the field of design history with an original methodological approach to the examination of Chandigarh Chairs using auction catalogues. Seitz' findings suggest that questionably moral and ethical—and perhaps illicit—practices surrounding the market for Chandigarh modernist furniture are ongoing. Equally enlightening is Seitz's discussion around the historic exclusion of designed objects as cultural heritage, rightly calling out the field for dismissing these objects from further ethical or legal considerations within the market.

Continuing the theme of auction catalogues, **Summer Austin**'s chapter offers a methodological approach to the use of digitised newspapers as a complementary empirical support for auction data. While the use of newspapers to research objects within the trade is a common tool for provenance practitioners, to date, there has been no published methodological approach or reflections on the use of newspapers as data for analysing the market for cultural heritage. Austin fills this methodological gap in the scholarship while also illustrating the potential for expanding the scope and potential for digital newspapers to not only contextualize objects and auctions but the market itself.

Following on the theme of markets and press coverage, **Neil Brodie**'s chapter offers a necessary examination on the use of investigative journalism for insights into the illicit antiquities trade. They rightly caution researchers and policy makers that the aims of investigative journalist are not always necessarily concordant with their own. Using press coverage of the ongoing case of thefts at the British Museums as their case study, Brodie demonstrates both the value and inherent limitations of investigative journalism. Context is everything, and while press coverage can offer valuable insights, it must be analysed and contextualized within the large picture.

Concluding this volume, **Melissa Metzgar** offers a useful legal prosecutorial focus by examining prosecuted antiquities trafficking cases in the USA from the MENA region, with the aims of both quantifying the impact of the illicit trade as well as measuring the effectiveness of a country's policies in reducing the illicit trade. Employing a quantitative data collection methodology, Metzgar's findings aptly illustrate that international conventions, bilateral restrictions, and US domestic laws are not reducing the illicit trade effectively and that the trade itself is not deterred by current policies, thus a need to reassess overall policy approach to combating the illicit trade.

As these chapters show, digital approaches clearly offer exciting new opportunities and insights for researchers investigating the trade in cultural heritage. This volume is but a first attempt at identifying and instructing on sources, methods and ethical and legal considerations for the use of open-source data. As we embark on an exploration of these digital approaches and their potential to research the (illicit) trade in cultural objects, we invite readers to consider not just the power of the tools presented here, but also their responsibilities as researchers and guardians of cultural heritage. We are excited to see the future directions of this field of enquiry, and how these initial chapters may further shape its development.

References

Altaweel M, Khelifi A, Shana'ah MM (2023) Monitoring looting at cultural heritage sites: applying deep learning on optical unmanned aerial vehicles data as a solution. Soc Sci Comput Rev 42(2):480–495. https://doi.org/10.1177/08944393231188471

Brodie N (2014) The antiquities market: it's all in a price. Heritage Soc 7(1):32–46. https://doi.org/10.1179/2159032X14Z.00000000017

Brodie N (2019) Through a glass, darkly: long-term antiquities auction data in context. Int J Cult Prop 26(3):265–283. https://doi.org/10.1017/S094073911900016X

Cairns S (2013) Mutualizing museum knowledge: folksonomies and the changing shape of expertise. Curator: Museum J 56(1):107–119. https://doi.org/10.1111/cura.12011

Casana J, Laugier EJ (2017) Satellite imagery-based monitoring of archaeological site damage in the Syrian civil war. PLOS ONE 12(11):e0188589. https://doi.org/10.1371/journal.pone.0188589

Cascone S (2022, October 16) An 'Architectural Digest' spread about two art collectors was photoshopped to obscure potentially looted cambodian statues in their home. ArtNet. https://news.artnet.com/art-world/looted-cambodian-art-architectural-digest-2160490

Dubberley S, Koenig A, Murray D (eds) (2020) Digital witness: using open source information for human rights investigation, documentation, and accountability. Oxford University Press

Dyer S, Ivens G (2020) What would a feminist open source investigation look like? Digital War 1(1–3):5–17. https://doi.org/10.1057/s42984-020-00008-9

Fabiani M, Smith E (2025) [in press]. In want of methodological rigor: a critique of Suber et al. (2022). Int J Cult Prop

Fabiani MD, Marrone JV (2021) Transiting through the antiquities market: a social network analysis of auctions. In: Oosterman N, Yates D (eds) Crime and Art, vol 1. Springer International Publishing, pp 11–28. https://doi.org/10.1007/978-3-030-84856-9_2

Fabiani MRD (2019) Building a baseline: unifying spatial and temporal methodologies to understand archaeological looting in Egypt [Digital Repository at the University of Maryland]. https://doi.org/10.13016/LNFJ-MKOP

Fenge LA, Oakley L, Taylor B, Beer S (2019) The impact of sensitive research on the researcher: preparedness and positionality. Int J Qualit Methods 18:1609406919893161. https://doi.org/10.1177/1609406919893161

Fiorella G (2022, November 23) How to Maintain Mental Hygiene as an Open Source Researcher. Bellingcat. https://www.bellingcat.com/resources/2022/11/23/how-to-maintain-mental-hygiene-as-an-open-source-researcher/

González-Ruibal A, Moshenska G (eds) (2015) Ethics and the archaeology of violence. Springer, New York. https://doi.org/10.1007/978-1-4939-1643-6

Guzman L, Dyer S (2020) 10 questions we're asking about ethics & open source research. The Engine Room. Retrieved 29 March 2025, from https://www.theengineroom.org/library/ten-questions-were-asking-about-ethics-data-and-open-source-research/

Hassan NA, Hijazi R (2018) Open source intelligence methods and tools: a practical guide to online intelligence. Apress L. P

Janssen M, Charalabidis Y, Zuiderwijk A (2012) Benefits, adoption barriers and myths of open data and open government. Inf Syst Manage 29(4):258–268. https://doi.org/10.1080/10580530.2012.716740

Jati PHP, Lin Y, Nodehi S, Cahyono DB, van Reisen M (2022) FAIR versus open data: a comparison of objectives and principles. Data Intell 4(4):867–881. https://doi.org/10.1162/dint_a_00176

Kersel MM (2023) Do the right thing. Levant 55(3):255–261. https://doi.org/10.1080/00758914.2023.2274666

Koenig A (2024) Ethical considerations for open-source investigations into international crimes. Am J Int Law 118:45–50. https://doi.org/10.1017/aju.2024.2

Lauricella A, Cannon J, Branting S, Hammer E (2017) Semi-automated detection of looting in Afghanistan using multispectral imagery and principal component analysis. Antiquity 91(359):1344–1355. https://doi.org/10.15184/aqy.2017.90

Malinverni ES, Abate D, Agapiou A, Stefano FD, Felicetti A, Paolanti M, Pierdicca R, Zingaretti P (2024) Significance deep learning based platform to fight illicit trafficking of cultural heritage goods. Sci Rep 14(1):15081. https://doi.org/10.1038/s41598-024-65885-6

Miller BH (2018) Open source intelligence (OSINT): an oxymoron? Int J Intell Counter Intell 31(4):702–719. https://doi.org/10.1080/08850607.2018.1492826

Murray D, McDermott Y, Koenig KA (2022) Mapping the use of open source research in UN human rights investigations. J Human Rights Pract 14(2):554–581. https://doi.org/10.1093/jhuman/huab059

University of California Berkeley (2022) In: Nationen V (ed) Berkeley Protocol on Digital Open Source Investigations: a practical guide on the effective use of digital open source information in investigating violations of international criminal, human rights and humanitarian law: advance version. Office of the High Commissioner for Human Rights

van Dijk JAGM (2006) Digital divide research, achievements and shortcomings. Poetics 34(4):221–235. https://doi.org/10.1016/j.poetic.2006.05.004

Vincent E, Saroufim M, Chemla J, Ubelmann Y, Marquis P, Ponce J, Aubry M (2024) Detecting looted archaeological sites from satellite image time series. arXiv. http://arxiv.org/abs/2409.09432

Whoriskey P, Woodman S, Politzer M, Sadek N (2022, 15 August) A luxury magazine photo hid relics Cambodia says could be stolen. The Washington Post. https://www.washingtonpost.com/business/2022/08/15/lindemann-cambodian-investigation-architectural-digest/

Woodman S, Politzer M, Whoriskey P, Sadek N (2022, August 15) Magazine spread of 'most beautiful house in America' conceals allegedly stolen Cambodian relics—ICIJ. International Consortium of Investigative Journalists. https://www.icij.org/investigations/pandora-papers/lindemann-cambodia-relics-altered-photo-magazine/

Yates D, Graham S (2024) Reputation laundering and museum collections: patterns, priorities, provenance, and hidden crime. Int J Herit Stud 30(2):145–164. https://doi.org/10.1080/13527258.2023.2284740

Emiline Smith is a Lecturer in Criminology at the University of Glasgow in Scotland (UK). She is a Fellow at the Centre for Criminology at the University of Hong Kong, and a member of the Scottish Centre for Crime and Justice Research, UK Blue Shield, the Trafficking Culture Research Consortium, and the Global Initiative Against Transnational Organized Crime. Combining a background in art history, archaeology, and criminology, Emiline's research concerns the protection, securitisation, and repatriation of cultural and natural resources. She fosters ethical, equitable collaboration between stakeholders in the protection of cultural and natural heritage, and has widely published on these topics. Emiline has extensive experience in the Asia-Pacific region.

Summer Austin is a PhD candidate at the University College London Institute of Archaeology. Her doctoral research Tut on Tour: 30 years of Demand Creation through Blockbuster Exhibition investigates the role of blockbuster museums exhibitions and how they influence the demand for cultural heritage on the market and the consequences for such demand. Summer holds an Art History MSc in Collecting and Provenance in an International Context from the University of Glasgow, and MSc in Archaeology from the University of Edinburgh. Her research interests include the art and antiquities market, looting and trafficking of cultural and natural resources, museums and the market, ethics of ownership, art crime and cultural heritage law.

Open Access This chapter is licensed under the terms of the Creative Commons Attribution-NonCommercial-NoDerivatives 4.0 International License (http://creativecommons.org/licenses/by-nc-nd/4.0/), which permits any noncommercial use, sharing, distribution and reproduction in any medium or format, as long as you give appropriate credit to the original author(s) and the source, provide a link to the Creative Commons license and indicate if you modified the licensed material. You do not have permission under this license to share adapted material derived from this chapter or parts of it.

The images or other third party material in this chapter are included in the chapter's Creative Commons license, unless indicated otherwise in a credit line to the material. If material is not included in the chapter's Creative Commons license and your intended use is not permitted by statutory regulation or exceeds the permitted use, you will need to obtain permission directly from the copyright holder.

Open-Source Intelligence (OSINT) for Researchers and Practitioners

Valerio Scuro

Abstract Intelligence is a powerful resource that is not only the exclusive prerogative of police, armed forces and government agencies, but it is also a valuable asset for analysts working in the private sector. The aim of this chapter is to provide an overview of open-source intelligence (OSINT) and its challenges and opportunities as part of a private sector analyst's operational experience applied to the analysis of companies and people. The sources, tools and techniques described can indeed be applied in many areas and contexts, including the analysis of actors and entities involved in the trafficking of cultural heritage. Furthermore, it presents an OSINT methodology suitable for practitioners and researchers who do not have access to law enforcement sources or classified information.

1 Introduction

Over the years, numerous definitions of intelligence have emerged, and many of these focus on the ability to acquire knowledge, apply it, solve problems, and adapt to the environment (Legg and Hutter 2007). This definition describes a cognitive process with several steps that humans engage in when facing new, unknown, or ambiguous situations and aim to acquire as much information as possible to predict the outcome of their actions. Beyond the individual level, organizations and countries also face situations of uncertainty that can impact people, citizens or employees, economic well-being, health, and safety. To address these challenges, organizations implement activities aimed at gathering information on topics of interest, their evolution, and the effect of possible actions to be taken. In this context, intelligence can be described as the process of collection, processing, analysis, evaluation, and interpretation of available information on a target, carried out by an individual or by a designed organization, whose output is a product that aims to reduce the level of uncertainty for a decision-maker (Bimfort 1958; Carlisle 2005;

V. Scuro (✉)
Independent Scholar, Rome, Italy

© The Author(s) 2026

E. Smith, S. Austin (eds.), *Researching a Rigged Game: Digital Approaches to Tracing the Illicit Trade in Cultural Objects*, Studies in Art, Heritage, Law and the Market 11, https://doi.org/10.1007/978-3-032-02014-7_2

Legg and Hutter 2007). The information used to support such intelligence can come from both open and classified sources.

The chapter aims to provide an introductory overview of the opportunities and considerations of open-source intelligence (OSINT). Unfiltered, raw information available from public sources is known as open-source data. While such data serves as the foundation for OSINT, they may not be immediately actionable in their original form. OSINT, on the other hand, is the result of systematically organizing and refining open-source data into a structured format. This transformed information consequently becomes valuable for various security-related activities and decision-making processes.

OSINT provides a wealth of publicly available information that can be leveraged to understand and track the illicit trade in cultural heritage, for example through social media monitoring, news and media analysis, and online marketplace surveillance (see Fabiani, this volume). Furthermore, OSINT research allows for network mapping of individuals and organizations involved in trafficking and provides contextual information for countries and stakeholders affected by or implicated in the trade in cultural heritage. Unlike classified intelligence, OSINT's open nature facilitates collaboration with diverse partners. It provides actionable intelligence to complement more traditional investigative methods, ultimately strengthening efforts to combat trafficking and theft of cultural heritage.

The following paragraphs will provide a critical overview of intelligence tools, methods, opportunities and challenges. The first part of the article contains the definition of intelligence, a description of its types, and the intelligence cycle. The second part, focused on OSINT, examines the different types of open data sources and proposes a classification based on their level of reliability, based on the author's experience as a private sector analyst. The third part examines some useful tools for conducting OSINT analysis and suggests a methodology that includes both the use of the data sources and the tools previously described. The final part presents some case studies of OSINT analysis taken from the author's work experience in the private sector.

1.1 The Intelligence Cycle

An intelligence analysis consists of different phases, the sequence of which is referred to as the intelligence cycle. Several conceptual models of the intelligence cycle exist (Jensen et al. 2017). However, generally, all analyses, from very simple cases of individual searches to more complex cases involving multiple stakeholders, contain several different stages, and each requires specific skills in order to be executed successfully (Phythian 2013). The intelligence cycle describes the steps involved in transforming raw information into finished intelligence for decision-makers and other stakeholders; this process applies not only to law enforcement and government agencies but also, in principle, to any form of intelligence analysis.

Several descriptions of the intelligence cycle have been proposed over time, depending on the number of stages listed in its composition (Phythian 2013; Sabry 2024). However, the intelligence cycle typically consists of five key stages (see e.g. Thomas Smith 2003): Firstly, there is the *Planning and direction* stage. This initial stage involves identifying intelligence needs and requirements set by decision-makers, including outlining sources, methods, and tools. If, for example, a private analyst is interested in investigating a news story about a company that is involved in the illicit activities, they must determine what information to look for, what sources to consult to find this information, and what tools to use to analyse it. Secondly, there is the *Collection* stage, when raw information is gathered from available sources. Continuing the previous example, the analyst will proceed to the collection phase, consulting the sources available to them, such as, but not limited to, public available databases and newspaper articles. In this way they will retrieve available data such as the names of directors and partners, names of other companies potentially linked to the illicit activity, addresses and other data. Thirdly, the *Processing* stage may involve converting the collected information, both unstructured and structured data, into a usable format through decryption, translation, or data reduction (Gibson 2004). In this phase, depending on the data obtained in the previous phase, the analyst may proceed to 'clean' the data: this may involve translation, decryption and data reduction to prepare the information for analysis. Fourthly, during the *Analysis and Production* stage, the data are integrated from multiple sources to identify patterns. This can be achieved by using, for example, software to link data together and to represent them graphically: a graph showing the evolution of a phenomenon over time, a network diagram highlighting connections between different entities or a geographical map where objects or events are positioned. This stage involves interpreting the significance of the gathered data and its implications. During the final step, *Dissemination*, finished intelligence is communicated to decision-makers in a format relevant to their needs. For example, a private researcher studying the illicit trade of cultural goods can disseminate the results of his research to other scholars, use it as a starting point for further investigation or send a report to the competent authorities of the country where an item originates from.

The intelligence cycle is designed to be a continuous, iterative process, with each stage informing and refining the others to produce increasingly accurate and relevant intelligence over time (Smith and Brooks 2013). Different projects will demand different intelligence collection disciplines, for which the 'intelligence problem' will be at the centre (Prunckun 2014). Understanding the intelligence cycle is crucial because, by knowing how intelligence is collected, processed and disseminated, individuals and organizations can structure their intelligence-gathering efforts, ensuring that they gather relevant information from all available sources and better assess the credibility and reliability of the information they encounter.

1.2 Types of Modern Intelligence

Since the twentieth century, with the advancement of technology, several specializations have been created within the intelligence sector, each focusing on different types of information collection and processing. The United States Department of Defense (DoD) categorizes the five primary intelligence disciplines based on their information sources. These disciplines are vital to national security and defence, providing critical insights into potential threats, vulnerabilities, and opportunities. By understanding the different types of information sources used by each discipline, policymakers and military leaders can make informed decisions and develop effective strategies to protect a nation (Thomas Smith 2003). While a researcher may not have access to all the intelligence sources available to government agencies, the following list provides a brief overview of the different types of information typically used in intelligence analysis:

- *HUMINT (Human Intelligence):* In the public security and military field HUMINT is a valuable tool for gathering information that cannot be obtained through other means (Trisolini 2020). It involves collecting information that are inaccessible to other methods from people as such as officers, agents, or informers.
- *IMINT (Imagery Intelligence)*: Intelligence collected by aerial/satellites images and geospatial information.
- *SIGINT (Signal Intelligence)*: Intelligence collected by means of intercepting and analysing electromagnetic signals.
- *MASINT (Measurement and Signature Intelligence)*: Intelligence collected by means of identifying the "signature" features of electromagnetic emissions.
- *OSINT (Open-Source Intelligence)*: Intelligence gathered from a variety of sources available to the general public, such as mass media, commercial information and visual imagery, official government reports, expert reports, and social media.

OSINT, SIGINT and HUMINT have dominated academic research (Henrico and Putter 2024). Although the definition of OSINT remains a matter of debate, this chapter considers the definition expressed by Coulthart and Nussbaum who, through a systematic literature review, define it as "legally obtained public or commercial information that has been validated, analysed and disseminated to fulfil an intelligence requirement" (Van Puyvelde and Tabárez 2025). This definition distinguishes OSINT by its reliance on legally acquired information, setting it apart from clandestine methods; its use of publicly or commercially available data, excluding confidential sources; and its purpose-driven nature, requiring a defined intelligence requirement, unlike other activities. Consequently, OSINT is typically employed by government agencies, private companies, and established civil society groups to address specific, identified needs.[1] This chapter focuses on the use of open-source intelligence (OSINT) in finding information on companies and individuals, which can be extremely beneficial in the study of trade of cultural heritage, for example when researching trafficking chains—whether physical, monetary or digital—and social network analysis. Some useful sources and tools for applying OSINT practices will be described below.

2 Focus on Open-Source Intelligence

There is a long history of gathering information for national security purposes (see e.g. Lowenthal and Clark 2015; Böhm and Lolagar 2021). However, with the proliferation of the internet, there has been an extraordinary growth of publicly available information: knowledge growth could even be doubling every 12 h in the near future (Pllana 2019, p. 32). Consequentially, OSINT has gained a position of great importance in the field of intelligence; so much so that Ghioni et al. (2023) have stated that OSINT is capable of meeting the majority of the information needs of law enforcement and intelligence services, i.e. between 70 and 90% of all contemporary intelligence material.

Today, a researcher or analyst from the private sector can perform valuable intelligence analysis when integrating online OSINT sources with offline material. There are several areas where OSINT can be particularly useful in the private sector: for example, when researching the details of an incident, such as where and how it occurred, who took part in it and formulating hypotheses about the reasons behind it trying to outline the trend or motivation behind a phenomenon (NATO OSINT Handbook 2002). Furthermore, OSINT can be useful in gathering publicly available information on a country, company or person—a particularly helpful tool when trying to outline how persons relate to each other (social network analysis) or to poll social opinion (e.g. Pastor-Galindo et al. 2020). In addition, OSINT can also be used to identify procedural vulnerabilities and potential intervention points for counter criminal endeavours (e.g. Senekal and Kotzé 2019; Chainey and Berbotto 2022). OSINT research has been especially beneficial in the study of cybercrime and cybersecurity (e.g. Tabatabaei and Wells 2016; Sari 2018; Hwang et al. 2022). As this Handbook shows, research using open-source data is a rapidly developing area in the study of trade of cultural objects, and so has much potential for intelligence related to cultural heritage.

[1] Interestingly, both the European Union and USA's Central Intelligence Agency (CIA) define open sources as those that are not classified, even if they are paid for (see e.g. European Union 2022; CIA 2024).

2.1 Categorizing Open-Source Intelligence Resources

One of the most challenging aspects of OSINT research is finding and accessing the data needed. The analyst-researcher of open sources, who wants to draw a complete picture about a specific event, country, company or individual, should be aware of the range of sources at their disposal. The following section outlines a wide range of sources available to the researcher, such as official registries, media, academic research, blogs, forums, and social networks. However, these sources must be triangulated: information found in one source should be confirmed by another source to avoid bias or misinformation and facilitate contextual understanding of the data (e.g. Dorton et al. 2019).

2.1.1 Official Registries

Public authorities possess a huge amount of detailed information that can provide the basis for comprehensive research. These official registries extremely valuable for investigators and analysts, as these databases offer comprehensive documents compiled by governmental institutions. However, there are vast differences in the ways in which data is recorded and what tools are used for recording, leading to cognitive and technical biases (Mariuta 2014; McDermott et al. 2021). Keeping in mind these limitations, these sources remain a valuable starting point for the collection stage, particularly when researching specific persons or companies.

2.1.2 Public Company Registries

Public company registries and commercial information providers offer valuable resources for uncovering connections within corporations.[2] By searching company names or other identifying data, these databases provide a wealth of information, including company activity, the identity of shareholders and directors, headquarter and branch locations, company's financial results including bankruptcies, and connected businesses. Each piece of information can be used as a starting point for further inquiries, expanding the understanding of the target entity.

By analysing leadership structures, physical locations, and individual affiliations, it is possible to uncover previously unseen relationships that might reveal overlapping interests, hidden agendas, conflicts of interest or even illicit activities. For example, art dealers involved in the illicit trafficking of cultural goods can create new companies to hide their identity and continue to operate on the market, without buyers being able to connect the company to their name (FATF Report

[2] A valuable link to the company registers of different countries is provided by the Institute of Chartered Accountants in England and Wales at https://www.icaew.com/library/research-guides/company-information/sources-by-jurisdiction.

2023). In this case, the researcher can use the data of public registers to undercover the involvement of a dealer behind newly established companies, and the potential involvement of other parties, such as collectors, restorers, transporters, etc. Similarly, analysis of the physical co-location of companies can offer illuminating clues: shared office spaces might hint at deeper collaborations or strategic partnerships, potentially influencing market dynamics and competition. Uncovering a competitor sharing space with a seemingly unrelated supplier could raise questions about potential collusion or non-compliance with non-compete agreements.

Revealing corporate connections can be a difficult task, as the available data and its granularity significantly vary depending on jurisdiction and corporate structure. While some nations oblige certain company types to publicly disclose their information, others offer less clarity or even permit anonymous company formation (e.g. Pacini and Stowell 2020; Montenarh and Marsden 2024). This necessitates an extensive understanding of the specific legal landscape and the type of company to maximize data accessibility.

2.1.3 Real Estate Registry

Beyond its function as a repository of property records, the real estate registry can provide analysts and researchers with a large amount of useful data. By querying the registry for a person or company of interest, it is possible to uncover a picture of their property holdings, including co-ownerships. This information can offer interesting insights into previously unknown connections based on shared ownership or other linked involvement, serving as a starting point for further exploration. Moreover, personal details in purchase agreements and inheritance documents can provide an understanding of past relationships, potentially revealing long-forgotten business dealings or familial ties.

2.1.4 International Sanction Lists

International sanctions lists are important tools for sustaining global peace and security, implemented by governments and international organizations. These comprehensive databases identify individuals and entities subject to restrictive measures due to recognized involvement in activities considered detrimental to international security or stability, such as terrorism, weapons proliferation, or drug trafficking (Clifton et al. 2023). Inclusion on a sanctions list carries significant consequences, as it prevents listed entities from participating in international trade and financial transactions. Assets held overseas might be frozen, travel restrictions implemented, and business relationships with reputable corporations hampered or blocked. In essence, sanctions represent a powerful tool for exerting pressure and influencing behaviour on the global stage. Two prominent examples include the European Union sanctions list and the United States Office of Foreign Assets Control (OFAC) sanctions list.[3] While each government maintains its own list, several commercial providers, such as Moody's, Dow Jones, and Lexis Nexis, offer consolidated databases aggregating data from numerous countries and international organizations, simplifying compliance efforts to search for the name of an entity on the sanctions lists of multiple countries at the same time. For entities engaging in international trade and finance, regular screening against sanction lists is not only a prudent safeguard but also a demonstration of due diligence (Preble and Early 2023). Sanctions lists can be a valuable resource for OSINT research, as they can provide crucial information about individuals and entities subject to restrictions. This can therefore be used for initial screening or risk assessments, as well as for network mapping and relationship analysis.

2.1.5 Court Trial Archives

To get a comprehensive understanding of the legal and reputational aspects of individuals and companies, court trial archives are an essential source. Some countries and organizations make these archives publicly accessible and searchable. Researchers can obtain key details about their target, such as associations in criminal networks, financial misconduct, or patterns of illicit behaviour potentially relevant to their analysis from these records. Analysing the names of individuals and companies mentioned within the proceedings can lead to the discovery of previously unknown associates, collaborators, or even co-conspirators.

2.1.6 Official Reports from Public Authorities

Documents published by public bodies such as government agencies and law enforcement contain research findings, statistics, and detailed reports on a wide range of topics, from country analyses and political organizations to security assessments and social situations. Some of these data could serve as both the foundation and supplementary elements for research into specific companies and individuals, although like official registries, these reports can be biased because of stakeholder priorities and resources.

2.1.7 Visual Imagery

Commercial images are a complementary source to documentary data that can provide visual verification of certain information or provide new research insights (Kovarik 2011). Images can be seen as a bridge between textual data and tangible

[3] OFAC's Sanctions List Search tool is available at https://sanctionssearch.ofac.treas.gov. EU Sanctions Map tool is available at https://www.sanctionsmap.eu/#/main.

realities on the ground. Commercial images encompass a varied landscape, including aerial, satellite and street-level views, to suit different needs and budgets: free services such as Google Street View provide readily available snapshots, while purchasable high-resolution satellite data allow for sharper detail. Historical archives can also provide valuable image data no longer otherwise available. By relating visual evidence with public records, media, and other investigative tools, researchers can paint a much clearer and more comprehensive picture of the subject at hand. For example, it is possible to conduct due diligence on a potential target individual, verifying their physical presence, assessing the scale of their operations, or gaining insights into their supply chain infrastructure, analysing their facilities, identifying potential risks, and gathering evidence to support your findings.

2.1.8 News Media

News media coverage can include events that are often absent from official registries, particularly regarding legal proceedings and corporate activities. Journalists, particularly investigative journalists, piece together narratives, enrich their reports with field interviews and use confidential sources, offering perspectives on hidden aspects of events not otherwise obtainable (Hunter 2011). In addition, articles often provide valuable details such as chronology of events and actions, descriptions and even personal information (Marsh and Melville 2019). These details allow researchers to cross-reference and deepen their analyses and gain a better understanding of the entities involved. For instance, the identification of personal data within articles can act as a key to link individuals to other sources, such as official records, allowing researchers to distinguish between individuals with similar names. An analyst who finds in an article the name of a person involved in illicit trade of cultural objects may have difficulty locating them in the public registers with accuracy if they has a very common name; but if, in addition to the name, the article also mentions the date of birth or other identifying features, it facilitates identifying the person in the public registers. This could uncover information such as whether the individual has been involved in illegal activities, is a member of a criminal network, or has been prosecuted or convicted in a court of law.

The location of a crime can be very important in understanding the nature of the crime itself: for example, if clandestine archaeological excavations are happening in the same place or in nearby places, it could be a sign that there is a specific interest in certain typology of objects (see Mura, chapter X). It could also mean that the site is not being adequately protected, or that there is a criminal group in the area targeting the site (Pastore 2011).

Media research can be done manually by searching the internet but also by using specialized databases: commercial online platforms as such as Dow Jones Factiva and Nexis Diligence+ offer extensive archives of diverse publications, spanning vast historical periods. These platforms provide access to both current and historical data, often covering newspapers, magazines, television transcripts, and radio broadcasts, giving the possibility to researchers to conduct in-depth investigations across various media types and timeframes. However, although news media can provide a valuable source of information, they can also be used to spread misinformation and 'fake news' which can have far-reaching consequences for OSINT research (see e.g. Mpala 2023; Oakley and Rogg 2024). It is therefore important to triangulate any news media used.

2.1.9 Academic Literature

Academic articles, essays and journals can contain valuable and reliable information. However, the specialized language and thematic focus can present accessibility challenges. Articles written by industry experts help provide practical insights and current trends through industry journals and trade publications, although potential biases aligned with the author's industry or affiliation necessitate careful evaluation. Peer review ensures a high standard in academic journals, while trade and general interest publications may require additional scrutiny.

2.1.10 Blogs and Social Media

With the rise of the internet, websites such as blogs, forums, and social networks have proliferated, generating a huge amount of data. This user-generated content presents valuable opportunities for researchers to uncover detailed information not readily available elsewhere (Golbeck 2015). However, extracting information from social media comes with ethical and practical limitations: for example, researchers need substantial platform expertise to effectively navigate and find relevant content, and critically evaluating user comments (Rønn and Søe 2019). This process can be time-consuming and further complicated by the subjectivity of user-generated content, while also raising questions about the standalone value of social media taken out of context (e.g. Trottier 2015). Beyond textual data, researchers can also obtain useful insights from multimedia content like videos and photographs, and this can be particularly useful when depicting locations, situations, or individuals of interest that the researcher might not be aware of beforehand.

2.2 *Evaluating Available Sources*

The pillars of any intelligence process are sources, software, and analysis. As mentioned above, an analyst must be aware that not all sources have the same degree of reliability. Intelligence units within law enforcement and government agencies commonly assess both the reliability of the source and the validity and accuracy of the information using formally recognized evaluation systems such as the 6×6 (see

Table 1 The 6 × 6 system from the Human Intelligence Collector Operations Field Manual by the US by the Department of the Army (Available at https://irp.fas.org/doddir/army/fm2-22-3.pdf)

Evaluation of source		Evaluation of information	
A	Reliable	1	Confirmed by independent source
B	Usually reliable	2	Probably true
C	Fairly reliable	3	Possibly true
D	Not usually reliable	4	Doubtfully true
E	Unreliable	5	Improbable
F	Reliability unknown	6	Difficult to say

Table 1).[4] Here, 'evaluation of source' refers to assessment of the credibility of the source, based on factors such as their expertise, experience, and track record. For instance, an expert in a particular field, regardless of their personal reliability and trustworthiness, may not be competent to understand and report information pertaining to another field of study. Evaluation of information then refers to the assessment of the accuracy and truthfulness of the information provided, based on factors such as its consistency with other sources, its level of detail, and its plausibility.

Employing Table 1, each data source can be assigned a grade based on the combination of the level of reliability of the source and the plausibility of the information itself: for example, a piece of information with value A1 would be far more reliable than another assessed as C3. These models are used by intelligence units to facilitate the collection, selection, and evaluation of information from a wide variety of sources.

3 Overview of OSINT Tools

Diverse software and platforms support analysts in the collection, visualization, and analysis of information, reducing the time required to analyse them and increasing the amount of information that can be processed. Among the tools that can be most useful to the analyst are search engines, visual analysis software, indexing platforms, and geographic analysis software. In addition, there are numerous tools available online, both free and paid, that allow the analysis and consultation of data of the most diverse types: IP addresses, Internet domains and subdomains, email addresses, phone numbers, usernames, Bitcoin addresses and more. The following section will introduce some types of these tools for collecting, visualizing and analysing research data and information, in order to provide an overview of their characteristics.

[4] See NATO "Communicating uncertainty, assessing information quality and risk, and using structured techniques in Intelligence analysis" (2016).

3.1 *Visual Analysis Software*

Visual analytics software, such as IBM's i2 Analyst's Notebook, Maltego, or Gephi, help to manage and to analyse huge data sets by employing interactive visualization technologies and human cognitive capabilities (Lavigne and Gouin 2014). For example, such software can create interactive graphs in which each node represents an element of interest (person, company, address, and so on); these nodes are interconnected by lines, symbolizing relationships such as ownership, management, residence, or personal ties. Such charts can be constructed manually or expanded dynamically through the automatic acquisition of data from a database. This integration enables seamless data visualization and research expansion with minimal effort and saves a great deal of time in creating an analysis perimeter. The true value of this approach lies in its ability to present the entire investigative context in a single, comprehensive picture that helps analysts identify potential targets, assess connections, and determine the need for further exploration (Tominski and Schumann 2020). For example, a researcher looking into suspected trafficking of cultural heritage by a company can exploit visual analysis by linking the software to the company register and obtaining a complete graph that automatically populates with relevant nodes representing shareholders, directors, and other connected companies. Exploring these connections could uncover previously unknown collaborators, potentially exposing a vast criminal network. An analysis could start with the graphical representation of companies mentioned in the provenance of lots included in auction catalogues, expanding the provenance beyond the mere name of the company, but instead to the complete corporate structure. Visualizing the connections between the company and its related entities may reveal red flags such as involvement in illicit activities, the presence of anonymous companies or companies based in tax havens.

3.2 *Search Engines*

In the expanded landscape of the internet, search engines are indispensable tools for researchers and investigators. Search engines continuously scan and index countless web pages, building a comprehensive map of the online world - although even search engines come with bias (e.g. Goldman 2006). Regardless of the platform chosen, a basic understanding of search engine functionality is necessary for researchers to become skilled navigators capable of finding, if they exist, the desired results, efficiently uncovering valuable information and conducting extensive investigations. For example, in order to refine a search, the analyst can use commands to be entered in the search bar that allow us to find results that are more precise and in line with what is desired. By adding text strings or symbols, it is possible, for instance, to search for pages that contain an exact phrase, to exclude pages that contain certain words, to search for files with a certain extension (pdf, doc, ppt, and so on), and to obtain results only from a specific site.[5]

Effectively combining search operators requires practice and various attempts in order to maximize desired results while minimizing extraneous information. However, search engines also present challenges because the huge volume of results can be overwhelming, requiring careful selection to identify relevant information. Additionally, ranking algorithms prioritize factors like page authority and backlinks, not necessarily information accuracy so that highly ranked results may not be the most reliable. To mitigate these limitations, researchers can employ indexing platforms for analysis of large text volumes, while focusing on critical thinking and verification techniques to ensure information accuracy.

3.3 Indexing Platforms and Databases

Beyond simple keyword extraction, semantic search engines based on Artificial Intelligence and indexed databases such as *Factiva* or *AlphaSense* demonstrate a high capacity for understanding, accurately identifying named entities such as people, companies, and places within the text (Subham et al. 2019). Furthermore, they can classify documents according to thematic content, identifying topics ranging from legal issues and economic reports to news articles and scientific publication. This functionality allows analysts to conduct precise and efficient searches: through the platform's filtering capabilities, analysts can find documents and articles on specific topics, relating to specific locations or featuring people of targeted interest. This significantly reduces search time and makes the investigative process faster. However, AI-enabled search engines inherently contain algorithmic bias: bias in humans leads to bias in AI systems (Evangelista et al. 2021; Kartal 2022; Plant et al. 2022). The use of AI should therefore be paired with an understanding of the potential bias of this system, and how this can impact decision-making (Osoba and Welser 2017).

3.4 Geographic Information System (GIS)

A geographic information system (GIS) is a system that creates, manages, analyses, and maps all kinds of geographical data (Pesaresi 2017). With a GIS system, it is possible to have a digital representation of one or more geographical maps and to add to them representations of a wide range of physical features (such as terrain types, altitude), socio-economic features (administrative boundaries, population

[5] The list of advanced search operators is available at https://support.google.com/websearch/answer/35890?hl=en.

data) and objects on the territory (buildings, natural features, archaeological areas). In addition to the representation of these elements, the GIS can store sets of attributes for each of them and perform spatial analyses that help the analyst interpret the phenomena of the examined territory (Salerno and Guandalini 2014). Such spatial data raises questions about privacy, transparency and digital equity (e.g. Curry 1995; Pickles 1995). One example of using geographic information system is to overlay events that have occurred in a specific geographic area and see how they are distributed spatially. For example, by entering events of cultural heritage looting with their geographical coordinates, it is possible to see where they are most concentrated and how the different types of looting and theft are distributed across a territory (see Fabiani and Mura, this volume). On the basis of this, an analyst can draw hypotheses about the looting taking place and propose to the decisionmaker tailored countermeasures (Chainey and Ratcliffe 2005).

The tools described above are by no means exclusive. As the data sources used by OSINT are open source, it is arguably the only fully legal method of intelligence collection, as long as it does not interfere with human rights (Hribar et al. 2014). Anyone can execute OSINT if they have access to the resources outlined above; the true value lies in the investigator's ability to interpret and contextualize data effectively. The distinction between rudimentary and comprehensive OSINT does not depend only on the accessibility of tools and data, but rather the quality of the analysis process.

Most importantly, these tools should be used in a safe and ethical manner. Operational security (OPSEC) is critical to any OSINT investigation, as it helps safeguard the techniques and tools used to gather intelligence and any resulting data. It also helps to keep the identities and activities of analysts secure. Following proper OPSEC procedures helps ensure intelligence research remains within legal and ethical boundaries (e.g. Rajamäki and Simola 2019). Key OPSEC practices for OSINT may include using secure, anonymized networks, employing dedicated research devices, careful management of digital footprints, regular security audits and updates, and proper data handling and storage procedures (e.g. Conway 2021; Lakomy 2023).

4 OSINT Application to Cultural Heritage Trade Research

OSINT can provide a valuable resource for researchers involved in studying a particular event, person, group or company. Its strength lies in the vastness of online sources and tools available: OSINT is a relatively low-cost, quick way of gathering intelligence. However, to fully utilize OSINT, it is essential to possess advanced and specific knowledge of the various sources and tools, as well as the ability to combine and analyse them effectively.

Applying OSINT to the trade in cultural objects can be particularly helpful in a multitude of ways: for example, when carrying out provenance research to identify and prove the origins of an object; when identifying stakeholders and stakeholder networks crucial for the illicit trade and trafficking of cultural heritage; when tracking the looting of a particular site or region; when analysing market trends so as to help identify a sudden influx of potentially looted material; or when monitoring online marketplaces and trade sites for illicitly-obtained cultural items.

The internet has dramatically altered the size and shape of the global trade in cultural objects, allowing new actors to participate, reaching a wider network of other potential stakeholders (Mackenzie et al. 2020). It has also given rise to new ethical and legal dilemmas, particularly with regards to the use of auction sites and social media platforms for the trade of cultural heritage and ancestral remains (e.g. Paul 2018; Huffer et al. 2019; Votey 2022; Huffer and Graham 2023). Because of the specialized nature of the cultural objects traded and the fluid structure of the network that supplies illicit cultural objects (Campbell 2013), OSINT takes on a heightened importance as it allows identification of illegal objects and practices in an otherwise legal market (Alder and Polk 2007) through both textual and visual data. We have only scratched the surface of the possibilities of OSINT in this field. By leveraging the OSINT tools and techniques mentioned in the chapter, analysts can gather valuable information to trace and counter the illicit trade in cultural objects.

References

Alder C, Polk K (2007) Crime in the world of art. In: Pontell HN, Geis G (eds) International handbook of white-collar and corporate crime. Springer Science+Business, pp 347–357

Bimfort MT (1958) A definition of intelligence. Stud Intell 2:75–78

Böhm I, Lolagar S (2021) Open source intelligence: introduction, legal, and ethical considerations. Int Cybersecur Law Rev 2:317–337

Campbell P (2013) The illicit antiquities trade as a transnational criminal network. Int J Cult Prop 20(02):113–153

Carlisle R (2005) Encyclopedia of intelligence and counterintelligence. Routledge

Chainey S, Berbotto A (2022) A structured methodical process for populating a crime script of organized crime activity using OSINT. Trends Org Crime 25:1–29

Chainey S, Ratcliffe J (2005) GIS and crime mapping. John Wiley & Sons

CIA (2024) The IC OSINT Strategy 2024–2026. https://www.cia.gov/static/9d89dd9a4fe41b63cfab00c5191a8803/IC-OSINT-Strategy.pdf

Clifton MT, Syropoulos C, Yotov V (2023) Economic sanctions: evolution, consequences, and challenges. J Econ Perspect 37:3–30

Conway M (2021) Online extremism and terrorism research ethics: researcher safety, informed consent, and the need for tailored guidelines. Terror Polit Viol 33(2):367–380

Curry MR (1995) Rethinking rights and responsibilities in GIS: beyond the power of imagery. Cartogr Geogr Inf Syst 22:58–69

Dorton SL, Frommer ID, Garrison TM (2019) A theoretical model for assessing information validity from multiple observers. In: 2019 IEEE conference on cognitive and computational aspects of situation management (CogSIMA) 2019:52–58

European Union (2022). What is OSINT: Open-source intelligence? European Data. https://data.europa.eu/en/publications/datastories/what-osint-open-source-intelligence

Evangelista J, Sassi R, Romero M, Napolitano DM (2021) Systematic literature review to investigate the application of open source intelligence (OSINT) with artificial intelligence. J Appl Secur Res 16(3):345–369

Financial Action Task Force (FATF) (2023) Annual Report 2022–2023. https://www.fatf-gafi.org/en/publications/Fatfgeneral/FATF-Annual-report-2022-2023.html

Ghioni R, Taddeo M, Floridi L (2023) Open source intelligence and AI: a systematic review of the GELSI literature. AI & Soc 39:1827–1842

Gibson S (2004) Open source intelligence. RUSI J 149:16–22

Golbeck J (2015) Introduction to social media investigation: a hands-on approach. Syngress Publishing

Goldman E (2006) Search engine bias and the demise of search engine utopianism. Yale J Law Technol 8:188–200

Henrico S, Putter D (2024) Intelligence collection disciplines—a systematic review. J Appl Secur Res 19:1–25

Hribar G, Podbregar I, Ivanuša T (2014) OSINT: a "Grey Zone"? Int J Intell Counterintell 27:529–549

Huffer D, Graham S (2023) These were people once: the online trade in human remains, and why it matters? Berghahn, New York. https://doi.org/10.1515/9781805390879

Huffer D, Wood C, Graham S (2019) What the machine saw: some questions on the ethics of computer vision and machine learning to investigate human remains trafficking. Internet Archaeol:52. https://doi.org/10.11141/ia.52.5

Hunter, ML (2011) Story-Based Inquiry. A Manual for Investigative Journalists. UNESCO

Hwang Y, Lee I, Kim H, Lee H, Kim D, Huo Y (2022) Current status and security trend of OSINT. Wirel Commun Mob Comput 2022:1–14

Jensen CJ, McElreath DH, Graves M (2017) Introduction to intelligence studies. Routledge, London

Kartal E (2022) A comprehensive study on bias in artificial intelligence systems: biased or unbiased AI, that's the question! Int J Intell Inf Technol (IJIIT) 18(1):1–23

Kovarik V (2011) Imagery intelligence (IMINT). University of Defence, Brno

Lakomy M (2023) Open-source intelligence and research on online terrorist communication: identifying ethical and security dilemmas. Media War Confl 17(1):23–40

Lavigne V, Gouin D (2014) Visual analytics for cyber security and intelligence. J Def Model Simul 11:175–199

Legg S, Hutter M (2007) A collection of definitions of intelligence. Front Artif Intell Appl 157:17–24

Lowenthal MM, Clark RM (2015) The five disciplines of intelligence collection. Sage

Mackenzie S, Brodie N, Yates D, Tsirogiannis C (2020) Trafficking culture: new directions in researching the global market in illicit antiquities. Routledge

Mariuta S (2014) Principles of security and integrity of databases. Proc Econ Finance 15:401–405

Marsh I, Melville G (2019) Crime, justice and the media, 3rd edn. Routledge

McDermott Y, Koenig A, Murray D (2021) Open source information's blind spot: human and machine bias in international criminal investigations. J Int Crim Just 19:85–105

Montenarh J, Marsden S (2024) Unmasking the oligarchs - using open source data to detect sanctions violations. J Econ Criminol 3:100055

Mpala DK (2023) Combating disinformation in modern conflict reporting: how international media are using open-source intelligence (OSINT) in their coverage of the Russia-Ukraine war. https://nla.brage.unit.no/nla-xmlui/handle/11250/3119493

North Atlantic Treaty Organization (NATO) (2002) NOSINT Handbook. https://archive.org/details/NATOOSINTHandbookV1.2/mode/2up

Oakley DP, Rogg J (2024) Spreading the "smog of war": the impact of propaganda, social media, and OSINT on U.S. civil-intelligence relations. Intell Natl Secur 39(3):539–553

Osoba OA, Welser W (2017) An intelligence in our image. The risks of bias and errors in artificial intelligence. Rand. https://www.rand.org/pubs/research_reports/RR1744.html

Pacini C, Stowell NF (2020) Panama papers and the abuse of Shell entities. In: Purda-Heeler L, Saadi S (eds) Corporate fraud exposed. Emerald Publishing Limited, Baker, H.K, pp 361–382
Pastore G (2011) Archaeology and the problem of unauthorized excavation in Italy. J Art Crime 6:68–70
Pastor-Galindo J, Nespoli P, Gómez Mármol F, Martínez Pérez G (2020) The not yet exploited goldmine of OSINT: opportunities, open challenges and future trends. IEEE Access 8:10282–10304
Paul KA (2018) Ancient artifacts vs. digital artifacts: new tools for unmasking the sale of illicit antiquities on the dark web. Arts 7(2):12
Pesaresi C (2017) Applicazioni GIS. Principi metodologici e linee di ricerca. Esercitazioni ed esemplificazioni guida. UTET
Phythian M (2013) Understanding the intelligence cycle. Routledge
Pickles J (1995) Ground truth: the social implications of geographic information systems. Guilford Press, New York
Plant T, Vij A, Swack J, Hogan M (2022) Diplomatic Courier. https://www.diplomaticourier.com/posts/how-ai-bias-in-search-engines-contributes-to-disinformation
Pllana D (2019) Expanding entire volume of knowledge influences on incrementing individual knowledge. Glob J Human Soc Sci 19(8):32–42
Preble KA, Early BR (2023) Enforcing economic sanctions by tarnishing corporate reputations. Bus Polit 26:102–123
Prunckun H (2014) Scientific methods of inquiry for intelligence analysis. Rowman & Littlefield Pub Inc.
Rajamäki J, Simola J (2019) How to apply privacy by design in OSINT and big data analytics?. In: Cruz T, Simoes P (eds) ECCWS 2019: proceedings of the 18th European conference on cyber warfare and security. Academic Conferences International. Proceedings of the European conference on information warfare and security pp 364–371
Rønn K, Søe S (2019) Is social media intelligence private? Privacy in public and the nature of social media intelligence. Intell Natl Secur 34:362–378
Sabry, F. (2024). Gestione del ciclo dell'intelligence. Un Miliardo Di Ben Informato
Salerno G, Guandalini B (2014) Manuale ArcGIS 10: Guida pratica con esercizi svolti. Dario Flaccovio Editore
Sari A (2018) Context-aware intelligent systems for fog computing environments for cyberthreat intelligence. In: Mahmood Z (ed) Fog computing: concepts, frameworks and technologies. Springer, pp 205–255
Senekal B, Kotzé E (2019) Open source intelligence (OSINT) for conflict monitoring in contemporary South Africa: challenges and opportunities in a big data context. Afr Secur Rev 28:1–19
Smith CL, Brooks DJ (2013) Security science: the theory and practice of security. Butterworth-Heinemann
Subham R, Akshay M, Debabrata B, Surajit G (2019) An overview of semantic search engines. Int J Res Rev 6:73–85
Tabatabaei F, Wells D (2016) OSINT in the context of cyber-security. In: Open source intelligence investigation. Springer, pp 213–231
Thomas Smith W (2003) Encyclopedia of the central intelligence agency. Infobase Publishing
Tominski C, Schumann H (2020) Interactive visual data analysis, 1st edn. A K Peters/CRC Press
Trisolini, M. (2020). Intelligence di polizia: Le forze dell'ordine come human sensors. Società Italiana di Intelligence https://press.socint.org/index.php/home/catalog/book/2020_12_trisolini
Trottier D (2015) Open source intelligence, social media and law enforcement: visions, constraints and critiques. Eur J Cult Stud 18:530–547
Van Puyvelde D, Tabárez RF (2025) The rise of open-source intelligence. Eur J Int Secur:1–15. https://doi.org/10.1017/eis.2024.61
Votey M (2022) Illicit antiquities and the internet: the trafficking of heritage on digital platforms. New York Univ J Int Law Policy 54 659

Valerio Scuro received a Bachelor's degree in Economics and a Master's degree in Environmental and Development Economics from Roma Tre University and he holds a postgraduate one year course in Information Security and Strategic Intelligence from Sapienza University of Rome. He has over 10 years experience working as an Intelligence Analyst in the private sector. Since 2020, Valerio has been a student in Archaeological Sciences at Sapienza University of Rome, eager to apply his skills in the fight against the illicit trafficking of Cultural Heritage. To this end, he completed courses at the Association for Research into Crimes against Art (ARCA) and the Istituto per l'Arte e il Restauro Palazzo Spinelli of Florence.

Open Access This chapter is licensed under the terms of the Creative Commons Attribution-NonCommercial-NoDerivatives 4.0 International License (http://creativecommons.org/licenses/by-nc-nd/4.0/), which permits any noncommercial use, sharing, distribution and reproduction in any medium or format, as long as you give appropriate credit to the original author(s) and the source, provide a link to the Creative Commons license and indicate if you modified the licensed material. You do not have permission under this license to share adapted material derived from this chapter or parts of it.

The images or other third party material in this chapter are included in the chapter's Creative Commons license, unless indicated otherwise in a credit line to the material. If material is not included in the chapter's Creative Commons license and your intended use is not permitted by statutory regulation or exceeds the permitted use, you will need to obtain permission directly from the copyright holder.

The Power of Quantifying Open Sources to Create Robust and Reliable Cultural Heritage Data

Michelle D. Fabiani

Abstract Open-source information is everywhere—potential data sources continuously surround us. Yet, as the volume of available sources grows, the ability to effectively use and understand their contents becomes a struggle. One way to address this need to balance depth of understanding with breadth of collection is to quantify the open-source data into a dataset or database. Synthesizing diverse open sources systematically can create robust and reliable data. In turn, those data can make it easier to process large quantities of information and facilitate analyses of entirely new sets of questions. This chapter presents an instructional account of one method of quantifying open-source data, based on the Berkeley Protocols on Digital Open-Source Investigations and experience from the CURIA lab. It argues that a process that prioritizes transparency, triangulation, metadata, and sustainability ensures a robust and reliable result. It demonstrates this method in the creation of a spatiotemporal dataset of cultural violence in the Syrian Conflict from 2014 to 2017 and discusses some of the applications for the resulting quantitative data.

1 Introduction

Interest in open-source investigations (also called open-source intelligence—both referred to as OSINT) has surged over the last decade. The sheer quantity of data produced on a daily scale has made this both an increasingly important and useful form of information gathering and processing (Ghioni et al. 2023). Although the OSINT cycle ostensibly includes both the collection/collation and analysis of the

M. D. Fabiani (✉)
Department of Criminal Justice, University of New Haven, Henry C. Lee College of Criminal Justice and Forensic Sciences, West Haven, CT, USA
e-mail: mfabiani@newhaven.edu

© The Author(s) 2026

E. Smith, S. Austin (eds.), *Researching a Rigged Game: Digital Approaches to Tracing the Illicit Trade in Cultural Objects*, Studies in Art, Heritage, Law and the Market 11, https://doi.org/10.1007/978-3-032-02014-7_3

information, comparatively less attention has been explicitly paid to the analysis phase. Instead, it is often combined with the verification or dissemination stages (see for example, Bellingcat 2018; Dubberley et al. 2020; Pherson and Pherson 2021). Yet, analysis requires the same level of consideration as the rest of the process, otherwise the results could be unreliable, irreplicable, and unusable. This is particularly problematic when the results of OSINT are often used to inform policy decisions that impact people's lives on a very real level. A lack of critical focus on the analysis portion of OSINT can thus very easily lead to poor research, poor policy, and by extension unethical unintended consequences.

This chapter provides an in-depth look at the analytical stage of the OSINT process, focusing on the process of creating robust and reliable quantitative data from diverse open sources. It begins with an overview of open-source investigations and a discussion on how to quantify open-source data. Then, to illustrate this analytical process, it presents an example looking at open-source cultural heritage data from Syria during the height of the civil war (2014 to 2017). The chapter ends with a discussion of challenges associated with creating open-source data and how to address them.

2 Open-Source Investigation: An Overview

As described earlier in this volume (see Introduction and Scuro), "Open-source" data refers to information that is both "publicly available" and whose use is unencumbered (i.e., generally free to redistribute). Some debate exists on how to define "public" and "unencumbered" and where that line is will vary depending on the field.[1] Over the last decade, the amount of publicly available information has grown exponentially. According to some estimates (Armstrong 2019), by 2035, 2142 zettabyte (1 zettabyte = 1 billion terabytes) of data will be created annually. Data here refers to any piece of information available publicly online. Such exponential growth poses both a significant opportunity and challenge for analysts and researchers (Wilson et al. 2024).

[1] Those working in law enforcement and legal accountability settings will not be able to access anything that requires a login without prior judicial approval (often in the form of a search warrant). Those working in academia will require some form of institutional or ethics review before they can access areas of the Internet that are password protected. Others should consider the ethical implications of using aliases or other obscuring techniques to access semi-restricted areas (e.g., forums, marketplaces, social media sites) that may violate a user's "reasonable right to privacy" before engaging in this work.

2.1 Planning and Assessment

Before beginning any investigation, it is important to think through the entire process to weigh the availability of information against risk tolerances and questions of ethics. It can be helpful to have a set of guiding principles to work from for each investigation. One set that is very helpful in the context of this chapter comes from the Berkeley Protocol on Digital Open-Source Investigations ("Berkeley Protocols") because they aim to provide a holistic set of principles covering professional, methodological, and ethical[2] (see Fig. 1). These should apply across a variety of investigatory contexts (e.g., journalism, research, legal accountability) and provide a valuable framework for planning and executing a project.

In the professional category, consider who is holding you accountable for your work and are you bringing in the necessary skills to do the work objectively, legally, and in full awareness of the risk landscape. Methodologically, this framework encourages you to think through whether your work is accurate, uses the minimum amount of data necessary, secure in all components, and preserved to the standards of the criminal justice system. Finally, ethically, it challenges you to explore how your work accounts for the dignity of *all* human life, the humility needed to do this kind of work, make space for others, ensure that it is free from influence, and transparent for others to replicate. Combined, these principles aim to ensure that each investigation is conducted with the highest standards in mind (HRL & OHCHR 2022).

The Berkeley Protocols are not the only set of principles related to open-source investigations. However, they are the most comprehensive, coming from a desire to provide a common standard for social science researchers, investigative journalists, and those working in the criminal justice system (Koenig 2024) such that the results of an investigation would be useful for courts of law. Other approaches tend to be more targeted in their focus and intended audience (Akhgar et al., 2016; Bazzell

Professional	Methodological	Ethical
• Accountability • Competency • Objectivity • Legality • Security Awareness	• Accuracy • Data Minimization • Preservation • Security by Design	• Dignity • Humility • Inclusivity • Independence • Transparency

Fig. 1 Guiding Principles from the Berkeley Protocols (adapted from the Berkeley Protocols—see HRL & OHCHR 2022: pp. 22–29)

[2]To access the Berkeley Protocol, visit: https://humanrights.berkeley.edu/publications/berkeley-protocol-on-digital-open-source-investigations/.

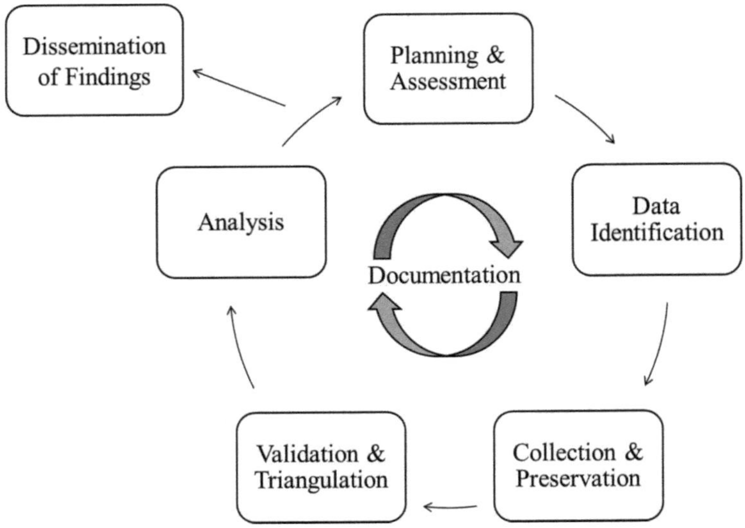

Fig. 2 Overview of the OSINT Process (adapted from the Berkeley Protocols—see HRL & OHCHR 2022)

2016; Bellingcat 2018; Hassan and Hijazi 2018).[3] The explicit and substantial focus on ethics is also a notable component of these principles. They centre the work around the experiences of those who have suffered the harm to seek justice (relating to the ideals of human rights) while balancing the ethical constraints of law enforcement.

With these principles in mind, the OSINT process begins with the planning stage identified in Fig. 2. This stage involves determining the availability of information, including identifying relevant sources and platforms, and relevant initial keywords and search strategies. This is also when any preliminary risk assessment is done to confirm the scope of the investigation.

Each investigation will carry its own set of risks that need to be fully understood. Digital risks include attempts by external parties to access your systems (brute force (DOS) attacks, phishing, malware/ransomware, man-in-the-middle, social engineering, etc.); manipulation of data or evidence during electronic transit; and attempts to compromise your identity or your team's identity. Not all targets will have sophisticated cyber capabilities, so it is important to assess the target every time, including any relevant geopolitical dynamics. For example, the organization or nation you are interested in may not have their own significant cyber capabilities, but if they are close or supported by someone who does have significant cyber capabilities, then you should treat your target as high risk. A thorough risk assessment will include bad actors, the

[3] Bellingcat (2018) provides a methodology specific for tracking the Russo-Ukraine war. Hassan and Hijazi (2018) emphasize intelligence on financial transactions, terrorism, and business. Bazzell (2016) provides a hacker-like approach to identifying and extracting personal information from open sources. Akhgar and colleagues (2016) emphasize the legal and theoretical frameworks for OSINT with a focus on data collection.

Fig. 3 Elements of Risk Assessment (adapted from Foundational Digital Open-Source Investigations Training by the Human Rights Center June 2024)

consequences of failure, requirements for adequate digital and physical protection, and the support and tolerance for risk personally and institutionally (see Fig. 3).

Open-source investigations for cultural heritage may not seem like a high-risk subject area initially—the work is done often remotely and may not appear to include obviously sensitive topics (e.g., violence against women and children). However, the situations most conducive to these investigations involve conflict in some capacity. Cultural heritage is always political in these contexts, making it a high-risk topic to investigate. Online platforms selling objects suspected to be looted or stolen by an aggressor (e.g., Russia allegedly stealing cultural heritage from Ukraine and selling it online, ISIS looting and selling antiquities, etc.). Monitoring the destruction and looting of cultural heritage as part of suspected targeted cultural cleansing campaigns. Identifying the perpetrators of looting of cultural heritage sites that may be tied to complicit or negligent government actors. These are not benign research contexts—they are actively fraught geopolitical landscapes that come with inherent risk.

Such risks include digital, financial, physical, psychological, and reputational and can affect individual investigators, their institutions, and those affected by the investigation (Dubberley et al. 2020; HRL & OHCHR 2022, pp. 56–66). Clicking on an unknown website in the context of data collection may inadvertently download a virus or ransomware, compromising the digital environment in which you work. Such viruses can easily exploit security networks at universities and other enterprise environments to take down the networks and steal information. Repeated clicking of links (e.g., if the investigator forgot to collect a site the first time and had to go back) can alert the domain owner or target that someone is looking into them and put *the investigator* on *their* radar. Once an investigator is visible to the target of the investigation, they may become the focus of the target's ire—they may try to intimidate you (physically or psychologically by letting the investigator know they can be found) or discredit them professionally to diminish the impact of the work. Remember: open-source investigations are not typically occurring within closed intelligence environments, whatever an investigator can see about the target of an investigation, it is likely they could find much more about investigators without much difficulty.

Exposure to fraught geopolitical contexts also brings those doing open-source investigations into more direct contact with the reality of war, through imagery, video, testimony, and any adversarial actions they experience. This can lead to psychological trauma that if not managed and treated, can impact the results of the investigation, lead to desensitization, and further risk-taking behaviour. Investigations into cultural heritage also run into risks associated with intention versus outcome. Well intentioned investigations that are carried out without careful thought may unintentionally make situations worse for those it aims to help on the ground. For example, an investigation seeking to prove that a certain group's cultural heritage is being targeted for destruction must be very clear on what the intended outcome is. Is it to stop the destruction and hold those responsible accountable in a court of law? Is that possible? Or is it to help the community preserve their heritage and rebuild it? What would the community itself prefer and is it possible to know? Investigating such a claim could lead to legal justice for the offenders; however, it could also lead to further retaliation against that group if not done carefully. It could also run the risk of running into Western saviour complex biases. It is thus important to go into any investigation with a clear picture of the amount of risk that it may pose to you, your institution, and those findings may touch.

The final element of the planning stage is to determine a process for data collection, preservation, and validation. Ideally, this includes the creation of metadata templates where information is documented about each piece of data collected, the verification of information, the search terms used to find the information, and how it will be processed later (in Sect. 2.4 Validation and Triangulation). It also usually includes the implementation of risk mitigations strategies. At a minimum, this usually includes the use of a secure browser, storage system, and a VPN to obscure your IP address.[4] In some cases, it may also involve the creation of aliases to access social media platforms and using a virtual machine (VM) alongside the VPN and secure browser. Institutions and funding agencies may also impose restrictions on the tools and systems that can be used, which will influence the "best" option.

[4] All recommendations are as of the date of publication. There are a range of secure VPNs available on the market. The more secure the network, the less access it is likely to have globally. Something like Express VPN, which requires a subscription, has more global access but may offer slightly less security. Similarly, Brave browser is considered one of the more secure browsers available. Regardless, you should still practice safe search methods and not use any personally identifying credentials when using conducting your investigation. Depending on the level of security required, a cloud-based system like Dropbox, Google Drive, or One Drive could be useful, particularly if at the enterprise level. At a minimum, the storage system should include multi-factor authentication and ideally encryption (e.g., SAML) to make it more difficult for unauthorized users to access. Proton is a particularly good free system that includes encrypted email, document storage, and a VPN.

2.2 Data Identification

The next phase of the OSINT process is to identify the data of interest for collection. Using the protocols and infrastructure previously determined, start searching for relevant information. Common sources for these types of investigations fall under four categories (Human Rights Center, UN OHCHR 2020): (1) primary (photos, videos, parliamentary records), (2) secondary (NGO reports, journalist accounts), (3) unique pieces of evidence (satellite imagery, social media posts), and (4) aggregated data (statistics composite images, video explainers). Boolean and search operators are effective tools for searching for data (HRL & OHCHR 2022, p. 56)—the terms used should be broad enough to capture the full range of possibilities and unique enough in combination to return the most relevant results. A common and effective strategy is to come up with a list of key words that when used individually are generic, but that become very specific when used together. It is also a good idea to use more than one search engine (e.g., Google and Yandex) and to vary where your IP registers with your VPN as it will alter the results you are shown. It is important to document the search terms used for each platform and how effective they are so that it is clear when a new strategy needs to be used (versus re-hashing the same results multiple times unintentionally).

2.3 Collection & Preservation

Data collection and preservation in the context of OSINT involves creating a local copy of each piece of information and storing it in a sustainable format. At a minimum, this can mean saving a PDF of a webpage or taking a screenshot of information. Neither of these options retains the metadata associated with the original source. If there is any possibility that the results of the investigation will be relevant for a legal setting (i.e., evidence in a court of law), it is necessary to create a clear digital chain of custody (Freeman 2020). A common way to do this is to save webpages and images as local copies (MIME HTML files, "mhtml") and to create a hash value[5] for each file individually (Freeman 2020, p. 126).

It is often not possible to find everything available on a topic—there is too much information to sort through and often not enough time or resources. This creates a tension between efficiency and thoroughness. If it is not possible to find the universe of information, how do you know when to stop? There is no single answer to this question—it will always be a trade-off. It is generally better to collect more than

[5] A Hash is a unique string of numbers and letters that act as the "fingerprints" of individual files. They are hexadecimal values created by an algorithm (usually SHA-256 or MD5) and attached as metadata to the file. Anytime anyone opens it or makes a change, the hash value will also change. Thus, in a court setting, if you can show the hash value has not changed from when it was assigned then it acts as a digital chain of custody. Hashes have been used since the ICC accepted digital evidence in 2013 (Quilling 2022).

you think you will need and then know you may have some irrelevant information (noise) than to collect too little, having to go back later. At the same time, OSINT investigations can be iterative so there may be multiple rounds of collection and validation before a final product is disseminated. Most important is that the collection process be thoroughly and transparently documented in the form of a collection metadata system. Ideally, this includes both information about the collection process (collector name, tool used (version), IP address of computer used, date and time), the digital item collected (specific URL; full page and source code (mhtml); separate media items like photos, videos; embedded metadata; and relevant contextual information like comments in a thread), and the hash value assigned to each item. This provides a transparent and complete accounting of the collection process.

2.4 *Verification & Triangulation*

After collecting and preserving data, the information contained within must be verified and triangulated. Verifying a digital item requires confirming that it: originated with the source you collected, talks about or depicts what it claims to be depicting, and is not AI-generated (HRL & OHCHR 2022). Verifying a source can involve reverse image searching, looking at the HTML source code, and performing geolocation. To confirm the details or content of the source often requires triangulation, here referring to building a consensus of the "facts" across multiple sources and types of sources. Triangulation involves not only looking across mediums (video, social media, primary, secondary), but also explicitly incorporating competing interests (Pherson and Pherson 2021). For example, to verify the details of an airstrike in Syria would require looking at Syrian government sources, non-state actor sources, and coalition reports of the event, depending on which countries are involved. Each one has a vested interest in framing an event within a specific narrative and that bias can distort the "facts" of interest. Sources that are verified are likely to be considered more accurate and thus may have more weight or validity (e.g., in a court of law, Freeman 2020).

As with collection and preservation, documentation and metadata tracking are extremely important here. Often verification and triangulation require additional searching and sometimes additional collection. It can be easy to go down a tangent without a clear goal. Spreadsheets and notes are very helpful to systematize the process—they create transparency and make it easier to trace back the work. It is also in this process that it becomes relevant and often helpful to think about quantification (see below).

2.5 *Analysis*

Analysis is the process of interpreting and drawing conclusions about the open-source data that has been collected and processed. While it often includes both qualitative (interviews, thematic analysis, case studies) and quantitative component, this chapter focuses on the quantitative approaches.

2.5.1 Why Quantify Open-Source Data?

The process of data collection in the context of open-source investigations focuses on acquiring diverse types of data while validation and preservation on sifting through to find relevant, accurate, and potentially actionable information. However, there is so much information, how does one process it all? How can the relevance of information be conveyed in a digestible format? Quantification is one way that scholars and practitioners can start to process information and find meaningful patterns while maintaining the metadata trail created through the OSINT cycle. For example, quantification allowed the first network analysis of an antiquities trafficking network (see D'Ippolito 2014). Relationships between actors in Giacomo Medici's personal circle were extracted from investigative journalist sources and news sources and compared to assumptions put forth by law enforcement at the time. Law enforcement assumed the group was hierarchically organized, like an organized crime group; the quantified data demonstrated it was likely more decentralized (D'Ippolito 2014).

A quantitative analysis of open-source data requires transforming it to extract relevant information and then synthesizing everything into a cohesive dataset. The end results will typically include information like locations and dates of events, types of damage, types of actors, duration, number and types of sources, reliability and veracity of sources. The Armed Conflict Location and Event Dataset (ACLED, ACLED 2024) and the Uppsala Conflict Data Program (UCDP, UCDP 2024) are two examples of quantifying open-source data to facilitate further analysis.

The goal in synthesizing diverse sources for quantitative analysis is to create something robust and reliable that can complement and add more weight to the findings of an open-source investigation. Finding a pattern of behaviour or actions in a mountain of evidence is useful but pairing that with a statistical analysis demonstrating that the pattern exists beyond what you would expect by random change is more powerful (Spiegelhalter 2017). This is particularly true if the findings can be presented in a compelling visual manner.[6] For example, it is interesting to suspect that two social media accounts are connected based on similar worldviews. It lends more weight to pair the semantic evidence with linguistic analysis of language simi-

[6] There are many visualization tools, depending on the desired end result. Good network analysis tools include NodeXL, UCINET, and R. Effective tools for creating charts and graphs are Excel and R. Flowcharts and diagrams can be easily created in Whimsical.

larities or backtrace the content to dates and times of posting (see e.g., Walsh et al. 2021). Building up datasets over time can also facilitate cross-national comparisons, assuming that the process follows clear principles of robustness and reliability.

The Cultural Resilience Informatics and Analysis (CURIA) lab[7] has developed a set of key principles of robustness (the longevity, replicability and sustainability of data) and reliability (the validity and transparency of process) that it employs in cultural heritage open-source investigations. These have been refined over ten years of interdisciplinary open-source research and include transparency, triangulation, metadata, and sustainability. *Transparency* refers to the ability to clearly communicate the assumptions, process, limitations, and implications of decisions. Often cultural heritage open-source investigations are initiated during urgent circumstances—during reconstruction or active conflict. This comes with a sense of urgency that can conflict with ideal research processes (see Greenland and Fabiani 2021) and can also come with the risk of incorporating unconscious bias or assumptions that may distort the data and findings. Thus, it is essential that the process be transparent for the work to be considered robust and reliable. *Triangulation* refers to the process of verification and validation, as discussed above. *Metadata* refers to the ability to trace-back the work and speaks the most directly to the reproducibility of the process. *Sustainability* refers to both the longevity and utility of the data in the long-term as well as the replicability of any analysis in the future. Figure 4, developed specifically for this chapter, outlines helpful guiding questions for each principle. These align closely with both the process of open-source investigations and the principles proposed by the Berkeley Protocols (HRL & OHCHR 2022)—at their core all these approaches advocate for a careful and complete adherence to best practice of research methods at every stage of the work.

In the process of quantification, every decision creates a carry-on effect that ultimately impacts the analysis. The specific focus of the investigation will determine the measures of interest and how the data should be structured. For example, if the investigative focus is on the actor or dynamics between actors (see for example Braithwaite and Johnson 2012), then the dataset should be constructed around them such that the unit of analysis becomes the actor (see the UCDP, 2024). This type of network dataset can then be used to model and visualize the patterns of aggression or relationships over time. If, as is more often the case with cultural heritage, the focus is on incidents of cultural heritage damage/destruction/change/loss and the circumstances around it, then the unit of analysis should be the event (more in line with the ACLED data). Regardless, any quantified dataset should include measures to assess the accuracy and validity of the data in space, time, and content so that future users are encouraged to use their own discretion to determine the degree to which they trust your work.

The data structure will then determine the (initial) unit of analysis and will impact how elements like multiple incidents, incident duration, and incident connections are treated. If the unit of analysis is an incident, then several incidents

---

[7] See https://curialab.org/.

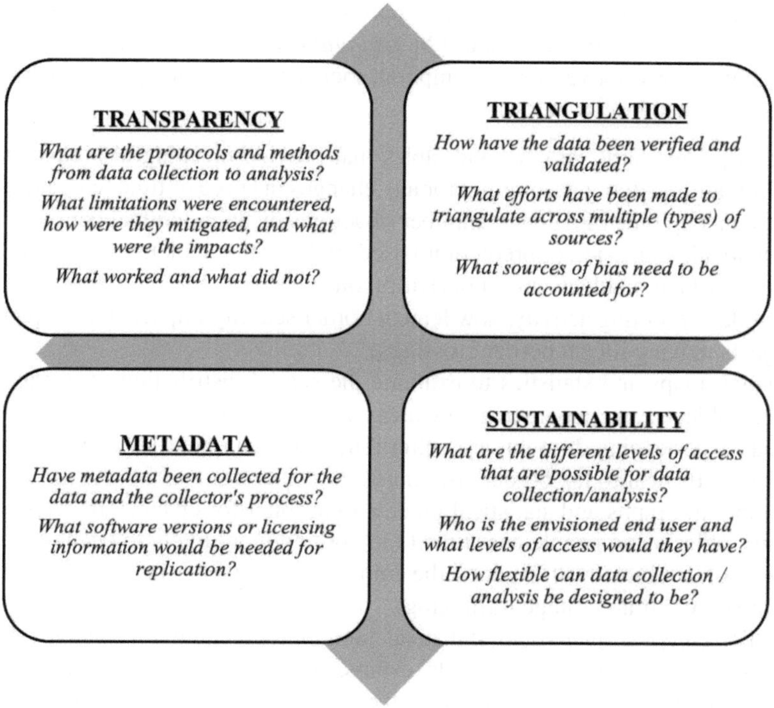

Fig. 4 Principles of Robust and Reliable Cultural Heritage Data Analysis

reported in a single source can be split out across multiple rows (one incident per row). If the unit is an individual, perhaps it becomes a tally of how many incidents that individual is involved in for a particular time. The same type of consideration applies to duration and whether and how to document connections between incidents (e.g., are a series of airstrikes coded as a single incident, a single incident with a long duration, or a series of linked incidents?). All these individual decisions will determine how the measures of interest can be operationalized as variables for analysis as well as how useful the data will be to others in the future. This is not a complete set of considerations—every investigation will run into unique circumstances that must be quantified and transparently documented.

2.5.2 Analytical Approaches for Cultural Heritage OSINT

Any analytical method that relies on quantitative data can be useful and used for cultural heritage OSINT. This includes descriptive graphs, tables, and charts, regression-based models, maps showing spatial distributions and statistics, temporal trends and analyses, spatiotemporal modelling, social network modelling, and more. The principles of transparency, triangulation, metadata, and sustainability apply equally to the analysis as they do to the data construction through how you document your process and how you approach your analysis. Specifically, in the context of analysis, findings should be *triangulated* or confirmed across multiple dimensions—descriptive, spatial, temporal, social, and spatiotemporal. Each dimension is described briefly below.[8]

- Descriptive: charts, graphs, and tables that provide meaningful breakdowns of information without accounting for any changes in space or time (e.g., number of incidents by type of damage, number of actions by an individual per month).
- Statistical: regression or prediction-based analyses that look to examine how cultural heritage incidents are impacted by other factors (e.g., how drought affects the odds of looting activity, how lenient border security impacts the frequency of objects making illegal border crossings).
- Spatial: maps and statistics to examine the spatial distribution of events, locations, objects, and people (e.g., are areas of higher looting activities located near areas experiencing drought, are cultural heritage communities most affected by prior thefts near to lax border crossings).
- Temporal: graphs and statistical models to account for changes in events, locations, objects and people over time (e.g., looting more likely to occur before the onset of conflict or after, does the implementation of a new law increase or decrease cultural heritage trafficking).
- Spatio-temporal: maps and statistical models to account for changes in both space and time for people, objects, events, and locations (e.g., are areas experiencing cultural heritage destruction the same as areas where civilians are targeted, how do changes in border access impact trafficking routes over time).
- Social: network-analysis diagrams and models that visualize the relationships between people, objects, and events. Useful for understanding flows of information or objects through people and places.

Not all dimensions will be relevant or even possible to analyse every time; however, an analysis that focuses only on one will be missing important nuance and could provide misleading results. For example, Fabiani (2019) examined the relationship between archaeological looting activity (operationalized as number of looting attempts) and conflict (operationalized as all conflict, violent, non-violent, and violence against civilians) in Lower Egypt from 2015 to 2017. The analysis looked at these two phenomena descriptively, spatially, temporally, and spatiotemporally. Theoretically, it was important to look across dimensions. A spatial analysis could find a statistically significant relationship between incidents that took place years apart; a temporal analysis could find a statistically significant relationship between incidents at opposite ends of the country. While it is not impossible that those relationships would be meaningful, it is unlikely. Only by looking across multiple dimensions could meaningful results be obtained (i.e. building consensus or

[8] Each of these dimensions are discussed in numerous textbooks and articles for specific fields. As an introduction to these analyses consider the following sources: Frey (2019) for descriptive, Brockwell and Davis (2014) for temporal, Darmofal (2015) for spatial, Diggle (2013) for spatio-temporal.

Table 1 Triangulation of Findings

Independent Variable	Spatial	Temporal	Spatio-Temporal	Descriptive
All Sociopolitical Stress	X		X	
Violent Conflict		X	X	
Non-violent conflict		X	X	X
Violence Against Civilians		X	X	

triangulating results). Table 1 demonstrates what this looked like. An "X" indicates an analysis found evidence of a relationship between archaeological looting activity and the independent variable (here the type of conflict). For example, Fabiani (2019) found evidence of a relationship between looting activity and all sociopolitical stress in spatial analyses and spatiotemporal analyses but not temporal or descriptive analyses. Plotting out the significant findings by dimension and type of conflict helped to clarify that the relationship between archaeological looting activity and conflict only holds for some types of conflict and not uniformly. This would suggest additional data collection and analysis could be helpful to tease out the relationship more fully.

2.6 *Disseminated Findings*

The final step of the OSINT process is to disseminate the findings. This may be by sending a digital packet of evidence to a criminal court with a cover letter. It may be through the creation of one-page briefs with diagrams, presentations, reports, or articles. The intended audience will determine which format is most appropriate. Across all formats, visual evidence can be especially compelling—charts, maps, tables—anything that helps to consolidate information to a more digestible form (Walsh et al. 2021). This is another area where quantitative analysis can be helpful. The outputs for many analyses are visual by design, making them easier to interpret than raw data files or the original sources. Regardless of how the findings are presented, it is important to balance being transparent with the limitations of the work and being authoritative about the conclusions. Too much hedging will undercut the confidence the reader will have in the conclusions of the investigation; too little and it may be misleading or overrepresenting what can be said. A helpful strategy is to lead with the main conclusions carefully worded to not mislead, then discuss how you arrived at those conclusions separately and include the limitations and caveats in that section (Pherson and Pherson 2021). For those who wish to know the details, the information is available. For those who do not, they can quickly get to the key points.

3 Example: ASOR-CHI Reports on Syria

Having provided a general understanding of the open-source investigative process, this chapter now turns to an illustration of quantifying open-source data for cultural heritage by the CURIA Lab, focusing on Syria at the height of the conflict from 2014 to 2017. The Syrian conflict includes multiple overlapping offensives and military campaigns, with many state and nonstate actors involved (Center for Preventive Action, 2024). Violence towards cultural heritage and civilians are both well documented in civil wars (see Besaw et al. 2023; Fjelde et al. 2016) as well as in Syria, specifically (see Bostad 2018; Guha-Sapir et al. 2018). Civilian violence—usually fatalities—is used to cleanse territories of heterogenous populations, force concessions from another party, help to assert control of a territory or population, and can serve as a form of terrorism (Stanton 2016). Cultural heritage attacks—most often seen as damage and destruction—serves to finance terrorism and further conflict (Losson 2016); is hypothesized to be a preamble to genocide (Bevan 2012); is used for propaganda and ritualization of motive (Shahab and Isakhan 2018); and can be seen as a form of cultural genocide and ethnocide (Isakhan et al. 2017; Post 2005; Van der Auwera 2012).

In Syria, from 2014 to 2017, targeted civilian and cultural violence occurred by multiple parties. The Syrian government was accused of using chemical weapons against areas where oppositional forces had strongholds (Solvang 2017). The Islamic State targeted specific cultural groups that went against their ideology (see Clapperton et al. 2017) and the Yezidis were specifically targeted based on their religion and cultural practices (see Amnesty International 2024). The destruction of their religious and historical material culture also happened concurrently with the mass rapes, kidnappings, and executions of Yezidi people (Borda, 2022; Cetorelli et al., 2017; Coppini, 2021). The weapons deployed most frequently in the Syrian war were explosive weapons including missiles, mortars, grenades, and bombs. Because these were often used in high-population urban areas, they killed people and destroyed the built environment—including buildings and monuments with historical and cultural value—indiscriminately. For example, the city of Aleppo was a stronghold for oppositional forces and was subjected to intense fighting with the Islamic State. The Islamic State also granted licenses and permission to loot archaeological sites throughout the country (see e.g., Brodie 2022; Cunliffe, 2014). This resulted in both the catastrophic loss of human life and severe damage and destruction to movable and immovable cultural heritage.

With this context, the CURIA lab sought to investigate the intersection of cultural heritage violence and civilian fatalities by creating a new incident-level geolocated cultural violence dataset in Syria from 2014 to 2017 and integrating it with known civilian fatalities data from the UCDP.[9] The motivating question for the

---

[9] The CURIA lab at the time was comprised of Dr. Michelle D. Fabiani and Dr. Fiona Greenland along with student research assistants. This project was funded by the National Science Foundation, award number 1948947.

investigation was: to what degree do incidents of cultural heritage attacks colocate with incidents of civilian fatalities?

The answer to this question could have significant sociopolitical ramifications. Cultural heritage sites designated as "no-strikes"[10] are supposed to be safe locations for civilians. If it is found that no strike locations were targeted and they aligned with incidents when civilians died, that is a potentially actionable war crime.[11] Similarly, it could be meaningful to understand (both for this conflict and for others, as in the ongoing Russo-Ukrainian war) what the microdynamics are for violence against civilians and against cultural heritage. Is it that cultural heritage sites are targeted first as a so-called "preamble" to civilian violence? If this were proven (i.e., a statistically significant relationship was found), then it could provide a new legal avenue for human rights organizations to advocate for earlier intervention and possible prosecution for war crimes after the fact. Alternatively, if such a relationship were found or if there is evidence that these two phenomena exhibit separate but parallel patterns, it would provide a more thorough understanding of modern conflict and the role that cultural heritage plays within it. Understanding any of these dynamics requires a quantitative and multidimensional modelling strategy. Yet the data available for this work is spread across multiple types of open sources. As such, the team took an OSINT approach with quantification of the data and analysis.

3.1 The Data

To assess this relationship, the team drew on diverse data sources on conflict, civilian casualties, cultural heritage damage and destruction, infrastructure, and protected civilian and cultural heritage locations. To capture the full set of constraints affecting when and where violence occurred in the conflict, the team incorporated data on the road network (obtained from *OpenStreetMaps*), populated places and administrative boundaries (downloaded from the United Nations Office for the Coordination of Humanitarian Affairs—OCHA), the ambient population (downloaded from the Oakland National Laboratories Landscan data), internally displaced person camp locations (synthesized from the Humanitarian Information Unit of the U.S. Department of State), and cultural heritage no strike list locations (acquired from personal contacts).

[10] No-strike locations are comprised of collateral objects defined by the Law of War as civilian or noncombatant in nature (DOD, 2015/2023). Cultural, religious, and historical institutions and structures are included in Category 1 of protected or collateral objects, which includes the most sensitive subject of objects defined by the Law of War (DOD, 2015/2023). The U.S. Department of Defense (2009: C-1) defines no strike entities as those "designated by the appropriate authority upon which kinetic or non-kinetic operations are prohibited to avoid violating international law, conventions, or agreements, or damaging relations with coalition partners and indigenous populations." Locations may be removed from the no-strike list if they are being used by the adversary intentionally, provided the adversary has been put on notice (DOD, 2015/2023).

[11] See for example, the 1998 Rome Statue of the International Criminal Court (ICC 1998).

Incidents of conflict, including those with civilian fatalities (representing targeted civilian violence), come from the Uppsala Conflict Data Program (UCDP). The UCDP tracks organized violence[12] and civil war around the world, using open sources of information that are systematically triangulated and verified (to the extent possible). The resultant data contains at least forty years of data on conflicts around the globe. These data are available in multiple levels of aggregation and include information on conflict dyads (the two sides of each conflict), duration, location of each incident, description of the incident.[13] The UCDP are exemplary open-source data (Höglund and Oberg 2011). They are one of the only sources to provide reliable estimates of civilian fatalities associated with conflict incidents as well as detailed incident-level information (latitude and longitude, date, duration, conflict dyad information, etc.). These data also have a robust, transparent, and replicable approach to the data creation (Sundberg and Melander 2013). Analysts from the UCDP worked on this project with CURIA to ensure that the cultural heritage data were comparable and could be integrated with the conflict data.

Incidents of cultural heritage damage and destruction (representing targeted cultural violence) were coded from the American Schools of Overseas Research Cultural Heritage Initiative (ASOR CHI) Reports. This group produced weekly and monthly reports from 2014 to 2018 as part of the "Safeguarding the Heritage of the Near East Initiative" project funded by the U.S. Department of State (Danti 2015). These reports provided a near-real-time assessment of damage and destruction to cultural heritage locations in Syria and Iraq.[14] They reflect reporting from a variety of sources—both verified and unverified—and were often treated as preliminary open-source intelligence briefs. The sources this group relied upon included governmental reports, news reports, social media, satellite images, personal images, and international NGO reports (Danti 2015). Later in the conflict (especially 2016—2017), updates to earlier incidents would be included as new information came to light. With some redactions, these reports are available to the public.[15,16]

[12] "The UCDP collects data on state-based armed conflict, non-state conflict, and one-sided violence" (UCDP 2024). These mutually exclusive categories are aggregated into "organized violence," and all share the same cut-off threshold of requiring a minimum of 25 fatalities in a calendar year.

[13] https://www.pcr.uu.se/research/ucdp/definitions/#tocjump_850943167861772_36.

[14] There is no specific definition of "cultural heritage" though the project did appear to take a wide view of the term, including everything from museums to archaeological sites to religious sites and general cultural sites based on the present data quantification.

[15] As of this chapter's publication, the reports are available at this link: https://www.asor.org/chi/reports/weekly-monthly/2014.

[16] A report could be redacted by the request of anyone in the State Department or the U.S. Government if it could potentially impact ongoing strategic initiatives or could impact the ability of commercial partners to make money off their products (e.g., satellite imagery) in the future. In the case of the ASOR-CHI group, most redactions concerned the publishing of satellite imagery online. This potentially affected the reliability of the data CURIA had to work with and could mean the final dataset underrepresents the true number of incidents of cultural heritage attacks. For an example of an ASOR-CHI report: https://www.asor.org/chi/reports/weekly-monthly.

These ASOR reports contain a plethora of detail and variable organization, requiring a detailed and careful coding to ensure the accuracy and validity of the resultant data. The rest of this chapter will focus on the process of coding and quantifying the ASOR data so that they could be integrated with the UCDP data and subsequently analysed and disseminated. The next section discusses the methodological framework for analysing the resulting database.

3.2 The Process

The process for creating the cultural heritage attacks data involved 5 steps: (1) establish a clear foundation with a living codebook and coding shell, (2) extract preliminary set of incidents from ASOR CHI reports; (3) verify geolocations (latitude and longitude) and record associated town locations; (4) review previous coding and code for measures of validity; and (5) validation of data coding. Such a multi-stage coding process allowed the team to work as efficiently as possible; each step is explored individually below.

3.2.1 Establishing a Clear Foundation: Living Codebook and Coding Shell

Having a clear foundation was the most important step of the process. A primary goal of the project was to create a robust dataset that could be used to analyse these incidents over space and time and to address any number of questions on cultural heritage attacks and conflict in Syria during the time frame. As such, it was essential that the data be constructed with an eye towards future scholarship and integration with other conflict datasets like the UCDP. The ability to seamlessly integrate data meant that any analysis would have a consistent level of validity and reliability, minimizing sources of unknown bias (Olteanu et al., 2019). This stage required a lot of forethought and design choices. For example, the team worked with the UCDP up front to design the scales for the Reporting Temporal Scale and the Incident Temporal Scale so that they conceptually aligned with the UCDP Location Precision Score.

To assist in designing a future-looking (i.e. sustainable) dataset, this project relied on a living codebook (Reyes et al. 2024)—a coding protocol that contained the goal of the project, the preliminary set of variables that should be present in the final dataset, and decision rules to be applied consistently. Using a living codebook allowed the team to maintain a balance between forethought of design, efficiency in coding, and the necessarily iterative nature of coding. Anytime a new situation needed to be addressed, the living codebook was updated so that it could be systematically applied both to what had already been coded and would be coded in the future. Each variable included the name, the coding variable name, its definition, a preliminary coding system (how information is documented), and any instructions for coding (nuances, exceptions, inclusion/exclusion criteria, etc.). Some variables were coded (or recorded) as numbers (e.g., days between), some were text-based sentences or descriptors (e.g., source type), and some were numbers representing other values (e.g., a scale or a category). Based on experience, it is better to create a numeric code for as many variables as possible—it makes the coding faster and minimizes cleaning of typos later. Document as much logic as possible at this stage so that it is available if needed later.

In this project, the protocol included three categories of variables, most of which were coded as scales or numeric categories. For example, the damage type variable was initially developed with a couple of known types of damage to sites in Syria (looting, artillery, and airstrikes). A numeric code was applied to each type of damage, starting with "1" so that as new types of damage were discovered, they could be added and have a number applied to them. In total, eleven types of damage were coded. Using a numeric code to represent this categorical variable also helped to increase the speed and efficiency of coding (and to minimize typos that would later cause problems).[17] The points below highlight the three categories of variables, with example variables from this project:

- ASOR Report Metadata: Variables that link each row coded back to the original source report and include the basic information from that report. Examples: ASOR Incident Number, ASOR Report Number, Report Date, Report Year, Report Month.
- Incident Information: Variables that describe the incident this project is interested in and that include both spatial and temporal elements. Examples: Unique ID, Incident Date, Incident Start/End Date, Source Type, Site Name and Variations, Actor Type, Site Date, Site Type, Damage Code, Location Name, Location Description, Town, Neighbourhood, Administrative boundaries (admin 1—4), Site Latitude and Longitude, Town Pcode (standardized unique ID for towns), Town Latitude and Longitude.
- Measures of Validity: Variables that allow analysts (on this project and in the future) to assess the amount of uncertainty they want to accept in their analyses and to explicitly model the impact of that uncertainty—these help to ensure that the data are not treated or interpreted as representing the complete objective "truth." Many of these followed the general approach of creating a scale where the lower the number the more precise/accurate the information (the exception is number of sources where a higher number indicates greater validity). Examples: Days Between (when the incident occurred and it was reported), Reporting Temporal Scale, Incident Temporal Scale, Unverifiable Sources, Number of Sources, Location Precision Score.

Alongside the living codebook, this project developed a coding shell that was used by all coders. This spreadsheet contained every variable in the codebook, starting

[17] The full coding protocol is available upon request. A sample of the data are available at curialab.org.

with a unique ID variable then proceeding in the order listed in the codebook, and ending with a "Notes" column. The unique ID allowed the coders to link and find information over time and was created from a concatenation (a string combination without spaces) of report, time, location information, damage type and incident type. For example, "14-002201482SHIDC15972AL" can be read as a combination of ASOR ID (14-002), year (2014), month (8) actor (2—nonstate), site type (SH—shrine), damage code (ID—intentional destruction), town code (1597), incident count (2), and governorate abbreviation (AL - Aleppo). This was the minimum number of discrete pieces of information that allowed every incident to be uniquely identified. The notes column provided a simple way to record relevant information or questions that might be useful in the future (e.g., for developing new variables or during recoding).

3.2.2 Preliminary Coding

During the initial round of coding, the goal was to identify as many incidents as possible from the reports and record the ASOR report metadata for each. The coding team involved several research assistants and so the protocols included a series of best practices in coding based on CURIA's prior experience in quantifying open-source data and detailed instructions on what to look for. These best practices are described below:

- *Before coding, read the full document.* The ASOR report content and structure evolved over time. Reading the full report before trying to code anything facilitates familiarity with the content and where there may be sticking points to investigate further.
- *Keep the coding protocol/instructions on hand.* Do not try to memorize the coding protocols. These reports contain a lot of noise for the purposes of coding, and it can be easy to go on a tangent, documenting irrelevant information. Referencing the protocols minimizes this potential issue.
- *Finding information.* If the structure of the document is difficult or you cannot find information easily, there are a couple of steps to take. First—search the report (using CTRL + F) based on a key word (e.g., a site name). The discussion of incident damage or date may be in an unintuitive location or even in an update report later. Second—if that does not work, communicate the issue with the team to troubleshoot. Never spend more than 30 minutes troubleshooting if you hit a brick wall before you reach out for help.
- *Do not try to be perfect, be transparent and communicate decision making.* This kind of coding is iterative and will evolve. Being transparent and documenting both the questions asked and the answers/adjustments to coding is essential. Others may have the same question, and it may reveal an area in the coding protocols that needs to be changed or updated. Communication is key.

- *Before submitting coding, double check it.* Coding is iterative. Make sure to go back and double check that all adjustments to the protocol are reflected consistently across the entire section.

Each row in the spreadsheet represented a single incident of cultural heritage damage or destruction. If the same site was reported to have two separate incidents of destruction, each was put in its own row. Similarly, an incident spread over multiple days and locations was split across multiple rows. Incidents dealing with Iraq, reconstruction, or where no damage or destruction was reported were *excluded*.[18] The following information was recorded for each incident at this stage: Unique ID, ASOR incident number, a count of coded incidents per ASOR incident number (e.g., if the team coded three incidents from ASOR incident SHI 16-0038), ASOR report number, ASOR report date, incident date, incident start date, incident end date, site name (and any variations), site historical period, type of site (e.g., shrine, church, tell), damage code, and location description. In total, the team coded 1,166 incidents of cultural heritage damage or destruction.

3.2.3 UCDP Reconciliation

Next, the team focused on confirming the location and start date of the incidents to the extent possible. Working with analysts from the UCDP, incident locations were geolocated and their start dates were verified through in-depth review of the ASOR reports and independent confirmation through other open sources. Having common understanding of the precision of where events occurred (locations) and when events occurred (the start of an incident) allowed for these two datasets to be combined analytically. The town geolocations were generally accurate; however, the site geolocations (the latitude and longitude for individual cultural heritage locations) were often hard to verify.[19] In these cases, both the site geolocation provided by ASOR, and the verified town geolocations were kept so that sensitivity analyses could be performed as needed. Finally, a measure of validity used by the UCDP was coded for each cultural heritage incident that could signal to a future analyst how precise the latitude and longitude are.

[18] The ASOR CHI reports looked at both Syria and Iraq as it related to the Syrian War. This project was focused only on Syrian cultural heritage, so Iraq reports were ignored.

[19] An archaeological site, which can take up several hectares of land will have a single set of coordinates associated with it—a single dot on a map. How and where that dot is placed on the site determines the precision of the resulting data. For example, is it placed at the "centroid"—the geometric center—of the site, or at the largest building, or at the entrance to the site? These same questions apply to geolocating incidents of cultural heritage destruction. The measures of validity developed for these data help to convey how certain the team was that this incident occurred at this specific location versus in the nearby vicinity.

3.2.4 Review and Coding for Validity

The UCDP geolocation process identified several incidents that needed to be split into multiple rows such as air strikes where the destruction is spread out across unique points. To fully capture each location of destruction, each row needed to have a discrete time *and* a discrete geolocation. The team used this as an opportunity to review the previous coding work (verifying the incident date, type of damage coded, and actor); verify all links and sources associated with each incident and code those variables (source types, number of sources); identify incidents to split out into multiple incidents; and to code the temporal validity measures. Two research assistants completed this new set of coding.

Two dimensions of time are relevant when dealing with near real-time reporting in a conflict. The first is how quickly information is reported in the aftermath of an attack. The second is how specific and precise the information is that gets reported. The first was captured by measuring the number of days between when an incident occurred and when it was first reported (the difference between the incident date and the report date). The second was captured by measuring how specifically the incident date was described. A one on this scale indicated that the exact start date is reported and five indicated that the start date was reported as somewhere in a one-month to one year time span (e.g., "sometime in the spring of 2016..."; zero indicated no date was ever reported). [The distinction between the incident date and the report date is especially important to capture, as discussed in Sect. 4.1.]

3.2.5 Coding Validation

To validate the coding, we drew a 10% random sample, five percent of each research assistant's work. This subset was coded from scratch and then the results were compared to the larger dataset. Any discrepancies were recoded after discerning the root of the error.

Throughout the process of quantification, CURIA applied the four principles discussed above: transparency, triangulation, metadata, and sustainability. All coding decisions and processes were recorded in living coding protocols and a final version is available with the data upon request (*transparency*). Verification checks were conducted on every link or reference provided in the ASOR reports and locations were validated between UCDP and ASOR (*triangulation*). All coding decisions and process decisions, including software versions, were recorded (*metadata*). Finally, all data were designed to be used to address a variety of cultural heritage questions and to be integrated with the UCDP and incorporated reliability measures to account for variation in sources. They also are posted in a de-identified manner to be available for future scholars (*sustainability*).

3.3 *Benefits of Quantification in the Case of Syria*

With these data it is possible to examine new questions and understand the dynamics of cultural heritage damage and destruction in conflict in new ways. At a basic level, they give a detailed view of incidents cultural heritage attacks during the Syrian conflict. In total, these data contain either 1166 or 1069 incidents of cultural heritage attacks across 11 distinct categories from 2014 to 2017, depending on whether you look at the report date or the incident date, respectively (see Fig. 4.1). The data are detailed enough so that one can look at the distribution of incidents by type of damage or destruction (Fig. 5) and by actor (Fig. 6).

It is also possible to look at the distribution of cultural heritage attacks in space to see how they relate to incidents of civilian fatalities and ambient population (Fig. 7). The flexibility and granularity of these data allow for deeper analyses that focus on microdynamics of conflict. Given the increasing frequency with which conflict is occurring globally, having data that can look at such detailed questions

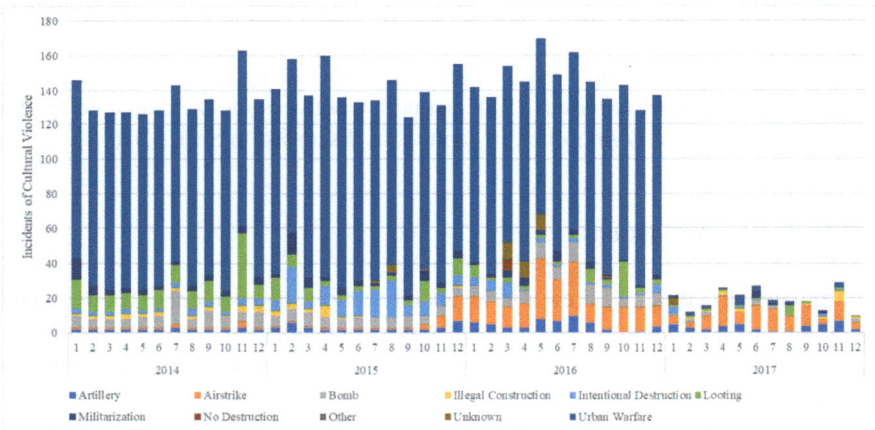

Fig. 5 Incidents of cultural heritage attacks over time and by type of damage or destruction

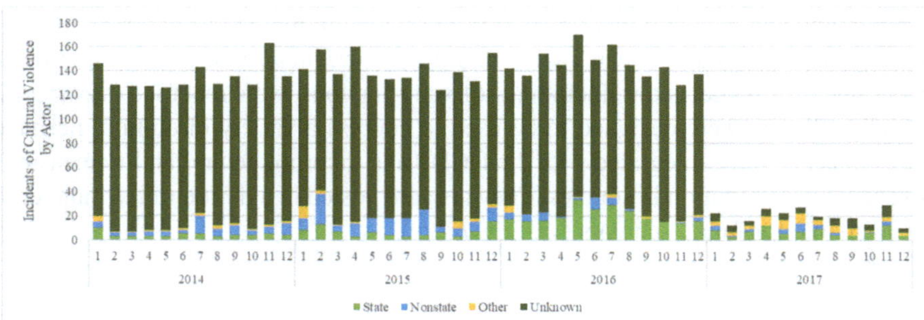

Fig. 6 Incidents of cultural heritage attacks by actor type over time

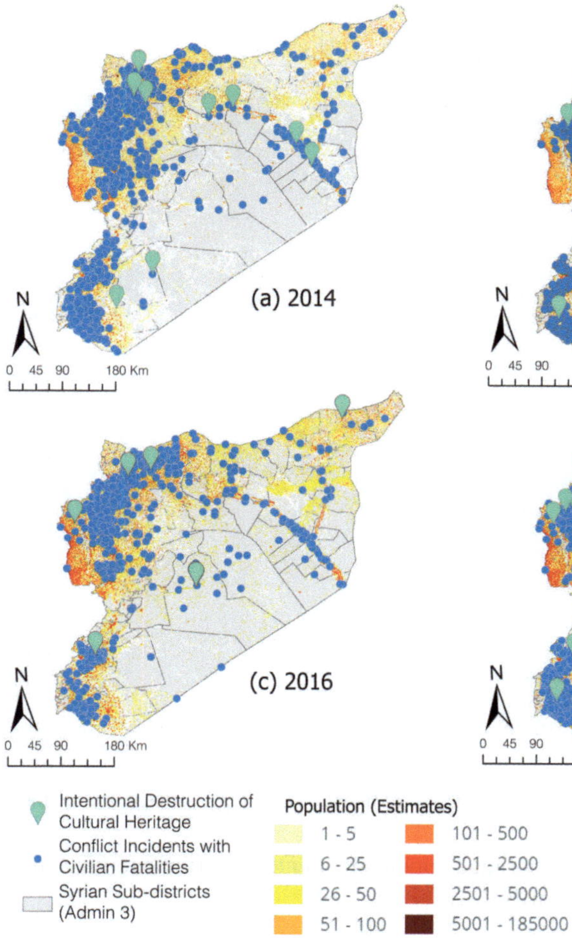

Fig. 7 Incidents of intentional destruction of cultural heritage compared to civilian fatalities and ambient population

related to cultural heritage is both timely and important. For example, one analysis examines whether civilian fatalities and cultural heritage attacks (measured as intentional destruction) colocate and whether they do so in areas where protected locations are prevalent. Based on preliminary results, the team finds no evidence of significant colocation of these two phenomena (Fig. 8) nor around protected locations (measured as cultural heritage no strike locations and internally displaced persons camps). These findings provide important evidence in support of the efficacy of no strike lists and other protected locations and counters arguments that international actors have intentionally targeted cultural and civilian locations as part of a cultural genocide (see Bokova 2015; Cuno and Weiss 2022; UNESCO World Heritage Centre 2015). Without empirically-sound evidence in support of such a

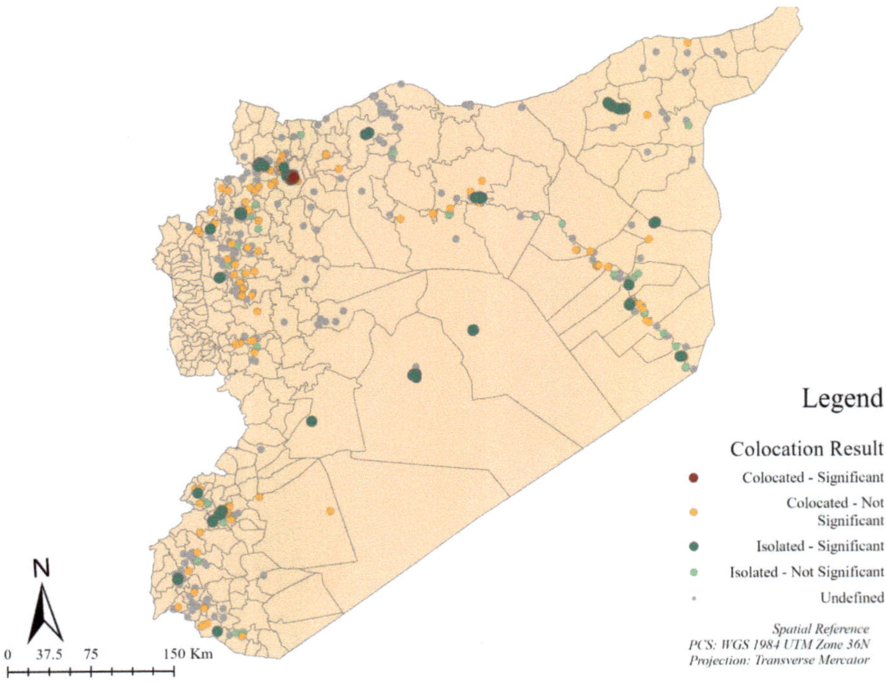

Colocation of Incidents of Cultural Heritage Damage (Incident Date) and Conflict with Civilian Deaths within 31 days. Neighborhood distance calculated as 1819 meters.

Fig. 8 Colocation of civilian fatalities and incidents of intentional cultural heritage destruction

claim, efforts to protect cultural heritage may inadvertently contribute to the expansion of these conflicts unnecessarily.

4 Addressing Challenges in Creating Valid and Reliable Data

The process of quantifying open-source information to create robust and reliable data can face many methodological and ethical challenges. Though they do not outweigh the benefits discussed above, it is important to discuss them and understand their potential implications for the data and future analyses.

In the case of the data discussed here, the team faced four significant challenges: (1) construct validity, (2) accuracy versus completeness, (3) geolocation, and (4) multiple incidents. First, when creating quantitative data, the goal is to capture information to convey specific concepts or ideas. The challenge is how to ensure that other scholars will be able to look at the final dataset and agree that what you have captured is what you intended to. This is the concept of construct validity, which is a significant challenge for many types of data collection (survey research,

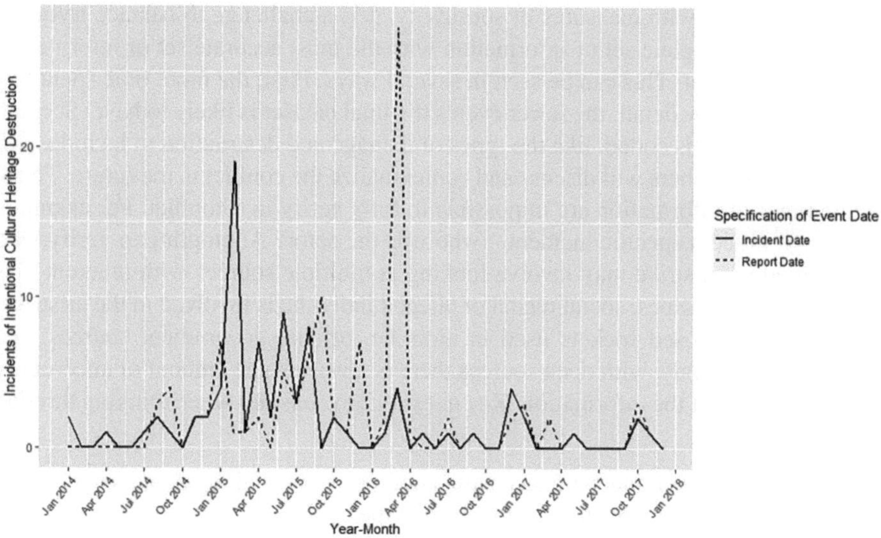

Fig. 9 Distribution of when incidents of intentional cultural heritage occurred from 2014–2017 based on the incident date versus the report date. The solid line indicates incidents coded based on their incident date. The dashed line indicates incidents coded based on their report date

secondary data collection, OSINT, etc.; Oleanu et al. 2019). In this case, the construct of interest was when and where an incident was occurring and what type of incident it was. In conflict settings, all three types of information are inherently difficult to know with any degree of certainty and the further the analyst is from the conflict, the harder it can be to truly verify details. To illustrate, the CURIA team incorporated both the date when the report was published (the report date) and an estimated date of when the incident took place (the incident date). Figure 9 shows a direct comparison of these two variables. The peaks in when large numbers of incidents occur are notably different between the two specifications, with the incident date peaks occurring largely from 2015 to 2016, while most events are clustered at the beginning of 2016 in the report date specification. The ASOR team was most active in reporting in early 2016, as more source information on earlier incidents became available. This suggests that the report is more likely capturing the activities of the ASOR team rather than when the incidents themselves likely occurred. Had the CURIA team only coded the report date or assumed the report date was "good enough" they would have been systematically capturing something different than intended—they would have created data with construct validity bias built in. The incorporation of measures of sensitivity are essential for mitigating this challenge. It signals to other scholars that those creating the data understand this difficulty and gives them the ability to choose where their tolerance for accuracy is. Scholars can include these measures directly in their models to empirically test whether the data collection or coding strategy affects the findings (see Dugan and Distler 2016).

Second, even with measures of sensitivity, it is a challenge to balance trying to get the most complete set of information with the most accurate set of information in the final dataset. This can be seen in several ways. First, the more time spent trying to verify every detail, the fewer events the final dataset is likely to have. Second, how information is coded, like the types of damage and destruction to include, will determine how others will discuss and contextualize the conflict in the future. Third, some types of information are impossible to fully verify in a conflict. For example, who committed a specific incident—who was the actor? Attempting to verify who committed an airstrike may involve looking at multiple sources with inherent bias and propaganda issues, social media of alleged individuals involved in the airstrike, pictures of supposed rockets used in airstrike, official government sources, and more. Unfortunately, with open sources there is always some amount of uncertainty in the accuracy of the information. Key questions to consider when thinking through accuracy include:

- Who has a vested interest in accusing another party or taking ownership?
- Who supplies the arms for each faction of the conflict?
- Who supplied the information contained in the source?
- Who funded the information or data collection, and do they have an agenda?

This uncertainty can create a secondary challenge—where is the line? *Should* all information be included, or should it be curated to some degree? Perhaps in an ideal world, all information would be included or only information that could create a perfectly balanced dataset would be included. Yet, even with the idea of a "balanced" dataset, it becomes an analytical choice how to define the term. Does it refer to the statistical notion of balance, where there are equal numbers of observations in treatment groups (Farrokhyar et al. 2010)? Or is it trying to balance the competing narratives present in the open-source information (for example by including both pro-Assad and anti-Assad propaganda in equal measure)? Every dataset will require a different answer; regardless of what the decision is, it will impact how the events documented will be framed for future scholars and what types of potential bias may be structured into the final dataset.

For example, the Syrian cultural heritage data discussed here tried to have the data be as complete as possible, meaning that balance was defined as representing as many different perspectives in the data as possible without overrepresenting one in particular. Since the CURIA team worked from a pre-curated set of open sources, they had to acknowledge and mitigate the potential for one narrative of the conflict to be more represented than others (e.g., if the Syrian government published more information, then it was possible it would be overrepresented by sheer volume). The team attempted to mitigate the issues of completeness vs accuracy and balance by including sensitivity measures plus detailed variables for the incident type, location, and time. However, when it comes to the actor variable, only include four options are included: state, nonstate, other, and unknown. This was an intentional curation of information and a statement on the accuracy of information that the team felt could be included. It was important to include some amount of actor information; however, it was not possible to say with any degree of certainty whether a given actor was any more specific than these categories. Doing so would require conducting deep dive open-source investigations into every incident and would potentially require crossing ethical lines. In particular, it ran the risk of assuming an individual was involved without any definitive proof or a conviction. Even with the vast amount of information available online, logically, it is not possible to say with absolute certainty that a given profile (for example on social media) belongs to a specific individual. It is too easy to create a fake profile or generate deep fake imagery in the current online landscape. To look at a historical event and prove someone was the perpetrator would require trying to navigate a potential historical bias (using knowledge of how events turned out to justify a claim) (Rivera 2018). Since due process requires innocence until proven guilty beyond a reasonable doubt and ethical standards (like international review boards in the United States) assume a reasonable right to privacy, there is no valid and ethical means of confirming a perpetrator's identity during a conflict like Syria. Attempting to do so runs the risk of violating someone's right to due process and crossing ethical lines that should not be crossed.

Third, as discussed above, geolocation is the process of identifying the latitude and longitude coordinates (the physical location on a map) of where an incident occurred. The uncertainty of information can present difficulties in finding and verifying the precise location of every incident (Hultquist 2020; Kuczyńska 2024). Another challenge involves choosing just one point to represent an incident spread over an area. For example, some incidents were discussed as "Aleppo experienced multiple airstrikes overnight." The location here is the city of Aleppo: not an overly large geographic area, but large enough that it makes pinning down the exact geolocation difficult. So, where should one place a pin on the map for the city? In the mathematical centre? In the centre where the alleged airstrikes occurred? Should each airstrike be geolocated individually? What if some of them cannot be? These are all questions that should be considered contextually and there is no single correct answer. It is more important that a decision be made, recorded, and applied consistently and transparently. In these data, the team included as precise a coordinate as possible along with a sensitivity measure to indicate how precise that point is—the specific location, the neighbourhood, the town, and so on. This was based off the UCDP approach, which is an internationally recognized standard for how to address geolocation challenges in open-source data (UCDP, 2024).

Finally, how you treat multiple incidents can affect how the data will be used. To continue with the example from above, namely 'should an airstrike be considered one incident or several connected incidents?' An airstrike is typically a series of missiles that are either fired in close proximity or sometimes can be a single missile that splits into multiple explosive components. How these are coded should depend on whether recording multiple connected impact locations is analytically relevant. That is, will it make a difference for any analysis if you treat them as one incident or several? Either way, it will affect how the data are constructed in other ways, such as how you will treat geolocation and what types of damage will be recorded. Then, make sure that the data are coded consistently, and the rules are transparently documented. In this project, airstrikes were typically considered as a single incident because they would all be launched at the same time; however, a series of airstrikes would be considered each their own incident. For example, "an airstrike was launched last night" would be considered a single incident; "multiple airstrikes were launched in three cities last night" would be treated as separate incidents in each location.

5 Conclusion

Open sources of information will only continue to become more prevalent and prominent as sources of cultural heritage data. Quantification is one important way of working with open-source information. First, it allows us to process and work with large volumes of information more easily. Once data are formatted as numbers, it is easy to create charts and graphs that make information more intuitively understood. Second, it enables more nuanced and complex analyses. This chapter demonstrated some abilities of data from Syria to look at the relationship between cultural heritage attacks and civilian fatalities. However, with standardized and transparent methods, it is also possible to create much-needed cross-national comparisons and analyses that move towards predictive modelling.

There are challenges associated with creating quantitative cultural heritage data that need to be considered—construct validity, balancing accuracy and completeness, geolocation, and handling multiple incidents. Yet, if the process is undertaken intentionally and follows the same principles of open-source investigations outlined here (transparency, triangulation, metadata, and sustainability) it should pose no difficulty to cultural heritage scholars. Doing so will allow cultural heritage scholars to address pressing questions about cultural heritage in crisis or in conflict quickly, at a high standard, and while accounting for the nuances inherent in such tasks.

References

ACLED (Armed Conflict Location and Event Data). (2024, October 14). ACLED. https://acled-data.com/

Akhgar B, Bayerl PS, Sampson F (2016) Open Source Intelligence Investigation: From Strategy to Implementation. Springer

Amnesty International (2024, July 30) Syria: Yezidi survivors of Islamic State atrocities abandoned to indefinite detention in north-east Syria. Amnesty International. https://www.amnesty.org/en/latest/news/2024/07/syria-yezidi-survivors-of-islamic-state-atrocities-abandoned-to-indefinite-detention-in-north-east-syria/

Armstrong M (2019, April 16) Infographic: global data creation is about to explode. Statista Daily Data. https://www.statista.com/chart/17727/global-data-creation-forecasts

Bazzell M (2016) Open source intelligence techniques: resources for searching and analyzing online information, 5th edn. CreateSpace Independent Publishing Platform

Bellingcat Global Legal Action Network (2018) Justice and Accountability Unit: Methodology for Online Open Source Investigations into Incidents Taking Place in Ukraine Since 24 February 2022. https://www.glanlaw.org/online-open-source-methodology

Besaw C, Ritter K, Tezcür GM (2023) Beyond collateral damage: the politics of civilian victimization in a civil war. Glob Stud Quart 3(3). https://doi.org/10.1093/isagsq/ksad050
Bevan R (2012, November 15) The role of cultural vandalism in genocide warning systems [Paper Presented at Symposium]. Cultural Heritage Protection in Times of Risk: Challenges and Opportunities, Yildiz Technical University, Istanbul Turkey
Bokova I (2015) Fighting cultural cleansing: harnessing the law to preserve cultural heritage. Harv Int Rev 36(4):40–45
Borda AZ (2022) Putting Reproductive Violence on the Agenda: A Case Study of the Yazidis. J Genocide Res 0(0):1–21. https://doi.org/10.1080/14623528.2022.2100594
Bostad EK (2018) Regime crackdown in Syria (2011–2017) – unpacking violence against civilians. In 18/01990. https://ffi-publikasjoner.archive.knowledgearc.net//handle/20.500.12242/2186
Braithwaite A, Johnson SD (2012) Space–time modeling of insurgency and counterinsurgency in Iraq. J Quant Criminol *28*(1):31–48. https://doi.org/10.1007/s10940-011-9152-8
Brodie N (2022) The looting and trafficking of syrian antiquities since 2011. In: Antiquities smuggling in the real and virtual world. Routledge
Center for Preventive Action (2024) Conflict in Syria. Global Conflict Tracker. Retrieved July 8, 2024, from https://cfr.org/global-conflict-tracker/conflict/conflict-syria
Cetorelli V, Sasson I, Shabila N, Burnham G (2017) Mortality and kidnapping estimates for the Yazidi population in the area of Mount Sinjar, Iraq, in August 2014: A retrospective household survey. PLOS Med 14(5):e1002297. https://doi.org/10.1371/journal.pmed.1002297
Clapperton M, Jones DM, Smith MLR (2017) Iconoclasm and strategic thought: Islamic State and cultural heritage in Iraq and Syria. Int Aff 93(5):1205–1231. https://doi.org/10.1093/ia/iix168
Coppini C (2021) Yezidi Cultural Heritage in the Sinjar Region: In K. Omarkhali & P. Kreyenbroek (Eds.), Yezidism (1st ed., pp. 135–150). Harrassowitz Verlag; JSTOR. http://www.jstor.org/stable/j.ctv2rr3gwx.10
Cunliffe, E. (2014). Archaeological Site Damage in the Cycle of War and Peace: A Syrian Case Study. Journal of Eastern Mediterranean Archaeology & Heritage Studies 2(3):229–247. https://doi.org/10.5325/jeasmedarcherstu.2.3.0229
Cuno J, Weiss T (Eds.). (2022) Cultural Heritage and Mass Atrocities. Getty Publications. https://www.getty.edu/publications/cultural-heritage-mass-atrocities
Danti MD (2015) Ground-based observations of cultural heritage incidents in Syria and Iraq. Near East Archaeol 78(3):132–141. https://doi.org/10.5615/neareastarch.78.3.0132
Darmofal D (2015) Spatial analysis for the social sciences. Cambridge University Press
Diggle PJ (2013) Statistical analysis of spatial and Spatio-temporal point patterns, 3rd edn. Chapman and Hall/CRC. https://doi.org/10.1201/b15326
D'Ippolito M (2014) New Methods of Mapping: The Application of Social Network Analysis to the Study of the Illegal Trade in Antiquities. In W. G. Kennedy, N. Agarwal, & S. J. Yang (Eds.), Social Computing, Behavioral-Cultural Modeling and Prediction (pp. 253–260). Springer International Publishing. https://doi.org/10.1007/978-3-319-05579-4_31
Dubberley E, Koenig A, Murray D (eds) (2020) Digital witness: using open source information for human rights investigation, documentation, and accountability. Oxford University Press
Dugan L, Distler M (2016) Measuring terrorism. In: The handbook of the criminology of terrorism. John Wiley & Sons, Ltd., pp 187–205. https://doi.org/10.1002/9781118923986.ch12
Fabiani MD (2019) Building a Baseline: Unifying Spatial and Temporal Methodologies to Understand Archaeological Looting in Egypt [Dissertation, University of Maryland College Park]. https://drum.lib.umd.edu/handle/1903/22107?show=full
Farrokhyar F, Bajammal S, Kahnamoui K, Bhandari M (2010) Practical tips for surgical research. Ensuring balanced groups in surgical trials. Canadian J Surg Journal Canadien DeChirurgie 53(6):418–423
Fjelde H, Hultman L, Sollenberg M (2016) Violence against civilians during civil war. In: Peace and conflict 2016. Routledge
Freeman L (2020) Prosecuting atrocity crimes with open source evidence: lessons from the international criminal court. In: Dubberley E, Koenig A, Murray D (eds) Digital witness: using open

source information for human rights investigation, documentation, and accountability. Oxford University Press

Ghioni R, Taddeo M, Floridi L (2023) Open source intelligence and AI: a systematic review of the GELSI literature. AI & Society. https://doi.org/10.1007/s00146-023-01628-x

Greenland F, Fabiani MD (2021) Collaborative practices in crisis science: interdisciplinary research challenges and the Syrian War. Sociol Sci *8*:455–479. https://doi.org/10.15195/v8.a22

Guha-Sapir D, Schlüter B, Rodriguez-Llanes JM, Lillywhite L, Hicks MH-R (2018) Patterns of civilian and child deaths due to war-related violence in Syria: a comparative analysis from the Violation Documentation Center dataset, 2011–16. Lancet Global Health *6*(1):e103–e110. https://doi.org/10.1016/S2214-109X(17)30469-2

Hassan NA, Hijazi R (2018) Open source intelligence methods and tools. Apress. https://doi.org/10.1007/978-1-4842-3213-2

Höglund K, Oberg M (2011) Understanding peace research: methods and challenges. Retrieved November 2, 2024, from https://www.routledge.com/Understanding-Peace-Research-Methods-and-Challenges/Hoglund-Oberg/p/book/9780415571982

Hultquist C (2020) Representation in geosocial data: grappling with uncertainty in digital traces of human activity. Int J Human Arts Comput 14:218–234. https://doi.org/10.3366/ijhac.2020.0253

Human Rights Center (HRL) & United Nations Office of the High Commissioner for Human Rights (UN OHCHR) (2022) Berkeley Protocol on Digital Open Source Investigations: A Practical Guide on the Effective Use of Digital Open Source Information in Investigating Violations of International Criminal, Human Rights and Humanitarian Law. UC Berkeley, School of Law and. https://humanrights.berkeley.edu/publications/berkeley-protocol-on-digital-open-source-investigations/

sakhan B, Zarandona A, Al-Deen T (2017) Cultural cleansing and iconoclasm under the 'Islamic State': attacks on Yezidi and Christian humans/heritage. In: Oruc F (ed) Pluralism and community in the Middle East. Hurst

Koenig A (2024) Digital Evidence and Open Source Information in Legal Practice [Training Presentation]

Kuczyńska H (2024) Digital evidence in investigations concerning Russian crimes in Ukraine. In: The Russian-Ukrainian conflict and war crimes. Routledge

Losson P (2016) Does the international trafficking of cultural heritage really fuel military conflict? Studies in Conflict & Terrorism, 484–495. https://doi.org/10.1080/1057610X.2016.1221255

Office of General Counsel of the Department of Defense (DOD) (2015/2023) Department of Defense Law of War Manual. United States Department of Defense

Olteanu A, Castillo C, Diaz F, Kıcıman E (2019) Social Data: Biases, Methodological Pitfalls, and Ethical Boundaries. Frontiers in Big Data, 2. https://doi.org/10.3389/fdata.2019.00013

Pherson KH, Pherson RH (2021) Critical thinking for strategic intelligence, 3rd edn. CQ Press

Post JM (2005) When hatred is bred in the bone: psycho-cultural foundations of contemporary terrorism. Polit Psychol 26(4):615–636

Quilling C (2022) The Future of Digital Evidence Authentication at the International Criminal Court | Journal of Public and International Affairs. https://jpia.princeton.edu/news/future-digital-evidence-authentication-international-criminal-court

Reyes V, Bogumil E, Welch LE (2024) The Living Codebook: Documenting the Process of Qualitative Data Analysis. Sociol Methods Res 53(1):89–120. https://doi.org/10.1177/0049124120986185

Rivera H (2018) Historian's fallacy. In: Arp R, Barbone S, Bruce M (eds) *Bad arguments: 100 of the most important fallacies in western philosophy*. John Wiley & Sons

Shahab S, Isakhan B (2018) The ritualization of heritage destruction under the Islamic State. J Soc Archaeol 18(2):212–233. https://doi.org/10.1177/1469605318763623

Solvang O (2017) Death by chemicals. Human Rights Watch. https://www.hrw.org/report/2017/05/01/death-chemicals/syrian-governments-widespread-and-systematic-use-chemical-weapons

Spiegelhalter D (2017) Trust in numbers. J Royal Statist Soc Ser Statist Soc 180(4):948–965. https://doi.org/10.1111/rssa.12302

Stanton JA (2016) Violence and restraint in civil war: civilian targeting in the shadow of international law. Cambridge University Press

Sundberg R, Melander E (2013) Introducing the UCDP georeferenced event dataset. J Peace Res *50*(4):523–532. https://doi.org/10.1177/0022343313484347

UCDP- Uppsala Conflict Data Program (2024). Retrieved November 2, 2024, from https://ucdp.uu.se/

UNESCO World Heritage Centre (2015, August 24) Director-General of UNESCO Irina Bokova firmly condemns the destruction of Palmyra's ancient temple of Baalshamin, Syria. UNESCO World Heritage Centre. https://whc.unesco.org/en/news/1339/

Van der Auwera S (2012) Contemporary conflict, nationalism, and the destruction of cultural property during armed conflict: a theoretical framework. J Confl Archaeol 7(1):49–65

Walsh EI, Sargent GM, Grant WJ (2021) Not just a pretty picture: scientific fact visualisation styles, preferences, confidence and recall. Inform Visual *20*(2–3):138–150. https://doi.org/10.1177/14738716211027587

Wilson H, Samuel O, Plesch D (2024) Open source investigations in the age of Google. World Scientific Publishing Company

Michelle D. Fabiani is a criminologist and interdisciplinary scholar focusing on quantitatively analysing cultural heritage crimes using open sources whenever possible. Combining a background in cultural anthropology, art history, and criminology with complex quantitative methods and open-source investigations, her research seeks to move towards proactive methodologies for cultural heritage protection and preservation. She is the co-director of the Cultural Resilience Informatics and Analysis (CURIA) lab, which seeks to support innovative analysis measuring the impacts of loss to culture including both property and heritage. CURIA uses data and analytical tools that are flexible and responsive to the needs of key stakeholders, supporting accountability and cultural justice processes related to cultural heritage crimes.

Open Access This chapter is licensed under the terms of the Creative Commons Attribution-NonCommercial-NoDerivatives 4.0 International License (http://creativecommons.org/licenses/by-nc-nd/4.0/), which permits any noncommercial use, sharing, distribution and reproduction in any medium or format, as long as you give appropriate credit to the original author(s) and the source, provide a link to the Creative Commons license and indicate if you modified the licensed material. You do not have permission under this license to share adapted material derived from this chapter or parts of it.

The images or other third party material in this chapter are included in the chapter's Creative Commons license, unless indicated otherwise in a credit line to the material. If material is not included in the chapter's Creative Commons license and your intended use is not permitted by statutory regulation or exceeds the permitted use, you will need to obtain permission directly from the copyright holder.

From Open-Access Spatial Data to Building a Typology of Looting Pits and Trends in Arid and Semi-Arid Landscapes

Mathilde Mura

Abstract Although understudied in the past, archaeological looting is now closely monitored constantly prompting new research. This chapter outlines a new methodological approach to the study of looting through the analysis of open-access satellite imagery and the statistical processing of the results obtained. Building on three regional case studies in Syria, Iraq, and Afghanistan, the chapter proposes a typology of looting and summarizes its main trends. The multiscale and multitemporal approaches highlighted in this chapter also enable intra-site case studies to be considered in a new light, as shown through an analysis of looting at Tell Senkereh-Larsa, a site located in southern Mesopotamia devastated by illegal excavations. This chapter demonstrates that by using archaeological methodologies and analysing looting pits, as if they were archaeological objects or structures themselves, allows for a more nuanced and detailed analysis of looting practices. Borrowing from spatial analysis, morpho-typologies and statistical analysis methods, it contributes to a greater understanding of the movements and targets of looters and how they operate from a social science perspective.

M. Mura (✉)
UMR 7041 ArScAn VEPMO and Archaïos, Paris, France

Bureau 278 UMR7299 Centre Camille Jullian Maison méditerranéenne des sciences de l'homme, Aix-en-Provence Cedex 2, France
e-mail: mathilde.mura@univ-amu.fr

© The Author(s) 2026

E. Smith, S. Austin (eds.), *Researching a Rigged Game: Digital Approaches to Tracing the Illicit Trade in Cultural Objects*, Studies in Art, Heritage, Law and the Market 11, https://doi.org/10.1007/978-3-032-02014-7_4

1 An Introduction to Studying Archaeological Looting in Relation to Illicit Trafficking

A substantial body of research into the illicit trade of cultural heritage has focused on the monitoring of illegal excavations perpetrated at archaeological sites during and post conflicts (Richason 2011; Cunliffe 2013; Parcak et al. 2016). Simultaneously, another angle grew from criminology, driving the analysis of the illicit trade into the direction of social sciences (e.g. Mackenzie et al. 2019; Hardy 2015), while looking for tools to identify provenience of the objects (Yates and Bērziņa 2022; Tompkins 2020; Huang 2013), stakeholders involved in the illicit trade of cultural objects, and more adequate legislation to convict those involved (Cornu 2018; Brodie et al. 2021).

Increasingly, illegal excavations are monitored efficiently with algorithms, change detection (Parcak 2007; Lasaponara and Masini 2010; Lauricella et al. 2017), and even exploring the field of artificial intelligence and machine learning (ALCEO project[1]; El-Hajj 2021; Vincent et al. 2024). While monitoring projects (like the EAMENA project, Wilson 2021) make remarkable amounts of data accessible, their aim is to detect incidents of unlawful excavations, but in many instances, they fail to discuss patterns, methods and therefore organization, context, and trends across looting incidents. So far, when typologies are considered, they aim at distinguishing different types of damage, their drivers and consequences, and looting is considered one type thereof (Cunliffe 2013; Zaina 2019). The data collected has yet to be utilized to their full potential, something that this chapter aims to demonstrate by considering looting the highest rank of typology rather than the lowest, so it can set the foundation for future research.

Using photointerpretation of open-access spatial data, ground truthing and bibliographical research, the study of looting pits—such as their shape, spatial distribution, time of emergence, types of sites where they occur, etc.—provides a rich source of information previously overlooked. It contributes to a better understanding of the social organization behind looting, the resources, motivations and organization of looters, and on large samples of sites, it allows to define the cross-regional trends of archaeological plundering. These trends are at the root of ongoing trafficking of archaeological objects and studying them can, to some extent, help predict the type and quantity of pieces that will reach the market in years to come. This will hopefully lead to more effective countermeasures across the trafficking chain.

The following chapter outlines a methodology to explore the spatial distribution, typology, and circumstances of looting on a large set of data from Syria, Iraq, and Afghanistan. By doing so, it underlines the still little-known trends and practices of looting in arid and semi-arid landscapes. The main objective of this research is to underline how the analysis of this open-air scavenging of archaeological sites can provide a useful avenue for research into the illicit traffic in archaeological material.

[1] More about the project https://www.iit.it/it/web/alceo and dataset https://iit-ccht.github.io/alceo/.

2 Photo-Interpreting Looting Events on Open-Access Spatial Data

2.1 *Data Sources, Use of Open-Access Data and Ethical Questions*

The study of archaeological looting events over long periods of time requires broad sources of imagery data (Parcak et al. 2016; Contreras and Brodie 2010). Multiscale and multitemporal data sets are needed and would be nearly impossible to compile if it was not for open-access resources. It should be noted that this chapter is based on open-access data rather than open-source data, meaning that they are freely accessible online or in archive repositories, but not freely redistributed or modified. Furthermore, although crucial to researchers, open-access data are not always sufficient and, in few instances, reliance on declassified state data or commercial data becomes necessary. For the case studies presented in this chapter, the main data sources that were used are described in Table 1.

Whether available in open-access or not, using aerial and satellite imagery in conflict areas poses several questions related to ethics: on the one hand, open-access data provides the framework for Findable, Accessible, Reproductible and Reusable research, following the FAIR principles (Wilkinson et al. 2016); on the other hand, it raises questions regarding the ethics of using oversight technologies to study conflict and post-conflict areas, when they are derived from military oriented devices

Table 1 Datasets of optical images used for the study, year covered, resolution and open-access status

Type	Source	Year	Resolution	Open-Access
Ground historical	Archives	/	/	Yes
Satellite historical	CORONA KH-4	1962–1972	0.6 m–2.75 m	Yes/No
Satellite historical	CORONA KH-7	1963–1967	0.6 m	Yes/No
Satellite historical	HEXAGON KH-9	1971–1986	0.6 m	Yes/No
Satellite historical	Google Archives	1984	70 m	Yes
Satellite historical and contemporary	Google Archives	2002–2024	0.3 m—5 m	Yes
Satellite contemporary	Copernicus (ESA) DEM	/	30 m	Yes
Aerial (UAV) contemporary	Orthophotographs and derived DTM (private compagnies)	2015/2016 /2019/2020/2021	4 cm	No
Ground contemporary	Ground photographs (various sources)	/	/	No

and sources of information (Meskell 2020). Both ethical conundrums will be discussed below.

Aerial and satellite imagery are not historically open source or open-access data. Produced either by states for intelligence purposes or by private companies, it has been a data source both difficult to access and prohibitively expensive for researchers to obtain. A first step towards accessibility of these resources was the declassification of spy satellite imagery from the CORONA program from 1995 onwards (some are accessible for free, and other at the rate of 30$ a tile) and the consecutive release of *HEXAGON* and *U2* imagery (Kennedy 1998; Ur 2003; Ur and Hammer 2018). The second major step was the creation of the *Google Earth Pro* program in 2001 and its *Historical Image* feature, allowing access to the imagery archives going back to 1984. These two milestones deeply transformed and shaped the discipline of archaeology (Herndon et al. 2023; Howey et al. 2020): although still not open-source, they made a colossal amount of data openly accessible and easily available to researchers. Since then, these data sources have been systematically used in the framework of large-scale archaeological surveys, conservation and damage assessments of archaeological sites (Ur et al. 2013; Giraud 2016; Zaina 2019), and as part of training programs for professionals in source countries (Hobson 2019). In addition, European satellite programs of the European Space Agency (ESA) are another open-access source of data for research purposes. The Sentinel and Pleiades programs can be used for detection purposes but were not available for the areas of interest for this study. The Copernicus program, also produced by ESA, provides open-access 30 m corrected DEM worldwide, with an improved quality since 2022 (Airbus 2022). This program was used when revisiting data collection through the study of looting at Larsa.

The *CORONA*, *HEXAGON* and *U2* programs, commonly used in archaeological practice, are three reconnaissance satellite programs implemented by the United States' Central Intelligence Agency (CIA) with support of the United States Air Force, which commenced during the Cold War (Kennedy 1998). In the broader context of studying the ties between military and archaeology or the military-industrial-academic complex as Meskell (2020) would define it, it has been debated whether these types of sources—as well as satellite imagery in general—should be used in conflict and post-conflict settings. Reflecting on the historical connections between archaeology, intelligence gathering and occupation in Western Asia, Meskell (2020) investigates how our discipline has borrowed from the military field, and argues that by using oversight technologies, archaeologists working on post conflict documentation are, to some extent, perpetuating colonial and imperialist approaches. This issue of using military data while studying conflict or post-conflict events, is indeed not acknowledged enough in the discipline of archaeology (Bernbeck 2012; Pollock 2016; Pollock and Bernbeck 2018). Even less debated is the use of unmanned aerial vehicles (UAV), i.e. drones, to produce new photographic records in post-conflict areas, when used in an area where they were used as weapons of war and where communities have been living under them, thus rightfully associating the device to traumatic events,[2] and therefore questioning the relevance of its use (Pollock and Bernbeck 2018). Conscious of these reservations, academia is nevertheless under serious funding constraint and the growing quantity of data made available open-access is a valuable source of information for research purposes, particularly in the fight against the trafficking of cultural and natural heritage.

Unfortunately, the present study is not immune to the methodological constraints outlined above. These data serve as powerful tools in the understanding of looting and protecting of cultural heritage. Every effort was made to use these data sources with care, emphasizing the importance of acknowledging their initial purpose. By doing so, the study would also like to put forward the idea that a minor counterbalance to its initial purpose lies in the open-access nature of the data, as it ensures replicability of the monitoring, analysing and subsequent protecting of their cultural heritage by source countries' professionals. The purchase of commercial satellite imagery was only carried out as part of this study in cases where a specific, dated event needed to be documented, and for which historical images from *Google Archives* were not available. Drone overflights were carried out with the support and agreement of and under the supervision of local colleagues and institutions, as part of a collaboration involving training in data collection for photogrammetry.

2.2 On the Geographical Restrictions Induced

In addition to accessibility, costs and ethical issues related to the use of aerial and satellite imagery, the data sources described above also induce geographical limitations. In order to investigate looting events on the base of photointerpretation, the damages have to be visible from the sky. This therefore excludes the study of cave looting, looting occurring inside buildings or looting concealed by vegetation cover or other obstacles.

As a result, the methodology presented below is best suited to arid and semi-arid landscapes, where the vegetation is not too dense and consists of crops, grass, shrubs or sparse trees. Mountainous landscapes, which contain rock shelters, caves, forest covered areas, where there is no visibility from an aircraft or satellite, would have to be investigated with specific tools such as on-board Light Detection and Ranging (LiDAR).[3] LiDAR is a radar system which enables the ground surface under the canopy to be modelled, but this technology is not yet widely or openly available in the examined area.

[2] The question is debated for instance within the framework of humanitarian activities using UAV to map disaster or deliver supplies (Wang et al. 2021; Resnik and Elliott 2019).

[3] This technique was implemented for instance in the study of looting of an Etruscan site covered by trees in central Italy (Danese et al. 2022) or in northern Guatemala (Canuto et al. 2018) or used within the OPTIMAL project (https://ccht.iit.it/it/web/optimal).

This chapter will build on the study of three specific regions: the Euphrates valley section located in the governorate of Deir-e-Zor in Syria, the Sharizor plain, in the south of the governorate of Souleymaniah in the autonomous region of Iraqi Kurdistan and the Balkh Oasis, spreading across the governorates of Balkh and Jowzjan in north Afghanistan (Fig. 1). These geographical areas are further introduced below.

In Syria, the study focused on the section of the Euphrates valley located in the governorate of Deir-e-Zor (Fig. 1a). More specifically, the geographical area covered by the corpus, i.e. the set of sites examined for this study, is bordered by the towns of Deir-e-Zor to the north and Abu Kamal to the south, an area with a very arid climate. The Euphrates and its valley are highly strategic in several respects. From an environmental point of view, it is a major water resource in the middle of the desert expanse that characterizes south-eastern Syria. From a geostrategic point of view control of the river, a major transport route, makes it possible to manage traffic and supplies and to cross the administrative border with modern-day Iraq.

The second study area is located in the north of Iraq in the autonomous region of Kurdistan (Fig. 1b). The Shahrizor plain forms the southern extremity of the Souleymaniah governorate and extends over three subdistricts (Souleymaniah to the

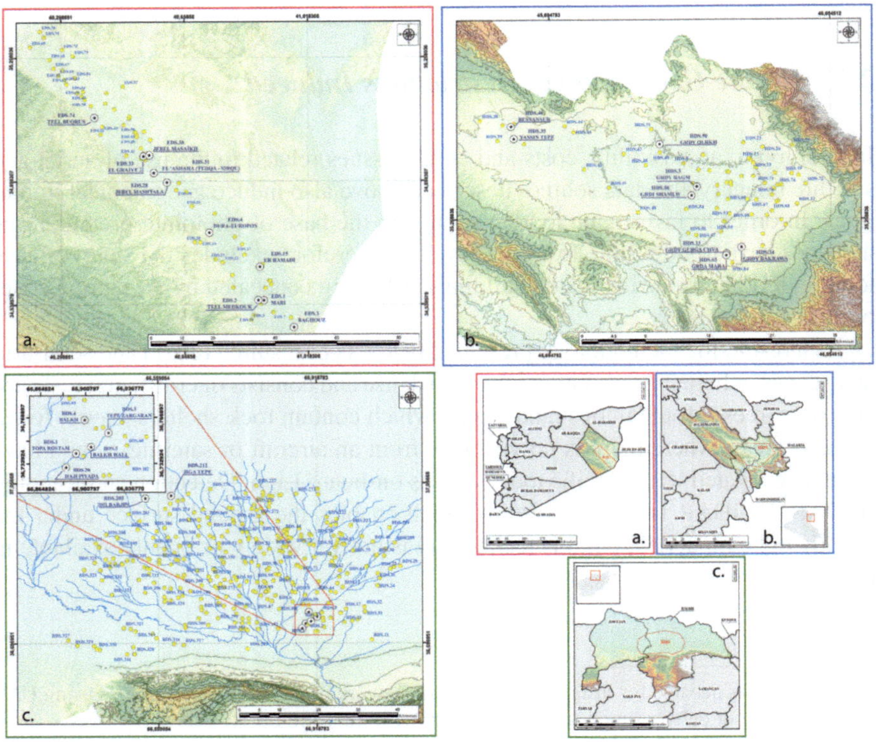

Fig. 1 Localization of the three areas of interest a. Syrian valley of the Euphrates b. Sharizor plain in Iraq c. Balkh Oasis in Afghanistan

north-west, Darband-i-Khan to the south and Halabja to the east). Geographically, it is a fertile plain between the foothills of the Zagros and the southern Kurdistan desert. Administratively, the plain is a pivotal area, bordered to the east by Iran, to the south by Federal Iraq and linked by the north and west to the rest of the autonomous region of Kurdistan. The Darband-i-Khan dam in the centre of the plain boosts agricultural productivity and adds strategic value to the region, as the dam controls the electricity and water supply to the wider region.

The third study area is the Balkh Oasis in Afghanistan (Fig. 1c), located north of the country, stretching as far as the border with Uzbekistan, in the districts of Balkh and Jowzjan. Set between a mountainous barrier to the south and an expanse of dunes to the north, Balkh Oasis is a wide plateau with a very gentle slope running from south to north. To the south, the highest point is the tip of the Hindu Kush. To the north, the dunes border the Oasis as far as the Amu Darya River, the natural border with Uzbekistan to the north, Turkmenistan to the north-west and Tajikistan to the north-east.

The next section will outline how these three case studies were analysed. The typology and trends defined in this study should not be bluntly applied to other geographical contexts without reassessment. Other areas, could be studied using the same replicable methodology, thus providing comparative data.

2.3 Analysis Method

To survey these vast open areas this study relied on photointerpretation, a method that has been widely used in archaeology for over 40 years (pioneering research in this field and for the study area can be attributed to Adams 1981; and Wilkinson 2003). This approach borrows from processes employed in geography, town planning, natural hazard monitoring and the military. At its core, the method employs images for visual analysis; previously these were physical images in photographic paper format, before this method was replaced by digital analyses or algorithms (Campbell and Wynne 2011). Visual analysis involves detecting points of interest on the images and then classifying, enumerating, measuring and delimiting them. To do this, all elements of the image must be considered, to define a 'signature'[4]: the tonality of the image (from lightest to darkest), the texture of the image (from smoothest to roughest), shading (angle, extent, etc.), repeating patterns, combinations, shapes and sizes. In the digital age, images are still analysed visually through a screen, but other methods are being developed to automate and speed up reading of images (Parcak et al. 2016; Casana and Laugier 2017; Lauricella et al. 2017).

Although considered very time-consuming, the study purposely relies on non-automated analysis of the satellite imagery. Indeed, many papers advocating for the semi-automatic reading of images demonstrate the opposite of their purpose

[4] On the topic of archaeological 'signatures" see Navalgund and Rajani 2017.

(Hammer et al. 2018; Lauricella et al. 2017; Parcak et al. 2016). When using semi-automatic methods to study archaeological looting, false positives are eliminated by successive, yet time-consuming manipulations of the image that limit the interest of a supposedly accelerating procedure. Often, visual evidence in academic papers, i.e. figures, show a mismatch between the vector or raster layer generated at the output and the initial raster, with false positives persisting (as noticed by Herndon et al. 2023) and true positives remaining undetected (Lauricella et al. 2017). For this reason, this study employed a visual and non-automated analysis of the images, to define a typology based on human analysis that could help refine digital algorithms in the future. This approach also improves the reproducibility of the method, even with limited technological expertise and resources.

During this study, known archaeological sites and potential new sites were identified and mapped using published regional archaeological maps and CORONA images. CORONA images were used to identify previously unnoticed anomalies that were characteristic of the presence of previous human occupation. These panchromatic images record the luminosity of the ground across the entire electromagnetic spectrum, and the so-called 'signatures' thus reflect the different types of soil occupation. Consequently, colorimetric anomalies can be studied in detail to identify distinct areas. This then informed the zoning of sites for this study's pedestrian survey. Sites are very diverse in terms of signatures and therefore morphology ranges from low mounds with a small surface area (comprising a single zone) to complex sites consisting of several mounds connected by flat occupied areas, i.e. low towns, subdivided into several zones (zoning >10 zones).

Following this first step, the corpus of sites was defined, it consists of 73 sites in the Euphrates valley, 75 sites in the Shahrizor plain, and 335 sites in the Balkh Oasis. Three extra sites were considered outside the main areas, one in each country (Ebla in Syria, Khorsabad in Iraq and Aï Khanoum in Afghanistan), bringing the total to 486 sites.[5]

Once archaeological sites of interest are located, recent imagery is needed to identify and assess looting. The accuracy of CORONA imagery and the shooting dates make it a marker of the pre-damage state of sites, but they become obsolete when it comes to the in-depth study of looting pits. On recent imagery, the following signatures are therefore sought: surface orifices, traces of soil cutting, modern on-site installations (buildings), etc. This initial photo-interpretation analysis enables to consider a sample of priority sites for ground-truthing. Ground-truthing involves selection of representative sites of the different intensities and concentrations of damage for each type of damage (shallow, moderately or very deep looting; shallow, moderately or very dense looting; diameter and number of impact zones, etc.). After this, all the sites were visited where the conditions allowed it. As a result, about a hundred of the 486 sites under study were ground-truthed, in the Shahrizor plain and the Balkh Oasis.

[5] For a complete list of analyzed sites and their locations see Mura (2021), vol.2 pp. 6–12.

Whilst in the field, the site is described in its entirety and then area by area: through this, the context in which the site is located, the geographical environment, the overall morphology of the site and the survey conditions (soil type, land use, level of vegetation cover, etc.) are described in detail. Then, for each area, the division is described according to its topographical, geometric or usage characteristics. Finally, the quantity of material discovered on the surface is assessed during the field, along with the damage present in the area. In the case of a damaged area, a specific spreadsheet has been developed to collect the data[6] including measurements (L, l, h) of looting pits, photographs (two to three shots per selected pit) and sketches (in plan and in lateral and transverse sections). Each distinctive pit was selected (smaller, larger and of average size, eroded or showing fresh tool marks, variable depths) to study looting. This strategy made it possible to create an exhaustive repository of traces. The following section will outline the typology built on the data collected at the 486 sites, remotely and on the ground.

Using these typologies, the methodology includes the creation of a destruction index to analyse a combination of information: it thus refers to the type, number, density, volume and impact of damage. A value of zero to four is assigned to each sub-index. The general criteria for the destruction index allocation are: (0) none; (1) presence of low-number and low-density damage: low impact; (2) presence of damage in small numbers, but in high density: average impact; (3) presence of damage in large numbers or very high density: strong impact; (4) near-irremediable damage.

Once the typology and destruction index were defined, the data obtained were statistically analysed using *Excel* for chi-square tests and *AnalysesSHS*[7] for factorial correspondence analysis and multiple correlations analysis. Chi-square test is a test of independence. It is used to check whether the frequencies observed in a sample differ significantly from the expected frequencies. The observed frequencies are compared with the expected one to define the deviation from independence. The test can be performed in any spreadsheet program, making it accessible and reproductible. If the chi-square test highlights a dependency between factors, a factorial correspondence analysis (for two factors) or a multiple correlation analysis (more than two factors) are relevant to discuss the decisive criteria of the dependence.

On an intra-regional scale, the spatial repartition of looting, relationship between morphology and damage, morphology and chronology, damage and academic knowledge were examined, carrying out chi-square tests and factorial correspondence analyses to understand whether the relationships are due to chance or not and thus trying to define the dominant trends.

---

[6] However, during this methodological research, careful attention was given to proposing a solution that could be integrated into traditional survey protocols. This solution has thus been permanently integrated into the Mission Archéologique Française du Gouvernorat de Souleymaniah (dir. J. Giraud) practices.

[7] *AnalysesSHS* is a web interface developed by the Pôle Informatique de Recherche et d'enseignement en Histoire of University Paris 1, Panthéon-Sorbonne, relying on R codes and packages: interface is available here http://analyse.univ-paris1.fr, as well as documentation related to the managed analyses http://analyses.univ-paris1.fr/documentation.html#AFC.

At the inter-regional scale, the results obtained in the three areas were compared, on the one hand, and all the sites in the corpus were treated independently of the region, on the other. The entire corpus was analysed using the same tests to establish the relationship between morphology and damage, morphology and chronology, damage and academic knowledge. These analyses enable to identify regional trends and cross-sectional patterns that would apply to the corpus as a whole. By examining intrinsic and extrinsic criteria, this methodology allows to identify which sites are most likely to be looted.

Although a social anthropology survey, based on qualitative interviews, was not planned at this stage, several villagers living in the vicinity of the studied sites came to provide additional information on looting events, during the field verifications. These exchanges, initiated by the villagers and never solicited, were translated on site, recorded in writing on the corresponding site spreadsheet and used with their agreement. Any information regarding looting came to light after the reasons for visiting the site had been explained. Deliberately, no personal information was collected, so as not to risk prejudicing participants who had admitted knowing someone who has or taking part themselves in looting activities for subsistence purposes (on the definition of subsistence digging see Hollowell 2006).

3 Building a Typology

Within the 486 sites, analysed in the three aforementioned regions, the study finds that looting greatly alters the surface morphology of sites—observable both in-person as well as through satellite imagery—and does so differently according to two dominant criteria, namely the morphology of the pits and their spatial distribution.

3.1 Morphology

Morphologically, the sample is divided between surface pits and tunnel types. Firstly, surface pit types correspond to all kinds of excavations made from the surface. It is the most easily identifiable type by remote sensing. Four types of surface pits can be defined (Fig. 2). The most common traces of looting are manual surface pits (*DMn*). Two subtypes are distinguished according to their opening size. An individual pit (*DMnIn*) is a hole excavated from the surface corresponding to the work of one individual. These independent holes have a narrow bowl or U profile. It can be either shallow (*DMnInd1*, Fig. 2A.) or deep (*DMnInd2,* Fig. 2B.).

The shallow manual individual pits (*DMnInd1*) do not exceed 50 cm in depth, have an average diameter of one meter and are made with shovels and pickaxes. Pits of slightly larger diameter, between one and two meter, and greater depth (*DMnInd2*), between 50 cm and 2.2 m, were also detected. By using remote sensing, the distinction between the two types can be established based on

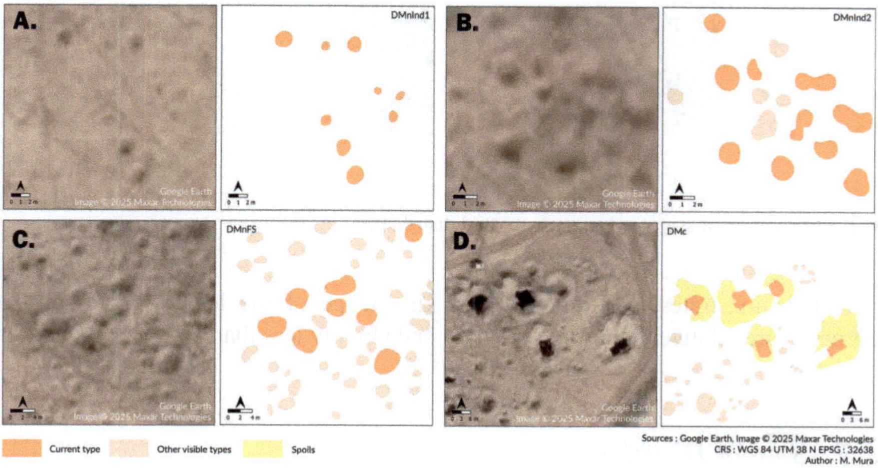

Fig. 2 Typology of surface looting, by morphology

assessment of the shadow cast inside the pit and the slightly larger diameter of *DMnInd2* types.

The third type of manual pit is both wide and deep (*DMnFS*, Fig. 2C), it is characterized by a wide U profile, a more rectangular notch in plan and rounded edges and 4-5 m diameter.[8] Discussions with nearby villagers allowed to determine that this type was made by a group of individuals (around 10 people depending on dimensions).

Surface pits can also be dug with the assistance of mechanical tools, making it the fourth type (*DMc*, Fig. 2D) of surface looting. They are characterized by sharper, vertical edges, and quadrangular shape. The profile is vertical on the edges and with curved angles on the sides perpendicular to the direction of the mechanical shovel. The pits show much greater depths (about 5 m minimum) with sides from 4 to 10 m at the surface.

Finally, the most invasive type of archaeological looting is also the most difficult to detect on satellite imagery, namely tunnels (*Tn*). Tunnels are implanted on the side of tells or at the bottom of topographical elements to penetrate the site further, and are thus less visible on vertical images such as satellite imagery. Tunnels are shaped as a cone with the entrance often larger than the end of the tunnel and no safety measures, such as scaffolding or consolidation, have been implemented by looters within the studied corpus. Unlike the surface pits, the construction of a

[8] These pits sometimes contain a rudimentary stairs shape, made of two to three steps, to facilitate removal of the rubble. In some instances, the pit follows very regular contours and corresponds to the outline of a room inside a building.

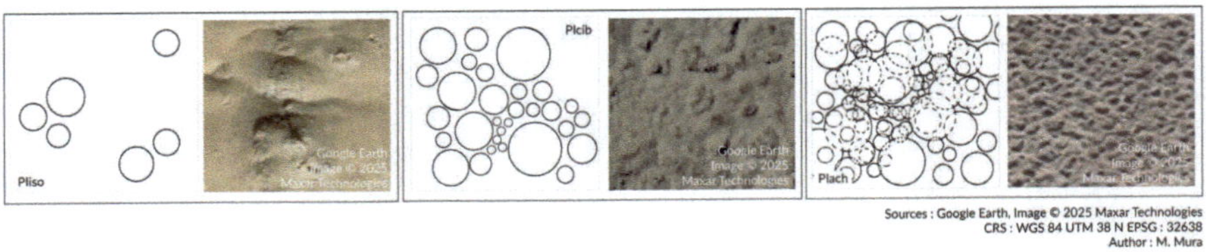

Fig. 3 Typology of surface looting, by spatial distribution

tunnel demonstrates a certain level of knowledge of the looters.[9] The tunnels observed are relatively constant in length and slightly less than 10 m.

3.2 *Spatial Distribution*

In addition to the morphology of stigmas of looting, the second criteria that was typologized is their spatial distribution. Three types of distribution have been observed in the corpus (Fig. 3): isolated looting (*PIiso*), targeted looting (*PIcib*) and relentless looting (*PIach*).

Isolated looting (PIiso) corresponds to a small number of pits, carried out on the periphery of a site. The second type (PIcib) is targeted looting, corresponding to a large number of pits, at a precise location and carried out side by side in a tight mesh. Relentless looting (PIach) consists of a very large number of holes, made at a specific location and for which the density of pits is such that they overlap each other, drawing coalescent circles.

3.3 *Destruction Index*

The specific criteria for assigning sub-indexes for looting are as follows and summarized in Table 2. Index 0 means that the site presents no sign of looting. Index 1 shows the presence of isolated looting (*PIiso*) regardless of morphology. Index 2 corresponds to the presence of targeted *PIcib* and manual *DMnInd1*, *DMnInd2*, *DMnFS* looting. Index 3 is either characterized by the presence of targeted looting *PIcib*, mechanized or tunnel *DMc*, Tn or by the presence of relentless *PIach* and manual *DMInd1*, *DMnInd2*, *DMnFS* looting. Index 4 considers as irremediable damage the presence of relentless *PIach* mechanized *DMc* looting, combined with targeted *PIcib* manual *DMInd1*, *DMnInd2*, *DMnFS* lootings.

[9] Tunnels documented in the study were systematically located between two archaeological floor levels visible in section or targeted piles of blocks or bricks that could be characteristic of funerary chambers.

Table 2 Attribution criteria for the looting destruction index

Index	Description	Looting Distribution	Looting Morphology
0	No signs of looting	None	None
1	Isolated looting observed, regardless of morphology	PIiso	Any type
2	Targeted looting and specific manual looting present	PIcib	DMnInd1, DMnInd2, DMnFS
3	Targeted looting with mechanized or tunnel methods, or relentless looting with manual methods	PIcib	DMc, Tn,
		PIach	DMnInd1, DMnInd2, DMnFS
4	Irremediable damage due to relentless mechanized looting, combined with targeted and specific manual looting types	PIcib and PIach	DMnInd1, DMnInd2, DMnFS, DMc

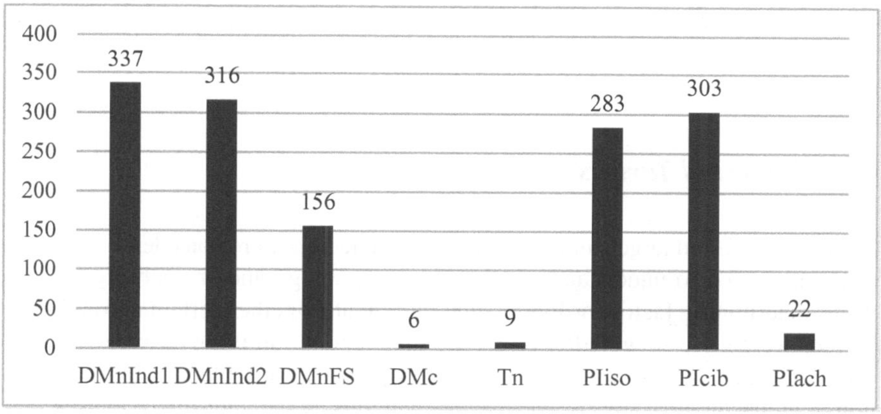

Fig. 4 Number of sites concerned per morphological types and spatial repartition types of looting

4 Towards a Better Understanding of Looting Practices

4.1 Preferred Methods

The results show that the sites in the corpus are predominantly looted manually and from the surface; according to our typology, they are affected by the *DMnInd1*, *DMnInd2*, and *DMnFS* types (Fig. 4). Tunnelling (*Tn*) and mechanized looting (*DMc*) are anecdotal in the corpus. Only nine sites show the stigmas of tunnels and six show notches characteristic of the use of mechanical shovels. Based on the unformal discussions that were conducted, types *DMnInd1* and *DMnInd2* are made by a single individual. The *DMnFS* type is achieved by a group. Individual pits are therefore the most widespread and group work at the pit scale is only represented in one third of the sites in the corpus. If we were to consider morphology alone, this could indicate most of the digging is carried out by single individuals.

But considering the spatial distribution within sites, our findings indicate that looting is a team effort. Indeed, the spatial distribution of targeted and relentless looting (*PIcib*, *PIach*) shows a density that is incompatible with operations undertaken individually. Two thirds of the sites are affected by targeted and/or relentless looting. In the case of targeted looting, corresponding to side-by-side pits, it is possible to assume the work was carried out by small groups, each making a hole in a tight cluster. Relentless looting, characterized by side-by-side and overlapping pits, corresponds more to collaborative work, but is only present in 4% of sites.

The most common modus operandus is therefore looting perpetrated by a small group working side by side to make shallow pits using common tools such as shovels and pickaxes (some traces of this could be identified on the surveyed sites). This division may mean that each person earns the profit from their own looting and that the profits are not centralized or redistributed. However, it is not possible to verify this hypothesis at this stage of our research. Thus, the evidence collected through the study of pit types and their distribution in space seems to indicate a predominant subsistence or opportunistic looting, organized within an already constituted social group (family, whole or sub-set of a village, etc.).

4.2 *Preferred Targets*

To define preferred targets intrinsic and extrinsic factors were considered. First, this study attempted to understand whether the morphology and/or visibility of a site was a determining factor for looting and investigate whether certain chronological periods were more sought after by looters than others, and if the degree of identification of the sites by the scientific community played a particular role in the perception of archaeological sites by local actors and thus on the intensity of looting.

Regarding the morphology of sites, the statistical analysis reveals that all morphological types of sites are potential victims of shallow damage. Yet low and flat sites (open-areas, or low tells) tend to be less damaged as a whole than large, mounded sites, or sites with apparent features, i.e. eroded architecture structuring the site[10] (Fig. 5). The less visible a site is in the landscape, the higher the probability of it being spared. Conversely, the more visible the site is, the higher the risk of looting.

When testing the sample of dated site (118 sites over the 486 studied), it seems that the presence of a specific period on a site is more significant than its proximity to the surface.[11] Three specific periods appeared to be favoured by looters within our study: the Early Bronze Age (from 3000 BC to 2100 BC), the Late Bronze Age/Iron Age transition (from 1500 BC to 600 BC), and the Classical Period (from 0 to

[10] A more detailed typology of site's morphology can be found in Mura (2021), which outlines plan and profile morphology and defines 39 types combining both.

[11] Unfortunately, it was not possible with our data to correlate the intensity of looting with the period most represented on sites.

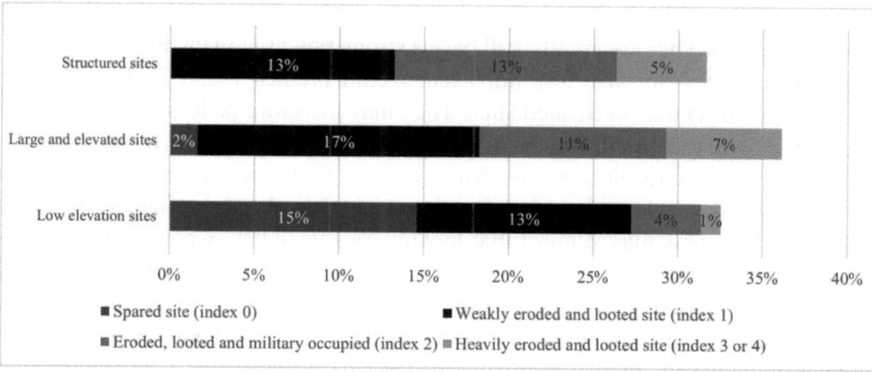

Fig. 5 Proportion and intensity of damage to the sites according to their morphology

Table 3 Number of sites per identification level by academics and destruction index

Index	Unknown sites	Identified sites	Surveyed sites	Excavated sites	Total
0	20	**32**	**55**	4	111
1	97	17	18	**8**	140
2	**147**	29	17	**10**	203
3	21	1	4	**5**	31
4	0	0	0	1	1
Total	285	79	94	28	486

300 AD), which correspond to periods rich in small objects such as cylinder seal, cuneiform tablets or coins, favourable to trafficking (Topçuoğlu and Vorderstrasse 2019).

Another objective was to examine the data available to address the relationship between the degree of knowledge by academics of a site and the intensity of looting (see data set in Table 3). For this purpose, four levels of identification were defined. Firstly, unknown sites are those identified remotely during this study, but that were not surveyed or referenced in publications to date. Secondly, identified sites were previously identified sites from remote sensing, although not surveyed their location was published. Thirdly, surveyed sites are those that were physically visited, their material collected, and the data published. Fourthly, excavated sites are those where at least a sounding was excavated, and results of the excavations were published.

On an inter-regional level, the independence test (chi-square) shows a dependency between the degree of knowledge of the site and intensity of looting, allowing for a factorial correspondence analysis of the data. The latter reflects the looters' primary attraction to safe values, i.e., sites that have been excavated, which indicates a certain form of archaeological richness. Identified or surveyed sites that have not been excavated are often ignored by looters. The absence of excavation thus appears to be considered locally as evidence of a rejection of the site by the researchers, and the site is therefore also deemed uninteresting to illegal excavators. Sites that are unbeknown to the scientific community (unknown sites) but discovered by the looters themselves are favoured over unexcavated sites. Having not been researched, these sites apparently still have a strong potential in the looters' opinion. Nevertheless, they are also less impacted overall (values 1 and 2 of the looting destruction index) than excavated sites. They may therefore be less rich in artefacts than the known, identified, and excavated sites.

Surprisingly, the results for sites that were identified remotely and published but not surveyed were closer to those for sites visited in the field than to those for unknown sites. This may suggest that looters are somewhat aware of publications but are still less interested in the identified sites that in those not been excavated.

This study finds that the more interest the scientific community shows in the site—namely by excavating it—the more likely it is that illegal excavators will plunder it intensively. In the lower valley of the Syrian Euphrates, where all the sites were at least surveyed, the contrast becomes clearer: surveyed sites are generally spared (values 0 and 1 of the destruction index linked to looting) and the scientifically excavated sites are looted (values 2 and 3 of the destruction index). In the Shahrizor Plain, the regional particularity lies in the fact that excavated and surveyed sites are equally affected to the first degree of the destruction index (value 1). But there is still a gradation in the degree of looting corresponding to the degree of identification. Thus, excavated sites are the most damaged (value 3 of the destruction index), surveyed sites are damaged to a lesser extent (value 2 of the destruction index) and sites identified but not surveyed are generally spared (value 0 of the destruction index). In the Balkh Oasis, there is an opposition between three groups (excavated, identified or surveyed, unknown) each located in an opposite quarter of the factorial correspondence analysis graph. Excavated sites are associated with a destruction index value of 4 (the highest). Identified or surveyed sites seem to be attracted mainly to the destruction index value 2. Index values 1 and 3 are indifferently associated with excavated or unknown sites. The preference of looters for excavated sites is also correlated in the Balkh area, therefore confirming that it is the richness of the site, demonstrated by excavations, that attracts local looters. This last finding highlights forms of knowledge of the looters other than archaeological knowledge per se. The latter appears to have a memory of the visits of scientific teams and of the sites that caught their attention. In addition to this knowledge, there are sometimes beliefs and superstitions that have a more anecdotal impact on looting and are difficult to quantify (Alva 2001; Karataş 2022). In the case of Afghanistan, the study found a consistency in looting tunnels on sites thought to be stupas, a phenomenon that could reflect a persistent belief that stupas contain a treasure at their core.

Overall, by analysing the multiple correlations between the looting destruction index values, the morphological types of the sites, the level of investigation on the sites and the identified periods, the study shows that three degrees of risk can be identified (Fig. 6).

A first group of sites distinguishes (Fig. 6: red limits), for which the risks of looting are very high. It concerns the high excavated tells, dated to chronological periods from the Early Bronze Age to the Iron Age, statistically attracted (close to each other on the graph) to the value 3 of the destruction index (the highest value of the index among the dated sites). A second group of sites concerns the intermediate risk

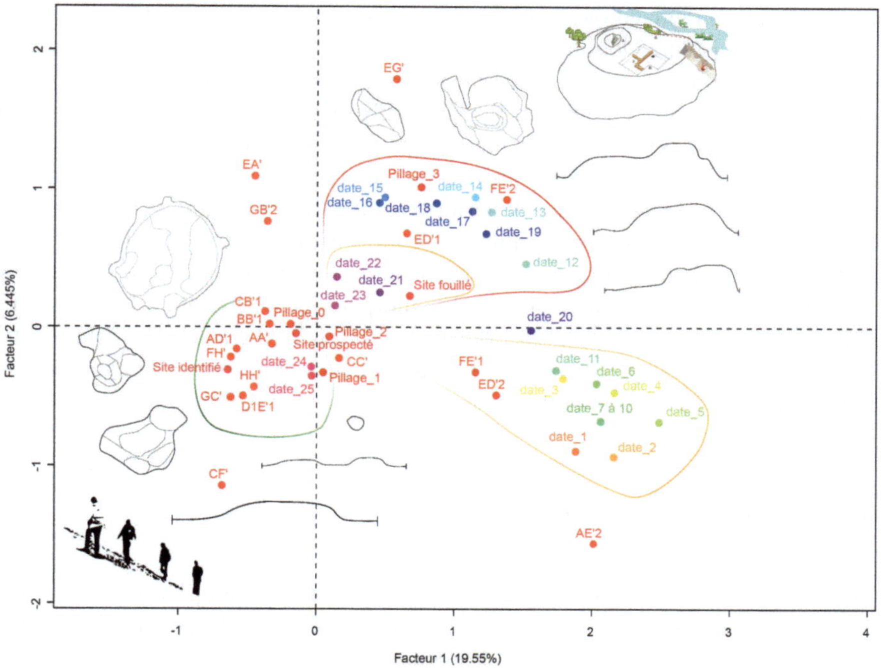

Fig. 6 Multiple correlations analysis graph showing correlation between looting index, site morphology, site chronology and level of academic knowledge on the deposit

sites (Fig. 6: orange boundaries). It is composed of two distinct sub-groups; on the one hand, the high tells from the Neolithic to the Chalcolithic, regardless of the level of investigation, on the other hand, the excavated sites from the Classical periods, and more specifically the Greco-Bactrian periods for the Balkh area, regardless of their morphology. The first sub-group is statistically attracted to the value 2 of the destruction index linked to looting. The second sub-group is statistically attracted to the destruction index value 3, but are closer to the origin of the graph than the high-risk sites, which indicates a lower probability of being looted. The third group of sites concerns sites relatively unaffected by looting (Fig. 6: green boundaries). It includes low sites, partially low sites, and structured sites, identified and surveyed, dating from the Islamic period. This group is statistically close to the values 0 and 1 of the destruction index. Without being completely risk-free, this group of sites nevertheless represents the most favourable combination of factors that put them at the lowest risk of looting.

The sites most favoured by looters are those that combine all three aggravating criteria: visibility, notability, and chronological period known for the presence and abundance of small objects. The sites for which the risks are moderate are groups for which one aggravating criterion is missing. In the first case, these are visible sites (high tells from the Neolithic to Chalcolithic period), which are tested despite the uncertainty of their richness, but which suffer less looting because they provide fewer objects in demand on the art market. This category is the most likely to bear the stigmas of isolated looting (*PIiso*), attesting to a failed attempt at identifying a sought period of occupation. In the second case, these are known sites rich in small objects, but whose morphology is not necessarily prominent (as for instance sites of the Classical periods). In this case, their lower visibility limits the number of looters and preserves sites that have not been excavated. The sites most likely to be spared are therefore those that combine at least two of the three mitigating criteria: invisibility, anonymity, and material culture of no known interest to the art market.

For the first time, looting targets have been identified according to several key and complementary criteria, including site morphology, visibility in the landscape, period of occupation and level of prior investigation by the academic community. Based on a statistical analysis of the data, these conclusions represent an important milestone in the protection of the most at-risk sites in the regions studied.

4.3 Larsa: A Case in Point

The site of Senkereh Larsa (Fig. 7) is located in southern Iraq, north-west of the modern city of Nassriyah. It is a low mound surrounded by a desertic landscape that used to be irrigated when the site was occupied (Vallet et al. 2019; Le Doaré et al. 2023). The site is not very visible in the landscape, but it is well known and has been the focus of archaeological excavations since shortly after its discovery by Loftus in 1854 (Loftus 1857). First sporadically at the beginning of the twentieth century by Andrae and Banks, and then in greater depth by French expeditions led by Parrot

Fig. 7 Oblique view of Larsa, showing the surface looting in the foreground and surrounding landscape of the site, courtesy of Joël Suire and MAFLU (Mission Archéologique Française de Larsa-Ueili)

from the 1930s to the mid-1960s, Margueron in 1969–1970 and Huot from 1974 until 1985 (Huot 2003; Margueron 1971; Parrot 1968). After more than 30 years of interruption, archaeological excavations resumed at Larsa in 2019.[12]

In addition to the known maximum extension of occupation from the Early Bronze Age to the Late Bronze Age, it appears that Larsa was at least partially occupied before and after these periods, from the time of Uruk to the Islamic period (Giraud et al. 2022). Unfortunately, this makes Larsa a site at the highest risk of looting. As a result, the successive conflicts that have shaken Iraq during the suspension period and lack of resources to protect archaeological sites have caused looting to rage on at Larsa. This was not the first wave of looting: illegal excavations were mentioned as early as A. Parrot expedition in the 1920s and in the decade that followed (Parrot 1933; Delougaz and Lloyd 1942). However, the recommencement of looting in recent times made it possible to undertake a thorough damage assessment of the site employing open-access data (Fig. 8).

The looting characteristics observed at Larsa correspond to four morphological types: *DMnInd1*, shallow individual manual pits; *DMnInd2*, individual deep manual

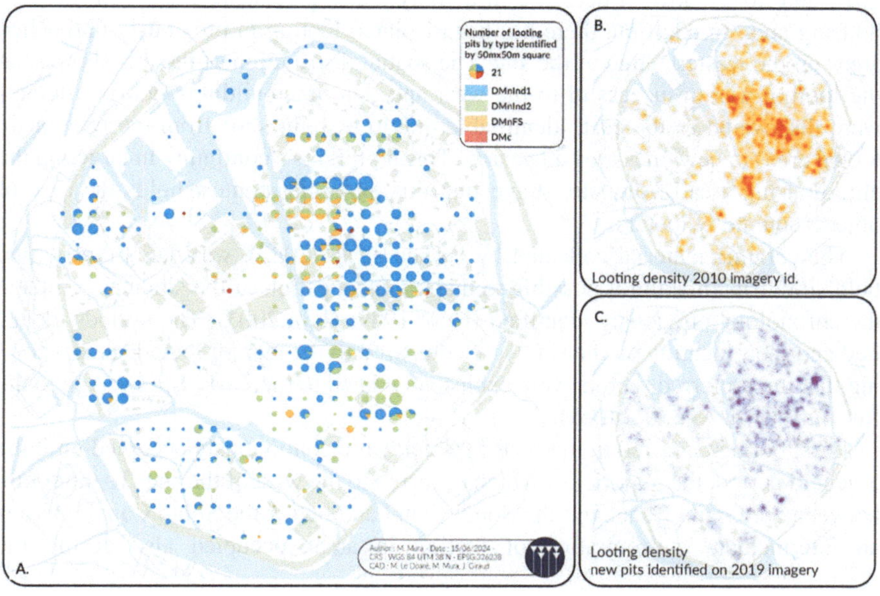

Fig. 8 Intra-site analysis of looting at Tell Senkereh-Larsa, A. Spatial repartition of looting pits as determined during the pedestrian survey (2019–2022); B. Looting density as identified in 2010; C. Looting density of new pits identified in 2019

[12] This study employs a pedestrian survey and dating of ceramic material that were executed as part of Vallet's research project (Vallet et al. 2019; Giraud et al. 2022), which allowed to reconsider the occupation of the site diachronically.

pits; *DMnFS*, large pits carried out by a group of individuals and *DMc*, mechanical cutting. No looting in the form of tunnels was identified.

The representation of the types decreases as the type became more invasive (Table 4), with a vast majority of pits being of the *DMnInd1* type. The largest manual types *DMnInd2* and *DMnFS* are concentrated in the area to the north-east of the ziggurat[13] and one particular type stands out: quadrangular manual pits instead of the traditional ovoid shape. Mechanized looting (*DMc*) is not very common on the site (only 7 occurrences).

The ground survey of the site enabled an in-depth study of the looters' strategy. It appears that the priority at Larsa was to target the visible elements on the site's architecture, which had not been excavated but had already been partly cleared by erosion. The north-western sector, which has no visible structures on the surface, was therefore relatively spared. A satellite image from 2010 shows effective, relentless looting concentrated on densely built-up areas (north-east sector of the elite residences). When looting is targeted, it corresponds to a large, clearly identifiable building, visible on satellite imagery and on the ground, with walls slightly flush with the surface. A comparison of the looting carried out before 2010 and between 2010 and 2019 shows a decrease in activity and a persistent interest in the elite housing area. In addition, there has been isolated looting in previously untouched areas on the western edge of the site. The spatial distribution of the pits shows that the looting was unsuccessful to the west and that new buildings rich in artefacts were discovered to the east, identifiable due to a slight shift from the previously looted areas to new ones located nearby. This highlights a continuity in targeting the elite housing area of the site, suggesting this particular context holds the type of objects sought by looters.

The ceramic material collected by Giraud et al. (2022). was dated during two field site visits, making it possible to map the occupation of the site and complete the chronology previously identified (Huot 1989; Huot 2003). The periods identified and their location on the site were compared to the map of looted areas, showing that the preferred sectors were exclusively dated to the Early Bronze Age to the Recent Bronze Age (north-east).

Less looting occurred in the sectors which were continuously occupied until the Seleucid period, the majority of which occurred to the west of the site. To the south, between the Grand Canal and the South Canal and below the South Canal, there is an intermediate concentration of looting in areas occupied also during the

Table 4 Number of looting pits per type identified during the pedestrian survey

	DMnInd1	DMnInd2	DMnFS	DMc
Number of pits	1046	471	154	7

[13] Monumental building characteristic of ancient Mesopotamia and earthen architecture. A Ziggurat is a multi-story tower or, more precisely, a superimposition of terraces of decreasing size, the last of which was most probably surmounted by a temple (Sauvage 1998).

Neo-Babylonian, Seleucid and Parthian periods. Where the material from the Parthian period is denser, the proportion of deeper pits (*DMnInd2*) is greater. Two findings therefore stand out: either, the looters are interested in two groups of periods (primarily the Bronze Age and Classical periods), or alternatively, the looters were only interested in Bronze Age objects and undertook deeper excavations to the south of the site in order to reach the remains of this targeted period. By comparing the data collected at Larsa with that from the main corpus of the study, both hypotheses remain plausible. Indeed, it has been shown that the periods targeted by looting were the Early Bronze Age, the Late Bronze Age/Iron Age transition and the Hellenistic/Parthian periods. Larsa hence fits perfectly in the defined perennial trend, with a slight preference for the Bronze Age at the intra-site level.

The types of objects extracted and targeted, taking into account the items discovered during excavations and pedestrian survey, are diverse: miniature items (zoomorphic figurines, carts, boats, furniture, found in large quantities all over the site during the survey); cylinder seals (two found during survey, in areas that had not been looted); cuneiform tablets (the presence of which is attested by excavations, but very rarely found during survey—only one fragmentary inscribed cylinder); votive plaques (the presence of which is attested by excavations and survey in non-looted areas); coins (the absence of which from survey could indicate systematic looting); or, on a smaller scale, beads (carnelian or shell), ornaments (metal rings) or arrowheads that were also found during excavations and survey. All these small objects are highly suitable for trafficking because of their volatile economic value, their size, which makes them easy to conceal and remove from the country and their presence over a wide geographical area, which makes it easier to falsify authentication documents (for instance by listing them as 'Western Asiatic' or 'Mesopotamian' see Topçuoğlu and Vorderstrasse 2019).

5 Open-Source Data Analysis Contributing to the Fight Against Illicit Trafficking of Archaeological Material

This chapter has shown that by using mostly open-access data, defining the typical signatures of different forms of looting and combining them to define a destruction index, it is possible to precisely identify the preferred targets of looting in a given region. These findings can be realistically used to improve countermeasures and protect at risk sites. By combining the study of three geographically distinct areas, each with their own wartime context and specificities, some common trends have also been identified, which are potentially relevant to other regions of the world.

The corpus, spanning over three conflict areas, has evidenced on each of them a primarily manual method of looting potentially corresponding to subsistence digging. And although time sequence could not be addressed in the framework of this chapter, the study evidenced the positive correlation between conflict and looting increase (as it was also highlighted by Fabiani (2018) in Egypt for instance). The analysis also highlights the existence of relentless manual looting combined with the introduction of mechanical means on some targeted sites. This represents a minority in terms of the number of sites concerned, but is not negligible in terms of its impact on the sites. This type of looting is concentrated in high-value targets, i.e. very well-known sites, previously excavated, and is commonly associated with a form of institutionalization of looting and the funding of terrorism or other organized criminalities (Mackenzie and Davis 2014; Shabi 2015; Sabrine et al. 2022). The proportion in which it does is yet to be defined (Yates and Brodie 2023), but within the studied data, only looting at Tell Harriri Mari in Syria has been positively correlated to the funding of such activities (for more details on the case of Mari see Butterlin and Mura 2019; Mura 2023).

The study examined a wide range of settlements, not all of which display monumental remains. The shape and spatial distribution of looting pits mostly encountered, are indeed not consistent with the removal of large-sized pieces, i.e. statues, mosaics, or architectural elements. This reflects the fact that, despite the focus on large items it is the smaller items that are most abundant on the market, objects resulting from archaeological looting, that are easily exportable, saleable and therefore small in size (Simpson 2017; Topçuoğlu and Vorderstrasse 2019). The small size of an object enables traffickers to smuggle it across borders, and the common nature of the piece makes it possible to falsify its provenance (Topçuoğlu and Vorderstrasse 2019). To be able to circumvent relevant legislation more easily, sites containing small common objects (coins, small and complete vessels, tablets, foundation nails, etc.) are looted preferentially. Previous research by Simpson (2017) established that as early as the 1980s, certain archaeological objects from Afghanistan transited through Iran, and once exported, they were identified as dating from the Elamite period and coming from an Iranian region, thus circumventing the laws protecting Afghan heritage. While these objects were likely to have come from the Balkh region, they could be sold on the legal market at a higher price (Simpson 2017, p. 142). More commonly, traffickers falsify the date of acquisition of a looted object to enter the legal art market (Brodie 2007). As most international conventions and national laws fighting against trafficking in antiquities are not retroactive and have a statute of limitations (Prott 2012), faking the date of acquisition is a way of laundering the piece so that it can be sold. Remote sensing of looted regions and sites can therefore be an important tool to date the event and prove that the illegal excavations occurred within the timeframe of a conflict for instance.

6 Conclusion

The aim of this chapter was to demonstrate the contribution of open-access data for this type of research project, i.e. its potential methodological contributions, its sociological potential, and its use as primary investigative technique. Firstly, the chapter provides a methodological framework to categorize looting stigmas by photointerpretation, to statistically analyse the results on a large sample of data and does so by reproductible means. Building on three case studies, it highlighted trends and patterns in the methodology of looters and their preferred targets, which can contribute to more effective targeting of countermeasures to protect at risk sites; and by identifying targeted periods and material culture associated to it, the last contribution of the study is to narrow down the type of objects susceptible to reach the market, in the years to come, by analysing key high-value targeted sites such as Larsa or Mari.

Overall, open-access satellite imagery enables unprecedented analysis of looting on a large scale within a collaborative research framework. By removing the barrier of satellite imaging costs, it allows everyone to contribute to data collection, enhancing our understanding of a global phenomenon that supports the cross-border issue of illicit antiquities trafficking. Using these resources to detect unlawful excavation, as well as discussing patterns, methods, organization, context, and trends across looting incidents, sets the foundation for future and more nuanced research into this international concern.

Acknowledgements This chapter is based on a study developed as part of a PhD thesis, defended in 2021, supported by a PhD contract from ED112 of University Paris 1 Panthéon-Sorbonne under the direction of Pascal Butterlin (Mura 2021). It was supported by the Mission Archéologique Française du Gouvernorat de Souleymaniah, directed by Jessica Giraud, and the Délégation Archéologique Française en Afghanistan, directed at the time by Julio Bendezu-Sarmiento. Analysis of the looting at Larsa was later incorporated thanks to the Mission Archéologique Française de Larsa-Oeili directed by Regis Vallet, whose study was financed by the Solidarity Fund for Innovative Projects, Civil Societies, Francophonie and Human Development (FSPI) of the French Ministry of Foreign Affairs (FSPI-2021-2019-41), as steered by the French Embassy in Iraq and the French Institute of the Near East (Ifpo). Archaïos, as one of the 4 operators of the project, contributed to the investigation on the looting at Larsa (under the author's supervision), oversaw the pedestrian survey of the site (dir. Jessica Giraud), and provided the research time to prepare this contribution.

References

Adams RM (1981) Heartland of cities: surveys of ancient settlement and land use on the central floodplain of the Euphrates. The University of Chicago Press, Chicago, USA

Alva W (2001) The destruction, looting and traffic of the archaeological heritage of Peru, in N. Brodie, J. Doole and C. Renfrew (eds) *Trade in illicit antiquities: The destruction of the world's archaeological heritage*, 89–96. Cambridge: McDonald Institute.

Airbus (2022) Copernicus digital elevation model. Product Handbook v4:36

Bernbeck R (2012) The political dimension of archaeological practices. In: Potts DT (ed) A companion to the archaeology of the ancient near east. Wiley-Blackwell, Chichester, pp 87–105

Brodie N (2007) Comment on 'irreconcilable differences?'. Pap Inst Archaeol 18:12–15

Brodie N, Kersel MM, Mackenzie S, Sabrine I, Smith E, Yates D (2021) Why there is still an illicit trade in cultural objects and what we can do about it. J Field Archaeol 47(2):117–130. https://doi.org/10.1080/00934690.2021.1996979

Butterlin P, Mura M (2019) Mari et la crise syrienne. In: Bessenay-Prolonge J et al (eds) Archaeology of conflict / archaeology in conflict - documenting destruction of cultural heritage in the middle-east and Central Asia. Routes de l'Orient Actes II. Association Routes de l'Orient, Paris, pp 199–224

Campbell JB, Wynne R (2011) Introduction to remote sensing. Guilford Press

Canuto MA, Estrada-Belli F, Garrison TG, Houston SD, Acuña MJ, Kováč M, Marken D, Nondédéo P, Auld-Thomas L, Castanet C, Chatelain D, Chiriboga CR, Drápela T, Lieskovský T, Tokovinine A, Velasquez A, Fernández-Díaz JC, Shrestha R (2018) Ancient lowland Maya complexity as revealed by airborne laser scanning of northern Guatemala. Science 361:1355. https://doi.org/10.1126/science.aau0137

Casana J (2015) Satellite imagery-based analysis of archaeological looting in Syria. Near Eastern Archaeol 78(3):142–152

Casana J, Laugier EJ (2017) Satellite imagery-based monitoring of archaeological site damage in the Syrian civil war. PLoS One 12(11):e0188589. https://doi.org/10.1371/journal.pone.0188589

Contreras D, Brodie N (2010) The utility of publicly available satellite imagery for investigating looting of archaeological sites in Jordan. J Field Archaeol 35(1):101–114

Cornu M (2018) Lutte contre le trafic illicite de biens culturels, la recherche de provenance et l'exercice de la diligence requise dans l'Union Europeenne Technical Report March 2018

Cunliffe E (2013) Satellites and site destruction: an analysis of modern impacts on the archaeological resource of the ancient near east, Durham theses. Durham University. Available at Durham E-Theses Online: http://etheses.dur.ac.uk/8472/

Danese M, Gioia D, Vitale V, Abate N, Amodio AM, Lasaponara R, Masini N (2022) Pattern recognition approach and LiDAR for the analysis and mapping of archaeological looting: application to an Etruscan site. Remote Sens 14(7):1587. https://doi.org/10.3390/rs14071587

Delougaz P, Lloyd S (1942) "Pre-Sargonid Temples in the Diyala Region", OIP 58, Chicago.

El-Hajj H (2021) Interferometric SAR and machine learning: using open source data to detect archaeological looting and destruction. J Comput Appl Archaeol 4(1):47–62. https://doi.org/10.5334/jcaa.70

Fabiani M (2018) Disentangling strategic and opportunistic looting: the relationship between antiquities looting and armed conflict in Egypt. Art 7(2):22. https://doi.org/10.3390/arts7020022

Giraud J (2016) Surface survey of the Dinka Settlement complex, 2013–2015. In: Radner K, Janosha Kreppner F, Squitieri A (eds) Exploring the Neo-Assyrian Frontier with Western Iran, The 2015 Season at Gird-i Bazar and Qalat-i Dinka. Peshdar Plain Project Publications, pp 29–35

Giraud J, Mura M, Le Doaré M, Coppini C, Oselini V, Havé A, Hashemi Z, Boudia S (2022) « Revitaliser la Valorisation du Patrimoine Archéologique de l'Irak » Programme FSPI. Rapport Final D'Activités Scientifiques 2019–2022, 196 p., Unpublished

Hammer E, Seifried R, Franklin K, Lauricella A (2018) Remote assessments of the archaeological heritage situation in Afghanistan. J Cult Herit 33:125–144

Hardy SA (2015) The conflict antiquities trade: a historical overview. In: Desmarais, France (eds) countering the illicit traffic in cultural goods: the global challenge of protecting the world's heritage. International Council of Museums Committee for Conservation, pp 21–31

Herndon KE, Griffin R, Schroder W, Murtha T, Golden C, Contreras DA, Cherrington E, Wang L, Bazarsky A, Van Kollias G, Alcover Firpi O (2023, 2023) Google earth engine for archaeologists: an updated look at the progress and promise of remotely sensed big data. J Archaeol Sci Rep 50. https://doi.org/10.1016/j.jasrep.2023.104094

Hobson MS (2019) EAMENA training in the use of satellite remote sensing and digital technologies in heritage management: Libya and Tunisia workshops 2017–2019. Libyan Studi 50:63–71. https://doi.org/10.1017/lis.2019.22

Hollowell J (2006) Moral arguments on subsistence digging. In: Scarre C, Scarre G (eds) . Cambridge University Press, The ethics of archaeology: philosophical perspectives on archaeological practice, pp 69–94

Howey MCL, Sullivan FB, Brouwer Burg M, Palace MW (2020) Remotely sensed big data and iterative approaches to cultural feature detection and past landscape process analysis. J Field Archaeol 45(S1):S27–S38. https://doi.org/10.1080/00934690.2020.1713435

Huang J (2013) Chasing provenance: legal dilemmas for protecting states with a verifiable link to underwater culture heritage. Ocean Coast Manage 84:220–225. https://doi.org/10.1016/j.ocecoaman.2012.11.007

Huot J-L (1989) Larsa: travaux de 1985, Bibliothèque de la Délégation archéologique française en Iraq, 5

Huot J-L (2003) Larsa: travaux de 1987-1989, Bibliothèque archéologique et historique de Beyrouth, 165

Karataş H (2022) Archaeological destruction and folklore: spiritual guidance and looting in Turkey. Trames 26(76/71):293–312. https://doi.org/10.3176/tr.2022.3.03

Kennedy D (1998) Declassified satellite photographs and archaeology in the Middle East: case studies from Turkey. Antiquity 72(277):553–561. https://doi.org/10.1017/S0003598X0008697X

Lasaponara R, Masini N (2010) Facing the archaeological looting in Peru by using very high-resolution satellite imagery and local spatial autocorrelation statistics. In: Computational Science and Its Applications–ICCSA 2010: International Conference, Fukuoka, Japan, March 23-26, 2010, Proceedings, Part I 10. Springer, Berlin Heidelberg, pp 254–261

Lauricella A, Cannon J, Branting S (2017) Semi-automated detection of looting in Afghanistan using multispectral imagery and principal component analysis. Antiquity 91(359):1344–1355

Le Doaré M, Mura M, Giraud J (2023) Contribution to the mapping of ancient watercourses of the Uruk—Larsa region (Southern Mesopotamia, Iraq) through remote sensing. J Archaeol Sci Rep 49. https://doi.org/10.1016/j.jasrep.2023.104021

Loftus WK (1857) Travels and researches in Chaldae and Susiana : with an account of excavations at Warka, the "Erech" of Nimrod, and Shúsh, "Shushan the Palace" of Esther. J. Nisvet and Co, London

Mackenzie D, Davis T (2014) Temple looting in Cambodia: anatomy of a statue trafficking network. Br J Criminol 54(5):722–740

Mackenzie S, Brodie N, Yates D, Tsirogiannis C (2019) Trafficking culture: new directions in researching the global market in illicit antiquities, 1st edn. Routledge. https://doi.org/10.4324/9781315532219

Margueron J-C (1971) Larsa. Rapport préliminaire sur la cinquième campagne. Syria 48-3-4:271–287

Meskell L (2020). Imperialism, internationalism, and archaeology in the un/making of the Middle East. American Anthropologist Distinguished Lecture https://doi.org/10.1111/aman.13413

Mura M (2021) Dynamiques des tells, Pillages et Destructions Militaires : étude comparative de l'évolution des tells archéologiques Moyen-Orientaux dans trois micro-régions de Syrie, d'Irak et d'Afghanistan. PhD Dissertation, Paris: Université Paris 1 Panthéon-Sorbonne. https://ecm.univ-paris1.fr/nuxeo/site/esupversions/89da0a6b-4690-46e2-b056-97ba195176ee

Mura M (2023) Mari, pillage et vandalisme de l'Etat islamique. Archeologia 623:28–43

Navalgund R, Rajani MB (2017) The science behind archaeological signatures from space. Curr Sci 113(10):1859–1872. http://www.jstor.org/stable/26494837

Parcak S (2007) Satellite remote sensing methods for monitoring archaeological tells in the Middle East. J Field Archaeol 32(1):65–81

Parcak S, Gathings D, Childs C, Mumford G, Cline E (2016) Satellite evidence of archaeological site looting in Egypt: 2002–2013. Antiquity 90(349):188–205

Parrot A (1933) Les Fouilles De Tello Et De Senkereh-Larsa: Campagne 1932-1933 (Rapport préliminaire). Revue d'Assyriologie et d'archéologie Orientale 30(4):169–182. http://www.jstor.org/stable/23284054

Parrot A (1968) Les fouilles de Larsa. Syria 45-3-4:205–239

Pollock S (2016) Archaeology and contemporary warfare. Annu Rev Anthropol 45:215–231. https://doi.org/10.1146/annurev-anthro-102215-095913

Pollock S, Bernbeck R (2018) Reflections on survey and surveillance in the archaeology of Western Asia. In: Frangipane M, Manzanilla L (eds) Prehistory and protohistory of ancient civilizations. Gangemi Editore, Rome, pp 93–108

Prott LV (2012) Strengths and weaknesses of the 1970 Convention: an evaluation 40 years after its adoption. Réunion des États parties à la Convention concernant les mesures à prendre pour interdire et empêcher l'importation, l'exportation et le transfert de propriété illicites des biens culturels, 2nd, Paris, https://unesdoc.unesco.org/ark:/48223/pf0000245258?posInSet=6&queryId=2ac483cd-2eb7-4b5a-b18f-a6b042030e7c

Resnik DB, Elliott KC (2019) Using drones to study human beings: ethical and regulatory issues. Sci Eng Ethics 25(3):707–718. https://doi.org/10.1007/s11948-018-0032-6

Richason BF (2011) Techniques of detecting and delineating archaeological site destruction using high resolution satellite imagery: an Iraq case study. In: American Society for Photogrammetry and Remote Sensing Annual Conference 2011, pp 426–436

Sabrine I, Abdo R, Brodie N (2022) Some new evidence documenting the involvement of Da'esh in Syria with the illicit trade in antiquities. J East Mediterranean Archaeol Herit Stud 10(2):115–136

Sauvage M (1998) La construction des Ziggurats sous la troisième dynastie d'Ur, vol LX. Iraq, pp 45–63

Shabi R (2015) Looted in Syria—and sold in London: the British antiques shops dealing in artefacts smuggled by Isis. The Guardian, 3 July 2015. https://www.theguardian.com/world/2015/jul/03/antiquities-looted-by-isis-end-up-in-london-shops

Simpson St. J (2017) Stolen, saved, Returned: Collaboration between the NMA, BM, UK Border Force, and Others in the Successful Return of Antiquities to Kabul. In: Stein G, Fisher MT, Latify AH, Popal N, Dupree NH (eds) Preserving the Cultural Heritage of Afghanistan: Proceedings of the International Conference Held at Kabul University, November 2014, 141–146

Tompkins A (2020). Provenance research today: principles, practice, problems. Lund Humphries in association with IFAR

Topçuoğlu O, Vorderstrasse T (2019) Small finds, big values: cylinder seals and coins from Iraq and Syria on the online market. Int J Cult Prop 26(3):239–263. https://doi.org/10.1017/S0940739119000213

Ur J (2003) CORONA satellite photography and ancient road networks: a northern Mesopotamian case study. Antiquity 77(295):102–115

Ur J, Hammer E (2018) Spatial Index of U2 Aerial photography of the Middle East, 1958-1960. Harvard Dataverse, V1, https://doi.org/10.7910/DVN/VD74QX

Ur J, de Jong L, Giraud J, Osborne JF, MacGinnis J (2013) Ancient cities and landscapes in the Kurdistan Region of Iraq: the Erbil plain archaeological survey 2012 season. Iraq 75:89–117

Vallet R, Abd-El-Ali J, Al-Debs R, Bachelot L, Charpin D, Darras L, Douche C, Giraud J, Herr J-J, Ibrahim C, Lisein J, Murad A, Mura M, Obreja S, Oselini V, Rasool A, Suire J, (2019) Preliminary Report on the XIVth and XVth Campaigns at Larsa, Sumer, LXVI. Unpublished

Vincent E Saroufim M, Chemla J, Ubelmann Y, Marquis P, Ponce J, Aubry M, (2024) Detecting Looted Archaeological Sites from Satellite Image Time Series, 2409.09432

Wang N, Christen M, Hunt M (2021) Ethical considerations associated with "Humanitarian Drones": a scoping literature review. Sci Eng Ethics 27(4):51. https://doi.org/10.1007/s11948-021-00327-4

Wilkinson M, Dumontier M, Aalbersberg I et al (2016) The FAIR guiding principles for scientific data management and stewardship. Scientific Data 3:160018. https://doi.org/10.1038/sdata.2016.18

Wilkinson TJ (2003) Archaeological landscapes of the eear East. University of Arizona Press, Tucson, AZ

Wilson A (2021) The use of remote sensing and digital tools for cultural heritage management and archaeological research. Levant 53(3):384–388. https://doi.org/10.1080/00758914.2022.2051901

Yates D, Bērziņa D (2022) Criminological frameworks for understanding Mexican antiquities in contemporary European auctions. In: Pérez-Prat Durbán L, Ruiz Z (eds) El Expolio De Bienes Culturales. Universidad de Huelva, Huelva

Yates D, Brodie N (2023) The illicit trade in antiquities is not the world's third-largest illicit trade: a critical evaluation of a factoid. Antiquity 97(394):991–1003

Zaina F (2019) A risk assessment for cultural heritage in southern Iraq: framing drivers, threats and actions affecting archaeological sites. Conserv Manage Archaeol Sites 21(3):184–206. https://doi.org/10.1080/13505033.2019.1662653

Mathilde Mura is a researcher focusing on the voluntary destruction of archaeological sites in times of crisis and investigating military damage and lootings as contemporary archaeological levels. She thus proposes a double vision of the destruction at archaeological sites, building a methodology to pursue traditional excavation at damaged sites, while considering damages like their latest level of occupation. This allows to consider looting and military occupation of archaeological sites from a social science perspective, replacing the events in their specific socio-economic and political contemporary background, and working on unveiling the means and motives behind it. Mathilde conducted her research at Archaïos (Archaeology, Culture and Heritage), and as an associate researcher of ArScAn-VEPMO team of CNRS and is currently Junior Professor at the University of Aix Marseille and Centre Camille Jullian (UMR 7299). She obtained her PhD in Archaeology at the University of Paris 1 Panthéon-Sorbonne in 2021.

Open Access This chapter is licensed under the terms of the Creative Commons Attribution-NonCommercial-NoDerivatives 4.0 International License (http://creativecommons.org/licenses/by-nc-nd/4.0/), which permits any noncommercial use, sharing, distribution and reproduction in any medium or format, as long as you give appropriate credit to the original author(s) and the source, provide a link to the Creative Commons license and indicate if you modified the licensed material. You do not have permission under this license to share adapted material derived from this chapter or parts of it.

The images or other third party material in this chapter are included in the chapter's Creative Commons license, unless indicated otherwise in a credit line to the material. If material is not included in the chapter's Creative Commons license and your intended use is not permitted by statutory regulation or exceeds the permitted use, you will need to obtain permission directly from the copyright holder.

RITHMS Digital Platform: Social Network Analysis for Intelligence-Led Policing of Cultural Heritage Crime

Madison Leeson, Michela De Bernardin, Riccardo Giovanelli, Sara Ferro, and Arianna Traviglia

Abstract The European Union-funded project RITHMS (Research, Intelligence and Technology for Heritage and Market Security) offers a network-focused approach to tackling cultural heritage crime, particularly trafficking. The project brings together a consortium of researchers, data analysts, law enforcement agencies, and scientific institutes across Europe to integrate interdisciplinary data in a platform to address the illicit trade using social network analysis (SNA). Data have been gathered from a range of open sources to enable reconstruction and examination of a sprawling network of actors involved in the circulation of cultural goods. Analysis of this network has the potential to reveal valuable information and insights about the circulation of cultural goods and the character of individual transactions. This chapter first offers theoretical background for the core concepts at the root of the project, namely trafficking, SNA, and the collection of open data. It then explores three case studies that highlight diverse approaches to data analysis which emphasise the value of open-source intelligence and promising methods for intelligence-led policing of and research into cultural goods crimes. This research reinforces the importance of an interconnected analysis among isolated datasets and encourages a broader approach to studying the circulation of cultural goods using these open sources.

M. Leeson · M. De Bernardin · R. Giovanelli · S. Ferro · A. Traviglia (✉)
Italian Institute of Technology (IIT) - Centre for Cultural Heritage Technology, Venice, Italy
e-mail: madison.leeson@iit.it; michela.debernardin@iit.it; riccardo.giovanelli@iit.it; sara.ferro@iit.it; arianna.traviglia@iit.it

© The Author(s) 2026

E. Smith, S. Austin (eds.), *Researching a Rigged Game: Digital Approaches to Tracing the Illicit Trade in Cultural Objects*, Studies in Art, Heritage, Law and the Market 11, https://doi.org/10.1007/978-3-032-02014-7_5

1 Introduction

The European Union (EU)-funded project RITHMS[1] (Research, Intelligence and Technology for Heritage and Market Security) offers a novel approach to tackling cultural heritage crimes, particularly trafficking and illicit trade (RITHMS 2024b). The analytical approach at the heart of the project is social network analysis (SNA), which investigates the structure of interactions among actors in a network using graph theory. Intended primarily for use by European law enforcement agencies (LEAs), the RITHMS platform builds a multi-layer social network graph (SNG) from structured and unstructured data collected from a range of diverse sources. Analysis of this network's layers has the potential to reveal valuable information and insights on the circulation of cultural goods and the character of individual transactions and relationships.

This chapter first offers a theoretical background for the key concepts at the heart of the RITHMS project, particularly cultural goods trafficking and social network analysis. This serves as a foundation for discussing the platform's key components, which comprise diverse functions for analysing the network dynamics of the art market. It then illustrates the methodological considerations which emerged relating to the consolidation of open data for addressing these activities, focusing on the integration of provenance databases and repositories of stolen and missing cultural goods. Three diverse case studies are used to demonstrate how the analytical approaches employed by RITHMS offer novel technological techniques and methods for enhancing intelligence-led policing of cultural heritage crimes. The chapter concludes by reflecting on the ethical considerations of these technologies, common limitations of SNA research, and additional opportunities for research and investigation. The insights for cultural heritage scholarship and law enforcement provided throughout the chapter highlight the value of an interconnected analysis among isolated open data sources and promote an interdisciplinary, semi-automated approach to studying the circulation of cultural goods.

2 Cultural Goods Trafficking

The term 'cultural goods' refers to objects that relate to human culture and the expression of cultural identity, including (but certainly not limited to) artworks, archaeological finds, coins, books, and jewellery (Europol n.d.; Lazăr 2015; Brodie et al. 2019). While there are significant overlaps with similar terms such as 'cultural

[1]This research is funded by the European Union, Horizon Europe, under the auspices of RITHMS project (2022–2025) (G.A. 101073932) and carried out at the Centre for Cultural Heritage Technology of the Italian Institute of Technology. Views and opinions expressed are, however, those of the authors only and do not necessarily reflect those of the European Union or the European Commission; neither the European Union nor the granting authority can be held responsible for them.

heritage' and 'cultural property,' these objects are commonly considered 'goods' in a commercial sense (particularly in policy and legislation) because of their commodification on the open market and susceptibility to illicit trade (Europol n.d.; Brodie et al. 2019; Hardy 2020). An international interest in thwarting the trafficking of these items has resulted in a sweeping set of policy and advocacy documents which include, in Europe, the EU Action Plan against Trafficking in Cultural Goods, the European Parliamentary Research Service's Briefing on the Illicit Trade in Cultural Goods, and the designation of 'cultural goods crime' as one of Europol's priorities in the fight against organised criminal activity (Europol n.d.; Zygierewicz 2017; European Commission 2022).

These efforts seek to disrupt a broad category of crimes that includes theft and looting, trafficking and smuggling, forgery, vandalism, destruction, and illegal import and export (Manacorda and Chappell 2011; Brodie et al. 2019; Fabiani and Marrone 2021). Of these, this chapter focuses on cultural goods trafficking: a blanket term that encompasses all unlawful activities related to the transfer of ownership of cultural objects (Boz 2018; Brodie et al. 2022; Erken and Turksen 2023). This category of misconduct is also closely linked to other typologies of criminal activity and occurs within a vast network of both licit and illicit behaviours; for example, the trafficking of cultural goods has been linked to the financing of extremist groups and organised crime syndicates as well as the perpetration of other criminal activities such as tax and sanctions evasion, drugs and weapons trafficking, and cybercrimes (Al-Azm and Paul 2019; Ermasova et al. 2019; Hardy 2021b). The criminal phenomenon of trafficking affects local communities, archaeological sites, cultural institutions, and art markets around the world and is frequently transnational, crossing borders to move goods from 'source' countries to 'market' countries where criminal actors can more easily find buyers for undocumented and unprovenanced items[2] (Chappell and Polk 2011; Campbell 2013). Increasingly, new technologies are being developed, tested, and implemented for the investigation and policing of these crimes to address their interdisciplinary and international nature (D'Ippolito 2014; Graham et al. 2023a, b; Giovanelli and Traviglia 2024), as will be discussed at length in the present chapter.

With the ratification of the 1970 UNESCO[3] Convention, an illicit system articulated in three stages (export, import, and transfer of ownership) was formally recognised at the international level as "one of the main causes of the impoverishment of the cultural heritage of the countries of origin" (UNESCO 1970, Art. 2.1). Now, 50 years later, the Council of Europe Convention on Offenses relating to Cultural

[2] This is a generalisation of trade patterns, which tend to flow from the Global South and East to the Global North and West. However, as Byrne (2016) has compellingly argued, this simplification of the international flow of looted antiquities often implies passivity on the part of 'source' countries, and "a grading of countries according to the consumability of their archaeology by Western collectors" (p. 349). For Thailand and the Philippines—the context in which he writes—this simplification replicates the global imbalance of economic power in the realm of cultural agency, diminishing local influence.

[3] The United Nations Educational, Scientific and Cultural Organization.

Property (the 'Nicosia Convention') is encouraging the criminalisation of a set of activities that represent the most harmful behaviours making up the illicit chain of trafficking: theft and unlawful excavation, illegal export and import, acquisition and placing on the market cultural objects of undocumented or illegal origin, falsification of documents, destruction and damage (which could occur in any stage), and aiding or abetting these criminal offences (Council of Europe 2017).

The various activities that enable this trafficking chain involve several distinct but connected actors. Of these, looters represent one of the greatest threats to archaeological sites—but they rarely work alone. Hardy (2021a) has illustrated how metal detectors, which would ordinarily be a huge investment for a full-time minimum wage-earner in lower-income countries, are often acquired through cost-sharing and profit-sharing arrangements among a group of would-be looters or between a dealer and a looter. He cites the examples of Croatia, Serbia, and Bosnia and Herzegovina, in which, at the time of writing, mean net monthly incomes of €905, €536, and €495, respectively, made individual ownership of a metal detector (priced around €650–750) nearly impossible (Ćirić et al. 2005; Hardy 2021a, p. 172, p. 184). Rather, cost-sharing arrangements make metal detecting a more accessible source of revenue for would-be looters in these countries and serves as evidence of collaboration among different actors in the trafficking chain. Such mutually beneficial relationships are not uncommon in the trafficking world, where each individual represents a link in a chain that connects the original, illicitly-acquired object with a final buyer (Watson and Todeschini 2007; Chappell and Polk 2011; Hardy 2021a, b); the division of labour represented by this chain similarly reflects the network's international scope, as goods acquired in so-called 'source' countries are transported to 'market' countries for sale (Chappell and Polk 2011; Campbell 2013; Palombo and Yates 2023).

Of course, dealers and looters are not the only figures fuelling and fostering the illicit flow of cultural goods. Other roles in the chain of trafficking are equally important, although more difficult to identify and prove in court (Mackenzie 2019, 2020). Indeed, a wide range of professionals can participate in trafficking networks, representing pivotal links that facilitate the illicit transit, acceptance, and commercialisation of the artefacts (Brodie 2005, 2011a, b, 2014a, b, c). For example, evidence has been collected of scholars providing false letters of expertise to produce fake provenance; auction catalogue authors manipulating provenance information by omitting certain locations or previous owners that could raise red flags; and restorers heavily intervening on cultural objects to hide evidence of illegal excavation or make them more difficult to identify (Watson and Todeschini 2007; People v. Wiener 2016; Mackenzie and Yates 2020). This creates an impression of collusion among trafficking networks and cultural heritage experts that threatens the legitimacy and authority of experts in the field. This has been reinforced by high-profile cases of scholars, historians, and other experts charged with abetment of trafficking activities, such as the 2005 indictment of Getty Museum curator Marion True and the 2019 case by New York prosecutors against British art dealer and author Douglas Latchford (Watson and Todeschini 2007; Brodie 2014b, c; Picciano 2023). Both cases also highlighted the international nature of cultural goods trafficking, which involved artefacts from Cambodia and southern Europe, respectively, illicitly acquired by buyers and museums in the United Kingdom (UK) and United States of America (USA).

Organised criminal networks habitually leverage the same routes for different categories of illicit objects, such as drugs and weapons in addition to cultural goods (Hardy 2021b; Hunt 2021; UNODC 2022). Further, high-profile cases of seizures and arrests often highlight the involvement of multiple countries, such as in a 2016 case where Ukrainian police recovered 17 artworks that had been looted from Castelvecchio Museum in Verona, Italy, and smuggled to Odessa via Moldova (Associated Press 2016). Similarly, Operation Pandora, coordinated by Europol each year since it began in 2016, has seen a crackdown on antiquities smuggling across Europe and led to the recovery of around 11,000 artefacts and the arrests of 60 people across 14 European countries in 2022 alone (Europol 2022; Begley 2023). Another accomplishment of the operation has been the identification of certain organised crime networks that have enabled the trafficking of cultural objects as well as other illicit goods including drugs, tobacco, and weapons.

This brief overview highlights the international and collaborative nature of cultural goods trafficking, which suggests equally interdisciplinary mechanisms are required to police cultural heritage crimes. New tools should promote collaboration among different law enforcement stakeholders, enable effective sharing of information and interoperability among existing open resources, and take advantage of promising new developments in technology which are enabling new avenues for data analysis. Able to highlight and reconstruct the often-obscure connections among various actors in the chain of trafficking, the network-focused RITHMS platform holds great potential for tackling such a diverse landscape of illicit activities.

3 Social Network Analysis and Other Analytical Methods

Viewing the trade of cultural goods as a complex network composed of nodes (actors) and edges (either inferred or known interactions and relations among actors) with notable topological characteristics fits well with foundational concepts of network analysis (Newman 2003; Barabási and Pósfai 2016). This analytical approach is well-suited to understand the flow of goods and information within markets because the methods and technologies it leverages allow for the extraction of insights on influential actors (individuals, organisations, and other entities) and a greater appreciation of how objects and information flow, the routes they take, and where bottlenecks in communication may exist (Granovetter 1985; Jackson 2010).

Network models have been applied to the analysis of art trade since the late 1960s, particularly within the realms of visual and contemporary art markets (Yogev and Grund 2012). They have also been explored in other disciplines of arts and humanities research, including investigations into archaeological and art world networks (Meirelles et al. 2014; Brughmans and Peeples 2023). Writing specifically on the illicit antiquities market, Campbell (2013) describes the network as 'fluid', highlighting the transnational nature of these systems (see also Palombo and Yates 2023). This fluidity is reflected, in part, by the ways in which various actors communicate and interact within the network, as outlined in the previous section. Further, as with trafficking networks for other goods, such as drugs and weapons, routes taken by traffickers are not permanent but rather evolve over time (Brodie et al. 2019). A holistic network model appreciates the ways in which systems transcend national boundaries and the various factors which impact their longevity, relying on a range of actors across a broad geographic and temporal scope.

Key applications of SNA include the work of D'Ippolito (2014), who designed two network models focused on the convicted antiquities smuggler and art dealer Giacomo Medici. These models demonstrated Medici's significant influence within the network and its fluid, non-hierarchical structure by employing measures like degree, eigenvector, betweenness, and closeness centrality. Similarly, Tsirogiannis and Tsirogiannis (2016) built network models on data surrounding the so-called 'Medici Conspiracy' (Watson and Todeschini 2007), creating new algorithms for transaction-based pathfinding and missing link prediction. Fabiani and Marrone (2021) showcased the potential of social network analysis by tracing over 30,000 individual items using catalogued provenance, shedding light on transit routes, pathways, and the connection between sale results and the recurrence of items in subsequent auctions. Their analysis also highlighted the role of private dealers in these networks. Further, Giovanelli and Traviglia (2024) have developed a semi-automated system to construct a knowledge graph (KG) of provenance events related to market-circulating objects, utilising existing named entity recognition (NER) techniques. This work projected both a bipartite actor-object network and a monopartite actor-actor network to reveal different patterns. Brennan and Tsirogiannis (2022) applied KGs specifically to the field by incorporating forensic data collected by Christos Tsirogiannis about 48 trafficked objects linked to Giacomo Medici, Gianfranco Becchina, and Edoardo Almagià (Giovanelli 2021; Pellegrini and Rizzo 2021). Finally, Graham et al. (2023b) have processed 129 entries from the Trafficking Culture Encyclopaedia, manually tagging entities and relationships and applying embedding modules for link predictions. This method revealed previously unknown connections between various actors, which led to identifying further patterns after deepened research (Yates and Graham 2023). To address the time-consuming nature of manual tagging, Graham et al. (2023a) subsequently explored automated KG population using prompts for large language models. Although less precise, this approach produced comparable results.

The value of SNA for investigations into cultural goods trafficking is, thus, increasingly recognised in interdisciplinary scholarship. The RITHMS project builds upon these innovative solutions and methods to streamline the intelligence and monitoring processes with research on the automation of data collecting and processing tasks. Although it will not be explored in detail in the present chapter, the project also proposes new opportunities for intelligence-led policing through the integration of open data with data from private sources (including mobile networks, satellite imagery analysis reports, and restricted police intelligence). These undertake to address a complex international criminal phenomenon with equally complex but promising technological solutions. What will be explored in this chapter is the promising opportunity for intelligence-led policing (see Scuro, this volume) presented by consolidated open datasets. Further, the data visualisation methods and tools that convey this research significantly enhance end-users' abilities to comprehend the valuable insights hidden within structured datasets, effectively transforming abstract statistics into actionable knowledge (Few 2014).

After a brief introduction to the platform itself, this chapter will outline the methods of data collection that fed this dataset as well as the legal considerations of automated and semi-automated research on open-source intelligence (OSINT). It then presents three case studies that demonstrate the value of these diverse datasets and reinforce the importance of SNA and other analytical approaches for research into the circulation of cultural goods. These studies relied on a range of methods and analytical approaches for researching cultural heritage crimes, including two different but complementary types of network analysis; *ego* network analysis examines an individual's role within a system and their influence on other individuals, while *whole* network analysis focuses on more general patterns of network dynamics and its overall structure (Perry et al. 2018). Both vantage points can offer valuable insights for investigations into the ways in which cultural objects flow through social systems. Complementing these are other analytical methods including exploratory data analysis, which was an important first step in identifying shared characteristics among datasets and highlighting patterns to investigate further (Chatfield 1986; Windhager et al. 2019). From this, and a combination of manual, semi-automated, and automated data processing operations, predictions are outlined for new opportunities for research, derived from predictive analysis based on historical trafficking cases (see also Graham et al. 2023b; Li et al. 2024). Land and other trade routes are equally important factors in this research, lending a dimension of spatial analysis to the case studies that sheds further light on the channels through which illicit cultural goods are transited (Brodie et al. 2019). Together, these methods offer promising opportunities for intelligence-led policing of cultural heritage crimes, of which cultural goods trafficking comprises a significant part.

4 The RITHMS Platform

At the core of the RITHMS project lies a sophisticated platform developed by a consortium of researchers, computer scientists, and law enforcement agencies across Europe. The tool, which will be used exclusively by law enforcement agencies, is designed to aggregate, correlate, and analyse OSINT with additional data from complementary sources as needed and/or by the end-users themselves, to construct a comprehensive KG and layered social networks. These layers yield crucial insights into trade patterns, allow the recognition of overlaps between licit and illicit activities, and facilitate the identification of individuals and patterns involved.

The platform features four main components. First, a set of automated data collection modules targets a diverse array of information sources, such as existing databases, specialised publications and newspapers, websites of market actors (e.g., auction houses and art galleries), social media, and other web-based public repositories. These modules comprise web scrapers (written in the Python programming language) that have been customised for each source to ensure accurate and comprehensive data collection; those discussed throughout this chapter were developed by the Centre for Cultural Heritage Technology (CCHT) of the Italian Institute of Technology (IIT). The second component, a core module, organises and manages the KG using a robust and detailed ontology. This ontology was designed by the European Software Institute (ESI)—the technical partner responsible for the development of the platform itself—around two main pillars. The first pillar is a domain-specific taxonomy that enables the classification of different types of actors such as individuals and organisations, cultural objects, dates, locations, and events. The second pillar is a complementary system of intelligence-based labelling that allows the end-users to assign specific interactions among the actors and patterns in these interactions. This structured approach enables seamless integration of diverse datasets while maintaining their inherent or hypothetical relationships. The third component comprises a multi-layered social network (Pio-Lopez et al. 2021) that correlates various patterns and applies different analytical algorithms, ranging from conventional SNA methods (Sandra et al. 2021) to advanced machine learning techniques such as graph neural network-based link prediction (Li et al. 2024). To tackle the unstructured nature of most of the data sources, the CCHT has fine-tuned natural language processing (NLP) models to autonomously generate nodes and relationships with contextual awareness (Ferro et al. 2025; Yang et al. 2021). The last component of the platform is a server-based desktop user interface engaged with data visualisation and data communication. It comprises diverse functionalities, allowing end-users (LEAs) to perform actions on the data, such as queries, traversals, and transformations on which to base analyses (e.g., topology analysis) and hypotheses (e.g., link prediction) about the interactions among data objects. Finally, the user interface allows for manual data entry to permit users to input and analyse other relevant data obtained from other, closed, sources.

While it is outside the scope of this chapter to present the platform in greater detail, this overview is essential for outlining the importance of open data to the project and contextualising the conditions within which these data were gathered and will be used. Further, this limited introduction draws connections between the analytical tools discussed in the previous section with the initial problem the platform aims to address: cultural goods trafficking. The methodology for data collection and the legal framework that enabled it will be detailed in the next section, while the opportunities, limitations, and ethical considerations of the platform's use are explored in the discussion that comprises Sect. 6. By enabling innovative analytical approaches towards the examination of open data on the circulation of cultural goods, LEAs will be empowered with enhanced investigative capacity to monitor, detect, analyse, and act on inexplicit patterns of illicit cultural heritage trade more effectively than ever before.

4.1 Methodology for Data Collection

In the initial phase of project development, the CCHT developed data collection modules to automate the gathering of information from 30 public databases of stolen, missing, unprovenanced, and protected cultural goods. These included the Federal Bureau of Investigation's National Stolen Art File, the German Lost Art Foundation's Lost Art Database, and the Romanian Police's public database of stolen cultural objects, as well as those discussed later in this chapter and many others. These tools are automated web scrapers that can be run manually, scheduled, and/or parametrised to limit the collection of data to certain results (for example, to only collect data on objects of type 'painting,' or to limit results to items stolen before a certain date). For the purposes of RITHMS project, all available data was gathered from each source, which in most cases included at least basic object data (for example, title, year of creation, author, materials or object type, dimensions, etc.) and in many cases also included information about the object's provenance or historical chain-of-ownership (for example, that a museum acquired the piece from a specific collector, or that an object was stolen from a private residence in Paris on a specific day). Data collection was performed with a combination of the *Requests*, *BeautifulSoup*, and *Selenium* packages of Python, depending on whether the data source was static (i.e., the page's source Hypertext Markup Language (HTML) could be automatically parsed) or dynamic (i.e., where the implementation of JavaScript in the page's source code necessitated the use of a web driver to replicate normal user behaviour). Additional methodological considerations for individual case studies presented in this chapter have been outlined in the corresponding sections below, to further contextualise and illustrate the individual procedures of data collection, processing, and analysis required for each case study.

Before discussing the legal framework within which data collection and analysis occurred, it is important to clarify the working definition of 'open data' used in this research. While 'open-source' and 'open' data are related concepts, 'open-source' data refers to data that is made available with a license that allows users to access, modify, and redistribute it, typically for software development or research purposes. In contrast, open data refers to data that is made available to the public for free and without restrictions, often with the intention of promoting transparency and public good. In our research, we utilised publicly available data within the broader context of OSINT research, where sourcing from openly accessible but legally bounded data is key. Legal considerations are crucial in both cases; open-source data may involve licensing agreements that dictate how the data can be used, while open data may be subject to privacy laws, data protection regulations, and restrictions based on intellectual property.

In terms of legal right to collect and process data, it should be noted that the activities conducted on public, open-access websites as part of the RITHMS project and the research presented here comply with EU Directive 2019/790 (Directive (EU) 2019/790, 2019, Title II, arts. 3–4), which has been transposed into Italian law through Legislative Decree 177/2021, specifically introducing articles 70-ter and 70-quarter into Italy's national Copyright Law 633/1941 (Legislative Decree n. 177, 2021, art. 1, par. 1(i)). Pursuing the lead institute's (the Italian Institute of Technology) legitimate interest to carry out scientific research (GDPR art. 6, par.1(f), Data Protection Commission 2019),[4] compliance with the key principles of the General Data Protection Regulation (GDPR) has also been ensured, particularly with regard to data gathering and storage, and an informative notice has been published on the RITHMS website in accordance with GDPR art. 14, par. 5(b) (RITHMS 2024a). Further, data collected for this chapter were restricted to only what was necessary for the immediate research need, and the mechanisms of data collection and processing were documented thoroughly to facilitate accountability and transparency. Additional ethical considerations on the use of open data for research on cultural heritage crimes and the ethical use of the platform are discussed in Sect. 6. Data collected for RITHMS project has produced the largest known consolidated non-police dataset of looted, missing, protected, and unprovenanced cultural goods (Leeson et al. 2025). Preliminary processing of this data facilitated the extraction of over two million entities (cultural objects, people, events, and other actors) linked to the circulation of cultural goods and the initial correlation and examination of object and entity data. Chronologically, this dataset includes information on the circulation of cultural goods from the year 1800 to the present day; geographically, Europe and the Americas are most well-represented, though data sources also include information on objects that originated in Middle Eastern, African, and southeast Asian contexts. While the ability to publicly reproduce the entire consolidated dataset is limited by copyright protections and pending reproduction rights from individual database managing authorities, the publication of an abridged version of this data is anticipated to follow the end of RITHMS project in October 2025. The following section discusses some of the initial case studies which have been conducted on this data, outlining the opportunities for intelligence-led policing of cultural heritage crimes and the value of automated and semi-automated analytical approaches for examining and visualising this information.

5 Case Studies

This section offers cursory analyses of several datasets collected within the scope of RITHMS project to highlight research prospects and the patterns that can be gleaned from the mechanisms implemented in the project. It draws attention to the ways in which different analytical approaches, including SNA, can highlight prospects for investigation into trafficking networks, grey areas of the market, and other problematic activities. Further, it reinforces the need for a consolidated dataset to minimise

[4] To ensure the lawfulness and compliance of the research process, IIT conducted a feasibility study and produced a corresponding Data Protection Impact Assessment (DPIA).

data siloes and complement existing research and investigation (Leeson et al. 2025). Through the project's collaboration with implementing LEAs across Europe, these initial opportunities can be translated into actionable results, contributing to the tackling of cultural goods trafficking and other criminal activities by bolstering mechanisms for intelligence-led policing.

Research on individual datasets collected for the project has shed light on the structure of elite social networks and networks of individuals active in the circulation of cultural goods. Leveraging the same methodology for automated data collection through web scraping, Leeson et al. (2024) reconstructed a social network of thousands of individuals who have been sanctioned for their support of Russian military action in Ukraine, including high-ranking oligarchs and individuals in the Russian state apparatus. This research highlighted the place of known art collectors within the network and, through centrality analyses and examination of acquaintance relationships among politically exposed persons, identified grey areas for the trade of cultural goods to continue in violation of international sanctions. Further, this research draws attention to the intersections between cultural heritage crimes and other clandestine activities, particularly white-collar crimes such as tax and sanctions evasion, money laundering, and fraud.

Similarly, Giovanelli et al. (2025) pursued the same methodology for automated data collection from the *Proveana* database of the German Lost Art Foundation, to reconstruct and visualise the networks of individuals, organisations, and events pertaining to the confiscation and circulation of cultural goods during the Second World War. By leveraging social network analysis, this research identified a single individual who served as a bridge between two major periods of state-led confiscations of cultural goods: the first under Nazi Germany during WWII and the second in 1962 under the German Democratic Republic's Ministry for State Security. This study produced insights that would not have been attainable using other methods of data collection or analysis, and this research highlights novel opportunities for research into the post-war provenance of looted objects, which is often incomplete, missing, or falsified (German Lost Art Foundation n.d.-a; Manikowska 2023).

These research projects, secondary to the development of RITHMS platform, leveraged the unique collection of open data to offer substantial insights on the structure and flow of the networks that feed the market for illicit goods. Similarly, the following case studies demonstrate how further research on other datasets collected for the project offers actionable insights on trade patterns and networks which can aid law enforcement efforts to tackling these types of criminal activity. The case studies are presented in reverse chronological order, first examining data on current trends in illicit trade, then considering data on post-1970 trafficking networks, and concluding with a case study on wartime looting during WWII.

5.1 Securius Datenbank

The Securius database is managed by the Federal Criminal Police Office of Germany (Bundeskriminalamt, also BKA) in collaboration with the German State Criminal Police Offices. The database holds records on thousands of cultural goods that have been confiscated by police departments across Germany and that are believed to be linked to criminal activity (Bundeskriminalamt 2024a). At the time of writing, the database holds 5260 object records, which include artworks, watches and jewellery, coins, gold bars, and other unprovenanced items seized during the carrying out of police activities (Bundeskriminalamt 2024a, b). The database is public, allowing anyone to browse the objects and submit a report if they identify an object for which previous ownership is known. Each object page includes at least one photo of the object, a brief description, details of the confiscation (date and place), and contact information of the police department involved, in most cases consisting of a telephone number, the department name, and its postal address. Keywords are also provided for the objects, for example 'coin', 'pendant', and 'gold,' which facilitate data querying and browsing in the raw dataset. While some of these items, particularly jewellery or watches, may not be typically included within the umbrella of 'cultural goods' or 'cultural heritage,' the present study has deferred to the BKA, which has included all such items under the umbrella of "art and valuables" (*Kunst und Wertgegenstände*) (Bundeskriminalamt 2024a). For the purposes of this research, data used were collected from Securius on 8 April 2024.

The development phase of RITHMS produced a data collection module that uses the *Requests* and *BeautifulSoup* libraries of the Python programming language to parse the HTML of each object record and retrieve all the available information. For the current analysis, the locations of all seizures were extracted and geolocalised to visualise the frequency of confiscations across Germany. Figure 1 shows the results of this processing, overlaid on a population density map. Cursory analysis reveals that the frequency of confiscations corresponds generally with the population density of Germany, with most seizures occurring in major cities and clusters that approximately reflect areas of greater concentration.

However, there are two major outliers that warrant further investigation. The first is the city of Hannover, which saw the most objects seized (at 1969; see Table 1). It is worth noting that Hannover is the thirteenth-largest city in Germany in terms of population size, but far exceeds larger cities—including Berlin, Cologne (Köln), and Frankfurt—in number of seizures. Hannover, and its region of Lower Saxony, does not have a particularly high regional crime rate, so the number of cultural goods seized is not a reflection of an overall higher rate of crime (McEvoy 2023). Further, Hannover is not a statistically significant hotspot for seizures of other illicit goods, such as drugs, so the high number of cultural goods seizures is notable (Bundeskriminalamt 2022, p. 59).

The most frequently confiscated items are jewellery and watches. Without further information, it is unclear in which context the cultural objects were confiscated. It is possible, however, that many were pickpocketed; this would explain why these

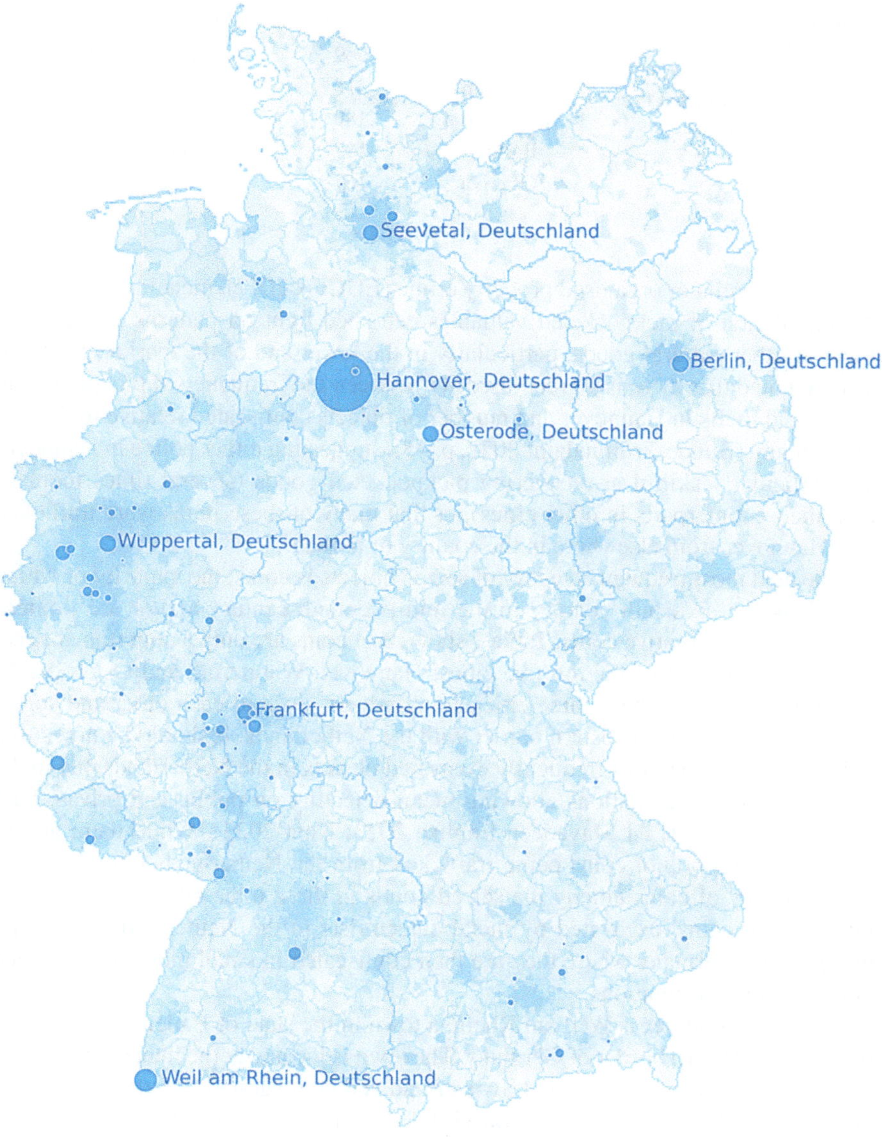

Fig. 1 Seizures of cultural goods in Germany, by city, as reported in the Securius database, with marker size proportionate to the number of seizures. Labels have been added for cities with more than 140 reported confiscations. Data were visualised using the *Geopandas*, *Matplotlib*, and *Shapely* Python packages

items, which for the most part are relatively low value, well-worn, not unique, and confiscated individually, would have been subjected to police seizure. While the practice of pickpocketing certainly has several important differences from the phenomenon of cultural goods trafficking, both are considered activities within the

Table 1 Cities with the most confiscated objects and the most frequently confiscated object in each, extracted from the Securius database

City	Confiscations	Most common objects
Hannover	1969	Jewellery, watches, coins
Weil am Rhein	315	Jewellery, watches
Wuppertal	180	Jewellery, coins
Berlin	177	Jewellery
Osterode	167	Jewellery, coins

broader umbrella of organised property crime (EUCPN 2017), meaning research on the circulation of pickpocketed valuables can shed light on patterns in the illicit trade of other cultural goods, particularly in the lower end of the market. It should also be noted that there is a great disparity between the frequency of pickpocketing events and thefts in Hannover and number of objects confiscated relative to the rest of Germany (Bundeskriminalamt 2022, p. 45), suggesting either police in Hannover are particularly skilful at recovering pickpocketed goods (several times more so than their counterparts in other cities), or that many of these items were trafficked into Hannover from elsewhere in the country or abroad.

The next most frequent category of seized objects is coins, the majority of which date from the sixteenth century to the mid-twentieth-century and/or are limited-edition commemorative coins. Table 1 shows that coins are only a common abstract object type in three of the top five cities: Hannover, Wuppertal, and Osterode. As illustrated in Fig. 1, these three cities are relatively close to each other and somewhat close to the northwestern border with the Netherlands. It should be noted that coins are one of the most frequently excavated objects in the Netherlands due to the country's lenient regulations allowing metal detecting on public and private land (PAN Project 2021; Al Mayadeen English 2023; Kuta 2023). While there are no recent news reports of coins being trafficked from the Netherlands into Germany, the frequency of coins among the seized goods in these three cities could suggest that modern coins, excavated by metal detectorists in the Netherlands, are being brought into Germany where they are then confiscated in small numbers by police during other investigations.

The second outlier is Weil am Rhein, a town in the state of Baden-Württemberg on the southeastern border of Germany. The town is located at the intersection of the borders of Germany, France, and Switzerland and is integrated into the local transport system of the Swiss city of Basel. Of the 315 objects in Securius that were confiscated in Weil am Rhein, most are wristwatches, and the second-most common abstract object type is jewellery. The high frequency of objects confiscated in Weil am Rhein could be explained by the town's location on the border of France and Switzerland and its integration in a Swiss transit system, which make it an advantageous passage for the trafficking of goods originating in these countries (or transiting through these countries from another source). Indeed, as reported in the Global Organized Crime Index report (2023, p. 4) on Germany, German police "have carried out multiple seizures of illegal gold and silver, highlighting the country's role in gold trafficking in the region" and drawing particular attention to recent "cases of gold trafficking between France, Germany, and Turkey" (see also Eurojust 2023). Further, it is reported that German customs agents seize thousands of counterfeit items at border points in the country, of which the most common types include jewellery and accessories (Global Organized Crime Index 2023, p. 3), echoing the insights provided by the data in Securius. This is further indication that lower-end goods (including counterfeits) tend to be targets for smugglers transporting relatively small and easily concealable valuables across borders within western Europe (Brodie et al. 2019, pp. 73–74).

Lastly, while the Securius database holds records on the unprovenanced and illicit cultural goods seized by German police, records on seizures of art and artefacts (as opposed to jewellery and accessories) are minimal. Of the over 5000 object records in the database, less than 1% are paintings and other pictures, another less than 1% sculptures, and only 5% coins; most of the remainder are wristwatches and jewellery. On one hand, this makes sense because unique artworks are more readily identified and returned to their rightful owner, leaving the non-unique goods to be registered on a database for public identification. However, a pattern can still be discerned from the locations with the most recovered paintings and sculptures: the cities where the most paintings have been recovered are Braunschweig and Hamburg, and the cities where the most sculptures have been recovered are Hannover and Neumünster. As illustrated in Fig. 2, these cities are all located in the north of the country and in relative proximity to one another. This might suggest that the north of Germany is a more frequent region for the looting or trafficking of these types of objects.

On the other hand, the German government has been criticised for misreporting the illicit trade in cultural goods with so-called "zombie statistics" (Bochereau 2020), and this dataset could be further evidence of that, challenging speculative claims that exaggerated the frequency of cultural heritage crimes in the country. In 2019, for example, the ILLICID project submitted a report that failed to find evidence of a billion-euro market for looted antiquities or proof that the illicit trafficking of cultural goods was financing terrorism and organised crime—claims that have been used to implement heightened regulations on the art trade and a new cultural property law (Fitz Gibbon 2019; Bochereau 2020).

Further, while the exploratory and spatial analyses discussed in this section do suggest a higher frequency of cultural goods crimes in the cities under examination than elsewhere in Germany, this research has been working with the BKA's definition of 'art and valuables,' which includes objects not typically considered by scholarship to fall within the definition of 'cultural heritage.' While much research and policy on the illicit trade tend to focus on art and antiquities, especially those with outstanding historic or artistic significance, jewellery and watches (which comprise the largest category of confiscated objects in Securius) tend to be classified instead as conspicuous or luxury goods (Oosterman and Angelini 2021; Blakeney 2023). The present study joins Oosterman and Angelini (2021) in advocating for more focus on the luxury goods market as a subset in cultural heritage crime research, because the patterns observed in this discipline have many similarities and overlaps with those affecting cultural goods trafficking. Further, it is well-established that

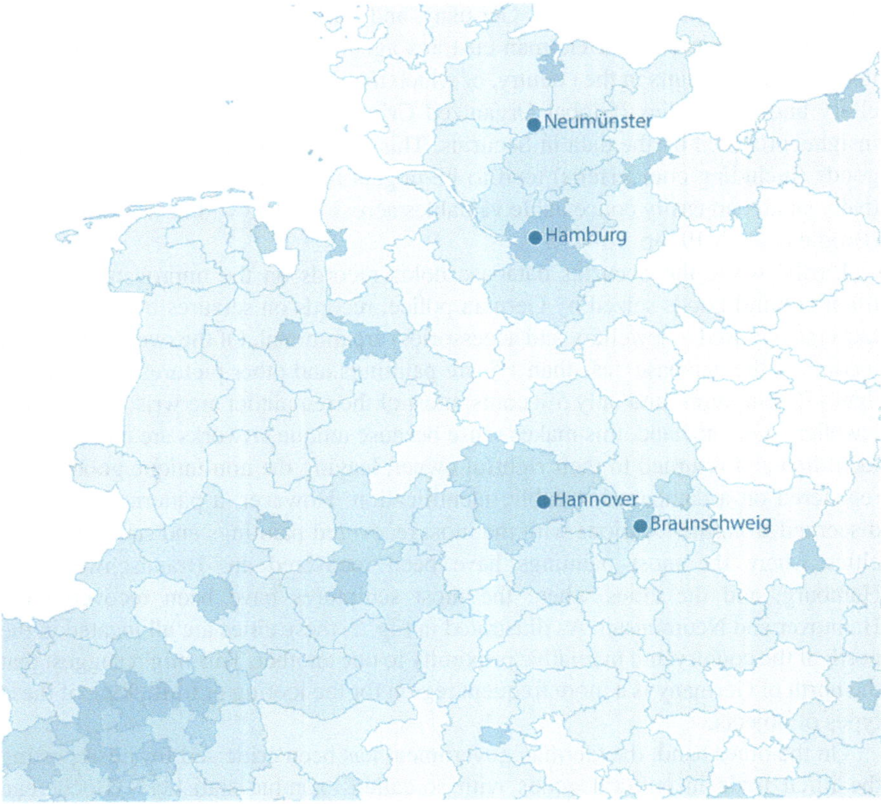

Fig. 2 Northern Germany, showing cities with the most seized paintings and sculptures: Braunschweig, Hamburg, Hannover, and Neumünster

trafficking networks tend to use the same routes for different types of illicit merchandise, including both cultural heritage and luxury goods as well as drugs, weapons, and other goods (Hardy 2021b; Europol 2022; UNODC 2022).

While this case study has highlighted some opportunities for additional investigation into trends of illicit trade, for example the likelihood of coins being smuggled into Germany from the Netherlands, or the increased frequency of art thefts in the country's north, additional research is needed to determine the context of these crimes and whether they are connected to broader trafficking networks across Europe. However, this analysis has reinforced the value of interdisciplinary approaches to open data on cultural goods crimes in Germany, including automated data collection and manual geospatial analysis. It also suggests greater focus be given to low-end cultural goods in scholarship on illicit trade for the patterns that these items can highlight within an international network of criminal activity.

5.2 AAMD Object Registry

The second case study is an examination of the Object Registry of the Association of Art Museum Directors (AAMD), a membership-based association linking the leadership of museums across North America. Within the Object Registry, the AAMD maintains two databases: the New Acquisitions of Archaeological Material and Works of Art database (of objects in AAMD member museums that were acquired after 2008[5] that lack pre-1970[6] provenance), and the Resolutions of Claims for Nazi-Era Cultural Assets database (of objects in AAMD member museums that were subject to claims of Nazi looting during World War II). The present research focused on the first database, which at the time of writing holds approximately 2300 object records. As the registry is continuously being updated, it should be noted that data used for this study were collected on 19 March 2024.

While most data gathered for the RITHMS project concern objects and collections within Europe, the AAMD and other non-European datasets complement these materials by expanding the coverage of the KG on which the platform relies. Specifically, they help mitigate a common weakness in social network analysis in which the restricted geographic scope of the network graph does not accurately reconstruct the network under study, which is rarely so limited. Rather, the integration of non-European datasets allows the visualisation of connections between trade routes in Europe and those elsewhere in the world, in this case the Americas. It also highlights the same patterns of trafficking which affect other regions, for example (as outlined below), the transit of illicit goods from looted contexts first to Europe and then to North American markets, which served to launder object provenance and disguise illicit origins. The inclusion of American data also helps link other datasets (of European scope) to high-profile trafficking cases, many of which have involved American galleries and museums. For example, the art and antiquities dealers Robin Symes, Robert Hecht, and John G. Bourne, all of whom have been implicated in international antiquities trafficking networks, feature in multiple object provenances in the AAMD Object Registry, problematising these objects and the channels that enabled their acquisition by reputable museums. Lastly, the enrichment of the RITHMS KG necessitated the automated extraction of entities and relationships from unstructured text to reconstruct the sequences of events which make up object provenances. The tool which enabled this was fine-tuned on the AAMD dataset and then further tested on other data gathered for the project, making the AAMD an important step in the technological advancement of the project's mechanisms for data processing.

As with the Securius database, a data collection module was developed that used the *Requests*, *BeautifulSoup*, and *Selenium* packages of Python to parse and gather all the available information on the objects listed in the database. One of the most

[5] The date of the last AAMD acquisition regulations.

[6] Referring to the landmark 1970 UNESCO Convention on the Means of Prohibiting and Preventing the Illicit Import, Export and Transfer of Ownership of Cultural Property.

interesting fields of data provided about the cultural objects is 'provenance,' which details the known ownership history of each item (not to be confused with 'provenience,' which refers to the object's place of origin). These fields are unstructured in the database, which means they consist of sentences or paragraphs of information from which specific entities (such as people, locations, and dates) must be extracted. For the purposes of RITHMS project, three natural language processing (NLP) models were fine-tuned to extract entities from the unstructured text integrated into the platform (Ferro et al. 2025). The development phase of the NLP models required annotating entities in the unstructured text, as illustrated in Fig. 3, where tags are displayed using the NER Annotator for Spacy software (NER Annotator for Spacy n.d.). This process trained the model to recognise and extract entities and has been implemented in the final RITHMS platform. Surprisingly, however, issues encountered during this phase were later found to highlight objects in the AAMD database with particularly suspicious provenance. Further examination indicates this methodology may successfully predict opportunities for further investigation into looted and trafficked goods.

In several instances, the NLP model returned errors because it was unable to parse distinct events within a provenance sample due to convoluted or opaque language. One of the records which returned such an error detailed a seated earthenware figure from the Jama-Coaque culture, originating in Ecuador and currently at the Walters Art Museum (see Fig. 4; AAMD n.d.-b). According to the 1970 UNESCO Convention, which recommends restrictions on which objects can be acquired by museums, this piece should not have been acquired by the museum because it lacks sufficient provenance from before 1970 (UNESCO 1970). Until 2008, however, AAMD guidelines for museums only required 10 years of provenance before the museum's acquisition (AAMD 2004). In 2008, these guidelines were updated to be in line with UNESCO's recommendations, requiring proof that the object was either already outside its country of origin by 1970, or that it was exported legally after this date (AAMD 2008). A revision to the guidelines in 2013 clarified that member museums may acquire such unprovenanced objects in cases where they were gifted or donated by bequest before the date of the new guidelines (2008), provided they are also logged in the Object Registry (AAMD 2013). This was the case for the earthenware figure, which, although it was not donated to the museum until 2013, was anticipated since 2005. The provenance listed for this piece is: "Arizona collection; Ron Messick Fine Arts, Santa Fe, New Mexico [date and mode of acquisition unknown]; John G. Bourne, October 3, 1998, by purchase; given to Walters Art Museum, 2013" (AAMD n.d.-b).

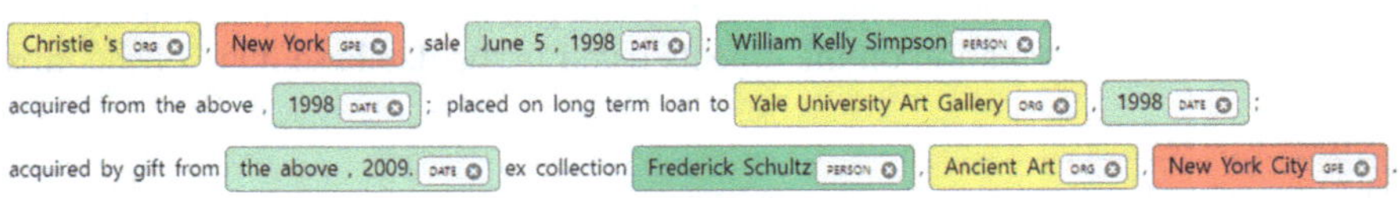

Fig. 3 Example of data annotated for NLP that tags organisations, locations, dates, and people as relevant entities, visualised using NER Annotator for Spacy

Fig. 4 Seated Figure Holding a Box, The Walters Art Museum. Earthenware, originated in Ecuador (photo by the Walters Art Museum, Creative Commons License CC0 1.0)

The reason the NLP model results were unsatisfactory for this object is that the structure of the provenance information is somewhat unclear, devoid of verbs, and includes in square parentheses irrelevant text. These factors all contribute to uncertainty on the part of the model (as well as for human researchers) trying to identify the events involved in the object's historical chain-of-ownership. There are multiple reasons why provenance texts may be vague, oddly structured, or otherwise confusing. In some instances, for example if an object were acquired illegally, ambiguous provenance may be a deliberate attempt to mask the illicit circumstances of the object's acquisition. In other cases, however, it may result simply from a lack of rigour or standards of documentation on the part of the reporting institution.

During manual attempts to reconstruct the chain of ownership that resulted in the object being acquired by the Walters Art Museum, it was ascertained that John G. Bourne is already known to the field of cultural heritage crime and provenance research (Yates 2014). In 1998, the Peruvian archaeologist Walter Alva identified objects in the New Mexico History Museum that he believed had been looted from the site of Sipán in Peru (Atwood 2003). An FBI investigation later determined that the objects had indeed been looted from the site in 1987; they were then trafficked out of the country, rerouted through the UK by an international smuggling ring, and sold to the American antiquities dealer Ben Johnson roughly 6 months later (Kirkpatrick 1992). Bourne purchased the items from Johnson shortly after. Curiously, he claimed to the FBI that the pieces had originated in a *different* looted archaeological site in Peru, La Mina, which exempted the items from emergency import restrictions that the US government had placed on artefacts from Sipán (Atwood 2003). Having acquired the objects before the formal imposition of import restrictions on Peruvian artefacts, and in the absence of proof that the objects originated in Sipán rather than La Mina, Bourne avoided charges, and the items returned to the museum (Constable 2008).

The New Mexico History Museum later announced that it would no longer welcome Bourne's anticipated donation of his personal collection of Mesoamerican artefacts. Bourne then turned instead to the Walters Art Museum, where he donated approximately 300 items from his collection and $4 million USD for a centre to focus on research of the ancient Americas (Yates 2014).

Further, Ron Messick, the New Mexico dealer from whom Bourne allegedly bought the earthenware sculpture under investigation, has also faced charges for trafficking artefacts that originated in looted Peruvian archaeological sites (The Washington Times 2005; Yates 2015, p. 41). The claim in the object's provenance field that Messick had acquired the items from an undisclosed "Arizona collection" is another example of a vague provenance that potentially covers up the object's illicit origins. The only publication provided to support the object's provenance is an overview of the John Bourne Collection, "Exploring Art of the Ancient Americas," published by the Walters Art Museum itself (Reents-Budet 2012).

While the earthenware figure at the centre of this study originated in Ecuador, not Peru, the actors involved in the object's historical chain of ownership are known to have participated in the trafficking of similar artefacts into the US and the fabrication of provenance to 'legitimise' these objects. Further, Bourne has participated in the laundering of items' provenance by donating them to museums (first the New Mexico History Museum and then the Walters Art Museum), the laundering of his own reputation through high-profile cash endowments, and the legitimisation of his collection through publishing activities, as demonstrated by the events related above. This object may not have drawn attention without being flagged by the NLP model currently in development, but research into this item and others like it have returned similar results that suggest the NLP model is able to predict promising opportunities for further research and investigation through the flagging of vague or deceptively worded object provenances.

5.2.1 The AAMD-Derived Network

This case study relies partly on analysis of the social networks that facilitated the circulation of these goods from their origins in Mesoamerican archaeological contexts, via trafficking networks which routed through Europe, to antiquities dealers and museums in the United States. Relationships among the actors involved can be studied further by conducting centrality analyses on the social network derived from the AAMD data to predict other opportunities for research into individuals and organisations who are closely related to those problematised above and/or that have significant influence in their networks.

After collecting data from the AAMD Object Registry using the automated web scraper described in the previous section, the refined NLP model was used to extract entities and relationships from all object provenances provided in the database. In the case of the provenance sample provided above, Table 2 lists the entities (and entity types) extracted, among which relationships were derived, for example that Ron Messick Fine Arts is located in Santa Fe, and that John G. Bourne gave the object to the Walters Art Museum in 2013. This procedure was repeated for all provenance samples in the database and resulted in a sprawling social network graph of 72,280 nodes (representing entities) and 111,863 edges (representing relationships among them) (Fig. 5). This method represents an innovative approach to enriching provenance data through the extraction of valuable data from unstructured texts (see also Giovanelli and Traviglia 2024).

Once this SNG is produced, different statistical analyses can be performed on the data to determine the centrality and influence of specific individuals, events, or organisations within the network. These results, in turn, can highlight opportunities for further research into those entities that have been central to the circulation of unprovenanced or under-provenanced objects. Notably, there are some limitations to this methodology which resulted from the nature of the source data; for example, 'private collection' (and variations, like 'collection', 'coll', and 'estate') is one of the most central entities in the network by most measures, reflecting the fact that many provenances have included an unspecified 'private collection' as one stop in their objects' ownership histories. However, this does not refer to the same private collection in every case; rather, dozens or even hundreds of unique private collections have been merged within a single node with the label 'private collection', reducing its value to the SNA of this graph.

One method for analysing influential entities is to calculate and compare each node's closeness centrality score; this reflects how close each is to the others in the network, and how many 'shortest paths' (the quickest way to move from one node to another within the system) pass through the entity. Unsurprisingly, the node with the highest closeness centrality score in the network is the auction house Sotheby's

Table 2 Entities extracted from the AAMD provenance sample by the NLP model fine-tuned for RITHMS project

Entity label	Entity type
John G. Bourne	Person
Ron Messick Fine Arts	Organisation
Walters Art Museum	Organisation
Santa Fe	Location
New Mexico	Location
October 3, 1998	Date
2013	Date

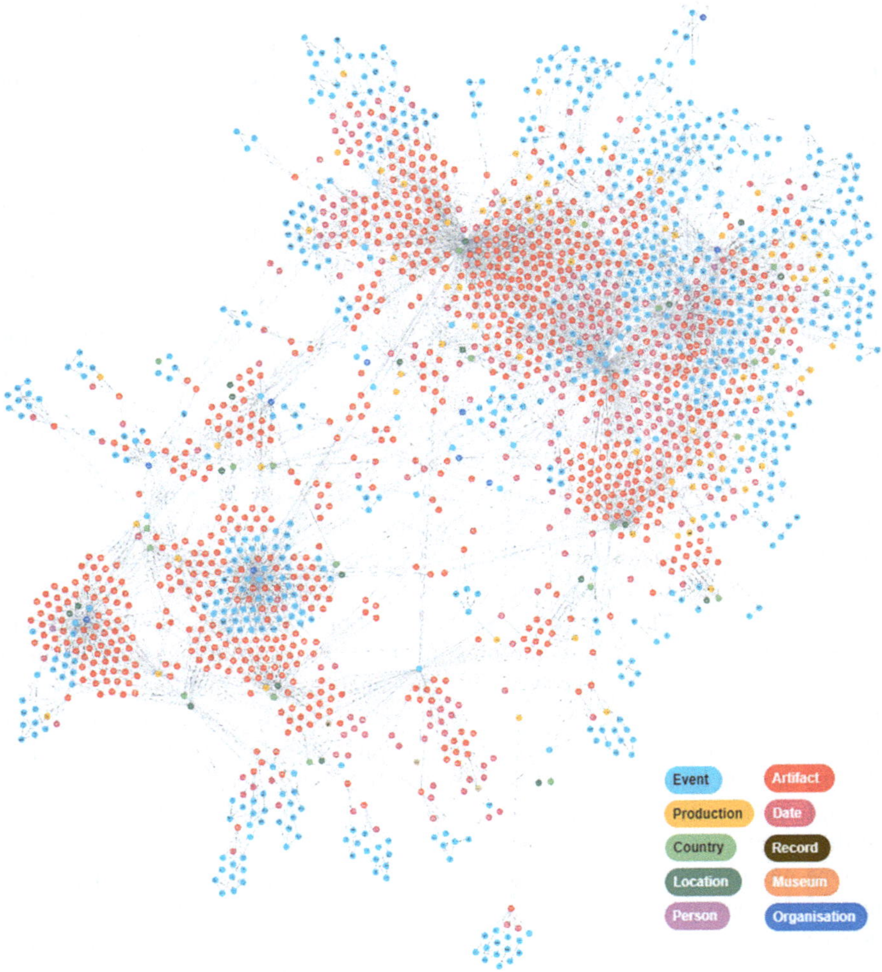

Fig. 5 SNG depicting a portion of the network derived from the AAMD dataset using the NLP model fine-tuned for RITHMS project, visualised in Neo4j

New York, which reflects its role as a broker and facilitator of a significant number of transactions in the cultural goods trade (Fabiani and Marrone 2021). Other nodes with an unsurprisingly high closeness centrality include Sotheby's London and Christie's auction house. More interesting is the fact that the former art dealer Nicolas Koutoulakis is within the top ten most central nodes according to this measure; Koutoulakis was named in the organigram of the Medici antiquities trafficking network and, along with his Paris-based gallery Segredakis, has been implicated in claims from Greece and Turkey for artefacts later determined to have been illegally removed from the countries and sold to the J. Paul Getty Museum in Los Angeles

(Watson and Todeschini 2007; Felch 2012). Through manual analysis of the nodes in Koutoulakis' immediate ego network (entities linked directly to him), Nanette B. Kelekian was identified as the most frequent buyer of his objects. According to the dataset, all the objects in the AAMD database that passed through Kelekian are now in the collection of the Metropolitan Museum of Art, which is known for its over-zealous acquisition practices, particularly in the 1970s (Hoving 1993; Watson and Todeschini 2007). Notably, the Kelekian objects were all acquired by the Met in either 2018 or 2020 from bequests expected before 2008, which permitted their acquisition according to the AAMD's most recent guidelines. Considering (i) Kelekian's proximity to Koutoulakis in the network, (ii) the fact that these objects all lack pre-1970 provenance and evidence of legal export from their countries of origin, and (iii) that she appears to be relatively unknown to scholarship on the illicit trade,[7] this is a promising lead for future research into objects believed to have entered the market illegally.

Another similarly influential node according to closeness centrality is the New York-based Merrin Gallery, which has also been linked to the Medici trafficking network (Giovanelli 2021, 2024). Specifically, the gallery was implicated in an investigation by the Manhattan District Attorney's Office into a group of ten objects that had been looted from Egypt, as well as a fourth-century BCE Greek artefact that had been sold to the gallery by Giacomo Medici himself (Giovanelli 2021, 2024). By following the same procedure as above, 46 objects were identified that passed through the Merrin Gallery, 33 of which were then sold by the gallery to an anonymous 'private collection' (which, as outlined above, may refer to the same private collection or unique ones) before being donated or gifted to the Walters Art Museum. Recall that it was the Walters Art Museum that accepted John Bourne's donation of approximately 300 items (and $4 million USD) after these objects, problematised by their proximity to an international trafficking network of Mesoamerican objects, were refused by the New Mexico History Museum (Yates 2014).

This brief foray into SNA of the AAMD-derived network demonstrates that closeness centrality, which is just one among many centrality measures, is a promising method of statistical analysis for both identifying known trafficking networks and flagging new individuals and organisations for further research. While it is outside the scope of this chapter to investigate these opportunities further, this section has highlighted the promise of this method for research into cultural heritage crimes. During deployment in the final RITHMS platform, these mechanisms have the potential to produce actionable intelligence for law enforcement agents investigating and tackling the illicit trade of cultural goods.

[7] Nanette Kelekian has been named in some scholarship, including Decamargo (2012), Jenkins-Madina (2000), and Thum (2022), but these works have only mentioned her in passing and focused more on the activities of her grandfather, the prolific collector and dealer Dikran Kelekian. It appears that the connections between Nanette Kelekian and Nicolas Koutoulakis have not been explored.

5.3 WWII-Looted Databases

As RITHMS is concerned with building a social network graph of historic chains of ownership, databases of cultural goods looted during the Second World War are an important addition to the knowledgebase. Fourteen databases of WWII-looted cultural goods were identified for integration with RITHMS, as indicated in Table 3; of these, the first six will be discussed in this section.

Partway through the data collection phase, several inventory and numbering systems were identified in use by multiple databases, suggesting the potential to correlate data objects across repositories to consolidate the available information on each item. Of the fourteen databases investigated for the project, the first six listed in Table 3 were found to use common systems; Table 4 provides a list of the various inventories (left column) and the databases that use them (header row). This final case study outlines the methodology used to correlate data objects among databases, offering new possibilities for research into the provenance and recovery of WWII-looted cultural goods.

Six different inventory and numbering systems were identified. 'Munich numbers' represents a numbering system used by Allied forces to consolidate Nazi-looted collections for repatriation. Following the end of the war, cultural goods were brought *en masse* to the 'Central Collecting Point' in Munich to determine their country of origin and rightful heirs (Enderlein et al. n.d.). Many of the artworks

Table 3 Databases of WWII-looted cultural goods identified for RITHMS project

Database	Managing authority
Hermann Göring Art Collection ("Göring Collection")	[Germany] German Historical Museum
Reichskunstdepot Kremsmünster – Paintings ("K-List Database")	[Austria] Leonhard Weidinger
Linz Collection	[Germany] German Historical Museum
Rose Valland MNR	[France] Ministry of Culture
Einsatzstab Reichsleiter Rosenberg Collection ("Rosenberg Collection")	Claims Conference and the United States Holocaust Memorial Museum
Tableau et dessin database ("TED Database")	[France] Commission for the Compensation of Victims of Spoliation
Cultural Goods of the Second World War	[Netherlands] Cultural Heritage Agency
Lost Art Database	[Germany] German Lost Art Foundation
The Central Registry of Information on Looted Cultural Property, 1933–1945	Commission for Looted Art in Europe
Art Database	[Austria] National Fund of the Republic of Austria for Victims of National Socialism
Catalogue of Wartime Losses	[Poland] Ministry of Culture, Division for Looted Art
Max Stern Art Restitution Project	[Canada] Concordia University
Degenerate Art Database	[Germany] Free University of Berlin
Nazi-Era Provenance Internet Portal	[United States] American Alliance of Museums

Table 4 Databases of WWII-looted cultural goods that use common inventory systems

	Göring Collection	K-List Database	Linz Collection	Rose Valland MNR	Rosenberg Collection	TED Database
Munich number	X	X	X		X	X
Linz number		X	X		X	
Aussee number		X			X	
Lv number		X				
ERR number					X	X
MNR number				X		X

confiscated by the Nazis during the war were intended for an unrealised 'Führermuseum' in Linz, Austria; these works were acquired by the 'Linz Special Commission' (*Sonderauftrag Linz*), which was established in June 1939 (Commission for Looted Art in Europe n.d.; Enderlein et al. n.d.; Leonhard Weidinger n.d.). Consequently, 'Linz numbers' represent the numbering system used for the full collection of these objects. Many of the items acquired for the Linz collection were, at various points during the war, stored at the Altaussee salt mine in Austria; these objects were inventoried using 'Altaussee' or 'Aussee' numbers (Leonhard Weidinger n.d.; Monuments Men and Women Foundation 2022). An alternate numbering system for objects stored in the mine is that of 'Lv numbers'; these were recorded by US soldiers upon reaching Altaussee, so it is possible they differentiate between objects originally brought to the mine for storage (the Aussee number) and those still in the mine when the Allies arrived (Lv number). Another department responsible for the acquisition of objects for the proposed museum in Linz was the *Einsatzstab Reichsleiter Rosenberg* (Special Purposes Reich Leader Rosenberg, ERR) office, which purchased and confiscated objects specifically from France; these items are identified by their 'ERR number.' Lastly, 'MNR numbers' refer to an inventory system for looted objects that could not, for various reasons, be returned to their rightful owners following the war and were entrusted to the care of French national museums (Ministère de la culture n.d.).

The databases used for this analysis are the Göring Collection, Linz Collection, Rose Valland MNR database, the so-called 'K-List' of looted works temporarily stored at the Kremsmünster Benedictine monastery, the Rosenberg Collection of works acquired by the *Einsatzstab Reichsleiter Rosenberg* task force, and the Tableau et Dessin database of claims for WWII-era compensation. It should be noted that data used for this research were collected between 12 February and 8 March 2024. Data were gathered using similar Python-based modules as those used for the Securius and AAMD databases. Following data collection, rule-based classification techniques were implemented using the *Pandas* package to normalise the data records and standardise inventory numbers; this enabled correlation across the six datasets as well as the identification of the most frequent values (e.g., most common artist or country-of-origin).

This approach identified hundreds of cases where records on the same object were provided by multiple databases. These examples were found by correlating the shared inventory numbers shown in Table 4, with the initial aim of consolidating all available information on each item. This mechanism provides additional opportunities for provenance research to leverage the consolidated open dataset of RITHMS by eliminating data silos and creating a central repository (Leeson et al. 2025). However, this approach found that many databases provided different data on the same item; inconsistencies ranged from minor variations in dimensions to significant discrepancies in title, provenance, materials, and other fields. Correlation of this data provides additional unforeseen advantages for research into looted goods, as indicated in the following example: a painting by the Dutch artist Pieter Aertsen, which is included in four databases with Munich number 11795.

Table 5 consolidates the different pieces of information provided by each database for this object, sourced from the Göring Collection, K-List database, Linz Collection, and Rosenberg Collection (ERR Project n.d.; German Historical Museum n.d.-a, n.d.-b; Leonhard Weidinger n.d.). It is outside the scope of the present study to determine the accuracy of the information provided by each database. Rather, this example shows that correlation of data between multiple sources can be used for two main purposes: to validate (or call into question) object data, and to improve the scope of object records by aggregating existing data. Consolidating all available information on this piece enables the reconstruction of the history of an extremely interesting object—something that would not be possible if provenance research relied on one database alone.

Jacques Goudstikker was a Jewish art dealer who owned and lived in the estate of Nyenrode Castle in Breukelen, the Netherlands. Following the German occupation of the Netherlands, which began in May 1940, Hermann Göring (one of the senior Nazi officers who oversaw the confiscation of thousands of artworks during the war) immediately acquired the full inventory of Goudstikker Gallery and integrated about 300 of the 800 paintings into his own personal collection (Köhler 2019). Those he did not retain (including the Aertsen painting), he consigned at various auction houses in Germany (German Historical Museum, n.d.-a, n.d.-b). The painting, which was taken from the Netherlands to Germany in July 1940, was consigned that same month to art dealer and director of the Göring Collection, Walter Andreas Hofer. It went unsold, however, and was later moved to the Altaussee salt mine to protect it from Allied bombing. In 1943 the work was consigned again to the Munich-based Galerie Marie Almas-Dietrich, where it again failed to sell. In February 1944, Göring used the painting (and 49 others) to barter for a highly sought-after Vermeer—a more desirable work, but one which was later found to be a forgery (Köhler 2019). The Aertsen was confiscated again, this time joining the Linz Collection of works intended to fill the anticipated 'Führermuseum' in Hitler's hometown of Linz, Austria. In 1945, however, following the end of the war, the

Table 5 Information provided on Aertsen's "Outdoor Kitchen" by each of the databases under examination

	Göring Collection	K-List Database	Linz Collection	Rosenberg Collection
Image	Yes		Yes	
Inventory numbers	Munich, Linz, and RM	Munich and Aussee	Munich and Linz	Munich and Goudstikker
Artist name	Pieter Aertsen	Pieter Aertsen	Pieter Aertsen	Pieter Aertsen
Artist lifespan	1508–1575		1508–1575	
Artwork title	Küche im Freien (Outdoor Kitchen)	Küche im Freien (Outdoor Kitchen)	Küche und Bereitung eines Mahles im Freien (Cooking and Preparing an Outdoor Meal)	Keukenstuk (Kitchen Piece)
Date			1533 (around)	
Material/ technique	Wood	Oil on wood	Wood	Painting Oil on Panel
Dimensions	59 × 137.5	59/138	59.5 × 138	59.5 × 138 cm
Previous owner	Collection Goudstikker		Jacques Goudstikker Collection/ Amsterdam 1940 (private collection Netherlands)	Jacques Goudstiker – Amsterdam, Netherlands
Previous location	Nyenrode Castle 1513			Nyenrode Castle, Breukelen, The Netherlands
Transfer type	Forced Sale		Forced Sale	
Consignment	Hofer, Walter Andreas/ Berlin, July 13, 1940		Galerie Maria Almas - Dietrich/ Munich 1943	
Transfer date		17 January 1941		
Transfer destination		Aussee		
Restitution	Netherlands		Netherlands	
Other notes	Delivery of Vermeer exchange on February 9, 1944 to Goudstikker-Miedl/Amsterdam, from there to the special order Linz (Linz 3031)		Acquired for Hermann Göring (RM 406)	

painting was brought to Munich where it was inventoried by Allied troops at the Central Collecting Point and where the decision was made to repatriate the piece back to the Netherlands (German Lost Art Foundation, n.d.-b).

The story does not end there. From the safekeeping of the Dutch government, one might assume the painting should have been restituted to Desirée Goudstikker, widow of Jacques and the major shareholder of the looted Goudstikker Gallery. However, the piece (and others repatriated like it) were instead sold at various auctions across the Netherlands in the 1950s (Köhler 2019). While it is known that the Aertsen painting was sold at Van Marle, de Sille and Baan auction house in Rotterdam between 20 and 22 December 1950, the buyer and subsequent provenance are unknown (German Lost Art Foundation n.d.-b). The painting, having survived so much during the war and having been repatriated to its country-of-origin, was returned to the market and its whereabouts are currently unknown.

This history could not have been reconstructed in such detail if provenance research had relied on just one of the databases mentioned above or was conducted without proper mechanisms to correlate data from different sources. In fact, additional context included here but not integrated in Table 5 was found in the Lost Art Database, yet another repository of WWII-looted cultural goods that could only be correlated with the others through manual analysis (German Lost Art Foundation n.d.-b; Köhler 2019). One limitation of this method—correlating objects using common inventory numbers—is that it does occasionally face collisions, where the same identifier has been assigned to multiple objects. While this can be resolved by comparing other object data to determine whether it is the same object, it means that the inventory code for these two items can no longer be used for correlation as it has been proven to not be unique. However, this still represents an opportunity for manual investigation to reconcile these errors, validate correct information, and further examine promising leads.

5.3.1 Network Analysis of WWII Data

Using the same methodology as that applied to the AAMD database, namely the automated extraction of entities using a fine-tuned NLP model, a similarly enriched network graph was generated that visualises the relationships among individuals, organisations, events, and other entities involved in the circulation of cultural goods during and after the Second World War. This builds on previous work, which has highlighted the ways in which looted and trafficking of cultural goods during the period relied on the same networks that enabled other war crimes (Giovanelli et al. 2025). In this study, one key individual, Walter Neuling, was found to serve as a bridge between Nazi looting activities and the mass confiscations of cultural goods realised by the German Democratic Republic in the 1960s, well after the close of the war. Neuling was found to be a crucial cut-point linking the two mass confiscations, both of which constituted nationwide appropriations of cultural goods (many of which in both cases were sold abroad to raise state funds) and were largescale examples of state crime disguised as actions in the national interest (Förster 2016; Giovanelli et al. 2025).

When consolidating data from multiple databases for SNA, an important consideration is the merging or linking of entities across sources. This would enable, for example, the linking of 'Walter Neuling' and 'Neuling, Walter' as the same individual. For this purpose, the CCHT developed a Python function for consolidating variations on individual names, factoring in string case, punctuation, and name order. This allowed for the merging of the following possible variations: 'Walter Neuling', 'walter neuling', 'NEULING, Walter', 'Neuling, Walter', 'WALTER NEULING', and so on. After implementing this function on the dataset collected from the *Proveana* database of WWII-era entities (including individuals, dates, and artworks), managed by the German Lost Art Foundation, an individual was identified who is also referenced in the AAMD database. This represents an insight that was largely unexpected and resulted from the unique combination of techniques and methods implemented for data processing within the RITHMS project: web scraping, consolidation of data from isolated sources, node linking, manual provenance research, and social network analysis (particularly centrality analyses).

The individual, Giorgio Sangiorgi, was a Rome-based art dealer and collector who mainly operated in the first half of the twentieth century (Dumbarton Oaks n.d.). To start, Giovanelli and Traviglia (2024) have reported that he has a relatively high closeness centrality score in a social network graph derived from auction house data, emphasising his efficient connections to other influential nodes in the network, including auction houses themselves as well as key individuals in the WWII-era trade of cultural goods. As a result, it is unsurprising that Sangiorgi also appears in the Office of Strategic Services (OSS) Art Looting Investigation Unit's (ALIU) final report on individuals implicated in the agency's investigations into Nazi-led confiscations (NARA 2016). The OSS was a special unit of the United States government tasked with researching looted art and identifying the individuals responsible who should be prioritised in postwar legal proceedings (Salter 2015). Sangiorgi was flagged because he, in his capacity as an art and antiquities dealer, regularly sold pieces to Walter Andreas Hofer, the primary agent of Hermann Göring (NARA 2016). Sangiorgi is also named in the AAMD dataset in the provenance of a first-century Roman marble urn currently in the collection of the Metropolitan Museum of Art, which was purchased by John J. Medveckis from Sangiorgi's son through Christie's auction house (AAMD n.d.-a). In sum, Sangiorgi is an important, influential node who links together multiple seemingly isolated datasets.

Rather than displaying evidence of wrongdoing, this analysis sheds light on the overlaps among diverse datasets and the value of consolidating seemingly unrelated open data—in this case, auction house records, databases of WWII-looted objects, OSS reports, and a North American registry of unprovenanced archaeological objects. This has provided unexpected insights into the ways in which networks extend across space and time and are rarely bounded by the constraints imposed upon them in typical social network analyses. The consolidation of data across multiple databases also offers other prospects for the recovery of WWII-looted objects. The Aertsen painting, for example, has been recorded with multiple titles, all of which can be used as possible aliases of the piece should it go back on the market. Similarly, the various repositories provide us with multiple different materials and slightly different dimensions, which allow the casting of a wider net when mining data from online auction houses or marketplaces for the painting. Interdisciplinary techniques and methods contribute to the further enrichment of the data and enable its reconstruction in a social network graph, allowing the visualisation of the network of actors and events around each item and providing additional prospects for correlation and investigation.

6 Discussion: Opportunities, Limitations, and Ethical Considerations

The case studies provided above offer initial insights gleaned from analysis of some of the databases integrated in the open dataset from which the RITHMS social network graph is derived. As indicated by the example of the WWII databases, the consolidation and correlation of data from multiple sources provides even greater opportunities for the provisioning of intelligence on looted goods. Other open sources include social media, news, and websites, each of which contributes further source layers to the network under examination.

Following the construction of the network, deep learning algorithms for link prediction can be leveraged to suggest connections that are likely to exist in the real world but are not present in the collected data. Yates and Graham (2023) have used a KG embedding model to suggest new relationships based on the known nodes and edges of a specific network: in their case, the organigram depicting the organisational structure of the Medici antiquities trafficking network. The model they used predicted a relationship between the notorious art dealer Leonardo Patterson and the Brooklyn Museum which, upon further investigation, turned out to be a promising lead for two objects connected to a known trafficking network. Crucially, the impact of this lead relied largely on the domain expertise of the authors, who leveraged their extensive knowledge of actors, events, and networks in the art trade to validate predictions made by the model. This experience reinforces the importance of interdisciplinary collaboration for intelligence-led policing to combine the domain-specific knowledge of researchers, the on-the-ground experience of LEAs, and the increasingly promising potential of new tools for machine learning, network analysis, and data mining.

While the opportunities for data-driven insights on the flow of cultural goods are promising, there are also some limitations to this research which should be noted. Certain constraints exist on all research that relies on OSINT sources and open data, some of which have already been acknowledged in this chapter. For example, in the case of the Securius database of police-confiscated objects, the extent of data coverage relies entirely on the diligence of police to voluntarily enter data on their confiscations. Consequently, a hotspot of seizures must be examined in relation to other sources of data to provide additional context on the confiscations and determine whether they truly reflect an increased number of looted or trafficked goods. Similarly, the AAMD database consists of information provided by the museums themselves, and OSINT research on this source depends largely on the willingness of museums to provide comprehensive provenance voluntarily. In this context, it is also critical to keep in mind that an item's or organisation's inclusion in the consolidated dataset or the RITHMS platform does not inherently imply misconduct or criminal activity, but rather serves as a mechanism for examining the routes through which cultural objects flow.

Similarly, while SNA offers some exciting opportunities for tracking and tackling the illicit trade of cultural goods, it has some limitations as an analytical tool that should be considered and mitigated, where possible, in scientific research and investigations. First, KGs and social network graphs inescapably oversimplify relationships among actors, which are significantly more complicated than what is drawn from SNA-based research. On the one hand, this is deliberate, as it allows for a macroscopic appreciation of the network, which can provide valuable context on the overall flow of goods and information. However, this also necessarily simplifies very complex relationships, the impact of which cannot be underestimated. As a result, SNA-based research should incorporate a range of data sources to examine both the characteristics of the network as a whole and the specificities of individual nodes or relationships that have been flagged by initial, macroscopic analysis. A similar challenge is the inability to accurately define the boundaries of a social network, so it must be recognised that the network constructed by the collected data only reflects a subset of the real-world interactions among actors, many of which do not leave a documentary record.

There are also several ethical considerations that must be kept in mind when conducting OSINT research in general, particularly in support of law enforcement efforts. First, results and insights should be discussed as such: they are not 'evidence' or 'proof' of wrongdoing until the appropriate investigations have occurred and a judicial authority has accepted that such intelligence constitutes evidence, in compliance with the relevant legal and ethical constraints. Similarly, research should be careful to not use dehumanising language when describing specific individuals, such as 'criminal' or other reductionist language that draws pre-emptive or unsupported conclusions. Ultimately, the RITHMS platform is intended as a tool for data management that has the potential to support law enforcement activities, but it does not create or generate evidence, and it does not make decisions or solve problems autonomously. Further, the platform will not be delivered with data and will only begin data processing after it has been installed within the secured premises of the implementing law enforcement agencies. A set of legal and ethical requirements for the project were also defined early in the development process and concern the assurance of security and best practices for the platform's use as well as the ethical and legal considerations of leveraging AI tools in the investigation of cultural goods trafficking (Díaz Castaño and Faraldo Cabana 2023; Faraldo Cabana et al. 2023a, b; García Adán and Fuentes Loureiro 2023).

The final challenge facing this research, and the RITHMS platform specifically, is the importance of ensuring end-users thoroughly understand and regularly use every available function. If officers and analysts were to not appreciate the full potential of the tools provided, or they were to fall into a routine of consistently relying on only one or two main functions, the impact of the project would be similarly limited. With this challenge in mind, a comprehensive plan for testing, validation, and training will allow LEAs to familiarise themselves with all the functions of the tool and promote understanding of how it can enable intelligence-led policing of trafficking networks. Conversely, enhanced collaboration between law enforcement and technical partners will ensure that the platform leverages systems of data classification and processes of knowledge discovery that LEAs already use in their real-world investigations of illicit activity. This safeguards the effectiveness of the tool and amplifies its relevance to end-users.

7 Conclusion

Cultural goods trafficking is a complex criminal activity that transcends national borders, increasingly exploits new technologies, leverages existing and clandestine transit routes, and overlaps with other typologies of both licit and illicit activities. The investigation and tackling of illicit trade and trafficking networks thus depend on the aggregation of expertise from a diverse range of stakeholders: domain experts, data analysts and technicians, law enforcement agencies, and actors from civil society. Research on the trade and trafficking of cultural goods must necessarily integrate data from similarly diverse sources and leverage new and promising technologies for data mining, analysis, and knowledge discovery. As the case studies in this chapter have demonstrated, open-source and publicly available data represent an increasingly valuable resource for the research of these activities.

The RITHMS project has already produced actionable insights on the movement of cultural goods through its leveraging of OSINT sources, SNA, NLP, and interdisciplinary methods of data analysis. This research emphasises an interconnected analysis of isolated databases and encourages a broader approach to studying the circulation of cultural goods using open sources. The platform developed by the Consortium is projected to provide further actionable intelligence on trafficking routes and, ideally, enable the dismantling of networks which have facilitated the illicit trade. Building on this project and the many opportunities presented by the integration of new technologies in cultural goods crime research, intelligence-led policing derived from analyses of open data offers promising opportunities for a network-focused approach to confronting trafficking and illicit trade.

References

AAMD. (2004). Report of the AAMD Task Force on the Acquisition of Archaeological Materials and Ancient Art. Retrieved October 22, 2024, from cms.aamd.org/sites/default/files/document/June%2010%20Final%20Task%20Force%20Report.pdf

AAMD. (2008). Report of the AAMD Task Force on the Acquisition of Archaeological Materials and Ancient Art (revised 2008). Retrieved October 22, 2024, from cms.aamd.org/sites/default/files/document/2008ReportAndRelease.pdf

AAMD. (2013). Introduction to the Revisions to the 2008 Guidelines on the Acquisition of Archaeological Material and Ancient Art. Retrieved October 22, 2024, from cms.aamd.org/sites/default/files/document/AAMD%20Guidelines%202013_0.pdf

AAMD. (n.d.-a). Object Information. Marble Cinerary Urn in the Form of a Tree Stump with Leaves and Grapes. Object Registry, New Acquisitions of Archaeological Material and Works of Ancient Art. Retrieved October 23, 2024, from https://aamd.org/object-registry/new-acquisitions-of-archaeological-material-and-works-of-ancient-art/6687

AAMD. (n.d.-b). Object Information. Seated Figure Holding a Box. Object Registry, New Acquisitions of Archaeological Material and Works of Ancient Art. Retrieved April 23, 2024, from https://aamd.org/object-registry/new-acquisitions-of-archaeologicalmaterial-and-works-of-ancient-art/484

Al Mayadeen English. (2023, March 11) 1,000-year-old medieval treasure unearthed in The Netherlands. Al Mayadeen English. Retrieved April 23, 2024, from https://english.almayadeen.net/news/art-culture/1000-year-old-medieval-treasure-unearthed-in-the-netherlands

Al-Azm A, Paul KA (2019) Facebook's black market in antiquities: trafficking, terrorism, and war crimes. ATHAR Project Retrieved May 5, 2024, from https://atharproject.org/wp-content/uploads/2019/06/ATHAR-FB-Report-June-2019-final.pdf

Associated Press. (2016, May 12). Ukraine tracks down $18.3 million in paintings stolen from Italy. NBC News Retrieved June 17, 2024, from https://www.nbcnews.com/news/world/ukraine-tracks-down-18-3-million-paintings-stolen-italy-n572521

Atwood R (2003) The Monkey's Head. Website of the Alicia Patterson Foundation. Retrieved June 14, 2024, from https://aliciapatterson.org/roger-atwood/the-monkeys-head/

Barabási A-L, Pósfai M (2016) Network science. Cambridge University Press

Begley I (2023, May 5) Gardaí seize archaeological objects in art trafficking crackdown. Extra.ie. Retrieved June 17, 2024, from https://extra.ie/2023/05/05/news/gardai-seizures-art-trafficking

Blakeney M (2023) Chapter 13: luxury goods. In: Counterfeit goods and organised crime. Edward Elgar Publishing, Cheltenham, UK

Bochereau, E. (2020, April 17). A new report says Germany is a hotspot for the illegal antiquities market. Here's why that's wrong – and dangerous. Artnet. Retrieved April 23, 2024, from https://news.artnet.com/art-world-archives/why-germany-is-not-a-hotspot-for-illegal-trade-1834536

Boz, Z. (2018). Fighting the illicit trafficking of cultural property: a toolkit for European Judiciary and law enforcement. UNESCO. Retrieved June 14, 2024, from https://unesdoc.unesco.org/ark:/48223/pf0000266098?posInSet=1&queryId=69eeca8c-383e-4b4f-b795-0e3dad58dab5

Brennan M, Tsirogiannis C (2022) Illicit antiquities network. Illicit Antiquities. Retrieved May 8, 2024, from https://illicitantiquities.net/about

Brodie N (2005) The circumstances and consequences of the British library's 1994 Acquisition of some Karosthi Manuscript Fragments. Cult Without Context 17:5–12

Brodie N (2011a) Scholarship and insurgency? The study and trade of Iraqi antiquities. Illicit traffic of cultural objects: law, ethics, and the realities. An Institute of Advanced Studies Workshop 4–5 August 2011. University of Western Australia, Perth

Brodie N (2011b) The market in Iraqi antiquities 1980-2009 and academic involvement in the marketing process. In: Manacorda S, Chappell D (eds) Crime in the art and antiquities world: illegal trafficking in cultural property. Springer, New York

Brodie N (2014a) Aramaic incantation bowls in war and in peace. J Art Crime 11:9–14

Brodie N (2014b) Auction houses and the antiquities trade. In: Choulia-Kapeloni S (ed) 3rd International conference of experts on the return of cultural property. Archaeological Receipts Fund, Athens, pp 71–82

Brodie N (2014c) Museum malpractice as corporate crime? The case of the J. Paul Getty Museum. J Crime Justice 37(3):399–421

Brodie N, Yates D, Slot B, Batura O, van Wanrooij N, Hoog G (2019) Illicit trade in cultural goods in Europe—characteristics, criminal justice responses and an analysis of the applicability of Technologies in the Combat against the Trade: Final Report. Publications Office of the European Union. Retrieved June 14, 2024, from https://publications.europa.eu/en/publication-detail/-/publication/d79a105a-a6aa-11e9-9d01-01aa75ed71a1/language-en/format-PDF/source-search

Brodie N, Kersel MM, Mackenzie S, Sabrine I, Smith E, Yates D (2022) Why there is still an illicit trade in cultural objects and what we can do about it. J Field Archaeol 47(2):117–130

Brughmans T, Peeples MA (2023) Network science in archaeology. Cambridge University Press

Bundeskriminalamt (2022) Police Crime Statistics. Federal Republic of Germany, Report 2020. V1.0. Wiesbaden. Retrieved May 27, 2024, from https://www.bka.de/EN/CurrentInformation/Statistics/PoliceCrimeStatistics/2022/pcs2022.html

Bundeskriminalamt (2024a). Confiscated items – "Securius" database. Accessed October 22, 2024, from https://www.securius.eu/de/informationen/

Bundeskriminalamt (2024b) Datenbank. Accessed October 22, 2024, from https://www.securius.eu/de/datenbank/

Byrne D (2016) The problem with looting: an alternative perspective on antiquities trafficking in Southeast Asia. J Field Archaeol 41(3):344–354

Campbell PB (2013) The illicit antiquities trade as a transnational criminal network: characterizing and anticipating trafficking of cultural heritage. Int J Cult Prop 20:113–153

Chappell D, Polk K (2011) Unraveling the "Cordata": just how organized is the international traffic in cultural objects? In: Manacorda S, Chappell D (eds) Crime in the art and antiquities world. Springer, pp 99–113

Chatfield C (1986) Exploratory data analysis. Eur J Oper Res 23(1):5–13

Ćirić A, Anastasijević D, Dekić S, Đikić I, Georgijev S, Limani Z, Popović G, Radu P, Raxhimi A, Skrozza T, Stanković S, Vasić M, Vasović-Mekina S, Vladimirova P, Xhara J (2005) Poluostrvo s blagom [a peninsula with a commodity]. Vreme, 3 November. Retrieved October 22, 2024, from http://web.archive.org/web/20170710032424/http://www.vreme.co.rs/cms/view.php?id=432410

Commission for Looted Art in Europe (n.d.) Hitler's Linz Collection. The Central Registry of Information on Looted Cultural Property 1933–1945. Retrieved April 23, 2024, from https://www.lootedart.com/P43P5J761921

Constable A (2008, May 30). Ancient Artifacts Returned to Owner. Santa Fe New Mexican. Retrieved June 17, 2024, from https://www.santafenewmexican.com/news/local_news/ancient-artifacts-returned-to-owner/article_26538e7a-cb78-56ff-a417-5cc510ba989c.html?mode=comments

Council of Europe (2017) Council of Europe Convention on Offences Relating to Cultural Property. CETS No. 221 and explanatory report. Council of Europe Publishing, Strasbourg

D'Ippolito M (2014). New methods of mapping. The application of social network analysis to the study of the illegal trade in antiquities. In: Kennedy GW, Agarwal N, Yang SJ (Eds) Social computing, behavioral-cultural modeling and prediction. Springer, pp 253–260

Data Protection Commission (2019, October) Quick Guide to the Principles of Data Protection https://www.dataprotection.ie/sites/default/files/uploads/2019-11/Guidance%20on%20the%20Principles%20of%20Data%20Protection_Oct19.pdf

Decamargo L (2012). Content and character: Dikran Kelekian and eastern decorative arts objects in America. PhD Dissertation, Corcoran College of Art. Retrieved October 23, 2024, from https://www.proquest.com/openview/f97847e872a70c4ab4d91830cef25505/1?pq-origsite=gscholar&cbl=18750

Díaz Castaño I, Faraldo Cabana P (2023, September 30) Deliverable 7.3: report on RITHMS social benefits and risks. RITHMS. Retrieved October 23, 2024, from https://rithms.eu/images/Public%20deliverables/RITHMS_D7.3_Social%20benefits%20and%20risks_v1.0.pdf

Directive (EU) 2019/790 of the European Parliament and of the Council of 17 April 2019 on copyright and related rights in the Digital Single Market and amending Directives 96/9/EC and 2001/29/EC (Text with EEA relevance) (2019) Official Journal of the European Union, 62, 17 May. Document L:2019:130:TOC, PE/51/2019/REV/1. Retrieved October 24, 2024, from https://eur-lex.europa.eu/eli/dir/2019/790/oj

Dumbarton Oaks (n.d.). Giorgio Sangiorgi (1886–1960). Retrieved October 23, 2024, from https://www.doaks.org/resources/bliss-tyler-correspondence/annotations/giorgio-sangiori

Enderlein A, Flacke M, Löhr HC (n.d.) Database on the Sonderauftrag Linz (Special Commission: Linz). Linz Datenbank. Retrieved April 23, 2024, from https://www.dhm.de/datenbank/linzdb/einleitunge.html

Erken E, Turksen U (2023) Countering the illicit trading of cultural goods: recent trends, emerging issues, and LEA Responses in Turkey. Trends in Organized Crime

Ermasova N, Haumann C, Burke L (2019) The relationship between culture and tax evasion across countries: cases of the USA and Germany. Int J Public Adm 44(2):115131

ERR Project (n.d.) Card ID 70874. Cultural Plunder by the Einsatzstab Reichsleiter Rosenberg: Database of Art Objects at the Jeu de Paume. Retrieved April 23, 2024, from https://www.errproject.org/jeudepaume/card_view.php?CardId=70874

EUCPN (2017) Pickpocketing committed by mobile organised crime groups. In: EUCPN Secretariat (eds) EUCPN Theoretical Paper Series. Brussels: European Crime Prevention Network. Accessed October 22, 2024, from https://tobias-lib.ub.uni-tuebingen.de/xmlui/bitstream/handle/10900/81670/theoretical_paper_pickpocketing.pdf?sequence=1&isAllowed=y

Eurojust (2023, June 16). Crackdown on a gold smuggling network in Italy, Germany and Switzerland. Press Release, Eurojust Retrieved April 23, 2024, from https://www.eurojust.europa.eu/news/crackdown-gold-smuggling-network-italy-germany-and-switzerland

European Commission (2022) Communication from the Commission to the European Parliament, the Council, the European Economic and Social Committee and the Committee of the Regions on the EU Action Plan against Trafficking in Cultural Goods. Document 52022DC0800, COM/2022/800 final. Retrieved October 21, 2024, from https://eur-lex.europa.eu/legal-content/EN/TXT/?uri=CELEX:52022DC0800

Europol (2022, March 9) A total of 52 arrests in operation across 28 countries targeting trafficking in cultural goods. Europol. Retrieved June 17, 2024, from https://www.europol.europa.eu/media-press/newsroom/news/total-of-52-arrests-in-operation-across-28-countries-targeting-trafficking-in-cultural-goods

Europol (n.d.) Cultural Goods Crime. Retrieved October 21, 2024, from https://www.europol.europa.eu/crime-areas-and-statistics/crime-areas/illicit-trafficking-in-cultural-goods-including-antiquities-and-works-of-art

Fabiani MD, Marrone JV (2021) Transiting through the antiquities market. In: Oosterman N, Yates D (eds) Crime and art. Studies in art, heritage, law and the market. Springer, pp 11–28

Faraldo Cabana P, Ferreiro Baamonde X, Puente Aba LM, Neira Pena A, Fuentes Loureiro MA, Rodríguez López S, García Adán A (2023a, March 31) Deliverable 1.1: initial legal requirements. RITHMS. Retrieved October 23, 2024, from https://rithms.eu/images/Public%20deliverables/RITHMS_D1.1_Initial%20Legal%20Requirements_v1.0.pdf

Faraldo Cabana P, Rodríguez López S, Fuentes Loureiro MA, Soto Díaz DJ (2023b, May 31) Deliverable 7.1: report on the legal framework. RITHMS. Retrieved October 23, 2024, from https://rithms.eu/images/Public%20deliverables/RITHMS_D7.1_Legal%20framework_v1.0.pdf

Felch J (2012, April 20) The Getty List: 10 Objects at the J. Paul Getty Museum that Turkey Says Were Looted. Chasing Aphrodite. Retrieved October 23, 2024, from https://chasingaphrodite.com/2012/04/20/the-getty-list-10-objects-at-the-j-paul-getty-museum-that-turkey-says-were-looted/

Ferro S, Giovanelli R, Leeson M, De Bernardin M, Traviglia A (2025) A novel NLP-driven approach for enriching artefact descriptions, provenance, and entities in cultural heritage. Neural Comput & Applic.

Few S (2014, January 1) Data Visualization for Human Perception. Interaction Design Foundation - IxDF. Retrieved June 14, 2024, from https://www.interaction-design.org/literature/book/the-encyclopedia-of-human-computer-interaction-2nd-ed/data-visualization-for-human-perception

Fitz Gibbon K (2019, July 14) Was ILLICID Report 'Buried' for Failing to Show Illegal Trade? Cultural Property News. Retrieved April 23, 2024, from https://culturalpropertynews.org/was-illicid-report-buried-for-failing-to-show-illegal-trade/

Förster A (2016) Treasure robber: the state security's search for Nazi gold. Ch. Links Verlag GmbH

García Adán A, Fuentes Loureiro MA (2023) Ethical and legal risks of algorithmic and AI tools developed to fight against trafficking in cultural property in the RITHMS Project. Proceedings XoveTIC 2023. Retrieved October 23, 2024, from https://ruc.udc.es/dspace/bitstream/handle/2183/34108/XoveTIC_2023_proceedings_Parte51.pdf?sequence=3&isAllowed=y

German Historical Museum (n.d.-a Data sheet LI003040. Linz Collection. Retrieved April 23, 2024, from https://www.dhm.de/datenbank/linzdbv2/queryresult.php?obj_no=LI003040

German Historical Museum (n.d.-b) Data sheet RMG00011. The Hermann Göring Art Collection. Retrieved April 23, 2024, from https://www.dhm.de/datenbank/goering/dhm_goering.php?seite=5&fld_0=RMG00011

German Lost Art Foundation (n.d.-a). "I have made abundant use of everything Berlin offered me in terms of science and art." The case of Walter Neuling (1894–1973). Proveana. Retrieved October 22, 2024, from https://www.proveana.de/en/project/i-have-made-abundant-use-everything-berlin-offered-me-terms-science-and-art-case-walter

German Lost Art Foundation (n.d.-b) Keukenstuk / Kitchen Scene (Outdoor Kitchen). Lost Art Database. Retrieved April 19, 2024, from https://www.lostart.de/de/Verlust/583903

Giovanelli R (2021, December 21). 150 oggetti trafficati in 30 anni di attività da Almagià potranno tornare in Italia. J Cult Herit Crime. Retrieved May 8, 2024, from https://www.journalchc.com/2021/12/21/150-oggetti-trafficati-in-30-anni-di-attivita-da-almagia-potranno-tornare-in-italia/

Giovanelli R (2024, May 9) Manhattan District attorney announces return of ten Egyptian antiquities. J Cult Herit Crime Retrieved October 23, 2024, from https://www.journalchc.com/2024/05/09/restituzione-antichita-egizie-trafficate-negli-usa/

Giovanelli R, Traviglia A (2024) AIKoGAM: an AI-driven knowledge graph of the antiquities market: toward automatised methods to identify illicit trafficking networks. J Comput Appl Archaeol 7(1):92–114

Giovanelli R, Leeson M, De Bernardin M, Ferro S, Traviglia A (2025) Social network analysis on the Proveana database: insights on the circulation of Nazi-looted cultural goods during and after WWII. Appl Netw Sci, in review

Global Organized Crime Index (2023) Germany. Global Initiative Against Transnational Organized Crime. Retrieved April 23, 2024, from https://ocindex.net/assets/downloads/2023/english/ocindex_profile_germany_2023.pdf

Graham S, Yates D, El-Roby A (2023a) Investigating antiquities trafficking with generative pre-trained transformer (GPT)-3 enabled knowledge graphs: a case study [version 1; peer review: awaiting peer review]. Open Res Europe 3(100)

Graham S, Yates D, El-Roby A, Brousseau C, Ellens J, McDermott C (2023b) Relationship prediction in a knowledge graph embedding model of the illicit antiquities trade. Adv Archaeol Pract 11(2):126–138

Granovetter M (1985) Economic action and social structure: the problem of embeddedness. Am J Sociol 91(3):481–510

Hardy SA (2020) Private 'Rescue'-by-purchase of stolen cultural goods: the material and social consequences and the complicity of Europe and North America. Int J Crime, Justice and Social Democracy, pp 1–18

Hardy SA (2021a) It is not against the law, if no one can see you: online social organisation of artefact-hunting in former Yugoslavia. J Comput Appl Archaeol 4(1):169–187

Hardy SA (2021b) Organized crime in trafficking of cultural goods in Turkey and interconnections between antiquities trafficking and narcotics trafficking, arms trafficking and political violence. In: Traviglia A, Milano L, Tonghini C, Giovanelli R (eds) Stolen heritage: multidisciplinary perspectives on illicit trafficking of cultural heritage in the EU and the MENA region. Fondazione Università Ca' Foscari, pp 115–156

Hoving T (1993) Making the mummies dance. Simon & Schuster, New York

Hunt J (2021, May 27) Did Paying a Ransom for a Stolen Magritte Painting Inadvertently Fund Terrorism? Vanity Fair. Retrieved June 17, 2024, from https://www.vanityfair.com/style/2021/05/did-paying-a-ransom-for-a-stolen-magritte-painting-inadvertently-fund-terrorism

Jackson MO (2010) Social and economic networks. Princeton University Press

Jenkins-Madina M (2000) Collecting the "Orient" at the met: early tastemakers in America. Ars Orientalis 30:69–89

Kirkpatrick S (1992) Lords of Sipán: a true story of pre-Inca tombs, archaeology, and crime. William Morrow and Company

Köhler JT (2019) Goudstikker Art Research Project: The Missing Paintings from the Jacques Goudstikker Collection. Lost Art Database. Retrieved April 19, 2024, from https://www.lostart.de/sites/default/files/attachment/document/2024-01/sobj_28888_79531.pdf

Kuta S (2023) 1,000-Year-Old Gold Earrings and Silver Coins Unearthed in the Netherlands. Smithsonian Magazine, 14 March. Retrieved April 23, 2024, from https://www.smithsonianmag.com/smart-news/1000-year-old-gold-earrings-and-silver-coins-unearthed-in-the-netherlands-180981792/

Lazăr A (2015) Illicit trafficking in cultural goods in south East Europe: 'Fiat Lux!'. In: Desmarais F (ed) Countering illicit traffic in cultural goods: the global challenge of protecting the world's heritage. The International Council of Museums, pp 107–124

Leeson M, Giovanelli R, De Bernardin M, Traviglia A (2024) War, art, and sanctions: social network analysis on the NACP'S databases of sanctioned Russian individuals and art collectors. Int J Dig Human 6:189–215

Leeson M, Giovanelli R, Ferro S, De Bernardin M, Traviglia A (2025) Overcoming data siloes in cultural heritage crime research: a consolidated OSINT-derived dataset on art, antiquities, and the trade in cultural goods. Arch Sci 25

Legislative Decree n. 177 (2021) Implementation of Directive (EU) 2019/790 of the European Parliament and of the Council of 17 April 2019 on copyright and related rights in the Digital Single Market and amending Directives 96/9/EC and 2001/29/EC (21G00192) Retrieved October 23, 2024, from https://www.normattiva.it/uri-res/N2Ls?urn:nir:stato:decreto.legislativo:2021-11-08;177

Leonhard Weidinger (n.d.) Reichskunstdepot Kremsmünster - Painting: "K-List." Leonhard Weidinger Wien. Retrieved April 23, 2024, from https://leonhard.weidinger.wien/daten/kremsmuenster-gemaelde

Li J, Shomer H, Mao H, Zeng S, Ma Y, Shah N, Tang J, Yin D (2024) Evaluating graph neural networks for link prediction: current pitfalls and new benchmarking. Adv Neural Inf Proces Syst 36

Mackenzie S (2019) Trafficking antiquities. In: Natarajan M (ed) International and transnational crime and justice. Cambridge University Press

Mackenzie S (2020) Transnational criminology: trafficking and global criminal markets. Bristol University Press

Mackenzie S, Yates D (2020) Researching the structure of the illicit antiquities trade. In: Tompkins A (ed) Provenance research today: principles, practice, problems. Lund Humphries, pp 162–171

Manacorda S, Chappell D (eds) (2011) Crime in the art and antiquities world: illegal trafficking in cultural property. Springer, New York

Manikowska E (2023) The Washington principles à Rebours: explaining Poland's current restitution policy. Int J Cult Prop 30:42–61

McEvoy O (2023) Regional crime rate in Germany in 2022 (per 100,000 people). Statista, Germany. Retrieved April 23, 2024, from https://www.statista.com/statistics/1081057/crime-rate-in-germany/

Meirelles I, Schich M, Malina R (2014) Arts and humanities, complex network analysis of. In: Alhajii R, Rokne J (eds) Encyclopedia of social network analysis and mining. Springer, pp 56–60

Ministère de la culture (n.d.). Biens Musées Nationaux Récupération (MNR). Ministry of Culture. Retrieved April 23, 2024, from https://www.culture.gouv.fr/Nous-connaitre/Organisation-du-ministere/Le-secretariat-general/Mission-de-recherche-et-de-restitution-des-biens-culturels-spolies-entre-1933-et-1945/Biens-Musees-Nationaux-Recuperation-MNR

Monuments Men and Women Foundation (2022) Altaussee Salt Mines. Atlas Obscura. Retrieved April 23, 2024, from https://www.atlasobscura.com/places/altaussee-salt-mine

NARA (2016, August 15) OSS art looting investigation unit reports name index. College Park: The U.S. National Archives and Records Administration. Retrieved October 23, 2024, from https://www.archives.gov/research/holocaust/art/oss-art-looting-investigation-name-index3.html

NER Annotator for SpaCy (n.d.) NER Annotator for SpaCy (Version 1.4.0) [Computer software]. https://github.com/tecoholic/ner-annotator/tree/main

Newman MEJ (2003) The structure and function of complex networks. SIAM Rev 45(2):167–256

Oosterman N, Angelini F (2021). One flew over the Cuckoo's Clock. In: Oosterman N, Yates D (eds) Crime and Art. Studies in Art, Heritage, Law and the Market, vol 1. Springer, Cham

Palombo C, Yates D (2023) Digital transit ports for the illicit trade in antiquities: the case of the 'Afghan Genizah.' Dig Scholarship Human 38(1):257–276

PAN Project (2021) Metal detection in the Netherlands: Code of conduct and rules for responsible metal detecting in the Netherlands. Retrieved April 23, 2024, from https://www.portable-antiquities.nl/pan/resources/downloads/Metaaldetectie_EN_sept2021.pdf

Pellegrini M, Rizzo D (2021) The Italian archaeological heritage abroad between agreements, debates and indifference. In: Traviglia A, Milano L, Tonghini C, Giovanelli R (eds) Stolen Heritage. Multidisciplinary perspectives on illicit trafficking of cultural heritage in the EU and the MENA region. Edizioni Ca' Foscari, pp 97–112

People of the State of New York v. Nancy Wiener, No. SCI-05191-2016 (N.Y. Crim. Ct. filed Dec. 21, 2016). Retrieved June 17, 2024, from https://s3.documentcloud.org/documents/3245935/Wiener-Complaint.pdf

Perry BL, Pescosolido BA, Borgatti SP (2018) Ecocentric network analysis: foundations, methods, and models. Cambridge University Press

Picciano PJ (2023) Laundered: An Analysis of Antiquities Trafficking Networks and the Illicit Market. PhD Dissertation, Rutgers the State University of New Jersey. Retrieved October 22, 2024, from https://www.proquest.com/openview/9343a25b0dbbf47456d0d0fe958eb0f2/1?cbl=18750&diss=y&pq-origsite=gscholar&parentSessionId=DQgtNo7m%2FhAp0xbPx29k0MUwyluYOTW2ZDEnaqyhFKQ%3D

Pio-Lopez L, Valdeolivas A, Tichit L, Remy É, Baudot A (2021) Multiverse: a multiplex and multiplex-heterogeneous network embedding approach. Scientific Reports, 11

Reents-Budet D (2012). Exploring art of the ancient Americas: the John Bourne collection. Walters Art Museum, Baltimore

RITHMS (2024a) Information on the Processing of Personal Data. Retrieved October 29, 2024, from https://rithms.eu/images/Privacy%20GDPR/GDPR%20%20PRIVACY%20Informative_RITHMS_IIT_Update.24.10.18.pdf

RITHMS (2024b) Research, Intelligence and Technology for Heritage and Market Security. Retrieved June 17, 2024, from https://rithms.eu

Salter M (2015) A critical assessment of US intelligence's investigation of Nazi Art looting. J Int Crim Just 13:257–280

Sandra L, Trisetyarso A, Ramadhan A, Abdurachnan E, Lumbangaol F, Isa SM (2021) Social Network Analysis Algorithms, Techniques and Methods, 2021 International Conference on

Advanced Mechatronics, Intelligent Manufacture and Industrial Automation (ICAMIMIA). ICAMIMIA, pp 182–189

The Washington Times (2005, July 26). Colonial artwork stolen in 2002 returned to Peru. The Washington Times. Retrieved April 23, 2024, from https://www.washingtontimes.com/news/2005/jul/26/20050726-113114-5091r/

Thum J (2022) Chapter 11. Learning from the Lintel of Ptahshepses Impy at the Harvard Art Museums. In the House of Heqanakht. Brill, Leiden, the Netherlands

Tsirogiannis C, Tsirogiannis C (2016) Uncovering the hidden routes: algorithms for identifying paths and missing links in trade networks. In: Brughmans T, Collar A, Coward F (eds) The connected past: challenges to network studies in archaeology and history. Oxford University Press, pp 103–120

UNESCO (1970) Convention on the Means of Prohibiting and Preventing the Illicit Import, Export and Transfer of Ownership of Cultural Property. Retrieved October 22, 2024, from https://www.unesco.org/en/legal-affairs/convention-means-prohibiting-and-preventing-illicit-import-export-and-transfer-ownership-cultural

UNODC (2022) False Trades: Uncovering the Scale and Scope of Trafficking in Cultural Property. Knowledge Gaps and Future Directions for Research. UNODC Research. Retrieved June 17, 2024, from https://www.unodc.org/documents/data-and-analysis/briefs/Trafficking_in_cultural_properties_brief.pdf

Watson P, Todeschini C (2007) The Medici conspiracy: the illicit journey of looted antiquities from Italy's Tomb Raiders to the World's Greatest Museums. BBS Public Affairs

Windhager F, Federico P, Schreder G, Glinka K, Dörk M, Miksch S (2019) Visualization of cultural heritage collection data: state of the art and future challenges. IEEE Transact Visual Comput Graph 25(6):2311–2330

Yang B, Wang L, Wong DF, Shi S, Tu Z (2021) Context-aware self-attention networks for natural language processing. Neurocomputing 458:157–169

Yates D (2014) John Bourne Collection. Trafficking Culture: Researching the global traffic in looted cultural objects. Retrieved April 23, 2024, from https://traffickingculture.org/encyclopedia/case-studies/john-bourne-collection/

Yates D (2015). Illicit cultural property from Latin America: looting, trafficking, and sale. In: Desmarais F (ed) Countering illicit traffic in cultural goods: the global challenge of protecting the world's heritage. International Council of Museums, pp 33–46

Yates D, Graham S (2023) Reputation laundering and museum collections: patterns, priorities, provenance, and hidden crime. Int J Herit Stud 30(2):145–165

Yogev T, Grund T (2012) Network dynamics and market structure: the case of art fairs. Sociol Focus 45(1):23–40

Zygierewicz A (2017) Illicit trade in cultural goods. Brussels: European Parliamentary Research Service. Retrieved October 21, 2024, from https://www.europarl.europa.eu/thinktank/en/document/EPRS_BRI(2017)603259

Madison Leeson is a historian of the modern Middle East, focusing on the ways in which cultural heritage is leveraged for political legitimacy. She holds a PhD in Archaeology and History of Art from Koç University (2022), specialising in Cultural Heritage Management and focusing on cultural governance in modern Iraq. Her research into cultural heritage crime emphasises the historical conditions that have enabled the trafficking of cultural goods. Other research interests include developments in museum studies, particularly concerning restitution and repatriation, and the role of objects in the manifestation of power. Her current work combines many research interests—heritage management, antiquities protection, archival research, and innovative technologies—in support of the RITHMS project to tackle the illicit antiquities trade.

Michela De Bernardin is an ancient historian and classical archaeologist with honours from the University of Pisa and the Scuola Normale Superiore, where she also obtained her PhD in Ancient History and Archaeology within a joint program with the Ruprecht-Karls-Universität Heidelberg.

After a specialised postgraduate course at the Centro Studi Criminologici in Viterbo, she completed a two-year postgraduate program at the University of Roma Tre addressing the illicit trade of Palmyrene funerary portraits and the impact of numismatic forgery on the art market. She co-founded and is now the secretary of the Art Crime Project APS organisation. Since 2020, she has been collaborating with the Centre for Cultural Heritage Technology (CCHT) of the Italian Institute of Technology (IIT). Her research stretches from provenance, looting, and forgery studies to the dynamics of illicit trafficking. Currently, she is a Postdoctoral Research Fellow at the CCHT and the Scientific Project Manager of the HE RITHMS project.

Riccardo Giovanelli an archaeologist specialising in Egyptology and Roman Provinces, directed his research towards investigating the looting and illicit trafficking of cultural artefacts in 2011, prompted by the widespread looting of museums and archaeological sites in Egypt during the Arab Spring. He is now a Postdoctoral Researcher at the Center for Cultural Heritage Technology (CCHT) in Venice. He researches practical application of advanced digital methods and Knowledge Graph frameworks towards the challenges associated with preserving cultural heritage and curbing the trade of looted artefacts. He is the President of the civil society organisation 'Art Crime Project', and actively engages in initiatives aimed at raising awareness, involving the broader public and fostering collective action to prevent and counter art-related crimes across various dimensions.

Sara Ferro a Control and Automation Engineer specialising in Machine Learning and Deep Learning models applied to sequential data, focused her research on developing innovative models for the automatic digitalisation of historical documents written in Western Latin-based languages. She earned her PhD in Computer Science from Ca' Foscari University of Venice, where her doctoral program was conducted in collaboration with the Center for Cultural Heritage Technology (CCHT) of the Italian Institute of Technology, based in Venice, Italy. Her thesis introduced new procedures, methods, and models to accurately transcribe historical texts by leveraging contextual information within the data, an important concept in Computer Vision and Natural Language Processing research. She is a Postdoctoral Researcher at CCHT, working under the EU Project RITHMS to utilise and define new Natural Language Processing models for extracting information from online sources to help create a Knowledge Graph database for the RITHMS platform.

Arianna Traviglia is the Director of the Centre for Cultural Heritage Technology (CCHT) at the Italian Institute of Technology (IIT). Her work focuses on integrating advanced technologies into the study, protection, and conservation of cultural heritage. With expertise in archaeology and imaging technologies, she leads interdisciplinary research in Artificial Intelligence, Nanotechnologies, and Robotics for material culture and ancient landscape studies. Over the past decade, Dr. Traviglia has led or contributed to numerous EU-funded projects on cultural heritage preservation. Currently, she coordinates the RITHMS project, which uses social network analysis and knowledge graphs, in collaboration with seven European police forces, to combat cultural property trafficking. She also leads the ALCEO project, funded by the European Space Agency (ESA), employing satellite imagery to detect archaeological looting. Dr. Traviglia has held academic positions in Italy (University of Venice) and Australia (University of Sydney, Macquarie University) and collaborates with the Council of Europe, contributing to the upcoming guidelines on AI for cultural heritage. Recognised with several awards, she also serves as Chair of the technical-scientific committee for the Cassa Depositi e Prestiti Foundation.

Open Access This chapter is licensed under the terms of the Creative Commons Attribution-NonCommercial-NoDerivatives 4.0 International License (http://creativecommons.org/licenses/by-nc-nd/4.0/), which permits any noncommercial use, sharing, distribution and reproduction in any medium or format, as long as you give appropriate credit to the original author(s) and the source, provide a link to the Creative Commons license and indicate if you modified the licensed material. You do not have permission under this license to share adapted material derived from this chapter or parts of it.

The images or other third party material in this chapter are included in the chapter's Creative Commons license, unless indicated otherwise in a credit line to the material. If material is not included in the chapter's Creative Commons license and your intended use is not permitted by statutory regulation or exceeds the permitted use, you will need to obtain permission directly from the copyright holder.

Detecting Deception in the Art Trade: A Computational Approach to Uncertainty, Unreliability, Anonymity and Red Flag Names

Laurel Zuckerman

Abstract This chapter presents an innovative computational method for detecting possible deception in the provenance texts of artworks. This is important because false ownership histories can conceal the kind of textual "red flags" that alert experts to potentially looted art. The first section presents the study's scope, context and approach to automating the detection of Nazi-looted art by analysing provenance texts and explains the urgency of solving the problem of deception. The second part presents provenance datasets, and a digital tool developed for counting words linked to unreliability, uncertainty or anonymity, which may indicate potentially deceptive language. The third part analyses the strengths and weaknesses of this methodology, exploring lessons learned. Benefits of the methodology described here include transparency, objectivity and replicability, as well as the generation of quantitative and Boolean metadata for artworks that can be fed into ranking applications, recommender systems, knowledge graphs, and AI, in order to potentially quantify deception within the art market. Challenges include optimization of ranking methods and the tension between open data and closed archives, which complicates the verification of the artworks flagged. The chapter concludes with opportunities for future developments in different domains.

1 Introduction

Between 1933 and 1945, the Nazis perpetrated the "largest campaign of persecution and dispossession the world has ever seen" (Schumacher 2024, p. 83). In Hitler's Third Reich, Jews were targeted for persecution: homes, businesses, real estate, financial assets, furniture, jewellery, clothes, books, ritual objects, musical instruments, and artworks of all kinds—paintings, sculpture, decorative objects, clocks—were systematically plundered from individuals of Jewish heritage, initially under a legal veneer, and then outright (Kulturgutverlust and Baresel-Brand 2005). During

L. Zuckerman (✉)
Bry-sur-Marne, France

© The Author(s) 2026

E. Smith, S. Austin (eds.), *Researching a Rigged Game: Digital Approaches to Tracing the Illicit Trade in Cultural Objects*, Studies in Art, Heritage, Law and the Market 11, https://doi.org/10.1007/978-3-032-02014-7_6

the Holocaust, theft and genocide were inextricably linked (e. g. Dean et al. 2008; Friedländer 2008, p. 497; Eizenstat 2009).

Schumacher argues that the origins of modern provenance research is a response to this massive plunder, beginning with the London Declaration in 1943 and continuing to the present day (Schumacher 2024, p. 50). The Allies deployed the Monuments, Fine Arts, and Archives group (MFAA), popularly known as the "Monuments Men", to preserve, recover and restitute looted art after the Second World War (WWII) to the countries from which they were looted, though not to their individual owners. Elaborate research and restitution efforts ended with the closing of the Munich Central Collecting Point in 1951, and the shift of geopolitical concerns to the Cold War (Nicholas 2017). After that, the looted art issue largely disappeared from public view (Petroupolis 2017). State archives, including those documenting looted art market networks, were sealed in Germany for fifty years (EPRS 2022, p. 5).

It was not until the 1990s, after the fall of the Berlin Wall and the dissolution of the Soviet Union, that Nazi looting, including of art, returned to the public consciousness (Masurovsky 2020). WWII archives, long closed, began to be declassified. A series of scandals and lawsuits, which received substantial media attention, reawakened public interest in Nazi looting (e.g. Feliciano 1998; Eisenstat 2004; Goodman 2016; O'Donnell 2017) In 1998, 44 countries convened at the Washington Conference on Holocaust Era Assets (Holocaust Expropriated Art Recovery Act 2016). Concerning looted art, they agreed on a non-binding commitment to opening archives, provenance research, transparency and restitution (Office of the Special Envoy for Holocaust Issues 1998). As Schumacher (2024, p. 60) notes, art became part of the investigation into Holocaust era assets "not because American museum directors campaigned for it, but because newspaper reports increasingly highlighted that artwork belonging to victims had found their way into the galleries of American Museums. The new technologies of the internet facilitated further searches, as museums began publishing information about their collections online. However, progress in restitution was slow (WJRO 2015; O'Donnell 2017; Schumacher 2024).

In 2013, news of the discovery in Munich of over a thousand artworks in the possession of Cornelius Gurlitt, son of Nazi art dealer Hildebrand Gurlitt, created headlines (Fisher 2013), and demands by the Claims Conference (2014) for greater transparency about the artworks and immediate restitution in cases where the heirs were known. Investigations into Gurlitt revealed, as Shalem (2017, p. 3) delicately expressed it, the "consciously veiled continuities of art dealerships and auction houses from the Nazi period into the Federal Republic" as well as significant attempts "to erase traces of provenance" (Hickley 2021a, b). In 2016, there were reports that looted art that was supposed to be returned to Jewish collectors had been given to the families of Nazis instead (O'Donnell 2017, p. 25).

In the USA, museums were criticized for using procedural technicalities to circumnavigate restitution claims and have them dismissed, instead of allowing them to be judged on merits, which many historians, legal experts and Jewish groups considered to be a breach of the Washington Principles (Cohan 2013; Meaney 2017). Anger at the use of such legal tactics by the Toledo Museum of Art, Detroit

Institute of Arts, Museum of Modern Art in New York, Museum of Fine Arts in Boston, and the Fred Jones Jr. Museum of Art at the University of Oklahoma (WJRO 2015) brought together a bipartisan coalition in Congress to pass the Holocaust Expropriated Art Recovery Act (S. 2763 HEAR Act) in 2016. The HEAR Act "expressly pre-empts all state statutes of limitations with respect to claims for Nazi-looted art" (O'Donnell 2017, pp. 26, 27). As Petroupolis (2017) points out, active deception by art market actors profiting from Nazi-looted art did not end with WWII. The following paragraphs will outline why this deception is important and how it can be detected in certain words of provenance texts.

2 Detecting Nazi Looted Art and the Problem of Deception

Provenance research is, as Stolberg and Lehmann (2020, p. 55) remind us, "a combination of art historical, historical, biographical and genealogical research". Best practice begins with a physical examination of the object and extends to documentation research of all kinds, of which digital resources are only a small part (Tompkins 2020, p. 55). In the specific domain of Nazi-looted art, the *AMM Guide to Provenance Research* (2024) recommends special attention to gaps in the ownership history between 1932 and 1945, the mention of certain "Red Flag Names" known to be involved in Nazi-looted art (ALIU 1946), artworks listed in lost art databases and the names of Jewish art collectors or dealers known to have been victims of spoliation (Masurovsky 2020).

Perfectly complete provenances are rare due to the passage of time and does not automatically mean that an artwork with an incomplete provenance is problematic. However, claims for restitutions have uncovered issues not only with the completeness but also with the reliability of postwar provenance texts, as red flags can be "obscured" and names of persecuted Jewish collectors omitted (Schumacher 2024, pp. 41, 102). Daix and Bourdaille's (1966) Picasso Blue Period catalogue, for example, omitted persecuted Jewish owners Dr Meyer-Udewald from the provenance of Picasso's *Still Life with A Portrait* and Paul Mendelssohn-Bartoldy from Picasso's *Boy with A Horse*, *Madame Soler*, and *Head of a Woman* (Daix 1967). Tobia Natter's 2017 Klimt catalogue raisonné omits Holocaust victims Irene Hellmann (144 and 87) and Nora Stiasny (165) (Natter 2017). Furthermore, false owners—that is, people who never owned the artwork in question—have been inserted in postwar provenances of the El Greco looted from Julius Priester (Boucher 2015), the Kirchner looted from Max Fischer (Crow 2015; Rother 2020) and the Gerard Ter Borch sold under duress by Max Emden (Jensen 2022). A Ruysdael owned by Ferenc Chorin was published with an incorrect image and description (Museum of Fine Arts Boston 2024). Inaccurate or misleading provenances were discovered during archival research for artworks claimed by the heirs of Siegfried Aram (Bowley 2020), Ferdinand Bloch Bauer (O'Connor 2015), Lea Bondi Jaray (O'Donnell 2017), Lily Cassirer (Court 2019), Max Emden (Foundation 2021), Adele Fischel (Solomon 2023), Emil Goldschmidt (Baily 2006), Friedrich Gutmann (Goodman 2016),

Madame Halphen (Beal 2018), Anna Jaffé (Robinson 2006), Serena Lederer (D'Arcy 2018), Heinrich Rieger (O'Donnell 2017), Paul Rosenberg (Washington 1999), Richard Semmel (Bührle 2023), Oscar Stettiner (Whoriskey 2021; Herzberg 2022) and Paul Westheim (O'Donnell 2017), to give but a few examples.

The scholarly research into the patterns of these Holocaust-linked provenance errors is thin: instead, most existing scholarship focuses on the deceptive tactics of auction houses and dealers in other art markets, such as that of antiquities (Gerstenblith 2018; Felch 2011). A systemic analysis of "widespread, carefully constructed and elaborate forged or false provenances" (Tompkins 2020, p. 10) enriches the scholarly literature for forgeries and antiquities trafficking. However, in the domain of Nazi-looted art, mentions of provenances errors tend to be anecdotal with comments like "a Weidler-based provenance could certainly not be true" (O'Donnell 2017, p. 18), referring to German art dealer and art historian Charlotte Weidler. Another example: "sometimes, an error in documentation is a simple error in documentation" (Stein 2019, p. 9). With a few exceptions that mostly focus on Nazi dealer networks (Petroupolis 2017; Polack and Dorléac 2019; JDCRP 2024; Lost Art Foundation 2024a, b), there have been few attempts until recently to develop a unified vision of false provenances for Nazi-looted art or specific tools for detecting them, especially in the postwar period. Part of this is structural. As Fuhrmeister and Hopp (2019, pp. 223–224) so cogently points out, "information, gathered in many different locations at considerable outlay in time and effort, is not networked or correlated from place to place. It is confined to its institutional or organizational silos as congealed knowledge that is neither able nor intended to flow".

To see any kind of pattern, one needs multiple instances. One method is to look at false provenances across many different artworks, such as those listed above; another is to examine multiple instances of false provenances for a single artwork. Both methods will be described below, taking a personal case as example.

3 Picasso's The Actor: How Layers of False Provenances Led to a Quantitative Approach

Picasso's *The Actor*, which once belonged to my great-grand uncle, Paul Friedrich Leffmann (1870–1956) of Cologne, Germany and for which I filed a lawsuit (Zuckerman v Metropolitan 2016), offers a rare opportunity to study a dozen false provenances created for a single artwork and to transform insights that can be gained only with knowledge of hard-to-access archival information into a method that can be applied to open source digital data.

3.1 A Catalogue of False Provenances

On October 4, 2004, I found *The Actor* on the website of the Metropolitan Museum of Art. Published in response to the Washington Conference, the provenance was: "P. Leffmann, Cologne (in 1912); Private collection, Germany (until 1938); [Hugo Pearls New York, in 1938]; [Paul Rosenberg & Co., New York, 1938-1941]; [M. Knoedler & Co., New York, in 1941]; Thelma Chrysler Foy, New York (1941-1952)" (Bowley 2016; Zuckerman 2022).

The words "Private collection, Germany" covered an important provenance gap during the Nazi era. It would take seven years and the intervention of lawyers for the Metropolitan Museum of Art to confirm publicly that this and many other provenances for *The Actor* were erroneous, and that, in reality, Leffmann had owned *The Actor* continuously from at least 1912 to 1938, when two art dealers jointly acquired it from Leffmann (Harvard Law Review 2020). Only in 2012 would the museum find an explanation for the erroneous insertion of a "private collection" in the form of handwritten notes inside a document created by a museum employee and accessible only to museum staff (Zuckerman 2022).[1] In the course of archival research across multiple countries, false provenances authored by more than a dozen different art market actors for this single painting were discovered (Table 1).

The layers of false provenances uncovered for this one artwork offer a mini case study of tactics used to conceal the itinerary of artworks that changed hands during the Nazi era: erasure of the Jewish owner; concealment of Nazi-era gaps with "private collector"; insertion of false "owners"; false pre-Nazi era sales date; and creation of fictitious events like inclusion in a (real) exhibition.

The succession of false provenances for *The Actor* between 1938 and 2010 offer the researcher the advantage of being exceptionally diverse. In addition, after confirming that Paul Leffmann had in fact owned *The Actor* continuously from 1912 to 1938, the Metropolitan Museum modified the provenance on its public website to remove the 1913 sale to a "private collector" (Metropolitan Museum of Art 2016; Zuckerman 2022), thereby confirming the provenance was indeed false. The evolution of these provenances provided is particularly interesting. Between 1938 and 2004, the false provenances were characterized by omissions, false information about transactions and owners, and the insertion of anonymous placeholder words such as "private" or "Italian collector" that appear to cover gaps while conveying no verifiable information. Use of these and similar words ("private collection", "property of a gentleman", or "art market") has long been criticized by art crime experts (Gill 2011). In 2005, after I began to ask the museum questions about the provenance, a new vocabulary of uncertainty and unreliability appears in the provenance

[1] The General Counsel of the Metropolitan Museum of Art (the Met) sent a photocopy of this letter to my lawyers, accompanied by a letter apologizing for not finding it seven years earlier. Unfortunately, this letter is not publicly accessible. In a personal email exchange with the Met in July and August confirmed that the letter is still not available, and requests go through their General Counsel.

Table 1 Overview of false provenances provided for Picasso's 'The Actor'[a]

Year	False provenance provided	Author/Editor	Source
1938	"Italian collector" is selling *The Actor*	Franz Perls	Private letter, July 26, 1938, to Walter Chrysler Jr.
1939	*The Actor* "Lent by Thannhauser"	James Thrall Soby (1939)	Published catalog, 1939
1941	"Collections Vollard – Directly from artist - Paul Rosenberg"[1]	Paul Rosenberg	Private letter, November 15, 1941, to Knoedler
1944	"from Vollard"	Thelma Chrysler Foy	Vogue Magazine, 1944 (Chase 1944, pp.72-73)
1967	"Coll. P. Leffmann, Cologne (1912); Private collection, Germany (1913-1938)"	Pierre Daix and Georges Boudaille (1967, p. 256)	Published catalog, 1967
1966-7	Perls bought *The Actor* "from a German professor in Solothurn, Switzerland who had been thrown out by Nazis"; "Joseph Müller from Solothurn lent to an exhibition in Zurich in 1932"	Hugo Perls as told to and written down by Margaretta M. Salinger	Unpublished, closed museum archives: unique draft catalog with hand-written annotations by curator, 1966–1997. Permission from Metropolitan Museum of Art General Counsel required.
1967	Paul Leffmann sold The Actor to a "private collector" in 1913	Charles Sterling and Margaretta M. Salinger	Published catalog, 1967 (Sterling, C., & Salinger, M. M. (1967), pp. 231–232)
1996	Pierre Leffmann sold The Actor to a "private collector" in 1913	John Richardson (1996)	Published biography of Picasso
2004	"P. Leffmann, Cologne (in 1912); Private collection, Germany (until 1938); [Hugo Pearls New York, in 1938]; [Paul Rosenberg & Co., New York, 1938-1941]"	Metropolitan Museum Website (2004)	Public museum website, October 4, 2004
2005	"[Vollard (directly from the artist)]; P. Leffmann, Cologne (by 1912); Private collection, Germany until 1938 (?)"	Metropolitan Museum Website (2005)	Public museum website, January 25, 2005
2010	"Paul Leffmann, Cologne (by 1912-13); private collection, Germany (1913-1938)"	Gary Tinterow, editor Christel Force, research (e.g. Tinterow et al. 2010, p. 67)	Published exhibition catalogue, 2010

[a]The 2010 catalogue mentions a version of this story: "When Paul Rosenberg sold the painting in 1941, he stated that Vollard had bought it directly from the artist, but in fact the first owner was Frank Burty Haviland who almost certainly acquired it from Picasso" (Tinterow et al. 2010, p. 66)

texts. In addition to "private", words such as, "probably", "likely", "ca.", "?" and other terms indicating uncertainty concerning owners, events and dates appear in the texts. For example, in 2004, the Metropolitan Museum of Art website published the painting's provenance as: "P. Leffmann, Cologne (in 1912); Private collection,

Germany (until 1938). The year after, the provenance text was changed to "[Vollard (directly from the artist)]; P. Leffmann, Cologne (by 1912); Private collection, Germany until 1938 (?)" – this text contains two words, namely 'private' and '?' as indicators of uncertainty (Metropolitan Museum of Art 2005). In their publication of a Picasso exhibition catalogue (Metropolitan Museum of Art 2010), the published provenance showed as "Frank Burty Haviland, Paris and Céret (ca. 1905–1911 or 1912; probably acquired from the artist); Paul Leffmann, Cologne (by 1912–1913); private collection, Germany (1913–1938)". In this case, five indicators of uncertainty, unreliability and anonymity—namely 'ca', '-', 'or', 'probably' and 'private'—are used. If one focuses, not on content, but on abstractions like the size of the text or the number of certain kinds of words, patterns emerge. This was the inspiration for the methodology presented here.

Given the knowledge that all these provenances have been proven to be false, can these word frequency patterns be used to detect deception? Are there words that appear in the false provenances of *The Actor* that also appear in false provenances written for other Holocaust-linked artworks? In a larger sense, can word frequency patterns observed in provenances known to be false, help to detect false provenances texts for other artworks? This chapter will attempt to answer these questions. The following sections present the initial datasets, methods, results, and lessons learned.

4 Experiments in Counting: Approach, Methods, Dataset and Results

In response to the moral commitments to transparency agreed on in 1998 at the Washington Conference, the American Alliance of Museums (AAM) created the Nazi Era Provenance Internet Portal (NEPIP) on September 8, 2003 (Association of Art Museum Directors 2024). Until it was archived in 2024, the NEPIP provided the only cross-museum "searchable registry of object in U.S. museum collections that changed hands during the Nazi era (1933-1945)" (American Alliance of Museums 2024). Over the past two decades, 165 U.S. art museums have listed 28,000 objects on the NEPIP (Association of Art Museum Directors 2024).

The data published on the NEPIP included the title, artist, creation, date, accession number, and museum of a particular object. However, the NEPIP did not include provenance information. To create a database of provenance information for NEPIP items, as was done for this study, it was necessary to retrieve that information from the open-source data provided separately by each individual museum and to match it, via the accession number, to the information published on NEPIP. When no provenance information was publicly available, the item was not included in the final dataset. In some cases, museums maintained public provenance research projects that referenced items not found on the NEPIP. These were included in the dataset. The initial dataset thus constructed included 21,000 NEPIP items, enhanced with provenance texts from museum websites.[2] In addition, the United Kingdom's Collections Trust published as open data provenance information on 17,496 artworks in a public database called Spoliation Reports from UK Museums (Collections Trust 2024). Some tests included these items as well (Zuckerman 2024).

In 2020, as part of the Swiss Open Data Cultural Hackathon called Swiss GLAMHack, I worked with a volunteer team composed of Birk Weiberg[3], Julia Beck, and Tamalera on a project to create a program to rank provenance texts by the probability that they were linked to Nazi-looted art (GLAMHack 2020).[4] The approach was to count certain indicators in the text: Art Looting Red Flag Names (ALIU 1946)[5], the names of persecuted Jewish collectors, and words conveying uncertainty, unreliability or anonymity. This chapter focuses, in particular, on the part of the tests that concerned the latter: words of uncertainty, unreliability or anonymity. The method was to compare two csv files. The first contained the provenance texts to be analyzed and the second contains a list of words or strings to be counted (word) and the category to group the counts in (type of flag).

To test the program during the hackathon, I would send the programming team a CSV test file with provenance texts, and they would run the code and send me a CSV file with the results for verification. We would then work together to improve the program in an iterative process. Each file upload and download had to pass through the programmers, because there was no user interface for non-coders. This version also included an experimental Named Entity Recognition (NER) component which linked Red Flag names to Wikidata identifiers.

The following year, at GLAMHack 2021, the project goal was to enable anyone, including non-coders, to easily access and use the counting program. The programmer Rae Knowler[6] added a user interface and web-based app which invited users to upload their own provenance files and gave them the option of replacing the default list of words and categories with their own lists of words to count, as well (ETH-Bibliotheck 2021, 1:12:21–1:17:30). In this version we opted to deactivate the Named Entity Recognition component because the process was not sufficiently

[2] This data was retrieved from the websites of the Detroit Institute of Arts, Yale University Art Gallery, Kimball Art Museum, Toledo Museum of Art, Norton Simon Museum, Museum of Modern Art, Nelson-Atkins Museum of Art, Art Institute of Chicago, Harvard University Art Museums, Museum of Fine Arts Boston, J. Paul Getty Museum, National Gallery of Art, Carnegie Museums of Pittsburgh, Cleveland Museum of Art, Metropolitan Museum of Art, Philadelphia Museum of Art, and Indiana University Art Museum.

[3] Project Manager at the SAPA Foundation, Swiss Archive of the Performing Arts (SAPA).

[4] The Swiss Open Cultural Data Hackathon is an annual event organized by the Swiss OpenGLAM Working Group. Known as GLAMHack, in 2020 it was held online due to the COVID pandemic. Anyone could pitch a cultural heritage-related challenge, and software developers, digital humanists, artists, Wikipedians or museum people could volunteer to collaborate for two or three days on making it a reality (Glamhack 2020). I pitched the idea of a word and name counting program for detecting looted art from provenance texts and offered datasets of the 21,000 provenance texts.

[5] List of people that the Art Looting Investigation Unit investigated in 1946 for involvement in the Nazi-looted art trade.

[6] Software developer at Liip.

transparent and the results, though very promising, were not always accurate (Zuckerman 2021a).

Testing this version was a simpler process than before because all the users had to do was upload files and click on "Click to Run". The program did the calculations, added them to the original input file and downloaded the results file automatically. One did not have to know how to code to upload files and run the program. We ran many tests, starting with small files and working up to a file with 60,000 provenances. We also tried different kinds of word lists, and different kinds of groupings of words within the word lists.

All input and output files were in CSV format, so that the users could upload the output file into the program of their choice for ranking and analysis. The input CSV file for provenances can include many columns in addition to provenance. The input CSV file for the word lists, called a Custom Indicator File, has a specific format that must be respected (Table 2). To upload, the word list CSV must have two columns titled "word" and "type of flag". The user can put any values in these columns. The program counts the words in the "word" column and groups them by "type of flag". Each "type of flag" adds a new column, which contains the corresponding word counts for every row of provenance, to the results file.

The experimental word frequency counting program was called the 'Looted Art Detector' and was made freely available for use by anyone on the internet. The python code was published on GitHub and hosted on PythonAnywhere (Zuckerman 2021b).[7] The objective was to offer a powerful tool to enable anyone—cultural heritage organizations, claimants, researchers, activists, journalists, citizen scientists—to analyse provenance files in whatever manner they saw fit (Zuckerman 2021b, c).

The program did not automatically create a ranking. The user could use the categorized data for this simply by sorting a category, or by applying filters or adding columns with additional calculations. Table 3 (below) shows a ranking by uncertainty for artworks in American museums that were analysed using the initial word flags in Table 2. Longer texts tended to contain more flags. To correct for this and normalize the ranking, the uncertainty flag count was divided by the total number of words in each provenance, providing a measure of the prevalence of potentially deceptive words. The 'uncertainty index' is therefore the number of uncertainty words divided by the number of words in the provenance texts.

The highest "Uncertainty Index" (50%) in Table 3 contains a very short text with two names, each followed by a question mark (which is considered an uncertainty "word"), indicating that the author of the provenance was not certain about any of the information provided. In addition to uncertainty flags such as "?", "probably", and "likely", one observes that these texts also contain anonymity words such as "private collection" and "art market" as well as unreliability words like "by 1926", "by 1932" and "until at least".

[7] The datasets used in this study (provenance files, wordflag files and results files) are published as open-source data on the Harvard Dataverse (Zuckerman, Harvard Dataverse 2024) and a demonstration is included in a dedicated video presentation (Zuckerman 2023c).

Table 2 Word flags used in the initial 2020 GLAMHack tests[a]

Word	Type of flag
Likely	flaguncertainty
Probably	flaguncertainty
Possibly	flaguncertainty
Maybe	flaguncertainty
?	flaguncertainty
Private collector	flaganonymity
Anonymous	flaganonymity
Art market	flaganonymity
Unidentified	flaganonymity
Unknown	flaganonymity
Property of a European collector	flaganonymity
Private collection	flaganonymity
Property of a lady	flaganonymity
Anon.	flaganonymity
?	flagpuncutation
[	flagpuncutation
Transfer	flagmove
Removed	flagmove
Telephone	flagreliability
To at least	flagreliability
Until at least	flagreliability
By 19	flagreliability
Before 19	flagreliability
According to	flagreliability
Said to have	flagreliability

[a]"Punctuation" varied too widely between countries and institutions, and "Move" was too vague to be useful and was abandoned (ParisData 2020). After we ran the tests, more words suggesting unreliability came to our attention: "by error", "erroneously", "mistaken", "by mistake"; however, these were not counted in the Glamhack2020 project; they were added later

The names in these top ranked provenances provide additional context. Grassi, Contini Bonacossi and Eugenio Ventura were both identified in 1945–1946 by the Art Looting Investigation Unit (ALIU) as "Red Flag" names (ALIU 1946). Frederick Mont (Boucher 2015), Edward Speelman (Malvern 2017; Lost Art Foundation 2022) and Kornfeld (Hickley 2017; Bragg 2023) are linked to several Nazi looted art cases, although they are not ALIU Red Flag names. Thus, the eight provenances with the highest "Uncertainty Index" score also contain six names related to Nazi era events. As Yates and Graham (2024) point out, a methodology must produce more than random results, which this result appears to do.

Table 3 Results: top ranked by uncertainty index (selected American museums), Swiss glamhack2020 (Zuckerman 2023a, b, c)

Uncertainty Index (uncert./qty words	Museum URL ID	Provenance	Uncertainty Count	Word Count
50.00%	NGA 47183	Pierre Ivanovitch Sevastianoff? (Lugt 2338?)	2	4
16.13%	Metropolitan 438407	?Curt Benedict, Villa de Sachs, Paris, later Zürich (sold to Meissner), [Kurt Meissner, Zürich, in 1961,?sold to Oppenheim],?Hans Oppenheim,?[Edward Speelman, London],?Colonel Hudson, Pershore, Worcestershire, England, Herman and Lila Shickman, New York (1971–2001)	5	31
15.79%	Toledo PDF	1968 or Sale conducted by;1969 (?) Maître Blach (?),Versailles;1968 or Dealer: Adolphe Stein, Paris;1969 (?);Dealer: Colnaghi;1971 Toledo Museum of Art	3	19
13.33%	Metropolitan 437083	[Luigi Grassi, Florence,?in 1924],?[conte Alessandro Contini Bonacossi, Rome], Maitland F. Griggs, New York (by 1926–d. 1943)	2	15
13.04%	Metropolitan 436497	?church of San Niccolò, Fabriano (until at least late 19th century),?barone Alberto Fassini, Rome,?[Eugenio Ventura, Florence], Mrs. W. Murray Crane, New York (by 1932–69)	3	23
11.36%	DIA 61539	Genoa, private collection;Wien?;Lucerne, 1925?;Berlin?;Paul Bottenwieser (dealer, based in Munich, Berlin, New York), likely January 1928;Sold to Julius H. Haass, Detroit, 1928;by descent to (?) Mrs. Lillian Henkel Haass, 1940;Newhouse Galleries, New York, 1957/58;Frederick Mont, New York;Detroit, DIA (presented by Mr. and Mrs. Henry Ford II).	5	44
10.34%	Getty 103R2A	Provenance -;Paignon-Dijonval, French, 1708–1792, (?), Paris -;Vicomte Charles G. Morel de Vindé, (?), Paris -;P. P. Steven, (?), Douvre December 12, 1986;Christie's (London), lot 322 -;Art Market, Boston	3	29

(continued)

Table 3 (continued)

Uncertainty Index (uncert./qty words	Museum URL ID	Provenance	Uncertainty Count	Word Count
10.00%	MOMA 82651	Kornfeld and Klipstein, Bern, ?; to H. Hoffman, Hamburg, 1971; to Private Collection, ?; to Kunsthandel Wolfgang Werner, Bremen, 1986; to Diethelm Hoener, ?; to Phillips de Pury & Luxembourg, New York, 2001?; to The Museum of Modern Art, 2001	4	40
10.00%	MOMA 64218	Probably Fred Jahn, Munich, ?. David Nolan, New York, ? ; sold to The Museum of Modern Art, New York, 1986	2	20

These results are replicable if one starts with the same dataset for 21,000 provenances and word flags (Table 1) and applies the same filters and sorts. To obtain the ranking in Table 3, the results were first filtered to keep only the artworks referenced in NEPIP and then sorted by the number of uncertainty flags, keeping only the top 500. After that they were sorted again, but this time by uncertainty index. This made the provenances with the highest concentration of uncertainty flags rise to the top of the ranking. One can further segment the datasets for analysis, for example by types of artworks or the period.

The distribution of flags in a dataset can help to guide the analysis, because it gives us an idea of which indicators stand out. That is important for deciding which criteria to use in ranking and how to segment data for meaningful results. In early tests, "Uncertainty" and "Unreliability" appeared far less frequently than "Anonymity".[8] Less than 20% of the artworks had uncertainty flags, which made that flag particularly useful in detecting outliers (ParisData 2020).

Figure 1 shows, for example, for one American museum, the different distribution of uncertainty flags depending on how old the painting is. We see that uncertainty flags are much rarer for recent paintings than for older paintings: more than 80% of artworks created after 1950 had 0 uncertainty flags. This tells us that an artwork from this period with one or more uncertainty flags is relatively unusual, and that we should pay attention to more recent artworks that have one or more uncertainty flags.

[8]After we ran the tests, more words suggesting unreliability came to our attention: "by error", "erroneously", "mistaken", "by mistake"; however, these were not counted in the Glamhack2020 project; they were added later.

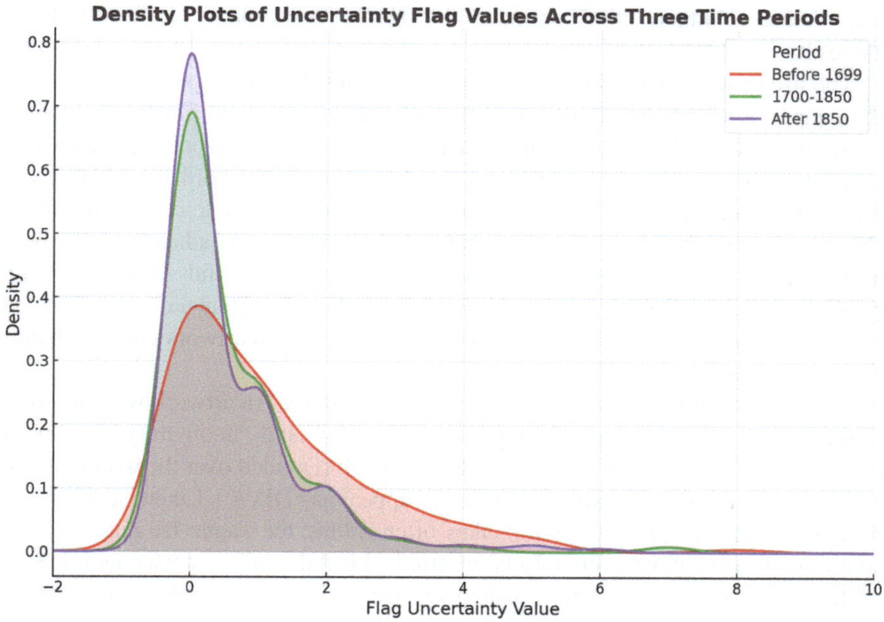

Fig. 1 The distribution of flags helps to guide the analysis

5 Observations, Lessons Learned, Practical Considerations and Challenges

Counting, which provides raw data for ranking, has significant advantages. It is objective, flexible and replicable. Counting generates quantitative and Boolean data well-adapted for integration into metadata, as well as for machine learning, recommender systems, knowledge graphs and AI. Given the same list of words, the same provenance texts and the same counting programs, the results will not vary. They are independent of the user. Counting works well on uncleaned, unstructured, unmediated texts. This removes a big barrier because it can be used on any CSV file with no preparation. Users can group words in categories in whatever way they like according to their analysis needs: although the Detector function proposes a default, anyone can load their own CSV file with the words grouped according to their own analytical concerns.

The counting approach works not only for words like "probably" or "?" but also for names. In 2020 and 2021, before the advent of Artificial Intelligence LLMs, counting last names of Art Looting Red Flag Names and Persecuted Jewish Collectors outperformed Named Entity Recognition (NER) (Zuckerman 2021d, e) both in accuracy and—even more importantly—in transparency, so we temporarily disabled the NER component. the vestiges of which still appear in several columns in the results file generated by the Looted Art Detector (The user can ignore or delete these columns: "# of commata"; "# of to"; "# red flags total"; "# red flag names").,

The use of word lists which can be published and shared as open data has many advantages. One can create separate lists for investigations into forgeries or looted antiquities, whose flags differ from those of Nazi looted art. Anyone can improve or adapt the list of words to count in any language; different word lists can be run against the same dataset, as more information becomes available or research focus changes. As patterns in provenance narratives emerge, one can adapt lists of words to track these patterns, creating, for example, a list of names falsely inserted into provenances, or a list of words such as "debt", "loan", "financial", "owed" and "reimbursement", to identify provenances that assert that an artwork changed hands as a reimbursement for a loan.

However, counting as methodology also has its limits. An artwork with no provenance at all will have "uncertainty", "unreliability" and "anonymity" counts of zero, which could be misinterpreted as a good result (Divided over the wordcount to normalize for the size of texts, the result will appear as #DIV/0). Likewise, forgeries pose a challenge. Provenances for fakes often mimic the vague language we are counting; forgers have even falsely inserted "Flechtheim", a persecuted Jewish dealer, into provenances to trick collectors ("Alfred Flechtheim" 2024). If the user's goal is to restitute looted art to families, it is important to avoid wasting time on forgeries, but it is currently not yet clear how to identify these unless museums state that they are forgeries.

Ranking, which uses the results of counting as input, has the goal of providing actionable information in the real world. We want our ranking to put artworks that are most likely to have been looted at the top. Ranking can be as simple as, for example, sorting artworks by most "uncertainty" or "unreliability" or "anonymity" wordcount from high to low.[9] Or it can be as complex as optimizing the mix of criteria using machine learning and adding contextual information from domain experts or knowledge graphs. How one implements ranking, and which criteria one chooses to weight more heavily, will depend on what one is trying to achieve: this is also why contextualization of the rankings is so important.

Dealing with speculative words such as "probably", "possibly" and "likely" poses a challenge, because it is difficult to prove definitively that a speculation could not possibly be true. In the Knoedler forgery case, for example, the forger Rosales simply added a name whenever her fake provenance was challenged to throw researchers off (Kallir 2021). It is not easy to avoid this trap. However, one can, as a first step, focus attention on verifying the references that are supposed to support the assertion in question. One can also search provenance databases to see whether the inserted name appears elsewhere, and whether those provenances turned out to be accurate. For example, the 2010 catalogue of the Metropolitan Museum of Art stated that Leffmann sold *The Actor* in 1913, a statement which has been proven to

[9]A practical approach is to start by normalizing scores to create an index such as the "uncertainty index" (uncertainty/word count), then sort from largest to smallest and filter for certain names >1 if lists of names were also counted.

be false. However, in the same provenance, a new name, Frank Burty Haviland, was introduced into the ownership history, accompanied by the words "ca.", "or" and "probably" ("ca. 1905-1911; probably acquired from the artist"; see Tinterow et al. 2010, p. 67). As Table 1 shows, six owners are known to have been falsely inserted into the provenance of *The Actor* between 1938 and 2010 ("Italian collector", "Vollard", "Thannhauser", German professor in Solothurn", "Joseph Muller", "private collection") so verification of a new name added to the ownership history when the painting is 105 years old would adhere to good practice. If one verifies in the archives the references cited in the 2010 catalogue, one will find a mention of "a Picasso" but not specifically of *The Actor*. A search to see where else the new name "Haviland" appears will lead to a Modigliani sculpture called *Woman's Head*, which was donated to the museum by Mr. and Mrs. Klaus G. Perls in 1997 and which has three mentions of "private collection" in the provenance (Metropolitan Museum of Art 2024). A wider search for Modigliani's *Woman's Head* will lead to a magazine article (Connolly 1992, p. 59) entitled "Scumbag Descending a Staircase" which tells how, in 1990, the art dealer Klaus Perls was tricked into buying a fake Modigliani sculpture called *Woman's Head*. If one studies Klaus Perls' social network, one will find he is the son of Hugo Perls and the brother of Frank Perls, whose false provenances for *The Actor* are listed in Table 1. Who decides what to do with this knowledge? The counting method can point the researcher towards a subject to be verified but cannot go further.

Another way to assess the success of the counting methodology outlined here, is to study artworks' provenances whose history has been thoroughly researched from the time before their true history was known, to verify how such provenances are worded. Do the earlier provenances also contain red flags or deceptive language? If we had looked at word frequencies then, would they have ranked high enough to be flagged?

It is in the verification process that one sees the tension between open data provenances and the closed world of the archives which contain the documents necessary to verify these statements. The Washington Conference Principles emphasized the importance of open access to archives. Yet, despite progress, many crucial archives necessary for Nazi-era provenance are neither digitized nor accessible without a series of permissions which the institution in question can and often does refuse. In the case of *The Actor*, for example, the proof that the museum's provenance was false was discovered in archives that were closed when I started the research. The existence of a key source, the Metropolitan curator's unique annotated draft of the 1967 French Paintings catalogue, was physically located inside the Metropolitan, known only to the Metropolitan, and, even in August 2024, was authorized for departmental use only and required special permission from the museum's general counsel to be accessed.

In addition to the problem of inaccessible archives, the verification process also highlights the problem of authority. There are, for example, two competing explanations for how artworks from the collection of Holocaust victim Fritz Grünbaum came into the possession of the Swiss art dealer Eberhard Kornfeld. One version is that the artworks were looted from Grünbaum by Nazis and surfaced, postwar, at

Kornfeld's; and the other is that Grünbaum's sister-in-law obtained the artworks "as a gift" from the Grünbaums and sold them after the war to Kornfeld (O'Donnell 2017, p. 13). Only one of these stories can be true. Who decides? On what authority? In 2023, the Manhattan District Attorney seized from public and private collections several artworks it believed were looted from Grünbaum (Bragg 2023). Five museums and two private collectors returned the artworks to the Grünbaum heirs (Sutton 2023). One museum—the Art Institute of Chicago—refused (Mashberg and Bowley 2024a). If, ignoring this, one applies to the contested artwork, *Russian War Prisoner*, the method of examining earlier provenances for signs of potentially deceptive language, one finds, in 2002, three "probably" terms in one paragraph about the provenance (Bogdanos 2024 p. 139). It is not, however, the Manhattan D.A. or the Grünbaum heirs who control the provenance that is published on the Art Institute of Chicago's website (Art Institute of Chicago 2024). And the Art Institute of Chicago states that it was not looted (Mashberg and Bowley 2024b).

The US National Academies of Science, Integrity in Scientific Research defines a conflict of interest in research as a situation in which an individual has "interests in the outcome of the research that may lead to a personal advantage and that might therefore, in actuality or appearance, compromise the integrity of the research. (…) A key feature of this situation is that the same individual is involved in two competing interests, one of which could possibly corrupt the motivation of the other and introduce bias in his or her professional judgement" (US National Academies of Science 2002).

Assessing the reliability of information in provenances requires understanding of stakeholders' roles and potential conflicts of interest (Tompkins 2020). In the realm of Nazi-looted art, it is not uncommon for defendants in civil lawsuits to state that their employees or service providers have conducted provenance research and concluded that the defendant has good title to the artwork in question (MFAH 2024). How might this triple role—cultural heritage institution, scholar and defendant—impact provenance texts written by the defendant's employees? Museum officers, employees, service providers, donors, dealers, art historians, collectors, claimants, defendants and their representatives may have financial, social or other interests that could influence how information is presented. Additionally, power dynamics mean that influential stakeholders, like museums or auction houses, can control narratives, leaving smaller actors underrepresented. This is particularly true where museums, collectors, dealers and auction houses control access to crucial closed archives and some stakeholders hold sway over others. At the intersection of litigation, reputation, money, and scholarship, provenance research is difficult to assess without transparency.

How to distinguish good faith from deception? Yates and Graham suggest that a machine-learning approach to provenance "could allow the detection of broader patterns of unethical or even criminal behaviours that are embedded in the relationships underpinning museum collections" (Yates and Graham 2024, p. 1). This suggests that there is scope for improvement in our methodology, which will be discussed below.

6 Further Areas of Research

Improvements to the Looted Art Detector could include automating the calculation of indexes, reintroducing named entity recognition, optimizing ranking by using machine learning and adding contextual information from knowledge graphs. The methods of provenance research require a detective work so complex "that one may miss the forest for the trees", Shalem (2017) warns us. Data visualizations are a way of stepping back and gaining perspective on patterns, and there is much work to do here. If one animates the data visualization with a time slider, for example, once can see how and when names are inserted, removed, or replaced by vague or anonymous language over time. An open data typology of false provenance statements and a dictionary of words and names associated with them could help all stakeholders. One can broaden the application of the methodology. At the collection level, for example, one can count the number of artworks with no provenance, and, for these items, the number of years between the creation date and the acquisition date to obtain a collection's total provenance gap in years. To assess the credibility of references, one can count the number of years between an event and the creation of the source used as a reference for that event. For artworks whose provenances change significantly, with names appearing and disappearing and sales dates moving, one can count the number of different versions. There may be insights here as well for other digital projects. The information provided by words such as "possibly" or "probably" highlights the importance of preserving provenance texts in their original form with all their errors and ambiguities when they are digitized and published as structured data. Quantitative measures of uncertainty, unreliability and anonymity could be placed at the top, most visible level of an artwork's metadata, with a suite of ready-to-run queries to explore connections and patterns. This differs somewhat from an approach in which qualifiers like "probable" are deeply nested within CIDOC-CRM or presented as part of a competing or alternative view (Mariani 2022). The conversion of text into quantitative features paves the way for machine learning and AI to predict looted art (Agarwal et al. 2024; Revell 2017). Given a training dataset of provenances tagged "true" or "false", AI should be able to predict false provenances using word frequency counts and other indicators. LLMs could even be prompted to automatically identify and rank texts by qualities such as uncertainty, anonymity, unreliability and to rank artworks for deceptive language.

7 Conclusion

This chapter explores some possibilities offered by a computational approach to identifying Nazi looted art. The methodology proposed involves counting key words associated with deception in provenance texts, and flagging key names associated with Nazi looting. Tools were developed and tested on 60,000 provenance texts, to produce a ranking of potentially looted art. The lessons learned and issues encountered, including the challenges of verifying assertions and the multiple roles of stakeholders, were discussed. Further avenues of development of the methodology are highlighted, both in terms of wider applications and in terms of expanding the computational power with the help of computer scientists into machine learning and AI. There are many ways to research this rigged game. Counting is but one of them.

References

"Alfred Flechtheim" (2024) The Jägers Collection. Retrieved from: http://alfredflechtheim.com: http://alfredflechtheim.com/en/reception/the-jaegers-collection/

Agarwal N, Huang R, Moehring A, Rajpurkar P, Salz T, Yu F (2024) Comparative advantage of humans versus AI in the long tail. AEA Pap Proc 114:618–622

ALIU (1946) Post-War Reports: Art Looting Intelligence Unit (ALIU) Reports 1945-1946 and ALIU Red Flag Names List and Index. Retrieved from lootedart.com: https://www.lootedart.com/MVI3RM469661

American Alliance of Museums. (2024) The Nazi-Era Provenance Internet Portal Project. (A. A. Museums, Producer) Retrieved May 2024, from NEPIP: http://www.nepip.org/

Art Institute of Chicago (2024, April 9) Russian War Prisoner. Retrieved from artic.edu: https://web.archive.org/web/20240409074325/https://www.artic.edu/artworks/25342/russian-war-prisoner

Association of Art Museum Directors. (2024) Resolutions of Claims for Nazi-Era Cultural Assets. Retrieved from aamd.org: https://aamd.org/object-registry/resolution-of-claims-for-nazi-era-cultural-assets/more-info

Baily M (2006, November 26) LootedArt.com. Retrieved from Revealed: National Gallery's Cranach is war loot: https://www.lootedart.com/news.php?r=O97FMI255891

Beal G (2018) Restitutions: Four Cases from Four Museums, Four Results. Looted Art, October 2024, Retrieved from: https://www.lootedart.com/web_images/pdf2018/Beal1.pdf.

Bogdanos M (2024) In the matter of an application for a warrant to search the premises located at the Art Institute of Chicago, 111 South Michigan Avenue Chicago, IL60603, application for turnover order Alvin Bragg, Jr. District Attorney New York County, by Matthew Bogdanos. Retrieved from AAID: https://acrobat.adobe.com/id/urn:aaid:sc:us:7e92b4b1-e138-4003-8652-71abf3a245d2?viewer!megaVerb=group-discover

Boucher B (2015) El Greco Stolen by Nazis and Sold by Knoedler Returns to Rightful Owners. Artnet, March 24. Retrieved from: https://news.artnet.com/market/el-greco-nazis-loot-returned-280817

Bowley G (2016) Met Picasso Belonged to Family That Fled Nazis, Suit Says. New York Times, September 30. Retrieved from: https://www.nytimes.com/2016/10/01/arts/design/metropolitan-museum-of-art-picasso-the-actor-lawsuit.html#:~:text=The%20estate%20of%20a%20German,low%20price%20after%20fleeing%20the

Bowley G (2020) Met Museum Adjusts Painting's History to Note Former Jewish Owner. New York Times, February 26. Retrieved from: https://www.nytimes.com/2020/02/26/arts/design/Metropolitan-Museum-Jewish-Owner.html

Bragg A (2023) D.A. Bragg: Seven Pieces of Nazi Looted Art Returned to Relatives of Holocaust Victim. Manhattan DA, September 20. Retrieved from: https://manhattanda.org/d-a-bragg-seven-pieces-of-nazi-looted-art-returned-to-relatives-of-holocaust-victim/

Bührle FE (2023, September 24) Paul Gauguin The Road 1884. Retrieved from Emil Buhrle Collection: https://web.archive.org/web/20230924041145/https://www.buehrle.ch/en/collection/?tx_buehrlewerkliste_werkliste%5Bwerk%5D=65&tx_buehrlewerkliste_werkliste%5Baction%5D=show&cHash=eed000fb7ceaa552e7c305e47777939a

Chase EW (ed) (1944) They like to dine in cotton. Vogue 103(10):72–73. Condé Nast.
Collections Trust (2024). Spoliation reports from UK museums. Retrieved from Collections Trust: https://records.collectionstrust.org.uk/
Connolly J (1992) Scumbag Descending a Staircase. Spy Magazine, October
Court UC (2019) David Cassirer v Thyssen Bornemiszma Collection Foundation. Courthouse News, April 30. Retrieved from: https://web.archive.org/web/20200222153528/https://www.courthousenews.com/wp-content/uploads/2019/05/CassirerThyssen-JUDGMENT.pdf
Crow K (2015) Museum of Modern Art Returns Painting to Heirs of Man Who Fled Nazis. Wall Street Journal, November 16. Retrieved from: https://www.wsj.com/articles/museum-of-modern-art-returns-painting-to-heirs-of-jewish-collector-1447715089
Daix P (1967) Picasso: The Blue and Rose Periods, A Catalogue Raisonné of the Paintings 1900-1906. New York Graphic Society Ltd, Greenwich, Connecticut
D'Arcy D (2018) Austria returns wrong Klimt to wrong family. The Art Newspaper, November 13. Retrieved from: https://www.theartnewspaper.com/2018/11/13/austria-returns-wrong-klimt-to-wrong-family
Dean M, Goschler C, Ther P (2008) Robbery and restitution: the conflict over Jewish Property in Europe. Berghahn Books
Eisenstat S (2004) Imperfect justice: looted assets, slave labor, and the unfinished business of World War II. Public Affairs, New York
Eizenstat S (2009) Holocaust Era assets Conference Proceedings Prague June 26–30, 2009. Forum 2000 Foundation, Prague, p 69
EPRS S. E (2022) Jewish art collections – Nazi looting. Retrieved from European Parliament: https://www.europarl.europa.eu/RegData/etudes/BRIE/2022/698872/EPRS_BRI(2022)698872_EN.pdf
ETH-Bibliotheck (2021, April 20) GLAMhack2021 | Project Presentation [Video]. https://www.youtube.com/watch?v=Yld9FkDyMac
Felch J (2011) Chasing Aphrodite: the hunt for looted antiquities at the world's richest museum. Houghton Mifflin Harcourt, Boston
Feliciano H (1998) The Lost Museum: The Nazi Conspiracy to Steal the World's Greatest Works of Art. Basic Books
Fischer M (2013) Why Nazi-seized art is only now resurfacing – and how it will change the art world. Washington Post, November 6. Retrieved from: https://www.washingtonpost.com/news/worldviews/wp/2013/11/06/why-nazi-seized-art-is-only-now-resurfacing-and-how-it-will-change-the-art-world/
Friedländer S (2008) The years of extermination: Nazi Germany and the Jews, 1939-1945. Harper Collins
Fuhrmeister C, Hopp M (2019) Rethinking provenance research. Getty Res J 11:213–231. https://doi.org/10.1086/702755
Gerstenblith P (2018) Provenances: real, fake, and questionable. Int J Cult Prop 26(3):285–304. https://doi.org/10.1017/S0940739119000171
Gill DW (2011) Polaroids from the Medici Dossier: Continued Sightings on the Market. The Journal of Art Crime, 29-32. Available at: https://www.artcrimeresearch.org/wp-content/uploads/2012/09/JAC-Spring-2011-eVersion-Final.pdf
Glamhack (2020) Hack.glam.opendata. Retrieved from Glamhack2020: https://hack.glam.opendata.ch/project/7
Goodman S (2016) The Orpheus clock: the search for my family's art treasures Stolen ny the Nazis. Scribner
GovTrack (2016) S. 2763 (114th): Holocaust Expropriated Art Recovery Act of 2016, Bills & Resolutions Summary, Gov Track US, Retrieved from Bills & Resolutions Summary, Gov Track US: https://www.govtrack.us/congress/bills/114/s2763/summary
Harvard Law Review (2020, April) Civil procedure — equitable defenses — second circuit holds that the holocaust expropriated art recovery act of 2016 does not preclude application of laches

defenses to nazi-looted art recovery claims. — Zuckerman v. Metropolitan Museum of Art, 928 F.3d 1. Harv Law Rev 133:2196 (Harvard Law Review), 2197
Herzberg N (2022) 'Panama papers': a clearer picture on the hidden Modigliani. Le Monde, March 3. Retrieved from: https://www.lemonde.fr/en/archives/article/2022/03/23/panama-papers-a-clearer-picture-on-the-hidden-modigliani_5979049_113.html#
Hickley C (2017) Gurlitt's Swiss dealer breaks silence on his client. Swiss Info, October 12. Retrieved from: https://www.swissinfo.ch/eng/-degenerate-art%2D%2D_Gurlitt-s-swiss-dealer-breaks-silence-on-his-client/43590572
Hickley, C. (2021a) Bern Art Museum restitutes two Otto Dix to presumed owners. Swiss Info, December 25. Retrieved from: https://www.swissinfo.ch/eng/culture/bern-art-museum-restitutes-two-otto-dix-to-presumed-owners/47197012
Hickley C (2021b) In the battle against antiquities trafficking, Germany develops app to identify looted cultural heritage. The Art Newspaper, January 5. Retrieved from: https://www.theartnewspaper.com/news/germany-develops-app-to-identify-looted-heritage
Holocaust Expropriated Art Recovery Act of 2016, S. 2763, 114th Cong. (2016) https://www.govtrack.us/congress/bills/114/s2763/text
JDCRP (2024) Pilot Project: The Fate of the Adolphe Schloss Collection. Available from: pilot-demo.jdcrp. https://pilot-demo.jdcrp.org/essays/european-art-market-networks/#postwar-networks-in-munich-silvano-lodi-and-the-abel-grimmer-paintings
Jensen N (2022) Max Emden's heirs to revive Nazi loot claim against the National Gallery of Victoria. The Australian, September 20. Retrieved from: https://www.theaustralian.com.au/arts/visual-arts/max-emdens-heirs-to-revive-nazi-loot-claim-against-the-national-gallery-of-victoria/news-story/3d4e9ef7a132b21d744961d527ec1c8c?amp&nk=021e6102ced70fd7a82ea63654089521-1680155380
Kallir J (2021) Why do forgeries sometimes deceive even the most venerable experts? Because We All Want to Believe. Artnet, August 8. Retrieved from: https://news.artnet.com/art-world-archives/jane-kallir-op-ed-1995928
Kulturgutverlust KF, Baresel-Brand A (2005) Entehrt, Ausgeplündert, Arisiert. Entrechtung und enteignung der Juden. Koordinierungsstelle für Kulturgutverlust
Lost Art Foundation (2010) Jüdische Sammler und Kunsthändler (Opfer nationalsozialistischer Verfolgung und Enteignung). Lost Art, July 30. Retrieved from: http://web.archive.org/web/20100730000859/http://www.lostart.de/Webs/DE/Provenienz/JuedischeSammler/Index.html
Lost Art Foundation (2022) Kastel Nijenrode aan de Vecht / Schloss Nijenrode an der Vecht Lost Art-ID 585618. Retrieved from: Lostart.de: https://www.lostart.de/de/Verlust/585618
Lost Art Foundation (2024a) Lost Art Database. Retrieved from lostart.de: https://www.lostart.de/de/start
Lost Art Foundation (2024b) Proveana Provenance Research Database. Retrieved from proveana: https://www.proveana.de/en/start
Malvern J (2017) Painting looted by Nazis found on Lord Mayor of London's wall. Looted Art Commission, November 6. Retrieved from: https://www.lootedartcommission.com/SQ8EC033952
Mariani F (2022) Introducing VISU: Vagueness, incompleteness, subjectivity, and uncertainty in art provenance data. Dans J. 0.–1. COMHUM 2022: Workshop on Computational Methods in the Humanities (Éd.), COMHUM 2022: Workshop on Computational Methods in the Humanities, June 09–10, 2022, Lausanne, Switzerland https://ceur-ws.org/Vol-3602/paper5.pdf. Lausanne, Switzerland.
Mashberg T, Bowley G (2024a) Investigators Say Chicago's Art Institute Is Holding onto 'Looted Art'. The New York Times, February 23. Retrieved from: https://www.nytimes.com/2024/02/23/arts/investigators-say-chicagos-art-institute-is-holding-onto-looted-art.html
Mashberg T, Bowley G (2024b) Investigators Say Chicago museum says investigators have no evidence art was looted. The New York Times, April 24. Retrieved from: https://www.nytimes.com/2024/04/24/arts/chicago-museum-schiele-court.html
Masurovsky M (2020) Cultural Plunder by the Einsatzstab Reichsleiter Rosenberg. (C. Conference, Producer). ERR Project, February 5. Retrieved from: errproject.org: https://www.errproject.org/

Meaney JE (2017) From platitudes to the passage of the HEAR Act: how procedural obstacles in U.S. courts have prevented the restitution of Nazi-expropriated art and Congress's efforts to provide a resolution. Univ Florida J Law Public Policy 28(2), Article 6. Available at https://scholarship.law.ufl.edu/jlpp/vol28/iss2/6

Metropolitan Museum of Art. (2005, January 25). Picasso The Actor. https://www.metmuseum.org/art/collection/search/488690

Metropolitan Museum of Art (2016, March 5) Picasso The Actor. Retrieved from Metmuseum.org Internet Archive: https://web.archive.org/web/20160305163052/https://www.metmuseum.org/art/collection/search/488690

Metropolitan Museum of Art (2024, October 26) Woman's Head. Retrieved from metmuseum.org: https://www.metmuseum.org/art/collection/search/486837

Monuments Men Foundation (2021) Monuments Men Foundation Analysis of the Museum of Fine Arts, Houston Research Report on Bernardo Bellotto, Marketplace at Pirna, prepared by Ms. Laurie Stein. August 30. Retrieved from https://6cc11eed-4e99-4b4c-8420-a45f580f84a9.filesusr.com/ugd/b39bbe_fa6170246dbd483192e13b3e6d2c601e.pdf

Museum of Fine Arts Boston (2024, October 19) Ownership Resolutions, 2021-View of Beverwijk (1982.396). Retrieved from: https://www.mfa.org/collections/provenance/ownership-resolutions

Museum of Fine Arts Houston (2024, May 30) mfah.org. Retrieved from MFAH Statement: "The Marketplace at Pirna," c. 1764, Bernardo Bellotto | The Museum of Fine Arts, Houston: https://www.mfah.org/press/mfah-statement-the-marketplace-at-pirna-c-1764-bernardo-bellotto

Natter T (2017) Gustav Klimt, tout l'oevre peint. Tachen, Köln

Nicholas L (2017) Markt und Macht: Der Kunsthandel im "Dritten Reich". Dans U. Fleckner, T. Gaehtgens & C. Huemer. De Gruyter.

O'Connor AM (2015) The Lady in Gold: The extraordinary tale of Gustav Klimt's Masterpiece 'Portrait of Adele Bloch-Bauer". First Vintage Books

O'Donnell NM (2017) A tragic fate: law and ethics in the battle over Nazi-Looted Art. American Bar Association

Office of the Special Envoy for Holocaust Issues (1998) Washington Conference Principles on Nazi-Confiscated Art. Retrieved at state.gov: https://www.state.gov/washington-conference-principles-on-nazi-confiscated-art/

ParisData (2020) GLAMhack2020 Github. Retrieved on Github.com: https://github.com/parisdata/GLAMhack2020

Petroupolis J (2017, July) Art Dealer Networks in the Third Reich and in the PostWar Period. J Contemp Hist, 52(3):546–565. www.jstor.org/stable/44504062

Polack E, Dorléac L (2019) Le marché de l'art sous l'occupation 1940-1944. Tallandier

Revell T (2017) AI detective analyses police data to learn how to crack cases. New Scientist, May 10. Retrieved from: https://www.newscientist.com/article/mg23431254-000-ai-detective-analyses-police-data-to-learn-how-to-crack-cases/

Richardson J (1996) A Life of Picasso, Vol II: 1907-1917 the painter of modern life. Random House

Robinson G (2006, June 6) Fort Worth museum plans to return looted painting. (F. W. Star-Telegram, Producer) Retrieved October 2024, from Lootedart.com: https://www.lootedart.com/news.php?r=MKT0F6398051

Rother L (2020) In: Tompkins A (ed) Provenance research today: principles, practice problems. Lund Humphries in Associate with IFAR, London, UK

Schumacher J (2024) Nazi Era Provenance of Museum Collections, A Research Guide. ULC Press.

Shalem A (2017) Nazi-looted art and its legacies: Introduction. New German Crit, 44(1), February 2017. https://doi.org/10.1215/0094033X-3705667

Soby JT (1939) Picasso: a critical estimate. Parnassus 11(8):8–12. https://doi.org/10.2307/772012

Solomon T (2023) Heirs of Art Dealer Persecuted by Nazis Claim Sotheby's Sold Prized Tiepolo with Misleading Provenance. ArtNews, May 22. Retrieved from: https://www.artnews.com/art-news/news/heirs-of-art-dealer-persecuted-by-nazis-claim-sothebys-sold-prized-tiepolo-with-misleading-provenance-1234669334/

Stein L (2019) Cassirer v Thyssen, Declaration of Laurie A. Stein [Docket No. 412] at 153. Case 2:05-cv-03459-JFW-E Document 621 Filed 04/30/19 Page 9 of 34 Page ID #:70376. (https://www.courthousenews.com/wp-content/uploads/2019/05/CassirerThyssen-JUDGMENT.pdf, Éd.) Retrieved from Courthouse News: https://www.courthousenews.com/wp-content/uploads/2019/05/CassirerThyssen-JUDGMENT.pdf

Sterling C, Salinger MM (1967) French paintings III: XIX & XX centuries. The Metropolitan Museum of Art / New York Graphic Society, pp. 231–232

Sutton B (2023) US authorities return seven Schiele works to heirs of cabaret performer murdered by the Nazis. The Art Newspaper, September 22. Retrieved from: https://www.theartnewspaper.com/2023/09/22/egon-schiele-works-returned-fritz-grunbaum-heirs-nazi-loot

Tinterow G, Daborwski M, Belloli L, Hollevoet C, Metropolitan Museum of Art, & Picasso, P (2010) Picasso in the metropolitan museum of art. Metropolitan Museum of Art, New York

Tompkins A (2020) Provenance research today: principles, practices, problems. Lund Humphries in association with IFAR, London, UK

US National Academies of Science Ii (2002) US National Academies of Science, Integrity in Scientific Research, 2002, US National Academies of Science

Washington UD (1999) Rosenberg v. Seattle Art Museum, 42 F. Supp. 2d 1029 (W.D. Wash. 1999). Retrieved from Justia: https://law.justia.com/cases/federal/district-courts/FSupp2/42/1029/2501685/

Whoriskey P (2021, October 5) Pandora Papers | A global investigation Global hunt for looted treasures leads to offshore trusts. Retrieved from Washington Post: https://www.washingtonpost.com/world/interactive/2021/met-museum-cambodian-antiquitie

WJRO CC (2015) U.S. Museums Fail to Address Holocaust Stolen Art Claims. Retrieved from: art.claimscon.org: https://art.claimscon.org/advocacy/u-s-museums-fail-to-address-nazi-era-stolen-art-claims/

Yates D, Graham S (2024) Reputation laundering and museum collections: patterns, priorities, provenance, and hidden crime. Int J Herit Stud 30. https://doi.org/10.1080/13527258.2023.2284740

Zuckerman, L. (2021a). Linked data and holocaust era art markets: gaps and dysfunctions in the knowledge supply chain. In Weber A (ed) COLCO 2020 Collection and Connect: Archives and Collecting in a Digital Age. 2810. Leiden: CEUR Workshop Proceedings ISSN 1613-0073. Retrieved from CEUR-WS.org: https://ceur-ws.org/Vol-2810/paper2.pdf

Zuckerman L (2021b) Looted Art Detector. ArtData. artdata.pythonanywhere.com: https://artdata.pythonanywhere.com/

Zuckerman L (2021c, July 18) Looted Art Detector Tool: Swiss GLAMHACK2021. Open Art Data: https://www.openartdata.org/2021/04/provenance-text-.html

Zuckerman L (2021d, July 21) Tutorial for the Looted Art Detector: using custom indicators. Retrieved from Open Art Data: https://www.openartdata.org/2021/07/Tutorial-Looted-Art-Detector.html

Zuckerman L (2021e, March 29) Where do fake art provenances come from? Open Art Data: https://www.openartdata.org/2021/03/fake-news-art-provenance.html

Zuckerman L (2022, April 8) Plunder, Restitution and the Challenge of False Provenances, 48th Annual Conference of the Association of Art History. [Video]. YouTube: https://www.youtube.com/watch?v=61n1uZbASDE

Zuckerman L. (2023a) Data Preparation: NEPIP items merged with Glamhack2020 computations, selected first for top 500 by number of uncertainty flags, then sorted by highest uncertainty index. Retrieved from: https://docs.google.com/spreadsheets/d/1bSMZqPf8jgUowPjEzO1gvn5xGSKaog8ULkod5mYRli4/edit#gid=254197731

Zuckerman L (2023b, September) Detecting deception: a computational approach to detecting Nazi-looted Art 14 September 2023. [Video]. YouTube: https://www.youtube.com/watch?v=AXwjBoC0Kp4

Zuckerman L (2023c) The error is the message: extracting insights from deceptive data for nazi-looted art. The Knowledge Graph Conference 2023: https://zenodo.org/records/7908630

Zuckerman L (2024, June 7) Harvard Dataverse. Retrieved from Replication Data for: Detecting Deception: Uncertainty, Unreliability, Anonymity and Red Flag Names, A Computational Approach, Harvard Dataverse: https://doi.org/10.7910/DVN/T03SVT

Zuckerman v. Metropolitan, Case No. 1:16-cv-07665-LAP (S.D.N.Y. Nov. 2, 2016). https://static1.squarespace.com/static/5e336b7aefe11e0fa31d8677/t/5e34c97e26acc86be0a95402/1580517759072/2016-Nov.-2-Amended-Leffmann-Complaint.pdf

Open Access This chapter is licensed under the terms of the Creative Commons Attribution-NonCommercial-NoDerivatives 4.0 International License (http://creativecommons.org/licenses/by-nc-nd/4.0/), which permits any noncommercial use, sharing, distribution and reproduction in any medium or format, as long as you give appropriate credit to the original author(s) and the source, provide a link to the Creative Commons license and indicate if you modified the licensed material. You do not have permission under this license to share adapted material derived from this chapter or parts of it.

The images or other third party material in this chapter are included in the chapter's Creative Commons license, unless indicated otherwise in a credit line to the material. If material is not included in the chapter's Creative Commons license and your intended use is not permitted by statutory regulation or exceeds the permitted use, you will need to obtain permission directly from the copyright holder.

Looking Across Collections: Ethical Challenges and Considerations of Using Museum Collection Data to Conduct Provenance Research at Scale

Isobel MacDonald

Abstract Collection databases, like the collections they record, are continuously changing entities shaped by human decisions and their cultural, economic and political contexts. Although analogous with collections, these databases have historically been used as management tools or for searching and sorting information related to objects. Over the past 20 years, recognition of the value of using collection data as a research tool for historical research, including provenance and the trade in cultural heritage, has grown. Through a comparative examination of projects that have used collection data within this context, this chapter will critically reflect on the ethical challenges and considerations of data integrity and data absence when working with museum collection databases. It will review projects based in the United Kingdom and Europe, that have engaged with diverse cultural heritage collections and their databases, timescales and perspectives, but share a common interest in looking across collections at scale. This chapter highlights the potential of large-scale analyses to augment what we can understand about museum collections and the wider art and antiquities market. Nevertheless, I argue that this potential is limited by the bias within, instability of and ultimately access to museums' digital collection records.

1 Introduction

Over the past six decades, paper records relating to objects within museums have been digitised to create digital collection databases, known as collections management systems (CMS). These were originally created as inventory, location and

I. MacDonald (✉)
Department of Greece and Rome, British Museum, London, UK
e-mail: imacdonald@britishmuseum.org

© The Author(s) 2026

E. Smith, S. Austin (eds.), *Researching a Rigged Game: Digital Approaches to Tracing the Illicit Trade in Cultural Objects*, Studies in Art, Heritage, Law and the Market 11, https://doi.org/10.1007/978-3-032-02014-7_7

collection management tools, as well as for searching and sorting information related to objects. More recently, their development has converged with an increase in researchers drawing on computational, numerical and quantitative methods to ask questions and look for patterns in collection data not visible through traditional qualitative analyses (Padilla et al. 2019; Greenwald 2019; Ahnert et al. 2023, p. 3). Whilst datasets have long been ubiquitous within the art world, it is their move to the digital that has offered new methodological opportunities for historical research, including provenance and the trade in cultural heritage. One such opportunity is the ability to look across collections and examine them on a large scale. This chapter critically reflects on some of the ethical challenges and considerations of using of collection data in this way.

The possibility of examining collection data on a large scale holds significance for provenance research. On an institutional scale, rather than focusing on individual collectors or parts of a collection, large scale data-informed analyses provide a context within which individual stories of the object, collection or collector can be further understood (MacDonald 2023). They can act to augment knowledge surrounding the historical processes of acquisition and the extent to which these are based on "strategic and calculated notions of value" (Berger 2023a, p. 2). Moreover, and within the context of colonial and imperial collecting, quantitative studies allow for a move away from ambiguous reflections and towards a systematic understanding of the "quantitative dimension of the appropriation of indigenous cultural assets" (Schmidt 2023, p. 2). Considering the provenance of collections on a large scale affords an ability to trace the changing uses and values of collections over time and allows for the illustration of trends that run across them, regardless of the type of object or what discipline it might fall into. Within the field of Cultural Analytics, the use of cultural data is valuable as a way "to start dealing with the scale of culture today" (Manovich 2020, p. 15). As noted by Ahnert et al. (2020, p. 92),

> Like aerial photographs, quantitative approaches in the arts and humanities do not seek to replace other methods, but to provide a powerful complementary approach that can facilitate the discovery of new case studies as well as give use to a vantage point from which local features merge into a more meaningful large-scale pattern.

The value of using collection data within this context then, is in its ability to act as a starting point for further research and questioning (MacDonald 2023, p. 308; Lok et al. 2023, p. 22).

There is a proliferation of data relating to museum collections now available within digital databases. Within the United Kingdom (UK)'s national museum context, the British Museum's (BM) database holds an estimated 4.5 million objects, the Victoria and Albert Museum (V&A) more than 1.25 million, and the National Museums Scotland 820,000 objects and specimens, to name just three examples (British Museum n.d.; Victoria and Albert Museum n.d.-a; National Museums Scotland n.d.). As these numbers suggest, the ability to comprehensively examine an institution's history of acquisition is limited by qualitative examinations of areas of a collection. Quantitative and numerical analyses of collection data held within digital databases unlock the ability to understand the shape of collections over time, which can in turn challenge assumptions surrounding the institutions' collection histories.

This chapter begins with a synthesis of the wider research context, including an outline of critical approaches to collection data within cultural heritage. An overview of projects that have used collection data as a tool for analysis to examine collection histories will then situate the varying ways in which digital cultural data has been used within a UK and European context. It will then undertake a comparative review of projects that have engaged with diverse cultural heritage collections and their databases, timescales and perspectives, but share a common interest in using data-driven methods to look across collections on a large scale. The purpose of this review is to critically reflect on two central ethical challenges faced when working in this context: data integrity and data absence. This review will draw out themes running across the projects regarding the specifics of using collection data and argue for the importance of transparency and the critical use of data. As I argue in this chapter, there remain limitations to large-scale approaches because of the biases within, instability of and access to museums' digital collection records. For this type of work to give a more detailed, nuanced and representative picture, museum and heritage institutions should follow "slow cataloguing" practices (Dalal-Clayton and Rutherford 2024, p. 234; Simpson 2024, p. 22) and prioritize transparent and equitable decision-making processes where collaboration with stakeholders in producing and sharing knowledge is central.

2 Critical Approaches to Collection Data

Digital collection databases, like the collections they record, are continuously changing entities shaped by human decisions and their cultural, economic, and political contexts. Goskar (2024, p. 11) demonstrated how the museum catalogue is "an active chronicle, a record of the museum's own social and cultural attitudes and the changes in them". She highlighted the continuous nature of documentation practices as a "curatorial ancestry", one that is "an unending story of collecting, organising and caring", and argues for institutional research to be considered in a similar way to family genealogy (Goskar 2024, p. 3). As suggested by this framing of collection data, it is much more than inventory records of objects within a cultural heritage collection. It is neither neutral nor static, but instead reflects a process of knowledge production and stewardship. Data available on backend collections management systems and frontend outputs like websites derive from the bulk transcription of historical paper records. Mak (2014, p. 1521) has argued that in the process of digitisation, the past and present are brought together and entangled. In other words, collection data is an abstraction of the historical paper records that pertain to objects within collections.

With each shift towards collections as data and the digital, there is a move away from the object and with that the people and places that it is connected to, including potentially problematic entanglements. Examining the history of documentation and record keeping in US ethnographic museums, Turner (2020, p. 4) argued that "institutional knowledge, particularly in museums, exists in the work of record keeping, data collection and (today) digitisation". This reflects the palimpsest nature of digital collections data, and in particular the harmful traces of colonial systems present within individual records from the transcription of historical paper systems. Modelled on eighteenth-century classification systems, the data includes historical and colonial biases, racist language and excludes many actors from the historical record (Lawther 2024). As a result, these records have, for some years, been criticised and challenged for their patriarchal Eurocentric origins (Dalal-Clayton and Rutherford 2024; Goskar 2021; Turner 2020; Collections Trust 2021; Rutherford 2021).

To summarise, the history of collection data is as complex and nuanced as the collections and objects it records. Its use on a large scale presents ethical challenges and considerations, particularly with regard to macro-level biases. Such large-scale methods raise the question of how individual erasures or biases can be accounted for, and indeed if using cultural heritage data as a research tool, replicates and reinforces innate power dynamics stemming from the erasure, misrepresentation or imperial classification of objects. Kizhner et al. (2020) argued, in line with Bode (2020), that in advance of quantitative or statistical analyses, work needed to be done to demonstrate, document and explain *why* chosen examples and certain data is assessed, and outline the criteria for its inclusion. Data cannot ever be completely objective and, in using it, we cannot forget the humans behind the records and their unconscious, or even conscious, bias. Through an analysis of the representativeness of Google Arts and Culture Kizhner et al. (2020, p. 4) demonstrate the importance of "documenting discrepancies, imbalances, and resulting biases in digitized content". When using collection data, it is imperative to critically reflect on the historical, social and political context in which the material was created. Following Lok (2022, p. 16), any analysis that uses collection data as a research tool must:

> …start from the assumption that information systems are never neutral or objective: that there will always be problems of bias, 'misclassification', and inconsistencies in data; and the so-called 'truth' of labels or categories can always be contested, whether they appear to be factual or speculative, conventional or controversial.

Such biases, misclassifications and inconsistencies raise challenges that need to be considered when undertaking this type of research. Central amongst these are questions surrounding how the material has been created and what is absent from the digital record.

3 Case Study: Hans Sloane and the Creation of Digital Collection Data

The collection of Hans Sloane (1660–1753) is exemplary for understanding the complex process of historical collection documentation becoming digital data. Sloane's global collection of natural history[1] and pharmaceutical specimens, ca. 50,000 books and manuscripts, ca. 30,000 coins and medals, 470 pictures, ca. 11,000 prints and drawings and just over 4700 antiquities,[2] was developed from the 1680s when he travelled to Jamaica as the new Governor, the Duke of Abermarle's (1652–1688), physician (MacGregor 1994). Sloane's ability to collect was enabled, in part, through colonial exploitation and the transatlantic trade in enslaved people (Delbourgo 2017). His collection embodies many forms of colonialism, including his work as a physician on a plantation worked by enslaved people, his ownership of plantations in Jamaica through his wife Elizabeth Langley Rose and his shares in the Royal Africa Company (Delbourgo 2017, p. 149). Upon his death in 1753, Sloane bequeathed his collection to the British nation, and this became the basis for Britain's first national museum: the British Museum.

During Sloane's lifetime he, along with his assistants, catalogued parts of his collection in a series of forty manuscript catalogues (MacGregor 1994; Enlightenment Architectures 2017). Many of the descriptions of the human-made objects, which include key provenance information, were created using information conveyed by the person giving or sending an object to Sloane. Sloane and his assistants relied heavily on this information that referred to the people associated with an object, its producer and where it was acquired from and copied it into the catalogues (King 1994, pp. 228–244). When his collection entered the BM, these catalogues were transferred to the institution along with the objects they recorded. The historical manuscript catalogues were by no means static within the museum, and across its history when departments were formed and changed, the catalogues were copied and divided. Sloane's original manuscript catalogues formed the basis for departmental registers in the museum, with Sloane descriptions copied directly into register books in the mid-nineteenth century. Added to this internal mobility of the collections, in the nineteenth century the BM collections were dislocated due to their increasing size and the lack of space at the Bloomsbury site. In 1880, the natural history specimens began their move to the British Museum (Natural History) at South Kensington (today the Natural History Museum, commonly referred to as NHM) and just under a century later the 1972 British Library Act signaled the

[1] This includes 8812 surviving specimens of vegetable substances, and 121, 506 specimens in the herbarium. These numbers were published in 2025 by Brad Scott, Victoria Pickering, Richard Coulton, Julianne Nyhan and Mark Carine in 'Collecting and cataloguing the world: the botanical collections of Hans Sloane (1660–1753). Their paper, which uses Sloane collection data pertaining to the Sloane botanic collections, undertakes a high-level analysis of the collection provenance; facilitating an understanding of the collections at scale for the first time (Scott et al. 2025).

[2] This figure was generated by totaling up the number of entries in two of Sloane's historic manuscript catalogues: 'Miscellanea' and 'Intaglios, Cameos & Rings'.

departure of the printed book and manuscript collections within the BM, with the material making its move to the new British Library (BL) at St Pancras in the early 1990s (Wilson 2002). When these parts of the collection left the BM at the Bloomsbury location, so too did their supporting documentation which included the original historical Sloane manuscript catalogues. Today these are divided between the BM, NHM and BL. This highlights the complexity of the analogue and historical records that relate to just one individual's collection within each of these institutions (Vlachidis et al. forthcoming). The object descriptions held in these historic manuscript catalogues were used as the basis for early understanding of the objects within the Sloane collection; this knowledge has in turn fed into the descriptions now found in digital catalogues pertaining to the institutions within which the Sloane collections are now held. Today, Sloane's collection is digitally recorded across five different digital cataloguing systems, each of which reflects its individual institutional siloes, disciplines and histories. The 'Sloane Lab: looking back to build future shared collections' project, funded by the AHRC Towards a National Collection Programme (referred to as TaNC henceforth), has re-established these broken links between Sloane's catalogues and collections across relevant institutions and digital projects, including digital editions of five of Sloane's historical catalogues created by Enlightenment Architectures; the key public interface for making the historical provenance information of the Sloane collections accessible in a visible and searchable format (Enlightenment Architectures 2017; Nyhan et al. 2022, 2023).[3]

It is not only the complexity of this process of the historical documentation made digital that must be considered, but also those individuals and communities absent from Sloane's original records of the objects within the collection. It is important to remember that both Sloane's historical data and the digital collection data are recorded from a Eurocentric perspective; a perspective that has its origins in Enlightenment ideals that sought to other, erase or hide the narratives of the global majority. As Turner has argued "records and objects […] may have been taken from communities without their consent" (Turner 2020, p. 7). A common absence within Sloane's historic manuscript catalogues is "accurate or detailed provenance and transit information […] primarily regarding the non-Western or socially 'inferior' contributors to his collection" (Ortolja-Baird and Nyhan 2021, p. 851). Examining two of Sloane's manuscript catalogues, Ortolja-Baird and Nyhan extracted ca. 3000 people and 600 geographical locations, giving a quantitative indication of the geographical spread of Sloane's network which they argue "attests a discrepancy of people and places in colonial and imperial contexts" (Ortolja-Baird and Nyhan 2021, p. 855). Following Onuoha, who has highlighted the need to foreground absences within data-saturated systems (Onuoha 2016), theirs was an attempt to trace individuals not recorded by name within this historical record. Hughes and Metilli's research as part of the Sloane Lab project has built on Ortolja-Baird and

[3] See 'The Sloane Lab Knowledge Base', https://knowledgebase.sloanelab.org/resource/Start (accessed 14.03.25).

Nyhan's analysis; looking across the data environment of the Sloane collections as a whole to consider absences in provenance in terms of objects, people, places and time through visualisation[4] and data quantification (Hughes and Metilli forthcoming).

This example of the Sloane collections has demonstrated the need to understand the inherent bias and limitations of digital collection data before analyses are conducted at scale. It also emphasises the need to understand the original circumstances in which provenance information was generated and recorded (Vancisin et al. 2023, p. 1322). This data, created by humans, is not neutral and must be used critically, with full transparency and acknowledgement of its shortcomings. The next section of this chapter will provide an overview of projects that have used collection data at scale, with reference to the way in which this data has been used to generate a broader understanding of collection and provenance histories of museum collections.

4 Projects: The Use of Collection Data at Scale

The following section critically provides a comprehensive review of recent and ongoing projects based in the UK and Europe, that have engaged with diverse cultural heritage collections and their databases, timescales and perspectives, but share a common interest in looking across collections at scale. This review is not exhaustive, nevertheless the projects highlight the potential of large-scale analyses to augment what we can understand about museum collections and the wider art and antiquities market.

4.1 Relational Museum

The use of statistics to examine an individual collection's history through digital collection data was pioneered by Alison Petch as part of the *Relational Museum* project at the Pitt Rivers Museum (Petch 2006; Gosden and Larson 2007). The project focused on human and institutional relationships that created the collection between 1884 and 1945, highlighting links between makers, collectors and museum staff through six case studies of major collectors (Petch 2006, p. 149). The impetus from the project derived from the digital availability of records. In the 1920s and 1930s the Pitt Rivers systematically documented its collections, creating accession books both retrospectively and for new accessions and card catalogue systems. In the 1980s, these paper records were transferred onto a digital platform, resulting in a "complete, and complex, computerised collections management databases for all

[4] See Hughes and Metilli's visualisation of absence in terms of objects in the Sloane collections, https://knowledgebase.sloanelab.org/resource/?uri=http%3A%2F%2Fsloanelab.org%2FD1%2Fmiscellanea (accessed 14.03.25).

its objects" by the mid-1990s (Petch 2006).[5] These were accessible both internally and externally via online versions. The database holds one record for each object in the collection, with a total of 512,866 records. Each record holds the following information relating to the object: collection type, description, geographical reference, dimensions, date made, date collected, acquisition information, materials and processes, object numbers, alternative names and people associated with the object.[6] As with most collection management systems these include structured and unstructured data: either standardised predefined vocabularies to be chosen when creating an entry, or free text fields where any amount of descriptive text can be added.

The *Relational Museum* project used this collection data to question when objects came into the museum, where they came from and through whom they entered the collection. In 2003, a copy of the database was downloaded, and data was collected from five key areas. These included: the 'Continent' and 'Country' field relating to an object's geographical provenance, the accession date of an object, the 'A/E' field which distinguishes archaeological from ethnographic objects, the 'People' fields and the 'Class' field which tags each object to a standard set of thematic classes (Gosden and Larson 2007, pp. 27–28). Their research found, for example, that 53 per cent of the material collected between 1884 and 1945 was archaeological material and 41 per cent ethnographic (Gosden and Larson 2007, p. 46); that the top three professions of those contributing to the Museum collection, where known, were archaeologists (23.7 per cent), army or navy officers (14.8 per cent) and natural historians (10.1 percent) (Gosden and Larson 2007, p. 49). Individuals facilitating acquisitions were also examined by how many were collecting in different regions of the world (Africa, Americas, Australia, Europe and Oceania). Over the period and Gosden and Larson highlighted that the number of people collecting in these locations remained relatively constant over the period examined (Gosden and Larson 2007, p. 56). Slight increases were seen in individuals collecting in Africa during the twentieth century and Asia in the 1920s and 1930s, and the research showed that 73 per cent of all Asian accessions in the 1920s were of Indian objects. The purpose of this statistical approach to the collection's history was to facilitate "a means of looking at the collections as a whole and their changing nature over time" (Gosden and Larson 2007, p. 29) by decade between 1884 and 1945.

4.2 England: The Other Within

The method of evaluation used by Petch, Gosden and Larson was foundational for studies of collections that seek to use collection data as a research tool. Defined as an "exploration process", their intention was to uncover patterns to be analysed in

[5] The Pitt Rivers Museum uses the *Filemaker-Pro* database.

[6] Potential people fields include maker, field collector, other owners (who owned an object before it entered the collection) and PRM source (the person or institution from whom Pitt Rivers acquired the object).

more depth (Gosden and Larson 2007, p. 29). The extent of this exploration can be seen through the 2009–2012 *England: The Other Within* project that sought to use the Pitt Rivers collection data to examine the shape of the Museum's English collections since 1884 (England: the Other Within 2012). Developed from findings from the *Relational Museum*, the project built on its predecessor's examination of relationships and networks central to this area of the collection's development (Wingfield 2011, p. 120). Wingfield situated the museum as a node in a collecting network, using the database to examine 44,133 objects with a geographical provenance of England. Rather than examine the volume of objects acquired by each individual or organisation, he focused on 'acquisition events', in which objects are examined by their accession to the museum (Wingfield 2011, p. 127). In other words, they were grouped to the individual or organisation (in this case the PRM source) who facilitated their entry to the institution by donation, sale, bequest, transfer or exchange. Some acquisition events included multiple objects and others just one. The use of collection data allowed for this examination across the museum's English collections through the extraction and statistical analysis of data from the 'PRM source' field and the individual object accession numbers. Wingfield's (2011, p. 131) findings demonstrated that half of the acquisition sources for the English material in the Pitt Rivers Museum were one-off contacts with the museum, and that most of these facilitated the acquisition of only one or two objects. His use of quantification highlighted the importance of smaller transactions for the development this area of the Museum collection; a pattern that is consistent with the wider Pitt Rivers collection (Gosden and Larson 2007, p. 39).

4.3 Science and Technology Collections of the National Museums Scotland

Beyond the Pitt Rivers Museum, projects that have adapted this use of collection data as a research tool include Phillipson's (2019) numerical analysis of the Science and Technology Collections of the National Museums Scotland (NMS) since 1855. Phillipson's (2019) research considered the historical patterns of collecting and disposal of science and technology objects by the museum as a means of determining their influence on present day collections development practice. Examining 65,751 records held on the NMS collection database, *Adlib*, Phillipson collected data relating to each item's year of accession, acquisition method, legal status, year and method of disposal, current location, and display information. This data was then analysed by mixed date groupings, ranging from single years to the entire period encompassing 1855 to 2019. The analyses questioned the way in which objects entered the collection and when, highlighting connections between methods of acquisition, display and deaccession. Graphs visualising the history of the acquisition of the collection by single year between 1855 and 2019 identified patterns which enabled six unequal periods to be grouped for further analysis. As noted by

Phillipson, the data-driven analysis revealed "traces of changing policies, activities and personalities" (Phillipson 2019). Phillipson's research, enabled through a numerical approach to the NMS collection data, showed that objects purchased were more likely to be displayed and retained by the Museum than donations or material "found in the collections or which was accessioned without the provenance being recorded" (Phillipson 2019). This significant finding not only shows the possibility of this method to uncover patterns in the history of a museum's collection, but it also reiterates the importance of recording provenance information in analogue and digital systems as objects divorced from their provenance were found to be more vulnerable to disposal.

4.4 Counting When, Who and How? Re-examining the History of the British Museum Collection

Between 2020 and 2022 the BM ran a pilot project entitled *Counting when, who and how? Re-examining the history of the British Museum collection* that assessed the value and possibility of using the collection database, *MuseumIndex+* (MI+), as a research tool to analyse the Museum's history of acquisition from 1753 to 2019 (British Museum 2022; MacDonald 2023). The BM's digital collections database originated in the late-1970s after decades of requests from the Parliamentary Committee of Public Accounts for the audit of its collection (Wilson 2002). Today MI+ holds over half of the estimated count of objects within the British Museum's collection (8 million). At almost 5 million objects, held in around 2 million object records it is a large and complicated data set. The scope of the Museum's collections covers not only examples of works of art and antiquities from across the world but also examples of archaeological and cultural artefacts. Records relating to the objects stewarded by the BM evolved alongside changes in departmental structures, with many objects being transferred between departments as these were divided or new departments were created across the Museum's history. The complexity of the BM documentation history meant that in creating a digital system it was not a straightforward case of one framework of documentation working across departments. As a means of building more structure into the database authority fields were developed centrally, with contributions from across the eight object-specific departments, to ensure they correctly and efficiently reflected the requirements of the collection. These "authority" fields are terminology, reference information, person information, place information, location information, dimension unit, field help and procedure definition. Each entry on MI+ has a predetermined set of variables which includes information such as: the object number, object name, physical description, location, production place, date of production, findspot, field collector, acquisition data, acquisition source and acquisition association (a structured field that records the information of how an object entered the BM collection, i.e. through donation or purchase), amongst many others. These set variables allow for some consistency across the database.

The *Counting when, who and how?* project aimed to examine the value and possibilities of using the database as a research tool to explore large scale trends in the BM's history of acquisition from its foundation in 1753 to 2019. The study asked simple questions of the data running across time, departments, and material: for example, when objects entered the collection, from whom the BM acquired objects and how they entered the collection. The decision to ask straightforward questions of when, how, and from whom was derived from the availability of data within MI+. Data was collected from three data variables that were connected to these questions: acquisition date, acquisition association (a structured field that records the information of how an object entered the BM collection), and acquisition source. The quantitative study examined the history of acquisition by decade. The intention behind the analysis was to facilitate an understanding of the shape of the collection and provide a context for individual holdings and areas of the collection. This data-led approach enabled the visualisation and understanding of acquisition patterns not visible through traditional qualitative approaches that focus on individual collectors, objects or parts of a collection. The findings brought into view the shape of the BM collection for the first time, allowing for an understanding of when the museum acquired more or fewer objects (MacDonald 2023, p. 307). It found that the BM collection grew actively and rapidly in the mid-nineteenth century, and that the biggest spike of acquisitions by volume of objects was found at the end of the twentieth century (MacDonald 2023, p. 308). It revealed patterns in the way in which objects entered the collection and illustrated that "although acquisition sources associated with large collections may have shaped the collection by volume, in each decade analysed around 30 per cent of all acquisition sources are associated with just one object record" (MacDonald 2023, p. 317). This analysis suggested the opportunity that quantification can offer to think beyond the celebrated individual, and to begin to understand the quantity of people, organisations and communities that have shaped the collection. It enabled stories of the individual—collector, collection or object—to be understood within an institutional context.

4.5 British Museum AHRC Collaborative Doctoral Partnership Projects

Other projects, funded through AHRC Collaborative Doctoral Partnerships, used the BM collection database and data-led methods to examine specific areas of the BM collection. For example, Elizabeth Wilkes's (2016) project 'Polished axes: object biographies and the writing of world histories' focused on an individual object type, assessing the history of the polished axe collection at the BM through a mixed-method approach using both collection data and the artefacts themselves. The collection data was used by Wilkes as a starting point in her methodology, searching across collections to determine the museum's holdings. Looking across the collections was needed because no collection sold or donated to the museum in its history consisted solely of polished axes; these were acquired as individual objects, or as a part of a wider collection. Through a data-informed study by object type, acquisition date and acquisition association, Wilkes was able to survey the entire collection (Wilkes 2016, pp. 32–35). In addition, Niti Acharya's ongoing project 'Gender, empire and material culture: Women Collectors of South Asia'[7] uses the BM collection data as a means of understanding the shape of the BM collection in relation to women and South Asian material between 1818 and 2019 (Acharya 2024). For Acharya (2024), the data is also a starting point to identify themes for further research. She created a dataset of over 12,000 object records from across the BM database, pulling together biographical, object-based, and geographical data variables, including acquisition source, acquisition association, life dates, postal addresses, biographical notes, object type, production date, production place, findspot, curatorial comment, acquisition date and department. This dataset is used to find new ways to answer the project's research questions.

Similarly, in her project 'The Global and the Local: South Asian collectors at the British Museum', Kajal Meghani[8] created a dataset collating data relating to relevant BM collectors based on their nationality, as a means of analysing the contributions of South Asian collectors to the BM collection. Meghani's main source for such information is MI+ Authorities; the BM's thesaurus for biographical data of people and organisations associated with the collections (Meghani 2024). Common across all three projects is the dispersed nature of objects within the BM collection. Sitting in different curatorial departments, the researchers are looking for the particular within the wider institutional collection. Because of the size and scale of the BM's digital collections, data-informed methodologies thus offer an opportunity to explore a larger corpus of data.

In her research, Meghani (2024) faced the challenge of legacy data from paper records transferred onto the database. Legacy data includes names, places and narratives assigned to objects by collectors or museum workers (Turner 2020, p. 7). Meghani's examination of South Asia includes countries like Afghanistan, Bhutan, India, the Maldives, Nepal, Pakistan and Sri Lanka, many of which had been under some form of British colonial rule. In surveying and collecting the BM data to create her dataset, Meghani (2024) had to consider the possibilities of historical bias obscuring South Asian identities; for example, in the case of typos or misspellings of South Asian names where they had been recorded phonetically. This was

[7] Niti Acharya (University of Lincoln and the British Museum), 'Gender, empire and material culture: Women Collectors of South Asia'. Further information on Acharya's (2024) thesis relating to data integrity and data absence was gathered by consultation with Acharya via discussion and written email correspondence in 2024, henceforth referenced as "(Acharya 2024)".

[8] Kajal Meghani (University of Brighton and the British Museum), 'The Global and the Local: South Asian collectors at the British Museum'. Further information on Meghani's (2024) thesis relating to data integrity and data absence was gathered by consultation with Meghani via discussion and written email correspondence in 2024, henceforth referenced as "(Meghani 2024)".

particularly prevalent in acquisitions from South Asia to the collection through British colonial governing bodies such as the India Office. Meghani (2024) noted that in general, this information appeared to be methodically transferred onto the database and could at least allow for the identification of relevant individuals and their contributions, as a starting point for further research. Nevertheless, these misspelling incorporated in analogue records would then also be incorporated into the digital database, leading to misrepresentation and Indigenous data erasure (See e.g., Adams-Campbell et al. 2014; Couldry and Mejias 2019; Roxanne 2019; Landström 2021; Basu 2024).

4.6 Victoria & Albert Museum Doctoral Training Programme Projects

In addition to the projects outlined above, two doctoral provenance projects, hosted by the Victoria & Albert Museum Doctoral Training Programme, have tackled the lack of digitally recorded provenance data held within the Victoria & Albert Museum (hereafter V&A) database,[9] with focus on the East and South Asian collections (Fraser 2023a, b; Gupta 2024). Outputs from both projects included the transfer of data from paper registers to the digital database. Gupta's (2024) research concentrated on the provenance of the ca. 13,000 objects from South Asia that entered the V&A's collection between 1879 and 1947. Her work has enabled all provenance information contained in the museum's central Inventory records and the Asia Department Acquisition records for objects acquired between 1880 and 1922 to be transferred onto the collection database. Fraser's (2023a, b) research[10] considered the dealers that the V&A had purchased East Asian objects through during the first sixty years of its history. Understanding how the objects came into the museum, and who was involved in their acquisition, is a key step towards furthering knowledge of their provenance.

The objects from China, Korea and Japan which Fraser (2023a, b) focused on, and which are now held within the Asia Department, were spread across museum departments until the 1970s. When objects were transferred to the East Asia collection in 1970, departmental register entries were photocopied to create collated Acquisition Register files used by the Asia Department today (Fraser 2023a, b). The registers include an object's unique museum number and a physical description. Additionally, they can record notes on the object, and information not yet recorded digitally, for example purchase price or the source of acquisition (Fraser 2023a, b). The V&A also holds 60,000 people history files that identify the names of

[9] The V&A also uses *MuseumIndex+* for its Collections Management System.

[10] Tullia Fraser (University of Glasgow, National Museums Scotland, and Durham University), 'Searching for dealers in the V&A's East Asia collection'. Further information on Fraser's project relating to data integrity and data absence was gathered by consultation with Fraser via discussion and written email correspondence, henceforth referenced as "(Fraser 2024)".

individuals and institutions it has interacted with. Using these in conjunction with the Acquisition Registers, Fraser collated a list of 300 individuals and organisations that contributed East Asian material to the V&A between 1852 and 1912. The information gathered from these sources has since been added to the digital database within the 'Object History' field. Fraser used this now digitally recorded data from the registers and people history files to examine patterns in the provenance of the V&A's East Asian collection. Her numerical analysis quantified the number of objects associated with each dealer, and the ways in which objects entered the collection through these individuals (Fraser 2023a, b).

4.7 Cross-Examining Collections

A growing number of projects have used digital collection data to trace patterns running across multiple collections. Recent scholarship within the history of collecting field argues for the need to look beyond the accumulation of individual collections, and highlight the mobility of collections (Driver et al. 2021). Objects within museum collections are not static entities, historically they have moved between collections through transfer, exchange, sale, loss and theft. Moreover, objects within European collections originating from around the world have been accumulated by different agents and means, and have entered institutions either through donation or sale, or via the arts and antiquities market. The line from an object's original creation to the museum collection is not linear, and involves stages of exchange and acquisition, including, but not exclusive to, looted, confiscated, stolen, gifted, purchased and inherited objects.

Projects focusing on collections of objects with specific geographical provenance within UK and European museums have used data-informed approaches to compare the history and provenance of how and why these collections entered different institutions (Dixon 2023; Berger 2024; Schmidt 2024). For example, Dixon (2023) cross-examined the collecting of Indian Ocean boat models by thirteen UK museums between 1820 and 2003. From each institution she collated data into a dataset of 648 boat models, which recorded object description, date of production, field collection, location, acquisition details, and object measurements where available (Dixon 2023, p. 20). Her intention was to build up a more comprehensive understanding of the collecting patterns and provenance of watercraft models in and across UK museums. Dixon's data-informed methodology offered an insight into when these objects were produced and collected, where in the Indian Ocean they were made, how they entered British collections and through whom. Her analysis highlighted peaks in the acquisition of these watercraft models between 1880 and 1909, a period concurrent with British imperial rule in the Indian Ocean. Through her data-informed approach Dixon identified trends for further study, for example the links between British rule, the importance of boats to Indigenous communities and the interest of Western collectors (Dixon 2023, p. 26).

In addition, Frieda Schmidt's (2024) doctoral research project 'Quantifying Colonialism: European Practices of Mass Appropriation of Indigenous Cultural Objects in nineteenth and twentieth Century Australia'[11] aggregated data from the 13 largest national collections of EU Member States, to create the European Museums Collection of Aboriginal Material (EMCAM) dataset (Schmidt 2024). The dataset records standardised data on 4862 indigenous cultural objects from Australia through sixty-five different variables, as well as information on thirty-five exhibitions relating to the material, and 101 individuals who acquired the objects during European colonial rule in Australia. Her research argues for the use of mixed-methods, structured data collection and standardised analytical procedures to augment transparency in the (re)examination of sensitive historical events and to avoid arbitrary case selections (Schmidt 2023, p. 2). Analysis conducted using the EMCAM dataset uncovered patterns of the appropriation of Indigenous Australian material culture, the development of European museum collections in this area and the individuals at the centre of these collections (Schmidt 2024).

4.8 *Between Canon and Coincidence: Using Data-driven Approaches to Understand Art Worlds*

Using a similar pan-European approach, the 'Between Canon and Coincidence: using data-driven approaches to understand Art Worlds' project[12] examines the collection of precolonial Latin American material by European museum collections between 1850 and 2000 (Berger 2024). The project analyses over 400,000 objects held across twelve museums in nine countries. Through a numerical and statistical analysis of the history of acquisition of Indigenous Latin American material culture, it will provide new insight into the way in which these collections now found in European museums were formed, questioning who acquired these objects and when, as well as how they entered museum collections. Berger's data-led approach raises the question of what numerical studies can tell us about museums as actors in the market for this material across Europe (Berger 2023a, b, p. 2). Latin America presents an interesting case study, because the countries considered within Berger's analysis were independent by 1821. The period under investigation (1850–2000) thus presents a different picture to the appropriation of material from colonial con-

[11] Frieda Schmidt (TU Darmstadt), 'Quantifying Colonialism: European Practices of Mass Appropriation of Indigenous Cultural Objects in nineteenth and twentieth Century Australia'. Further information on Schmidt's thesis relating to data integrity and data absence was gathered by consultation with Schmidt via discussion and written email correspondence in 2024, henceforth referenced as "Schmidt (2024)".

[12] Martin Berger (Leiden University), 'Between Canon and Coincidence: using data-driven approaches to understand Art Worlds'. Further information on Berger's research relating to data integrity and data absence was gathered by consultation with Berger via discussion and written email correspondence in 2024, henceforth referenced as "(Berger 2024)".

texts seen in large parts of Africa, Southeast Asia and India, where countries were still subjugated under European imperial rule in the twentieth century (Berger 2024).

Berger's initial focus examined two museums in the Netherlands—the National Museum of Ethnology (NME) of the Netherlands in Leiden and the Wereldmuseum in Amsterdam (formerly known as the Tropenmuseum; Berger 2023a, b). The NME was founded in 1837 through a collection acquired by the German physician Philipp Franz von Siebold (1796–1866), who had worked at the Dutch trading post of Dejima in Nagasaki, Japan. Siebold's collection focused heavily on East Asia and Indonesia, a former Dutch colony. The Wereldmuseum in Amsterdam was founded in 1926 to promote ethnographic and economic knowledge of the Dutch colonies. A continuation of the Colonial Museum in Haarlem (founded in 1871), it formed part of the Colonial Institute—a training institution for colonial officers. The foundations of both collections are thus entangled with colonial systems and histories. Berger (2023a, b, p. 4) highlights how neither institution had a clear interest in precolonial Latin American material culture from the offset and active periods of acquisition did not occur until the mid-twentieth century. Instead, their focus was on Indonesia because of the colonial connections. Nevertheless, whilst the Mesoamerican archaeological material acquired by these museums was from a post-colonial context, it still entered an internally colonial system of categorisation within the museums. This example highlights the complexity of collection data, and the importance of understanding it and the objects it records both within the local context of its geographical provenance and history, as well as the context of the country and museum within which it currently resides (Berger 2024).

The projects outlined here have engaged with diverse cultural heritage collections and their databases, timescales and perspectives. Common to each is their interest in looking across collections at scale. Whilst the scales examined are diverse, ranging from 648 objects to over 4.5 million, the intention across projects remains consistent: to understand the broader shape of collection histories, using collection data as a tool to inform research questions and case studies for further analysis. This chapter now turns to a comparative analysis across the projects of the ethical considerations and challenges discussed above that researchers face when using collection data as a tool for research. In doing so, I highlight the limitations of these types of analysis because of the biases within and instability of museum collection data. It is important to remember that data-informed approaches rely on the strength of the datasets they analyse. Considered within the context of the critical approaches to collection data outlined above, I argue that for such approaches to enable more in depth and nuanced explorations of the provenance of collections at scale, heritage institutions need to prioritise cataloguing strategies that better represent the complex global histories, people and communities to which the objects within collections belong.

5 Discussion & Critical Reflection

The projects outlined above can broadly be classified according to four different analytical foci: geographical provenance of objects, individuals associated with institutions, object types and institutional histories. Within each of these overlapping areas, three overarching themes are traced: considerations of the way in which data was created, the data absences found within digital records and access to museum collection data.

When using collection data for analysis, it is important to consider the context within which an object record was created and the decisions that shaped it (Drucker 2021, p. 22). Schmidt (2023) noted the significance of identifying bias and the importance of a critical look at sources. In the creation of the EMCAM dataset, she identified three levels of conscious and unconscious bias found across the 13 museum databases from which her data was collected. First, in terms of the historical sources and paper records, object descriptions, documentation, reports and other written sources that form the basis for online data. Second, present day political and economic contexts that influence museum policy and resourcing. And third, during the digitisation processes undertaken by externally commissioned technical experts (Schmidt 2024). Schmidt foregrounds the importance of data criticism as a means of increasing awareness of bias and being accountable for those that are unavoidable. Hers is a call, in line with Plets et al. (2023, p. 244) to consider the digital collection database as "a social construct, defined by a set of complex and highly culturally specific internal workings and standardisations". As noted at the beginning of this chapter, museum collection data was created as a means to manage and inventory collections. When using data as a research tool for analysis it is thus imperative to understand how and why it was created and not just consider what it details.

Acharya's methodology also critically reflected on this question of how the digital information was created. As noted above, Acharya's ongoing doctoral analysis of women collectors of South Asian material within the BM collection considers objects spread across the Museum's eight curatorial departments. In the early stages of her research, she identified the movement and internal transfer of objects between departments.[13] These transfers would be updated in the database, however, associated documentation and archival records pertaining to the objects often remained with the department that had originally acquired them (Acharya 2024). Paired with the different types and amount of information recorded across the different records she examined; Acharya illustrated the need to map the history of paper and digital cataloguing systems within an institution both at an organisation and department level. Assessing when, how and who transferred handwritten records to the digital, which records were used for the transfer, and which fields were populated, can augment our understanding of why collection data appears the way it does today, which

[13] For an overview of the history of BM departments from 1753–2002, see Wilson (2002, p. 379).

in turn informs how we use and approach the datasets held within departments and institutions (Acharya 2024).

As a means of making the process of data creation visible to the researcher, the V&A have included provenance statements for some of their object records that identify where the information has come from and when it was created. Provenance information is added to the 'Object History' free-text field in short, uniform statements. This is an outcome of the two aforementioned DTP research projects that examined the provenance of East and South Asian collections at the museum (Fraser 2023a, b; Gupta 2024). The intention of these provenance statements is to layer information on top of the existing digital catalogue entries (Fraser 2024), as seen in the entry for a Jingdezhen Porcelain Jar with brass mounts made during the Qajar dynasty in Iran (V&A Object number 1566–1876). The provenance statement within the 'object history' field reads: "Purchased from Robert Murdoch Smith, accessioned in 1876. This acquisition information reflects that found in the Asia Department registers, as part of a 2022 provenance research project". Below this is recorded "Bought in Iran, 8s.;;", a piece of cataloguing done prior to Fraser's research and pointing to the object's initial purchase in Iran by Colonel R. J. Murdoch Smith, Director of the Indo-European Telegraph Department in Tehran (V&A n.d.-a). Such provenance statements act to complement ongoing research and make data collection records more transparent (Fraser 2024).

Within collection databases, data absence, uncertainty and instability is unavoidable. For example, Phillipson (2019) situated "[…] the fallacies and omissions of the digitisation of paper records, as well as the incomplete survival (or even generation) of these initial records" as one of the most significant limitations of her numerical analysis methodology. Similarly, Mariani (2023, p. 64) introduced the categories of VISU—Vagueness, Incompleteness, Subjectivity and Uncertainty—to art provenance data, highlighting the varying levels of missing or partial data that can be found within databases. Indeed, collections databases are continuously evolving, with new research and material being added to them by curators, collection managers, catalogue managers, researchers, volunteers and, in some cases, communities. When using collection data as a research tool it is important to take into consideration and be transparent about the absences and limitations of data as a means of ensuring that analyses are not skewed or partial.

As noted above, MacDonald's (2023, p. 314) quantitative analysis of the sources that facilitated acquisitions of objects into the BM collection highlighted that acquisition sources associated with ten or fewer object records accounted for the "majority of individuals, groups and organisations who built up the BM collection". A similar finding was established in Wingfield's (2011) analysis of the English collections at the Pitt Rivers Museum, where over half of the acquisition sources for this type of material were associated in transactions of one or two objects, the majority of which were one-off acquisitions. Whilst the number of individuals linked to smaller or one-off donations is significant in these findings, the information held within the collection databases detailing who these individuals were is limited. Indeed, Lawther (2024, p. 14) argued that: "Museums have historically recorded the contributions of only a very few individuals – those with the influence, wealth and privilege to collect, donate and ensure their names were remembered. Yet there were usually many other individuals who contributed to historic collections".

Across the projects discussed in this chapter, the consideration of the absence of information relating to individuals in the databases is prevalent. Acharya's (2024) scoping of the BM data relating to women collectors of South Asian material has highlighted that until the 1980s most women's first names were missing from the database, and after the 1980s their first names were included but not their titles. Across her dataset, 13 per cent of women have a well-outlined biography based on their own identity and achievements, whilst twenty-one per cent are qualified in relation to a male relative and sixty-five per cent of the female biographies hold no information (Acharya 2024). Added to this, whilst the BM biographical authority holds the option to include an individual's gender, this is not consistently applied across biographies. As such when collecting data, searches by gender do not return all possibilities (Avery-Quash and Riding 2020).

Similar absences in biographical data were noted by Meghani (2024) in terms of searching for individuals with South Asian heritage on the BM database. Her research used the database as a starting point to identify collectors to include in her dataset. However, searches by nationality rely on this information being held within a biographical authority record, which is dependent on the cataloguer knowing the nationality of an individual at the time of creating a paper or digital record. Whilst this information within a contemporary context is possible to gather, it becomes more challenging for historical acquisitions. Meghani noted that cataloguers rely on sources that privilege renowned individuals to record their nationality, but for lesser-known individuals, this information is difficult to find. Therefore, her method for identifying such individuals relied on her own South Asian heritage, which facilitated identifying names within the database or other paper documentation that sounded South Asian (Meghani 2024). As she reflected, this is neither wholly accurate nor without its own bias, however, it draws attention to the advantages of researchers and collaborators having diverse backgrounds, networks and lived experience when consulting Eurocentric collection data (Meghani 2024; Dalal-Clayton 2024, p. 227).

These examples point to the need to use mixed methods to collect, sort and analyse digital collection data. This is particularly significant when the subject of analysis is not a privileged or celebrated individual and looks to include those marginalised or excluded from traditional retellings of an institution's acquisition history. As noted by Schmidt (2024), the application of a mixed method design can enable gaps to be identified and, where the information is available, filled. Schmidt's process for creating the EMCAM dataset, in line with the approaches of Dixon (2023), Acharya (2024), Fraser (2023a, b) and Meghani (2024), combined data collection from museum databases with archival research and literature, as a means of filling the gaps present within the digital record. Schmidt's (2024) use of mixed methods holds relevance as the research can help to further verify or correct incorrect information. However, this information is not always found within data collections' supporting paper documentation. Returning to the V&A provenance statements, we can see an example of a continued absence within the digital system despite the use of mixed method research. The 'object history' entry for a Chinese wooden Ruyi (a sceptre) notes "Acquisition method and source not identified in the Asia Department registers, accessioned in 1852" (V&A n.d.-b, c). This example reinforces Mariani's (2023) statement that data absence within collection and provenance data is unavoidable. If the data was not recorded at the time of an object's acquisition in a paper register, then it may remain irretrievable in the present day.

Examining why data appears as it does within digital databases does not only encompass how the material was transferred from paper to digital systems, but also the ontologies and languages used to record and describe objects within it. Berger (2024) questioned the naming of ethnographic objects and collections within museum documentation, and specifically the transfer of a sacred or spiritually meaningful object from one system of knowledge production and understanding into a museum system. For the majority of museum databases, information is recorded in a single language—normally that of the country within which the museum is located. Indeed, Schmidt (2023) has argued for the importance of accessing databases in their national language, as translated English versions do not hold the same quality of information. However, Berger's project goes further than this in questioning how to address the absence of Indigenous languages held within databases. Examining collections on a large scale makes it challenging to capture these potential data absences. Yet they are essential to consider when using data.

Combating this type of data absence is not straightforward and requires equitable and transparent methodologies to include multiple perspectives. The TaNC Discovery Project *Provisional Semantics* examined this question of how museums can ethically produce catalogue entries and interpretation labels, "particularly in relation to the histories and artworks of racialised and minoritised people" (Dalal-Clayton and Rutherford 2024, p. 222). Discussing the importance of co-produced, "slow cataloguing" of heritage collections within museum databases in the context of a limited project budget and timescale such as TaNC, Dalal-Clayton and Rutherford (2024, p. 233) argue, "This fundamental work is typically side-lined in favour of digitisation that privileges images and limited metadata, but in our view, cataloguing should be regarded as a core output for funded collections-based projects".

This statement is of course true outside of a funded-project context. Citing the 2023 BM thefts as museum documentation's "surprise entry into the public consciousness" Lawther (2024) noted how for too long documentation has been undervalued and under-resourced within museums and heritage organisations. She highlighted that this vital area of museum work has traditionally been thought of as "back of house" work, yet access to collections "is virtually impossible if the collections in question are not properly documented. It is truly impossible if they are not properly located" (Lawther 2024). Announcing the BM's plans to digitise fully its collections Jones, the Interim Director of the BM in 2023, stated,

> Over the next five years we have set ourselves the objective of improving and completing the online record of every object in the British Museum's collection. It is a big task, with 2.4m records to upload or upgrade, but more than half is already done and when it is

> finished it will mean that everyone, no matter where in the world they live, will be able to see everything we have – and use this amazing resource in a myriad of ways. (Jones 2023)

This task of digitising 2.4 million records in just five years raises the question of what it means within this context for the digital record of each object in the BM to be "complete". Within a limited timeframe, any metric of completeness will be based on digitisation and inventory rather than slow cataloguing parameters. This suggests a side-lining of the co-production of cataloguing that the *Provisional Semantics* project demonstrated is necessary for such systems to be truly inclusive, nuanced and accessible to global communities.

An example of this type of co-produced cataloguing[14] within the BM's database is outlined by Christophe et al. (2024, p. 99), part of the Hawaiian language advisory and research group named *Keaukāna'I*, with the goal of integrating *'ōlelo Hawai'I* (Hawaiian language) descriptors into the BM database for *mea kupuna* (Hawaiian ancestral treasures) physically held at the BM. As well as restoring the use of *'ōlelo Hawai'i* descriptors for the *mea kupuna*, their work also aimed to provide a culturally relevant context within the digital space and create inclusive pathways of access for Hawaiian language speakers and cultural practitioners (Christophe et al. 2024, p. 99). As they argue, "The 'authority', the 'control', and the 'preference' invoked are those of the institution, and those who authorise, control, and determine preferences are therefore the members of staff who work on these terminologies on behalf of the institution at any given time" (Christophe et al. 2024, p. 105). According to the *BM Collections Online* there are ca. 1080 objects associated with the place term "Hawaii", on which the *Keaukāna'I* group worked over a three-year period (British Museum n.d.). If considered alongside the digitisation of 2.4 million objects in five years, the group's integrations of co-produced knowledge reinforce the extent to which the disruption of institutional authority is a slow, critical and careful process.

A final key consideration within the context of this book is the levels of "open source" that these datasets are. The examples used in this chapter require institutional access through backend databases or online via institutional websites, and as such are not open-source data. Open-source data, as understood within this volume, is data that is both freely and publicly accessible *and* its use and re-use is not limited or restricted. In the case of the BM, the database has been accessible on the museum's website since 2007 through Collections Online. The information available on both is from the same dataset, and entries are not rewritten for the public facing output (MacDonald 2023, p. 307). Nevertheless, the BM does not publish all the

[14] Two other projects undertaken by the Santo Domingo Centre of Excellence for Latin American Research (SDCELAR) at the British Museum are using participatory and co-produced methods for the documentation of collections. See: 'A 'hearth to hearth': Afro-Colombian dialogues around culinary practices' https://www.sdcelarbritishmuseum.org/news/afro-colombian-dialogues-around-culinary-practices/; and 'Relating to the territory': Remapping Amazonian collections through co-curation and participatory documentation https://www.sdcelarbritishmuseum.org/news/reinterpreting-amazonia-baniwa-perspectives-on-indigenous-curation-2/ (both accessed 147.03.25).

variables found within the back-end dataset. For example, it does not publish addresses of acquisition sources, locations of objects not on display, nor prices paid for objects acquired by purchase (unless the historical information is entered in a curatorial comment). Added to this, the data on the BM website is published under a Creative Commons Attribution-NonCommercial-ShareAlike 4.0 International Licence,[15] meaning that the museum still has some control over the use and reuse of its data. All of the institutions considered within this chapter have websites where a public version of their data can be accessed. However, this access to museum collection data is in itself biased to large or national institutions. In their 2022 Commissioned Report 'Digital Collections Audit' Gosling et al. (2022, p. 33) cited that 80 per cent of records and digital collection data in the UK are held by larger institutions located within cities. This raises a wider issue of what information is both accessible and freely usable and redistributable in digital format to researchers. Within databases that are available, it is important to consider what is shared by institutions or indeed withheld from public access, who holds the authority to share culturally sensitive data, and what in turn this might mean for this type of research. Returning to Christophe et al. (2024)'s discussion of the institutional 'authority' and 'control' of data held within museum databases, a pertinent question comes to the fore of the extent to which community generated knowledge should be open and accessible to all. Whilst open-source data affords the access and reuse of material relating to collections, its misuse can act to reinscribe and reinforce pre-existing colonial biases (Roxanne 2019, p. 71). As such, it is imperative that cultural heritage databases and digital archives allow access to culturally sensitive material to be restricted based on the criteria of source communities, rather than the licences of the institutions that currently steward the objects.

6 Conclusion

This chapter has reviewed and critically reflected on the use of collection data to conduct large scale analyses of collection and provenance histories of museum collections. The rich examples drawn on throughout this chapter highlight the breadth of possibilities offered by using quantitative and data-informed methods in this context. I argue that when using digital databases understanding why they appear the way they do as well as considering their limitations, historical biases and omissions is imperative. However, when working at scale it is not always possible to capture the granular instances of historically biased or absent data. Looking across 4.5 million objects held in over 2 million object records in my research at the BM, I illustrated the importance of reading a database as a "representation of the collection" in question at the point of analysis, and considering the patterns gleaned from the data as a high-level illustration of how a collection has been shaped over time (MacDonald 2023, p. 306). At just over half of the estimated count of the BM collection, this can

[15] See https://www.britishmuseum.org/terms-use/copyright-and-permissions (accessed 14.03.25).

be read as a partial recommendation. Nevertheless, my analysis clearly outlined the caveats of the data being used, highlighting the importance of transparency when undertaking this work. This type of research is complex and not straightforward, yet it offers the opportunity to look at collections differently. In this way it acts as a starting point for further analysis; it is not intended to give a final definitive picture but rather suggests areas to be further considered through granular, mixed method analyses based on pattern recognition and statistical findings.

My purpose in this chapter is not to dissuade collections researchers from using the collection database as a source. Rather it is to highlight the importance of using this source, as with any, critically. In the conclusion to my 2023 article, I argued: "Using the database in the way outlined within this chapter, supported by more granular provenance research of object and individual collection histories, has the potential to allow us to contextualise and address these issues at a high level" (MacDonald 2023, p. 317). The issues that I was referring to relate to the question of how the BM collection has come into existence across its history. On reviewing the projects consulted for this chapter I wish to build on this argument. Using the database as a research tool to examine large-scale patterns holds the potential to facilitate new understandings of museum collections and the art and antiquities markets within which they are located. For this type of research to reach its full potential, museums and heritage organisations need to follow sector-wide calls for "slow cataloguing", with transparent, equitable building of these catalogues where collaboration with stakeholders is prioritised.

Acknowledgements The author would like to thank Kajal Meghani, Niti Acharya, Tullia Fraser, Dr. Freida Schmidt, Dr. Martin Berger, Sean Cham and Dr. Alicia Hughes for their contributions: they played a pivotal role in bringing this chapter to fruition.

References

Acharya N (2024) Gender, empire and material culture: women collectors of South Asia. University of Lincoln and British Museum

Adams-Campbell M, Falzetti AG, Rivard C (2014) Introduction: indigeneity and the work of settler archives. Settl Colon Stud 5(2):109–116. https://doi.org/10.1080/2201473X.2014.957256

Ahnert R, Ahnert SE, Coleman CN, Weingart SB (2020) The network turn: changing perspectives in the humanities. Cambridge University Press

Ahnert R, Griffin E, Ridge M, Tolfo G (2023) Collaborative historical research in the age of big data: lessons from an interdisciplinary project. Cambridge University Press

Avery-Quash S, Riding C (2020) Two hundred years of women benefactors at the National Gallery: an exercise in mapping uncharted territory. J Art Hist 23

Basu P (2024) Towards the pluriversal museum: from epistemic violence to ecologies of knowledge. Mus Soc Issues 18:1–16. https://doi.org/10.1080/15596893.2024.2333658

Berger M (2023a) Between canon and coincidence. J Art Mark Stud 7(1). https://doi.org/10.23690/jams.v7i1.147

Berger M (2023b) Archaeologist Martin Berger explores Latin American collections with an ERC grant. Universiteit Leiden https://universiteitleiden.nl/en/news/2023/09/archaeologist-martin-berger-explores-latin-american-collections-with-an-erc-grant

Bode K (2020) Why you can't model away bias. Mod Lang Q 81(1):95–124

British Museum (2022) Re-examining the history of the British Museum collection. https://www.britishmuseum.org/research/projects/re-examining-history-british-museum-collection#:~:text=Re%2Dexamining%20the%20history%20of%20the%20British%20Museum%20collection%2C%20is,1753%20right%20up%20to%202019
British Museum (n.d.) Collections online. https://www.britishmuseum.org/collection
Christophe A, Ha'alilio Solomon N, Kneubhul H, Donnellan V, Caldeira L (2024) Hosting and integrating a Hawaiian language taxonomy in the British Museum's collection database. Collections 20(1):96–121. https://doi.org/10.1177/15501906241234945
Collections Trust (2021) Decolonising the database. Collections Trust https://collectionstrust.org.uk/decolonisation/
Couldry N, Mejias U (2019) Data colonialism: Rethinking Big Data's Relation to the Contemporary Subject. *Television & New Media 20(4)*. https://doi.org/10.1177/1527476418796632
Dalal-Clayton A, Rutherford A (2024) Provisional semantics: addressing the challenges of representing multiple perspectives within public collections. Collections 20(1):221–240. https://doi.org/10.1177/15501906241232427
Delbourgo J (2017) Collecting the world: the life and curiosity of Hans Sloane. Harvard University Press
Dixon C (2023) Sailing the monsoon winds in miniature: understanding Indian Ocean boat models. British Museum Press
Driver F, Nesbitt M, Cornish C (eds) (2021) Mobile museums: collections in circulation. UCL Press
Drucker J (2021) The Digital Humanities Coursebook: An introduction to Digital Methods for Research and Scholarship. Routledge
Enlightenment Architectures (2017) Enlightenment architectures: Sir Hans Sloane's catalogues of his collections. https://reconstructingsloane.org/enlightenmentarchitectures/2017/07/19/featured-content/
Fraser T (2023a) Searching for dealers in the V&A's East Asia collection. https://www.vam.ac.uk/blog/projects/searching-for-dealers-in-the-vas-east-asia-collection
Fraser T (2023b). Dealing and dealers: the East Asia collection. https://www.vam.ac.uk/articles/dealing-and-dealers-the-east-asia-collection
Gosden C, Larson F (2007) Knowing things: exploring the collections at the Pitt Rivers Museum, 1844-1945. Oxford University Press
Goskar T (2021) Ananda Rutherford on provisional semantics, documentation and decolonising collections management. Curatorial Research Centre. https://curatorialresearch.com/decolonising-practice/ananda-rutherford-on-provisional-semantics-documentation-and-decolonising-collections-management/
Goskar T (2024) Museums will forget: critical approaches to catalog-centered historical research. Collections 20(1):156–176. https://doi.org/10.1177/15501906231220974
Gosling, K, McKenna G, Cooper A (2022) Digital Collections Audit https://museumdata.uk/wpcontent/uploads/2023/11/Digital-Audit.pdf
Greenwald D (2019) Painting by numbers: data driven histories of nineteenth-century art. Princeton University Press
Gupta S (2024) Researching South Asia provenance. https://www.vam.ac.uk/blog/museum-life/researching-south-asia-provenance
Hughes A, Metilli D (forthcoming) Investigating absences in cultural heritage collections: a Sloane Lab case study
Jones M (2023) Press release: British Museum sets out plans to digitise fully the collection. British Museum. https://www.britishmuseum.org/sites/default/files/2023-10/British_Museum_sets_out_plans_to_digitise_fully_the_collection.pdf
King JCH (1994) Ethnographic collections: collecting in the context of Sloane's catalogue of 'miscellanies. In: MacGregor A (ed) Sir Hans Sloane: collector, scientist, antiquary, founding Father of the British Museum. British Museum Press
Kizhner I, Terras M, Rumyantsev M, Khokhlova V, Demeshkova E, Rudov I, Afanasieva J (2020) Digital cultural colonialism: measuring bias in aggregated digitised content held in Google arts and culture. Digit Scholarsh Hum 36(3):607–640
Landström K (2021) Archives, epistemic injustice and knowing the past. Ethics Soc Welf 15(4):379–394

Lawther K (2024) Documentation is central to the work of museums. Museums Association. https://www.museumsassociation.org/museums-journal/opinion/2024/01/documentation-is-central-to-the-work-of-museums/#

Lok S et al (2022) First report—transforming collections: reimagining art, nation and heritage. Towards a national collection. https://zenodo.org/records/7153482

Lok S et al. (2023). Second report - transforming collections: reimagining art, nation and heritage. Towards a national collection. https://zenodo.org/records/7967237

MacDonald I (2023) Counting when, who and how: visualising the British Museum's history of acquisition through collection data, 1753-2019. J Hist Collect 35(2):305–320. https://doi.org/10.1093/jhc/fhac034

MacGregor A (ed) (1994) Sir Hans Sloane: collector, scientist, antiquary, founding Father of the British Museum. British Museum Press

Mak B (2014) Archaeology of a digitisation. J Assoc Inf Sci Technol 65(8):1515–1526

Manovich L (2020) Cultural analytics. MIT Press

Mariani F (2023) Introducing VISU: vagueness, incompleteness, subjectivity, and uncertainty in art provenance data. In: COMHUM 2022: Workshop on computational methods in the humanities, June 9–10 2022. Lausanne, Switzerland

Meghani K (2024) The global and the local: south Asian collectors at the British Museum. University of Brighton and British Museum

National Museums Scotland (n.d.) Search our collections. https://www.nms.ac.uk/search-our-collections

Nyhan J, James H, Vlachidis A, Flinn A, Pearlman N, Carine M, Hill J (2022) First report—Sloane lab: looking Back to build future shared collections. Towards a National Collection. https://zenodo.org/records/7152459

Nyhan J, Vlachidis A, Flinn A, Pearlman N, Carine M, Hill J (2023) Second report—Sloane lab: looking back to build future shared collections. Towards a National Collection. https://zenodo.org/records/7995409

Onuoha M (2016) The point of collection. Data and society: points. https://medium.com/datasociety-points/the-point-of-collection-8ee44ad7c2fa

Ortolja-Baird A, Nyhan J (2021) Encoding the haunting of an object catalogue: on the potential of digital technologies to perpetuate or subvert the silence and bias of the early-modern archive. Digit Scholarsh Hum 37(3):884–786. https://doi.org/10.1093/llc/fqab065

Padilla T, Allen L, Frost H, Potvin S, Roke E, Varner S (2019) Always already computational: collections as data final report. https://zenodo.org/records/7883759

Petch A (2006) Counting and calculating: some reflections on using statistics to examine the history and shape of the collections at the Pitt Rivers Museum. J Mus Ethnogr 18:149–156

Phillipson T (2019) Collections development in hindsight: a numerical analysis of the science and technology collections of National Museum Scotland since 1855. Sci Mus Group J, 12. https://doi.org/10.15180/191205

Plets G et al (2023) De-neutralising digital heritage infrastructures? Critical considerations on digital engagements with the past in the context of Europe. In Harrison R, Dias N and Kristiansen K (eds) Critical Heritage Studies and the futures of Europe. UCL Press, pp. 243–262.

Roxanne T (2019) Digital territory, digital flesh: decoding the indigenous body. APRJA 16(1). https://doi.org/10.7146/aprja.v8i1.115416

Rutherford A (2021) Decolonising the database. Museum Data Laundry. https://museumdatalaundry.com/2021/07/07/decolonising-the-database-event-centre-for-design-history-university-of-brighton-july-5th-2021/

Schmidt F (2023) Das Quantitative Ausmaß europäischer Aneignungspraktiken ndigener Kulturgüter Australiens: Eine Genderperspektive. https://zenodo.org/records/8319631/files/Schmidt-Aneignungspraktiken_v1_1.pdf?download=1

Schmidt F (2024) Quantifying colonialism: European practices of mass appropriation of indigenous cultural objects in 19th and 20th century Australia. Universität Greifswald

Scott B et al (2025) Collecting and cataloguing the world: the botanical collections of Hans Sloane (1660-1753). Syst Biodivers 21(1):2455440

Simpson K (2024) Technology of recovery and discovery: the poetics of "artefacts". ARTLAS 13(1):2

Turner H (2020) Cataloguing culture: legacies of colonialism in museum documentation. The University of Chicago Press

Vancisin T, Clarke L, Orr M, Hinrichs U (2023) Provenance visualisation: tracing people, processes and practices through a data-driven approach to provenance. Digit Scholarsh Hum 38:1322–1339

Victoria and Albert Museum (n.d.-a) Explore the collections. https://www.vam.ac.uk/collections?type=featured

Victoria and Albert Museum (n.d.-b) Jar. Explore the collections. https://collections.vam.ac.uk/item/O33615/jar-unknown/

Victoria and Albert Museum (n.d.-c) Ruyi. Explore the collections. https://collections.vam.ac.uk/item/O461145/ruyi-unknown/

Vlachidis A et al (forthcoming) A Data Atlas method for analysing and visualising dispersed cultural heritage collections

Wilkes E (2016) Polished axes: object biographies and the writing of world prehistories. University of Southampton and British Museum

Wilson D (2002) The British Museum: a history. British Museum Press

Wingfield C (2011) Donors, loaners, dealers and swappers: the relationship behind the English collections at the Pitt Rivers Museum. In: Byrne S et al (eds) Unpacking the collection: networks of material and social agency in the museum. Springer

Isobel MacDonald is a specialist in the history of European collecting with a specific interest in mapping the processes and history of museum collections and the use of data-driven and numerical methodologies to conduct provenance research at scale. Her other interests include private collections brought into the public domain, the social life of collections, the psychology of collecting, the collector's interior, and the display of collections. She is current Project Curator of Documentation and Recovery in the Department of Greece and Rome at the British Museum. Before this she was a Research Fellow in UCL's Department of Information Studies, working on the Towards a National Collection 'Sloane Lab: Looking back to build future shared collections' project. Between 2020 and 2022 she was Project Curator: History of Collection at the British Museum, London, where she pioneered the use of quantitative methods to research the large-scale history of acquisition of the BM collection through its collection data.

Open Access This chapter is licensed under the terms of the Creative Commons Attribution-NonCommercial-NoDerivatives 4.0 International License (http://creativecommons.org/licenses/by-nc-nd/4.0/), which permits any noncommercial use, sharing, distribution and reproduction in any medium or format, as long as you give appropriate credit to the original author(s) and the source, provide a link to the Creative Commons license and indicate if you modified the licensed material. You do not have permission under this license to share adapted material derived from this chapter or parts of it.

The images or other third party material in this chapter are included in the chapter's Creative Commons license, unless indicated otherwise in a credit line to the material. If material is not included in the chapter's Creative Commons license and your intended use is not permitted by statutory regulation or exceeds the permitted use, you will need to obtain permission directly from the copyright holder.

Cataloguing Authenticity: Exploring Collection Engagement with Forged Papyri Through Online Catalogues

Richard A. D. Bott

Abstract In recent decades, an ever-increasing number of institutional collections have begun to comprehensively digitise their collections and make the resulting catalogues available freely online. These online catalogues have brought to light a number of objects that may have previously never been displayed and have allowed scholars to better understand the nature and scope of collections around the world. As such, they are a valuable source of open access data for those interested in the trade in cultural heritage and history of collecting. Focussing on forged papyri, this chapter considers the communication of (in)authenticity in online collection catalogues to better understand the reliability of the information they provide. It will be shown that although issues with authenticity appear to be recorded more often than current research would perhaps suggest, the reasons for presenting material as either authentic or inauthentic are frequently not made clear. As such, when forgeries are mistakenly presented as authentic in these online catalogues, their authenticity appears secure and there is little indication to anyone working from the catalogue that there might be some form of issue.

1 Introduction

In the study of the trade in cultural heritage, exhibition catalogues have long been considered a valuable source of data (Brodie et al. 2013). These catalogues, which often contain substantial discussion about the listed objects, have provided data allowing scholars to explore issues like the incidence of provenance, trends in acquisitions, and even the methods used to discuss provenience (e.g. Chippindale and Gill 2000; Marlowe 2016). Importantly, many of these studies have noted concerns around authenticity, given that most of the objects in these catalogues cannot

R. A. D. Bott (✉)
Department of History and Archaeology, Levels 1 and 2, Arts Precinct 25B, Wally's Walk, Macquarie University, Macquarie Park, NSW, Australia
e-mail: richard.bott@mq.edu.au

© The Author(s) 2026
E. Smith, S. Austin (eds.), *Researching a Rigged Game: Digital Approaches to Tracing the Illicit Trade in Cultural Objects*, Studies in Art, Heritage, Law and the Market 11, https://doi.org/10.1007/978-3-032-02014-7_8

be traced to an excavation, are almost never raised (Chippindale and Gill 2000; Marlowe 2016). On the basis of such observations, it is often suggested institutional collections are unwilling to discuss forgeries (e.g. Bonnie et al. 2020; Chippindale and Gill 2000; Marlowe 2016), while Muscarella (2000) has claimed that some actively suppress discussion about forgeries in their holdings. However, exhibition catalogues typically feature prestigious objects, which are carefully selected and studied before display and a potential source of great embarrassment should they be found to be inauthentic. It is perhaps of little surprise then that issues around authenticity are not raised in these catalogues. Moreover, given their parochial focus, it is difficult to say whether conclusions drawn by studying exhibition catalogues are representative of approaches across a collection. To better understand how authenticity is approached across wider collection records, this chapter explores the recording of forged papyri by institutional collections within their online collection catalogues.[1] It will be argued that, contrary to popular belief, collections are often willing to publicly identify forgeries in their online catalogues. However, the cataloguing of the material itself obscures, by omission, information necessary to understanding the processes of authentication.

As is well-acknowledged, and certainly laid bare by the British Museum thefts made public in 2023 (see Brodie, this volume), the material that appears in exhibition catalogues only ever represents a minute part of an institution's total holdings. In recent years, however, many institutions have begun efforts to digitise their entire collections and make the results available as open access databases and catalogues.[2] Designed to provide insight into the wider collection, these catalogues appear as a cross between the card catalogues that came into use in the late nineteenth century and the print catalogues associated with exhibitions. Typically, they contain the basic 'tombstone' data—dates, provenience, support, script, dimensions, and so on—and have space for more discursive discussion, as one might find in an exhibition catalogue. Given the open access nature of these catalogues, and the reported unwillingness of collections to discuss issues of authenticity publicly, one may expect very few forgeries to be discussed openly within them. However, as this chapter will show, this does not appear to be the case.

The papyri featured in the following analysis are not the high-profile, high-end forgeries that collections invest large sums of money in to acquire or that scholars excitedly announce to the media (see e.g. Brodie and Kersel 2012; Schøyen 2016 on the interest generated by biblical forgeries).[3] Instead, like most forged papyri, they

[1] 'Institutional collections' is used here to describe libraries, museums, or university departments that hold papyrus collections. 'Papyrus' is used according to disciplinary convention, and refers to texts produced, typically with ink, on moveable supports including papyrus, ostraca, wooden tablets, and parchment. See, for example, Bagnall (2009), Choat (2019b).

[2] A number of online collection catalogues still require potential users to seek permission to publish images, and so may not meet the strictest definition of 'open access'. However, for purposes here, these are still described as open access provided use of the metadata is unencumbered.

[3] The definitions of the terms 'fake' and 'forgery' are subject to some debate in current scholarship. Most often the two terms are used interchangeably. However, Charney (2016) uses 'fake' to

are either of low production quality or replicate lower-value texts, like mummy labels. In other words, they are low-end forgeries. Low-end forgeries, much like their authentic low-end counterparts (i.e. coins, cylinder seals, utilitarian ceramics), have received little consideration in scholarship.[4] Instead, existing scholarship has largely focussed on forgeries like the Gospel of Jesus' Wife, the post-2002 Dead Sea Scrolls, or the James Ossuary. While such 'high-end' forgeries, when thought to be authentic, have the potential to greatly influence academia, they should not be taken as representative examples of text-bearing forgeries. Because most forgeries are low-end, they do not have the potential to influence and distort understandings of antiquity and art history in the same way the Gospel of Jesus' Wife papyrus may have. This does not mean, however, that they cannot corrupt scholarship. When high-end forgeries are published, they are often met with fanfare and are consequently subject to intense examination and debate, which then results in their (eventual) de-authentication. In contrast, when low-end forgeries are mistakenly published as authentic, they are often subsumed into large datasets used to inform largescale analyses and will rarely have their individual characteristics examined in detail. As such, they can become a small, but corrupting, part of the academic bedrock with the potential to undermine a multitude of studies that may draw on these datasets.

As online collection catalogues make a wider range of objects available, a growing number of researchers have turned to them to view objects for historical research or as new sources of data to further understand the trade of cultural heritage. It is, therefore, important to understand how institutional collections are communicating information and the reliability of these records. This chapter begins with a brief discussion of online collection catalogues as sources of data by which researchers have explored collecting and the market for cultural heritage. This is followed by a brief introduction to the Forging Antiquity database, which was used to identify suspected forged papyri in collections, and authenticity markers, methods of presentation used in catalogues that communicate an object is authentic. Finally, this chapter examines the presentation of known or suspected forgeries in various online collection catalogues. The findings of this research suggest that institutional

describe authentic objects fraudulently altered to increase their value, while 'forgery' describes objects created in fraudulent imitation of existing authentic objects. Durney and Proulx (2011) and Passas and Proulx (2011), on the other hand, define 'forgery' as an object produced as a copy of an original but passed on as the original, whereas 'fake' is used for a fabricated object made in the same 'style' as an original and passed as authentic. Chappell and Polk (2009) take a different approach and ground their definitions in an analysis of case law. Although there were some inconsistencies, they found that 'fake' was largely used to describe fraudulent works of art, while 'forgery' was largely reserved to describe documents and writing. Although substantial discussion of the nuances of these terms falls outside the scope of this chapter, it is worth noting that 'forgery' is preferred here to discuss papyri as it is the more commonly used term when discussing ancient texts.

[4] Several recent examinations of the antiquities trade suggest the number of low-end fakes and forgeries on the market is increasing, and that between 30 and 70 per cent of the antiquities currently available on the online market are likely to be inauthentic. See Brodie et al. (2019), Sargent et al. (2020). There is also a growing body of work that has recognised that much of the antiquities trade is built around the sale of low-end antiquities. See, for example, Greenland et al. (2019) and Topçuoğlu and Vorderstrasse (2019).

collections are more willing to identify forgeries in their collections than current research would suggest (e.g. Chippindale and Gill 2000; Marlowe 2016). However, these same collections do not typically record why an object should be seen as a forgery or, and more concerningly, as authentic. As such, those who might rely on these records are not provided with information that would allow them to properly understand how of if (in)authenticity has been confirmed. Ultimately, these findings suggest that when using online collection catalogues as sources of data, scholars need to be wary of the information they are presented with.

2 Online Collection Catalogues as Sources

For institutional collections, documentation is crucial to the successful management and navigation of their often-vast holdings. While documentation within a collection can take various forms—such as field notebooks, register books, letters between collection staff and donors—it is a collection's catalogue that often takes centre stage (Jones 2022). In the mid-nineteenth century, an increasing number of institutional collections recognised the need to formally document their holdings. With the need for greater organisation, collections began to supplement their early register books with card catalogues and indexes, which allowed already collected objects and new additions to be reordered and properly grouped (Jones 2022; Turner 2020).

The physical catalogues that emerged from this early period remained the standard until the 1960s, when institutional collections began to explore the potential of computers as tools for object registration and cataloguing (Turner 2020). These early digital catalogues were largely based on the existing card catalogues, and thus the data fields and indeed the data recoded often reflected the physical limitations of the individual cards (Jones 2022; Turner 2020). Information was regularly constrained to limited descriptive text, while attributed data and larger narratives about the objects were minimised if not ignored (Jones 2018; Jones 2022).[5] These digital catalogues were, like their physical predecessors, initially designed as internal reference tools to be used by curatorial staff. However, in recent years, amid growing calls for improved access and collection transparency, an ever-increasing number of museums and libraries have begun to undertake projects to comprehensively digitise their collections and make the resulting catalogues available freely online (Palombo and Yates 2023; Rafii 2023). Through these, researchers and the public have been able to access antiquities that in previous decades may never have been physically displayed (MacDonald 2023; Rafii 2023). For those interested in the trade in cultural heritage and the history of collecting, these catalogues have also been used as valuable sources of data by which collections, their history, and

[5] Following Chenhall and Homulos (1978, p. 209), attributed data is "the body of information about the specimen that was recorded at the time it was collected."

relationship to the market might be further unpacked (e.g. MacDonald 2023; Tsirogiannis 2017; Yates and Graham 2024).

Although online collection catalogues are valuable sources of data, it does need to be acknowledged that they only provide readers with information that the collection has decided to record and share. It is, after all, the institution in possession of the object that ultimately dictates how others can interact with its digital facsimile and what aspects of the object they are shown (Rafii 2023). As such, despite increasing pressure on museums to be transparent, it is rare to find complete provenance records in a collection database.[6] Even in instances where collections seemingly provide detailed catalogues entries, some have argued that these records are manipulated to obscure problematic parts of an antiquity's history (see e.g. Tsirogiannis 2017; Marlowe 2023).[7]

Finally, the construction of some online collection catalogues and databases does not allow forgeries to be easily accessed, even if they are already tagged as such. The *Papiri della Società Italiana* (PSI) database, for example, contains at least one forged papyrus: PSI inv.384. Under the '*Contenuto*' (Content) field on this forgery's specific catalogue page it is identified clearly as a "*Falso*" (Fake). Yet despite this papyrus being listed in this database, and labelled as a forgery, the provided search criteria make it difficult to find. If one wishes to narrow their search using the content field, they are presented with three options: '*Qualsiasi*' (Any), '*Documentario*' (Documentary), and '*Letterario*' (Literary). As such, although '*Falso*' is the '*Contenuto*' descriptor used for PSI inv.384, it is not an available search option. Even using the '*Testo libero*' (Free Text) field to search the database for '*Falso*' does not yield results. Unless one has an inventory number for the specific forgery or is willing to search through each individual catalogue pages, finding this forgery is difficult. It seems, then, that the possibility of searching specifically for forgeries was not properly considered when the database was being designed. Not every

[6] For example, in their survey of 67 small museums in the United States of America, Thompson and Priest (2021) found many museums were not in compliance with the American Alliance of Museums (AAMD) guidelines, which stated member collections "should make [publicly] available the known ownership history of archaeological material and ancient art in their collections" (AAM Board of Directors 2008). Provenance was routinely not easily accessible and around a quarter of the surveyed museums even claimed they would only make provenance available on an 'object-by-object' basis. For scholars looking to trace the illicit antiquities market, such a requirement further complicates research (Thompson and Priest 2021).

[7] Tsirogiannis (2017) identified several antiquities in the Toledo Museum of Art's collection, using the museum's online catalogue, that passed through either Robin Symes or Nicholas Koutoulakis (and Giacomo Medici)—infamous dealers well-known for their involvement in the illicit trade. This information, however, was not provided in the Museum's online catalogue. Yet, when Tsirogiannis requested any further provenance information about the objects the museum had, the museum quietly updated its online records, suggesting it had this information but avoided making it public until fielding Tsirogiannis' requests. More recently, Marlowe (2023) noted that, following calls for its repatriation and seizures by the Manhattan District Attorney of other pieces looted from Bubon, the Cleveland Museum of Art changed the description and provenience on the online catalogue page for a bronze sculpture widely thought to depict Marcus Aurelius and to have been looted from Bubon in modern Türkiye.

online catalogue is subject to such drastic issues. More often, collections have simply employed a variety of terms to identify their forgeries as inauthentic, which are not communicated to anyone wishing to search the catalogue. For instance, a single collection might label their forged papyri with a number of related, yet different tags: fake, forgery, modern, and composite. Without clarity before searching the catalogue, it is entirely possible these entries might be missed.

Online collection catalogues and databases are valuable, yet somewhat underutilised sources for understanding behaviours relating to the collection of illicit antiquities (see also Turner 2016). Although institutions can tailor the information available through catalogues to tell particular stories, and can therefore never be wholly objective, they do allow open access to material that might otherwise never be displayed (MacDonald 2023). As such, online open access collection catalogues can provide possible insight into how wider collections have been assembled, discussed, and approached by collections staff (Turner 2016).

3 The Forging Antiquity Database and Forged Papyri

Although not always a popular topic, as Wirth and Rasmussen (2023) have pointed out, fakes and forgeries have value as objects of study in their own right. When the right questions are asked, examinations of how fakes and forgeries have been collected and engaged with, can offer valuable insight into the history of collecting (e.g. Bott 2024), the history of a discipline, and even the development of specific methodologies central to the study of the ancient world (Choat 2019a). Despite the value of forgeries as objects of study, previous studies concerned with collecting behaviours have largely avoided forgeries and focussed on how cultural heritage have broadly been collected, at most highlighting behaviours which may facilitate market participants' interaction with fakes and forgeries, such as their willingness to interact with poorly documented materials (e.g. Chippindale and Gill 2000). Even studies that have engaged with forgeries specifically to explore how issues of authenticity have been approached by those involved in the collection of antiquities have typically been rather parochial in scope, focussing almost exclusively on high-end forgeries (e.g. Klawans 2023). While such approaches have highlighted a number of methodological shortcomings relating to how the authenticity of these objects has been confirmed and reported (e.g. Justnes and Rasmussen 2017), it is difficult to ascertain whether these identified issues are general or only applicable when considering high-end forgeries.

This chapter proposes a separate approach, which looks at a broader range of "low-end" forgeries that would not otherwise attract scholarly attention, in an effort to better understand how collections deal with issues around authenticity. Forgeries, by design, can be difficult to identify, especially when working across large corpora. Naturally, this has prevented many previous studies from being able to consider how forgeries fit within collection catalogues and market supply. Nørskov (2002, p. 258), for example, when charting the supply of Greek vases for the market, stated that she had "not been able to take forgeries into account, as an inspection of every item would have been necessary, which…would not be feasible." To counter this issue, this chapter draws examples from the Forging Antiquity database.

The Forging Antiquity Database is one of the key outcomes for the Australian Research Council Discovery Project, *Forging Antiquity: Authenticity, Forgery, and Fake Papyri*.[8] This database is a list of all forged papyri known to the project, most of which were identified through targeted searches of discipline specific databases like Papyri.info or Trismegistos, online collection catalogues, and reviews of relevant literature. Others were identified during research undertaken by various project members, or via communications with curators and other individuals not directly involved in the project. The first edition of the database was published online in 2019, listing 214 suspected forgeries.[9] A forthcoming updated public version will list more than 540 forgeries. It is from this expanded version that the forgeries discussed in the current chapter were identified.

Because of the scope of the Forging Antiquity project, the database only records forgeries said to be from Egypt and largely excludes epigraphic material. As such, some well-known forgeries like the post-2002 Dead Sea Scrolls are not included in the database, nor are certain groups of text-bearing forgeries like the numerous fake ushabti or scarabs that were especially common on the Egyptian antiquities market in the nineteenth century and first few decades of the twentieth (Potter 2022; Tomorad 2014, 2017). Data on forgeries that collections have identified but not properly accessioned, and therefore are not found in publicly accessible collection records, has not yet been systematically sought. The database thus privileges forgeries that have been publicly acknowledged and catalogued and does not include those which have not been. Nevertheless, the database has value in providing a tangible—if in some ways limited—dataset on which conclusions may be clearly based, as opposed to the impressionistic nature of much of the existing work on forgeries.

Before continuing, it is worth briefly outlining what types of forgeries are covered in this study. Broadly, forged papyri can be divided into three categories (Choat 2019b; Coles and Gallazzi 1981; Lucarelli and Choat 2023). The following is a simplified version of the typology currently being developed by the Forging Antiquity project, which will be set out clearly in a future treatment.[10] First are nonsensical script forgeries (e.g. Fig. 1). Nonsensical script forgeries are the most common type of forged papyrus and are so-called because the text they feature does not make sense. The complexity of nonsensical scripts varies significantly, ranging from examples where the forger has produced some form of imaginary script

[8] This Australian Government-funded project (DP170104196) is based at Macquarie University and overseen by Malcolm Choat, Rodney Ast, and Rachel Yuen-Collingridge. The author has been involved in the Forging Antiquity project since 2018 and has been working with the database since 2020. For further information about the project see https://www.forgingantiquity.com/

[9] The database is available openly at https://www.forgingantiquity.com/forgeries

[10] A working version of the Forging Antiquity typology, which illustrates the immense variation across forged papyri, is available at https://www.forgingantiquity.com/typology

Fig. 1 P.Mich.inv. 1793. Nonsensical (simulated) script forgery. University of Michigan Library, Papyrology Collection. Courtesy of University of Michigan Library Digital Collections

resembling little more than scribbles, to those that feature letters from an identifiable alphabet (e.g. Coptic), but their arrangement does not form known words. The second group of forged papyri are composite support and text forgeries. These are forgeries constructed from smaller authentic fragments, which are glued together to give the appearance of a larger, or even complete document (e.g. Fig. 2). Importantly,

Fig. 2 P.Mich.inv. 2216. Composite support and text forgery comprised of at least nine authentic fragments from different papyri. University of Michigan Library, Papyrology Collection. Courtesy of University of Michigan Library Digital Collections

the fragments used in the construction of forgeries belonging to this group feature authentic text, although a forger may add additional 'text' to make the forgery appear more complete.[11] Like nonsensical script forgeries, composite support and text forgeries sit on a complexity scale ranging from examples like P.Mich.inv.2216 (Fig. 2) at the low-end, to high quality examples where the papyrus fragments are carefully cut and aligned, like PUG.inv.1330 (PUG.5.225; Fig. 3) in the Università di Genova papyrus collection, at the other.[12] The final group dealt with here are

[11] There are some forgeries that would belong to the other two groups that may make use of a composite support (i.e. a number of blank fragments are glued together to make a large blank sheet). For example, a number of the forgeries produced by Constantine Simonides were made in this way (aspirational text using a composite support), while inv.EC3452 in the Egypt Centre Collection at Swansea University is an example of a nonsensical script forgery on a composite support. On Simonides and his forgeries see Choat (2019b) and Wasserman and Choat (2020).

[12] For the sake of clarity, several different methods of referring to papyri have been combined in this chapter where appropriate. Given the focus of this chapter, and the wider volume, when referring to specific papyri in text their collection number has been used as their primary identifier (always indicated by the inclusion of 'inv.'). However, when possible, their publication abbreviation, as per papyrological practice, is also included in brackets immediately following the inven-

Fig. 3 PUG 5.225 (PUG. inv. 1330). Composite support and text forgery comprised of four fragments (all outlined). La collezione dei Papiri dell'Università di Genova (University of Genoa, Papyrus Collection). Courtesy of Università degli Studi di Genova - Dipartimento di Antichità, Filosofia, Storia

aspirational script forgeries: so-called because the forger has 'aspired' to replicate an ancient language (although mistakes often creep in). Again, there is a large degree of variation across this group, which includes those forgeries where the forger has simply copied an authentic text, through to the rarest examples where the forger has composed an entirely new text that can be understood.

tory number. Finally, when referring specifically to publications including the papyri a citation in the author-date format is also provided. Thus, PUG.inv.1330 refers to the inventory number used by the Università di Genova papyrus collection, while PUG.5.225 refers to the published edition of this papyrus. The abbreviations used follow the *Checklist of Editions of Greek, Latin, Demotic, and Coptic Papyri, Ostraca, and Tablets* available at https://papyri.info/docs/checklist (last accessed 21/06/2024).

4 Markers of (in)Authenticity

To unpack the presentation of forged papyri in collections, the analysis below considers the selections of authenticity markers visible in the catalogue pages for suspected forged papyri. Within the context of the market, which has been the focus of most previous discussions, authenticity markers can best be understood as techniques used by dealers and auction houses, including those operating on platforms such as eBay, in the presentation of antiquities that communicate to potential buyers an object is authentic (Villa 2021). These markers can take various forms and do not need to specifically discuss 'authenticity'. Sellers may employ any number of them in various combinations depending on the resources available, the venue of sale, and the likely customer. The images used in auction catalogues, for example, give buyers "the impression of walking into a 'fine art' gallery" and allow specific aspects of the antiquities that are considered typical of the relevant culture or object type, and thus indicative of authenticity, to be highlighted (Villa 2021, p. 143). In other instances, sellers may stress specific provenances that show an antiquity was once owned by a discerning collector or institutional collection, which helps communicate the value and thus authenticity of the object (Yates 2015). Ultimately, understanding what authenticity markers are favoured by the market and how they function has allowed scholars to assess the importance of academic expertise to the market, the various ways in which provenance and provenience are discussed, and, more broadly, how sellers navigate the uncertainty that stems from dealing with undocumented and likely looted materials (Brodie 2011a; Fay 2011; Villa 2021; Yates 2015).

Within the market environment, buyers rely on the information provided by sellers to guide their purchases (Mackenzie et al. 2020), and the choices made by sellers when presenting material impact how buyers engage with that object. Likewise, within a museum context, the institution takes on the role of educator with the public relying on the choices made by the institution when presenting antiquities to guide their interaction with them (Gurian 1991; Marlowe 2013). In both settings, decisions are made regarding how material is presented that impact how it is received. As such, given the similarities in the modes and style of communication it certainly seems appropriate to consider how institutional collections communicate authenticity by examining their use of authenticity markers when presenting forged papyri in their online catalogues (see also Joyce 2013).

Of particular importance to the following analysis is one of the most frequently discussed categories of authenticity markers: demonstrations of expertise. Within the market, indicators of expertise have manifested in a variety of ways. In some cases, sellers present themselves as the expert. Various dealers, for example, claim they hold higher degrees in a relevant field, cite published comparisons in the object descriptions in their catalogues to demonstrate their familiarity with the object, or refer to their longevity as a successful dealer in their catalogues or on their website (Dundler 2021). Auction houses, on the other hand, have in-house experts to call upon (Tremain 2017), and include descriptions written by these experts as part of the marketing of cultural heritage. Perhaps the most well-known marker used by sellers, but certainly the most criticised, is the market's use of university or museum-based experts to authenticate the offered antiquity (Brodie 2011a, b; Justnes and Rasmussen 2017; Smith and Thompson 2023; Yates 2015). How this is achieved can, of course, vary. If an antiquity has been published or exhibited, this is often stressed and operates as a form of "authentication by proxy" (Yates 2015, p. 75; see also Gill and Chippindale 1993; Tremain 2017). In other cases, the seller may claim an antiquity has been examined by an expert (Brodie 2011a, b), although the results of this examination are not always made explicitly clear nor is the expert always named. Ultimately, although displays of expertise can vary, they are one of the most effective categories of authenticity marker available to both the market and collections.

5 Analysis

5.1 Forged Papyri in Collection Catalogues

The following analysis is built around a sample of six open access collection catalogues: the Michigan University Papyrology Collection (Michigan Collection), the Yale Papyrus Collection (Yale Collection), the University of Pennsylvania Museum of Archaeology and Anthropology (Penn Museum), the Louvre; the Rijksmuseum van Oudheden in Leiden (RMO), and the British Museum. These collections were chosen for study following a consultation of the expanded version of the Forging Antiquity database, and a secondary search of the respective collections' online catalogues. These initial probes indicated that these collections maintained an online, open access, catalogue that contained observable forgeries. Each collection holds, at a minimum, 13 suspected forgeries known to the Forging Antiquity Project, which, importantly, can be found in their online catalogues.[13] Admittedly this is a rather small sample and so more extensive empirical research is needed. However, given the variety of collections covered, the results of the following analysis are revealing. Beyond sample size, the approach employed here does have several other limitations worth noting. First, this analysis relies heavily on forgeries already identified, either by the collection or in print, as forgeries. As such, it is almost certain that there are forgeries that have either not yet been identified as forgeries or that identifications have not been properly communicated, as Muscarella (2000) warns, which have been missed by this survey.[14] Secondly, given the size of the surveyed

[13] There are a number of collections that hold, or have been discussed in publication (often during the mid-twentieth century) as holding, interesting forgeries that were not considered for discussion here. Either these collections do not currently have an online catalogue, or their forgeries are not currently listed in their online catalogue. As such, it is not clear if they still own these forgeries.

[14] It is also possible that there are forgeries in these collections which have been identified, but these identifications have not yet been publicly known for whatever reason (i.e. waiting to publish).

collections, the various material supports covered, and the different terms used to identify forgeries it is also possible that forgeries correctly identified as inauthentic have also been missed.

Across the six collection catalogues considered, using the Forging Antiquity database, 254 examples of potential forged papyri were identified. Most entered collections in the first half of the twentieth century, although some were acquired as late as the 1990s. Determining whether these were suitable examples and whether the owner had identified the relevant papyrus as either authentic or a forgery was not always clear, and so occasionally the author made an informed decision. For example, under the 'Conservation Status' field on the catalogue page for P.Mich.inv.2216 (Fig. 2), the papyrus was described as comprised of "Medium-brown small pieces of papyri (c. 9) joined together to make a new sheet (composite fragment, doctored)." While the image makes it clear this piece is a composite support and text forgery, this description is the only indicator provided by the collection that this papyrus is a forgery. Traditional descriptive terms like 'fake' or 'forgery' are not used. Although there is a small possibility that a member of the public reading this may assume the construction happened in antiquity, for purposes here this description was recorded as an example of a collection identifying a forgery as inauthentic. More problematic were objects like the mummy labels in the Louvre. As will be discussed in greater detail later, a number of these were identified by Baratte and Boyaval (e.g., 1976) as being either forgeries or authentic. Because there is evidence that these pieces could be inauthentic, but these concerns were not communicated in the catalogue, such papyri were recorded as examples of suspected forgeries being presented as authentic.

Where possible, identifications made either in print or in the catalogues were checked by the author. At the time of writing, by way of example, a mummy label in the British Museum (inv. EA26450; T.BM Arlt 127) was identified by the author as being mistakenly labelled as inauthentic (Arlt 2011, pp. 87–88 no. 127). The British Museum was contacted for clarification and the author was informed that there was no evidence supporting the identification of this label as a forgery and it was seemingly a mistake made when cataloguing the label. It should be noted that some of the forgeries counted as part of the sample no longer exist as forgeries, having been disassembled after acquisition. For purposes here, these have been counted as forgeries and when institutions indicate that the authentic fragments came from a forgery, these have been recorded as instances of an institution identifying a forgery publicly. Only 15 instances of collections not acknowledging that authentic fragments came from the disassembly of a forgery were identified (14 in the Yale Collection and one in the RMO Collection), although more cases almost certainly exist.

Of the 254 suspected forgeries identified, just under seventy per cent (n = 175) were acknowledged in the respective collection's online catalogue as being inauthentic at the time of writing (Fig. 4). Of these, eighty (45.71 per cent) were

Examples of Forgeries Identified as Forgeries in Collection Catalogues			
Collection	# of (Suspected) Forgeries	# Identified as Forgeries	% Identified as Forgeries
Michigan Collection	56	56	100
Yale Collection	24*	7	29.17
Penn Museum	13	5	38.46
Louvre	61	9	14.75
RMO	54*	52	96.30
British Museum	46	46	100
Totals	254	175	68.89

Fig. 4 Forgeries Identified as Forgeries in Collection Catalogues. * Denotes totals that include disassembled composite support and text forgeries that are known to the present author but not mentioned in the collection catalogue

identified with language that indicated the object in question was a definite forgery,[15] while the remaining forgeries were identified as inauthentic but with varying degrees of certainty, which ranged from stating a papyrus is probably or possibly a forgery, noting some of the text is modern but the support and remaining text are ancient, to describing the papyrus with language that makes it clear the papyrus is not authentic but distances it somewhat from ideas of deception (i.e. P.CtYBR inv. 1865 in the Yale Collection is described only as "Modern").

In many cases, the inconsistent labelling appears to stem from the initial cataloguing of the forgeries or potential errors introduced when updating records. For example, across the current Michigan Collection catalogue, over fifty per cent of the forgeries are listed with some form of doubt expressed in the identification.[16] Although not evident from the catalogue pages themselves, when the related archival material is checked, it becomes clear that much of this can be traced to Harold Bell's initial descriptions of papyri in the British-American Papyrus Syndicate distribution lists, which were prepared rapidly and not designed to be catalogues but nonetheless formed the basis of Michigan's initial catalogue (Bott 2024; Heilporn 2000). Due to the size of the acquisitions made by the Syndicate and the speed with which Bell had to work, some of his identifications indicate that a papyrus is 'probably a forgery'. Because Bell's descriptions were usually repeated verbatim in Michigan's internal records, these labels have simply persisted through the various stages of digitising the catalogue with no further research to revisit the uncertainty.[17]

[15] That is, a papyrus was labelled as a 'forgery' with no additional qualifiers.

[16] This ranges from noting that a papyrus is "Probably a forgery rather well done" to the more simplistic "Modern fake?" See, for example, P.Mich.invs.3856 and 1793.

[17] The Michigan Collection acquisition reports can be found at: https://apps.lib.umich.edu/papyrology-collection/acquisition-reports (last accessed 06/05/2024).The Michigan Collection has made a substantial portion of the archival material relating to many of its papyrus acquisitions freely

5.2 Forged Papyri Listed as Forgeries

At their core, collections are seen by many as amalgamations of expertise (Biedermann 2022). As such, the public often assumes without question that the information they are provided by a collection must be true (Biedermann 2022). Perhaps unsurprisingly, then, the most common marker used to indicate the validity of the decision to identify a papyrus a forgery in collection catalogues is the projection of expertise. The suggestion of expertise in the deauthentication of forged papyri is projected in catalogue pages in a variety of methods. Most simply, this is achieved merely by labelling a papyrus a 'fake' or 'forgery' (or some variation thereof). In fact, 73.89 per cent of the time a forgery was identified as a forgery in one of the viewed catalogues, the only information conveying this to the reader was a simple descriptor listed somewhere on the catalogue page, without further indication as to who identified these papyri as forgeries or why. That this occurs is somewhat unsurprising as collection catalogues have historically included very little additional detail beyond basic descriptive data and an object's location within a collection (Jones 2018, 2022; Lawrence 1990). Although this might be standard behaviour within many collections, it does make it difficult to trace the sources of information. This is especially concerning when considering collections of cultural heritage, as many of these collections are predominantly comprised of undocumented materials, often acquired from the market (e.g. Chippindale and Gill 2000; Marlowe 2016). Because so few objects can be traced confidently to their origin, fakes and forgeries can enter the streams that supply these collections with relative ease. Without further clarification, it is difficult to determine if the reported identifications have come from the market or if they have been independently confirmed by experts (Marlowe 2016).

Within an online catalogue, applying a forgery label in isolation is both dependent on and reinforces the often-acknowledged power dynamic between a collection and the public (Alpers 1991; Gurian 1991; Kersel 2021). Because institutional collections are typically seen as both trustworthy and experts, the reputation of the institution acts in these situations as a proxy for arguments of inauthenticity and validates the provided information (Biedermann 2022; Gill and Chippindale 1993; Palombo and Yates 2023; Yates and Smith 2022). Readers are expected to accept the label simply because it has been applied by (someone working for) an important cultural institution (Kersel 2021; Palombo and Yates 2023).

Not every collection relies only on simple labels to convey inauthenticity: some demonstrate the expertise of collection staff by providing additional information, which can vary in detail, to expand on and explain the basic descriptors. Most often, collections provide brief descriptions of the issues with the papyrus that led to it being tagged as a forgery. The text of P.CtYBR.inv.5207, in the Yale Collection for instance, is described as "Random lettering perhaps imitating Coptic but including

available online. It should also be noted that the RMO has begun to digitise its vast archives. The results of this ongoing project can be found at: https://archieven.rmo.nl/ (last accessed 06/05/2024).

S from the Roman alphabet". Additionally, the description for the text of P.CtYBR. inv.5268 reads: "Strange symbols in three short lines. The lines each end before the break and were likely written after the papyrus was damaged. A probable fake." This practice is taken a step further in one instance by the British Museum, with EA76746 described as a fake "with [the] remains of 26 horizontal lines of fake Aramaic script, written in black ink… The text is a forgery imitating Aramaic writing (checked by Irving Finkel)." Although useful, this practice was infrequent across the studied catalogues, with just under twelve per cent (n = 20) of the catalogue pages for the recognised forgeries identifying the individual responsible for classifying the object as inauthentic.

Moreover, in some cases, when previous hard copies of a collection's internal catalogue could be consulted, it appears that the name listed with the information likely referred to the party who copied that data over when the catalogues were being digitised, not necessarily the original source of the identification. This appears to be the case for many of the forgeries listed in the Michigan Collection catalogue. As noted above, this catalogue relies heavily on Bell's initial identifications made in the 1920s and 1930s. However, Bell is almost never named as the identifying party, and instead the initials of the person seemingly responsible for copying the information over is often listed under the object description. That this might be the reason for naming an authority was never made clear, and anyone consulting the catalogue may very well assume the named party was responsible for the identification.

Just as publications can play an important role in the marketing of cultural heritage in auction and dealer catalogues—helping assure buyers the object in question is authentic—so too can they be used to help communicate the inauthenticity of a forgery in collection catalogues. If an antiquity features within a publication as authentic, then this is widely considered proof that the object is indeed authentic (Brodie 2009, 2011a, 2016; Gerstenblith 2022; Villa 2021; Yates 2015). Likewise, although many forgeries are not published, providing bibliography for those that have can act as a justification for identifying a papyrus as a forgery. This is perhaps most evident in the British Museum catalogue. As part of her 2011 study of the British Museum's demotic mummy labels, Arlt (2011) published several forged labels as forgeries. This publication is linked clearly with the forgery tag in the 'Curator's Comments' field on the catalogue page for these mummy labels (e.g. BM EA26674; T.BM Arlt F163). In lieu of a description indicating why these labels are problematic, the reader is offered a simple comment: "Forgery (Arlt 2011)." While such a comment is sparse in detail, it does convey to the reader that these labels are considered forgeries, and further discussion can be found in Arlt's work. In other instances, however, the link between the forgery identification and the publication may only be implied, with a bibliography listed on a catalogue page of a labelled forgery but no indication as to what the listed publications argue. References to external demonstrations of expertise are used in these instances as shorthand justifications for identifying these pieces as forgeries.

Another method used by collections to justify the labelling of a papyrus as a forgery is the use of comparative analysis, although this is rare. Such an approach is commonly used in scholarship in attempts to prove either authenticity or inauthenticity.[18] When employed within collection catalogues, the analysis tends to be between forgeries with the reader informed that the papyrus displays characteristics similar to another known forgery. One may consider, for example, the catalogue page for P.Mich.inv.4218, which reads:

> (Prof. Claudio Gallazzi's communication to N. Litinas) Fake sandal made from mummy cloth and papyrus, made in late 19th century, parallel to many such "artifacts" made at this time and sold to the European institutions. The letters (?) ink that we can see on the external leaf are just a fake. The same appears in a "mummy", published by Cl. Gallazzi in ZPE 112 (1996), pp. 183–188.

This information, provided to the Michigan Collection by Gallazzi and then shared on the catalogue page, informs the reader why this piece has been labelled a forgery, while also situating it within an identified means of forgery production through comparison with known examples. Although helpful, the use of comparisons found in external collections is extremely uncommon in the online catalogues: this was the only identified such instance across the six sampled catalogues. More often, although still far from regular, collections discuss similarities between forgeries within the immediate collection. The Penn Museum, for instance, has at least eight forged papyri seemingly produced by the same forger. On the catalogue pages for almost every papyrus, the reader is informed that other pieces in the collection also feature "the same peculiar script" along with the corresponding inventory numbers (Penn Museum invs. E16305K, E16411A, E16411B, E16411C, E16540A, E16540B, E16540C, E16757). While not every one of these eight forgeries has been identified by the Penn Museum as a forgery, an interested reader can quickly come to this conclusion for themselves because these links have been made apparent.

Identifying forgeries produced by the same forger across and within collections can increase awareness of a particular type of forgery or a particular forger's style. This, in turn, may help collections ensure forgeries produced by the same forger or using a similar method are identified quickly. Despite the benefits of such practice, however, the limited examples of this practice found across the surveyed catalogues suggests that collection staff rarely confirm (in)authenticity via comparison with other known forgeries. As such, there are instances where forgeries seemingly produced by the same forger, but spread across collections, have been identified inconsistently. In some cases, this inconsistency is minor. P.Mich.inv.1793 in the Michigan Collection catalogue, for example, is labelled as a "Modern fake?" Yet P.Mich. inv.2422, which features a similar script presumably produced by the same forger, is labelled clearly as "Two fake papyri, joined together with a tie." In other cases, however, the differences are much more substantial, as the extensive yet poorly defined corpus of forgeries produced by Hufuta of Hawara illustrates. Hufuta was identified by John de Monins Johnson (1914) in his report on the Egypt Exploration Fund's (now Society) excavations at Antinoë. Usefully, Johnson notes that one of Hufuta's distinctive forgeries had been published as authentic: P.Strassb.1.39A

[18] See, for example, Askeland's (2015) use of a clear forgery, the so-called Lycopolitan John fragment, to argue in favour of the Gospel of Jesus' Wife fragment being viewed as a forgery.

(Strasbourg, Bibliothèque Nationale invs. P.Gr. 762 & 788; Preisigke 1912). While Hufuta has been mentioned several times in general studies of papyrus forgery, no one has yet attempted to chart his forgeries and he is mentioned only twice in collection catalogues.[19] Because of this seeming lack of wider awareness, some collections have identified Hufuta's characteristic forgeries as forgeries, while others have misclassified them as either Aramaic or magical texts (cf. Penn Museum inv. E16525 described as written in "cursive Armenian (?)" and Pierpont Morgan inv. MS M.662B.14c labelled a forgery). Because collections have not typically sought to identify and link forged papyri that share similar characteristics across collections, or at least not communicated these links in their catalogues, the wider identification of these forgeries has been limited.

5.3 *Forgeries as Authentic Papyri*

Although many forged papyri are identified as such in the catalogues of institutional collections, some are recorded as authentic. The presentation of papyri as authentic in these venues tends to occur in a relatively uniform manner through the use of a fairly standard descriptive framework, even accounting for formatting idiosyncrasies across collections' catalogues. Papyri are typically assigned to a time period, a comment is made on the nature of the support (i.e. papyrus, ostracon, wood), the language or script is noted (e.g. demotic, Greek, Coptic), the content of the text might be identified,[20] a bibliography identifying publications that have featured the papyrus is often included if applicable, and provenance and provenience information can be provided. By describing forgeries using these same criteria, collections situate them alongside their authentic counterparts, without making an explicit comment relating to the specific object's authenticity. In doing so, collections create a "false equivalence" between (suspected) forgeries and authentic papyri with forgeries appearing functionally indistinguishable from their authentic counterparts (Palombo and Yates 2023, p. 267).

[19] The British Museum catalogue, after O'Connell (2014), suggests inv. EA75191 was produced by Hufuta. Following enquiries made by the author, the catalogue for the Egypt Centre Collection at Swansea University now also suggests inv. EC3452 may also be a forgery made by Hufuta. The corpus of forgeries produced by Hufuta will be the subject of a future treatment by members of the Forging Antiquity Project.

[20] The identification of content can range from general statements about the genre of text (e.g. receipt) through to full transcriptions and translations.

5.3.1 Engaging with Scholarship and Displays of Expertise

As discussed, when attempting to present an antiquity in a certain way, one of the most valuable tools available to justify this decision is engagement with scholarship. Listing publications that have featured an antiquity can help facilitate researchers' inquiries, demonstrate the importance of the object to the public, inform readers where a collection may have received information about the artefact, and of course help communicate (in)authenticity (Griffiths 2010). However, while the inclusion of bibliography is often a crucial part of the cataloguing process, and space is often left for such information in a catalogue page schema, there is no certainty that collections will engage with scholarship that suggest a papyrus might be inauthentic. In the Louvre's Département des Antiquités égyptiennes, for example, there are at least 57 mummy labels that have been identified as forgeries, or potential forgeries, in various publications (e.g. Almásy-Martin 2019; Baratte and Boyaval 1976, 1979).[21] These concerns of inauthenticity, however, are consistently not communicated in the Louvre's catalogue. Of the 57 suspected forgeries, only five had any indication that they are thought to be inauthentic, and one of these is listed as authentic albeit with some forged text.[22] The remaining 52 mummy labels are presented unequivocally as authentic. That these pieces are presented as unquestionably authentic is curious given that all bar five of the catalogue entries for the 'authentic' mummy labels include a reference in the bibliography section to the publication that suggested they were inauthentic.[23] Similarly, an ostracon (inv.F 1901/1.178; SB 10.10581) in the RMO collection was listed as a possible forgery by Pieter Sijpesteijn (1968) and a certain forgery by Bagnall et al. (1980) but is presented as authentic in the RMO's collection database despite both publications being listed on the catalogue page. In these examples, the relevant collection avoids mentioning that the authenticity of these objects has been questioned and instead only provides a reference to the publication(s) that raises these doubts, putting the onus on the reader to find this information.

Interestingly, many of the publications referenced avoided speaking of the authenticity of the suspect objects in absolutes. In the case of the Louvre's mummy labels, many were published under the heading "*ETIQUETTES PRESUMEES FAUSSES*" ('Labels suspected to be false'; Baratte and Boyaval 1979, pp. 288–289). Likewise, Sijpesteijn (1968) suggests the RMO's ostracon is either a forgery or an incomplete, incorrect receipt. These uncertainties, however, are not reflected in the respective catalogue pages. This notably differs from the recording of the viewed forgeries as inauthentic. When identifying a papyrus as inauthentic, collections often included some form of doubt in the labelling (i.e. 'probable forgery' or

[21] There are an additional four that have apparently not been published, but the Louvre's description of them would suggest they might be partial forgeries.

[22] Louvre invs: E 9335, E 9345, E 9355, E 9370, and E 9372.

[23] It is also worth noting that one of the scholars who first edited these mummy labels, and identified a number as problematic was François Baratte who worked at the time as a curator at the Louvre.

'possible forgery'). In contrast, when a suspected forgery was presented as authentic across the surveyed catalogues there was never any doubt expressed to suggest the authenticity of the papyrus in question might not be completely secure, despite there being grounds for concern.[24]

The limited engagement with the listed publications also means problematic, but illuminating, relationships between objects within the same collection may go unreported. For example, several of the Louvre's mummy labels were identified by Baratte and Boyaval as being of dubious authenticity because they featured identical (or nearly identical) text as another label in the collection: "Même main et même texte que le no 432 [= Louvre inv.293; T.Mom.Louvre 432]. L'un des 2 est un faux" ('Same hand and same text as no 432. One of the two is a fake'; Baratte and Boyaval 1976, p. 240 no. 945 = Louvre inv.E 9642; T.Mom.Louvre 945). Despite the clarity of such a relationship, and the fact other forms of relational metadata, such as names, have been indexed and exist in a searchable format in the Louvre's current catalogue, these problematic links are never made explicit and the respective labels are still presented as authentic. Given that the replication of text is often an indicator of inauthenticity for mummy labels (e.g. Boyaval 1987; Clarysse 1980; Vleeming 2011), by not making these links clear, information that throws the authenticity of these labels into question is somewhat obscured.

That collections may not engage with scholarship that suggest certain papyri might be forgeries does not mean that expertise is not visible within a catalogue. When suspect objects are presented as authentic, some form of expertise is always visible. As noted above, this can be as simple as a papyrus being presented as authentic and assigned to a (usually broad) time period, with the catalogue itself functioning as a proxy of authority and validating this information. In a few cases, however, more detailed information about a papyrus that seemingly better links it to antiquity is offered. For example, the catalogue pages for two of the Louvre's mummy labels, also featuring identical text (Louvre invs. E 20480 & E 20482; T.Mom.Louvre 1204 & 1206), provide information about the individual named on the labels: *"Achillas; Pakaltiane (père); Paniskos (brasseur)"* (see also Baratte and Boyaval 1979).[25] The translation of the names, and brief description of the familial dynamic, gives the illusion that these identical labels have been examined and are in fact authentic. The only way for an uninformed reader to learn that there is something problematic with these labels is to check the publication listed in the bibliography at the bottom of the catalogue page themselves or to come across both labels

[24] The closest example of a collection presenting a papyrus as authentic albeit with some doubt identified was P.CtYBR inv.578 in the Yale Collection catalogue. This papyrus is described as either a "Magical text (?) or fake (?)." There is, however, no further information like a date that would suggest this papyrus is authentic.

[25] The transcription and translation of the label was originally published by Baratte and Boyaval (1979, p. 286). The entry for T.Mom.Louvre 1204 (inv. E 20480) just included the translation, while the entry for T.Mom.Louvre 1206 (inv. E 20482) pointed out that the text between the two labels was the same and suggested "L'un des deux est un faux" ('One of the two is a fake').

in the database separately and recognise the connection themselves. Hardly a transparent undertaking.

The catalogue examples discussed above featured references to publications that suggested the relevant materials were forgeries, even though these arguments were not engaged with by the respective collection. This, however, is not a universal practice. The Yale Collection catalogue includes two nonsensical forgeries, P.CtYBR.inv.1797 and P.CtYBR.inv.1798, which are presented as authentic papyri. As is common, the reader is informed these objects have been published, with a short bibliography provided for each. These, however, are not exhaustive, missing references to the various publications that have discussed these pieces as forgeries (see e.g. Choat 2019b; Coles and Gallazzi 1981; Horak 1991, 2001).

The presentation of publications in the catalogue pages for these forgeries is interesting, with the catalogue distributed by the bookseller Hans Kraus to initially market these papyri featuring in the listed bibliography. To produce this catalogue, Kraus employed Theodore Petersen, an expert in the Coptic language, to help identify the papyri, and Petersen's identifications in the market catalogue have clearly influenced the presentation of the papyri in the collection catalogue. Following Petersen (1964, pp. 46–47 no. 59–60), these forgeries are both identified as magical texts written in an "Uncertain language." With no evidence provided to support viewing these papyri as authentic, even in the initial dealer catalogue, the acceptance of Petersen's dating and suggestion these forgeries were 'magical' texts is a clear example of how the uncritical acceptance of market-derived information by collection staff can result in forgeries entering collections as authentic objects. Regarding the unlisted publications, it is unclear whether omissions like these are the result of ignorance, resourcing issues, or if they are deliberate. Irrespective of the reason, however, the authenticity of these papyri is presented as secure.

In almost all catalogues considered, a specific field was available for collection staff to include more substantial discussion beyond the basic descriptive data found in the tombstone portion of a catalogue page.[26] Marlowe (2016) has argued that these discursive spaces play an important function within catalogues, allowing collections to communicate the reliability of a supplied provenience or provide comparanda to demonstrate the authenticity of unique, unprovenienced objects. However, just as Marlowe noted that this space was underutilised to justify the reliability of 'said to be from' proveniences, so too was it underutilised in the recording of forgeries. While occasionally collections used this space to provide longer explanations to justify labelling papyri as fakes, no evidence was found of them using this space to justify presenting a papyrus of disputed authenticity as authentic. As such, several collections described nonsensical scripts as 'magical', 'Armenian', or even 'unidentified' but still authentic, without providing comparanda or arguments in support. In fact, the only evidence ever provided on a catalogue page to justify presenting suspected forgeries as authentic is the recording of those

[26] The 'tombstone' portion of a catalogue page (or a museum label) refers to the section where basic metadata is often recorded (i.e. date of manufacture, findspot etc).

limited publications that included the suspected forgeries as authentic and, in the case of some objects in the Louvre catalogue, the inclusion of details derived from the text.

While around 70 per cent of known forgeries were labelled as forgeries, it is not quite so easy to affix a percentage to the number of forgeries presented as authentic. In large part, this is due to how institutional collections have dealt with composite support and text forgeries. Because composite support and text forgeries are comprised of authentic fragments, they have often disassembled after they were identified as inauthentic (Leach and Tait 2000; Choat 2019b). In such cases, the forgery itself no longer exists, and the various authentic parts are accessioned separately. Although some collections note when fragments came from a forgery, many do not. This makes it almost impossible to determine how many composite support and text forgeries a collection may have acquired or how certain collections have approached them. In theory, one could request conservation records, but, assuming such records exist and a collection would be willing to share them, to do so one would still first need to know what objects might be useful, which is difficult to determine. Other times, market records may bear fruit, provided one can access them. This is well-illustrated by the Yale Collection's 1964 acquisition of a collection of papyri offered by Kraus.

In 1964, Edwin Beinecke purchased the collection with the express purpose of immediately donating it to Yale. Of the one-hundred and forty lots offered by Kraus (most of which contained a single papyrus), around twenty appear to have been forgeries; 14 of these were composite support and text forgeries. The composite support and text forgeries were initially identified by Petersen (1964, introductory note), who noted they were "pasted together [in modernity out] of heterogenous pieces by wily Arab traffickers." Almost none, however, now exist in the state in which they were acquired (P.CtYBR.inv.1827 appears to be the only composite support and text forgery from this acquisition still intact). That the forgeries ever existed can only be found by examining the original dealer catalogue: such information is missing from the collection catalogue. While, again, the decision to disassemble these forgeries is understandable, by not communicating that the various fragments were once part of larger forgeries, potentially valuable information about their provenience and provenance is obscured. For instance, Albarrán Martínez (2023) has identified a number of composite support and text forgeries, which appear to have been the product of a single forger (or workshop) operating in the mid-twentieth century. Many of the fragments used in the examples discussed by Albarrán Martínez feature internal markers that link them to the archaeological site of Bawit in Egypt. On this basis, she suggested that the forgeries were likely produced somewhere nearby or by someone who had direct access to material being looted from the site. If accurate, Albarrán Martínez's findings, while also offering further insight into the nature of forgery production in the mid-twentieth century, may provide evidence helping to link other papyrus fragments used in such forgeries that are without the internal indicators of (likely) provenience to the site. Given that several of the forgeries acquired by Yale also contain fragments with text suggesting they came from Bawit, it is possible that at least some of the composite support and text forgeries acquired in the 1964 acquisition were also produced by this unknown forger. Further study of the various fragments certainly seems to be warranted.

Finally, because many identifications are routinely presented without supporting evidence, it can be almost impossible to determine whether forgeries were listed erroneously as authentic as the result of lax record keeping, information lost over time, or deliberate efforts by staff to avoid admitting that the collection has forgeries. While some have suggested that collection staff manipulate catalogue information to deliberately obscure problematic provenances and concerns around authenticity (Marlowe 2023; Muscarella 2000), it could not be determined how frequently such behaviour occurred for papyri on the basis of information derived from the catalogues. Moreover, on several occasions various collections were contacted and asked whether they had further information in their internal records to explain why a forgery had been presented as authentic. Of those that responded, none reported the existence of such records.

Perhaps the clearest examples of probable lax record keeping influencing how forgeries are presented were found in the Penn Museum catalogue. There are a number of nonsensical forgeries in the collection listed as authentic, which apparently display text in 'Armenian'. Between 2009 and 2010, Kraft (2010a, b) began to go through the papyri held by the Penn Museum. He correctly identified these pieces as featuring "fake writing." Although the Penn Museum is aware of Kraft's work, and his lists were still available online at the time of writing,[27] the Museum's collection catalogue has not been updated to reflect his findings nor is there any way to navigate from the catalogue to Kraft's lists. As such, unless one finds Kraft's lists independently and then checks them against the Penn Museum catalogue or has the necessary knowledge to identify the forgeries themselves, the provided interpretation of these papyri still appears correct.

5.4 *Value and Authenticity*

As part of his discussion on the prevalence of 'forgery culture', Muscarella (2000) claimed curators have presented material they know to be inauthentic as authentic to keep the donor happy, to protect predecessors, or to avoid negatively impacting their own professional reputation. Additionally, Potter (2022, p. 280) noted that museum staff were more willing to discuss inauthentic objects if they were described as 'tourist art' rather than as examples of fakes or forgeries because of the "perceived negative connotations surrounding the display of a fake." This belief that collections avoid acknowledging forgeries, or even suppress discussion about their existence, out of embarrassment or concern for the repercussions is often present in the scholarship examining the relationship between collections and the market, yet

[27] They are even hosted by the University of Pennsylvania, see: https://ccat.sas.upenn.edu/rak//ppenn/museum/fake/000-index.htm

the results of this survey suggest collections are more open about their forgeries than typically thought. Brodie (2019), however, has noted that several examinations of the market have not properly considered a range of potential casual factors when trying to explain their findings.

With this in mind, it is worth reiterating that most forged papyri are low-end, and a great number were acquired as part of large purchases undertaken with little oversight on the part of the buyer (see e.g. Bott 2024). When high-end forgeries, like a post-2002 Dead Sea Scroll, are found to be inauthentic after acquisition, institutional collections are effectively forced to admit they were duped into parting with a large sum of money and (often) that several noted experts were wrong. In contrast, there is considerably less reputational risk in admitting most forged papyri are inauthentic because they are lower in quality and financial value. It is possible, then, that it is not simply 'forgeries' in general that institutional collections are reticent to acknowledge, but rather those forgeries, which would be valuable if authentic. To a point, this is supported by the examples identified here of suspected forgeries being presented as authentic by collections despite their authenticity having been questioned or disputed elsewhere. Although these objects should still be understood as low-end forgeries, by virtue of either their manufacture or the involvement of academics in their sale they appear to have more intellectual value than the nonsensical script forgeries frequently identified almost immediately upon collection (Bott 2024). That is, they are of greater perceived value than many of the papyri tagged by collections as forgeries. For example, the Louvre only identified those labels featuring clearly nonsensical text as forgeries: those that have translatable text continue to be presented as authentic, even when obvious duplicates exist in the collection. Understandable text can more readily be situated within the framework by which the ancient world is understood, and these papyri are thus more likely to be valuable to academics, collections, and the market. A slightly different example can be found in the Yale Collection, where several nonsensical forgeries acquired from the dealer Kraus, continue to be presented as authentic papyri. It appears, here, the reception of these objects, including the interpretation of them as 'magical texts' has been heavily influenced by their presentation on the market. As noted above, prior to Yale's acquisition, Kraus employed Petersen, an academic expert, to help produce a sales catalogue. The descriptions Petersen (1964) provided were often substantial and, where the forgeries are concerned, created contexts within which the abnormalities that identify these pieces as forgeries could be explained. In doing so, Petersen made these forgeries appear as genuine products of antiquity, even if his analyses were problematic (Brodie 2011a).

While further research into the internal workings of the authentication processes employed by collections is required to properly understand why some of these papyri have been recorded as authentic, it seems possible, and perhaps likely, that the ambiguity created by the value of these objects also played a role. Yale's nonsensical Kraus forgeries were authenticated by an expert before entering the collection, while the RMO's ostracon and the Louvre's mummy labels were published as either forgeries or authentic texts. Even if incorrect, there were then grounds to argue that these papyri could be viewed as authentic. Moreover, it has been suggested that once published as authentic, antiquities become protected and will continue to be accepted without further analysis by others (Marlowe 2013, 2015). That is, the burden of proof is raised following publication, with those who wish to prove inauthenticity required to prove unequivocally that an antiquity is a fake even if no clear attempts to demonstrate authenticity have been made. Given some of the examples viewed here, however, it seems the limits for forgeries to receive such protection might be lower than often assumed. Most of the Louvre's disputed mummy labels were, after all, not necessarily published outright as authentic texts. It seems possible, therefore, that the simple fact that these forgeries entered a collection and were catalogued as authentic, raised the evidentiary threshold required to identify these objects as forgeries.

6 Conclusion

Although many studies considering the relationship between academia, institutional collections, and the market for cultural heritage have discussed the risk of encountering forgeries when interacting with undocumented objects, few have sought to provide evidence that might allow their statements to be confirmed. Using data derived from open access catalogues, this chapter has sought to offer some clarity to the situation and has explored the presentation of problematic papyri by collections to better understand how collections engage with, respond to, and record objects of dubious authenticity. A number of the examples discussed here provide cause for cautious optimism: for the most part, and certainly contrary to conventional wisdom, it appears that collections are in fact willing to acknowledge the existence of forgeries within their holdings, albeit with some variation between collections. Just under seventy per cent of the suspected forgeries across the six collections surveyed were identified publicly as inauthentic by the holding collection, and three of the six collections identified, at a minimum, an astonishing ninety-six per cent of their suspected forgeries as being of dubious authenticity. Although the forgeries held by these collections are often rather obviously inauthentic, these numbers are certainly promising.

Despite this, the ways in which both authenticity and inauthenticity for the forgeries considered was presented in the catalogues is concerning and illustrative of the wider issues with opacity within scholarship and trade of cultural objects. In their related studies examining exhibition catalogues, Marlowe (2016), and Chippindale and Gill (2000) noted that collections often do not provide evidence to justify claims made about the provenience ascribed to undocumented objects. As they highlight, this makes it difficult for outsiders to determine how reliable this information is, with market hearsay conflated with verifiable information. Similarly, when collections presented forged papyri as authentic, there was no evidence that the collection had considered the possibility of forgery and disproved such concerns, or any indication as to who was responsible for the identification. As such, it is often unclear exactly why a collection treated a papyrus as authentic. While the forgeries considered here are unlikely to be mistakenly accepted as authentic by anyone looking for publishable material, this is a further reminder that the information recorded by institutional collections, which both the public and academy could rely on, is not always infallible—especially where market derived antiquities are concerned. The results are, however, slightly better when collections identify forgeries. Although most of these identifications go no further than stating a papyrus is a 'forgery', a little over twenty-five per cent of the catalogue pages for these papyri included some form of explanation to justify this identification. While somewhat positive, this practice needs to become far more widespread to ensure the reliability of catalogue pages as sources of information for the listed antiquities, especially if the results presented here are in anyway indicative of how institutional collections approach fakes and forgeries more broadly.

Ultimately, this study suggests the treatment of forgeries within collections is perhaps more nuanced than typically portrayed. While some collection staff may be uncomfortable discussing the existence of forgeries (Potter 2022), many can be found relatively easily through the online catalogues most collections maintain through simple key-word searches. Despite this, collections do not typically indicate why they believe certain papyri to be forgeries and provide almost no evidence to justify the cataloguing of suspect objects as authentic. The issue, then, is not that collections are unwilling to admit to owning forgeries, but that they do not record and share why material is believed to be (in)authentic. In doing so, illicit cultural heritage objects are able to appear more secure than they should, and forgeries can become harder to identify. Although the behaviours discussed above can be considered broadly typical of cataloguing practice, they have made it difficult to accept collection data, especially for low-end objects, as reliable. To be able to properly understand and appreciate an object, one needs to be able to appreciate both the object itself and any data associated with it (Jones 2022). When one cannot be certain that even the authenticity of an object in a collection catalogue is secure, even if known forgeries are typically made apparent, the remaining data becomes immediately concerning. For those who wish to use online collection catalogues as a source of data to study the trade in cultural goods, this is worth remembering.

Acknowledgements This chapter is derived from research undertaken for my PhD thesis at Macquarie University, and under the auspices of a research project on forged papyri funded by the Australian Research Council (DP170104196). I would like to thank Malcolm Choat for reading earlier versions of this chapter and making helpful suggestions; Ziming Liu cast her critical eye over this work and her insightful comments and suggestions that improved it greatly; Ewan Coopey for his willingness to engage in numerous conversations about the place of open access data in archaeology; and finally, CJ Bott for her helpful proofreading. All remaining mistakes are my own.

References

AAM Board of Directors (2008) Archaeological material and ancient art. https://www.aam-us.org/programs/ethics-standards-and-professional-practices/archaeological-material-and-ancient-art/

Albarrán Martínez MJ (2023) Baouît dan la Collection Palau-Ribes: Un Corpus en Progression. In: Calament F, Hadji-Minaglou G (eds) Bouît (2008–2018), Panorama et Perspectives: Rencontre de l'Archéologie et des Textes. Institut Français d'Archéologie Orientale, pp 185–197

Almásy-Martin A (2019) Some remarks on bilingual mummy labels in the louvre. In: Naether F (ed) New approaches in demotic studies: acts of the 13th international conference of demotic studies. De Gruyter, Berlin, Germany, pp 16–38

Alpers S (1991) The museum as a way of seeing. In: Karp I, Lavine S (eds) Exhibiting cultures: the poetics and politics of museum display. Smithsonian Institution, pp 25–32

Arlt C (2011) Deine Seele möge leben für immer und ewig: Die demotischen Mumienschilder im British Museum. Peeters

Askeland C (2015) A Lycopolitan Forgery of John's Gospel. New Testament Studies 61:314–334

Bagnall R (2009) Introduction. In: Bagnall R (ed) The Oxford handbook of papyrology. Oxford University Press, pp xvii–xxi

Bagnall R, Sijpesteijn P, Worp K (1980) Greek Ostraka: a catalogue of the collection of Greek Ostraka in the National Museum of antiquities at Leiden with a chapter on the Greek Ostraka in the Papyrological Institute of the University of Leiden. Terra Publishing

Baratte F, Boyaval B (1976) Catalogue des Étiquettes de Momies du Musée du Louvre (C.E.M.L.) - Textes Grecs - 3ème Partie. Cahiers de Recherches de l'Institut de Papyrologie et d'Égyptologie de Lille 4:173–254

Baratte F, Boyaval B (1979) Catalogue des Étiquettes de Momies du Musée du Louvre (C.E.M.L.) - Textes Grecs - 4ème Partie. Cahiers de Recherches de l'Institut de Papyrologie et d'Égyptologie de Lille 5:237–339

Biedermann B (2022) Museum objects and fake authenticity. Representing museum objects in the virtual space. In: Salvadori M, Bernard E, Zamparo L, Baggio M (eds) Beyond forgery: collecting, authentication and protection of cultural heritage. Padova University Press, pp 217–226

Bonnie R, Goff M, Jokiranta J, Thomas S, Tzoref S (2020) Professional ethics, provenance, and policies: a survey of Dead Sea scrolls scholars. Dead Sea Discov 27(2):257–293

Bott R (2024) "Miscellaneous fragments" and "specimens of the Faker's art": Fake Papyri and the British-American papyrus syndicate. Bull Am Soc Papyrologists 61:335–367

Boyaval B (1987) Conclusions Provisoires sur les Étiquettes de Momies en Langue Grecque. Bulletin de l'Institut Français d'Archéologie Orientale 86:37–89

Brodie N (2009) Consensual relations? Academic involvement in the illegal trade in ancient manuscripts. In: Green P, Mackenzie S (eds) Criminology and archaeology: studies in looted antiquities. Hart Publishing, pp 41–58

Brodie N (2011a) Congenial bedfellows? The academy and the antiquities trade. J Contemp Crim Justice 27(4):408–437

Brodie N (2011b) The market in Iraqi antiquities 1980-2009 and academic involvement in the marketing process. In: Manacorda S, Chappell D (eds) Crime in the art and antiquities world: illegal trafficking in cultural property. Springer, pp 117–133

Brodie N, Dietzler J, Mackenzie S (2013) Trafficking in cultural objects: An empirical overview. In: Manacorda S, Visconti A (eds) Beni Culturali e Sistema Penale. Vita e Pensiero, pp 19–30

Brodie N (2016) Scholarly engagement with collections of unprovenanced ancient texts. In: Almqvist K, Belfrage L (eds) Cultural heritage at risk: the role of museums in war and conflict. Ax:son Johnson Foundation, pp 123–142

Brodie N (2019) Through a glass, darkly: long-term antiquities auction data in context. Int J Cult Prop 26:265–283

Brodie N, Kersel M (2012) The social and political consequences of devotion to biblical artifacts. In: Lazrus P, Barker A (eds) All the king's horses: essays on the impact of looting and the illicit antiquities trade on our knowledge of the past. The Society for American Archaeology Press, pp 109–125

Brodie N, Batura O, Op't Hoog G, Slot B, van Wanrooij N, Yates D (2019) Illicit trade in cultural goods in Europe. European Commission

Chappell D, Polk K (2009) Faker and forgers, deception and dishonesty: an exploration of the murky world of art fraud. Curr Issues Crim Just 20(3):393–412

Charney N (2016) Introduction to part I. In: Charney N (ed) Art crime: terrorists, tomb raiders, forgers and thieves. Palgrave Macmillan, pp 2–7

Chenhall R, Homulos P (1978) Museum data standards. Mus Int 30(3–4):205–212
Chippindale C, Gill D (2000) Material consequences of contemporary classical collecting. Am J Archaeol 104(3):463–511
Choat M (2019a) Dating papyri: familiarity, instinct and guesswork. J Study New Testament 42(1):58–83
Choat M (2019b) Forged antiquities: the case of papyrus fakes. In: Hufnagel S, Chappell D (eds) The Palgrave handbook on art crime. Palgrave Macmillan, pp 557–586
Clarysse W (1980) Forgeries and ghost-names. Zeitschrift für Papyologie und Epigraphik 40:76–77
Coles R, Gallazzi C (1981) Papyri and Ostraka: alterations and counterfeits. In: Bresciani E, Geraci G, Pernigotti S, Susini G (eds) Scritti in Onore di Orsolina Montevecchi. Clueb, pp 99–105
Dundler L (2021) #antiquitiesdealers: the construction and use of "dealer persona" in the internet market for antiquities. In: Oosterman N, Yates D (eds) Crime and art: sociological and criminological perspectives of crimes in the art world. Springer, pp 45–61
Durney M, Proulx B (2011) Art crime: a brief introduction. Crime Law Soc Chang 56(2):115–132
Fay E (2011) Virtual artifacts: eBay, antiquities, and authenticity. J Contemp Crim Justice 27(4):449–464
Gerstenblith P (2022) Hobby lobby, the Museum of the Bible, and the law: a case study of the looting of archaeological artifacts from Iraq. In: Hashemi L, Shelly L (eds) Antiquities smuggling in the real and virtual world. Routledge, pp 59–95
Gill D, Chippindale C (1993) Material and intellectual consequences of esteem for cycladic figures. Am J Archaeol 97(4):601–659
Greenland F, Marrone JV, Topçuoğlu O, Vorderstrasse T (2019) A site-level market model of the antiquities trade. Int J Cult Prop 26(1):21–47
Griffiths A (2010) Collections online: the experience of the British museum. Master Drawings 48(3):356–367
Gurian EH (1991) Noodling around with exhibition opportunities. In: Karp I, Lavine S (eds) Exhibiting cultures: the poetics and politics of museum display. Smithsonian Institution Press, pp 176–190
Heilporn P (2000) The Michigan papyrus collection. In: Clarysse W, Verreth H (eds) Papyrus collections world wide: 9–10 March 2000 (Brussels-Leuven). Universa Press, pp 55–60
Horak U (1991) Fälschungen auf Papyrus, Pergament, Papier und Ostraka. Tyche: Beiträge zur Alten Geschichte Papyrologie und Epigraphik 6:91–98
Horak U (2001) Fälschungen auf Papyrus, Pergament und Papier. In: Gastgeber C (ed) Kopie und Fälschung: Katalog zur Ausstellung. Akademische Druck- und Verlagsanstalt, pp 51–59
Johnson JD (1914) Antinoë and its papyri: excavation by the Graeco-Roman branch, 1913-1914. J Egypt Archaeol 1(3):168–181
Jones M (2018) From catalogues to contextual networks: reconfiguring collection documentation in museums. J Arch Rec Assoc 39(1):4–20
Jones M (2022) Artefacts, archives, and documentation in the relational museum. Routledge
Joyce R (2013) When is authentic? Situating authenticity in the itineraries of objects. In: Geurds A, van Broekhoven L (eds) Creating authenticity: authentication processes in ethnographic museums. Sidestone Press, pp 39–57
Justnes Å, Rasmussen JM (2017) Soli Deo Gloria? The scholars, the market, and the dubious post-2002 dead sea scrolls-like fragments. The Bible and Interpretation. https://bibleinterp.arizona.edu/articles/2017/11/jus418014
Kersel M (2021) Redemption for the Museum of the Bible? Artifacts, provenance, the display of the dead sea scrolls, and bias in the contact zone. Mus Manag Curatorship 36(3):209–226
Klawans J (2023) The magic of forgery: patterns of distraction in the authentication of suspicious objects. J Anc Judaism 14(2):291–320

Kraft R (2010a) Papyri with pseudo-writing in the University of Pennsylvania Museum Collection. https://ccat.sas.upenn.edu/rak//ppenn/museum/fake/000-index.htm

Kraft R (2010b) Provisional list of Papyri in the University Museum. https://ccat.sas.upenn.edu/rak//ppenn/museumlist.htm

Lawrence G (1990) Object lessons in the museum medium. In: Pearce S (ed) Objects of knowledge. The Athlone Press, pp 103–124

Leach B, Tait J (2000) Papyrus. In: Nicholson P, Shaw I (eds) Ancient Egyptian materials and technology. Cambridge University Press, pp 227–253

Lucarelli R, Choat M (2023) The art of forgery in the manuscript culture in antiquity. In: Lucarelli R, Stadler M (eds) The Oxford handbook of the Egyptian book of the dead. Oxford University Press, pp 556–567

MacDonald I (2023) Counting when, who and how: visualizing the British museum's history of acquisitions through collection data, 1753-2019. J Hist Collect 35(2):305–320

Mackenzie S, Brodie N, Yates D, Tsirogiannis C (2020) Trafficking culture: new directions in researching the global market in illicit antiquities. Routledge

Marlowe E (2013) Shaky ground: context, Connoisseurship and the history of Roman Art. Bloomsbury

Marlowe E (2015) Said to be or not said to be: the findspot of the so-called Trebonianus Gallus status at the metropolitan museum in New York. J Hist Collect 27(2):147–157

Marlowe E (2016) What we talk about when we talk about provenance: a response to Chippindale and Gill. Int J Cult Prop 23(3):217–236

Marlowe E (2023) A Cleveland Museum's bad bet on a looted Roman statue. Hyperallergic. https://hyperallergic.com/862516/cleveland-museum-bad-bet-looted-roman-statue/

Muscarella O (2000) The lie became great: the forgery of ancient near eastern cultures. Styx Publications

Nørskov V (2002) Greek vases in new contexts: the collecting and trading of Greek vases - an aspect of the modern reception of antiquity. Aarhus University Press

O'Connell (2014) John de Monins Johnson 1913/14 Egypt exploration fund expedition to Antinoupolis (Antinoë), with appendix of objects. In: Pintaudi R (ed) Antinoupolis II. Firenze University Press, pp 415–425

Palombo C, Yates D (2023) Digital transit ports for the illicit trade in antiquities: the case of the 'afghan Genizah'. Digit Scholarsh Hum 38(1):257–276

Passas N, Proulx B (2011) Overview of crimes and antiquities. In: Manacorda S, Chappell D (eds) Crime in the art and antiquities world: illegal trafficking in cultural trafficking. Springer, pp 51–67

Petersen T (1964) Catalogue 105: a collection of papyri: Egyptian, Greek, Coptic, Aramaic, dating mainly from the second century B.C. to the eighth century A.D. H. P. Kraus

Potter D (2022) A note on modern (fake) Shabtis as tourist art. J Egypt Archaeol 108(1–2):279–286

Preisigke F (1912) Griechische Papyrus der Kaiserlichen Universitäts-und Landesbibliothek zu Strassburg. J. C. Hinrichs

Rafii R (2023) Digitizing manuscripts and the politics of extraction. In: Brodie N, Kersel M, Rasmussen JM (eds) Variant scholarship: ancient texts in modern contexts. Sidestone Press, pp 235–245

Sargent M, Marrone JV, Evans AT, Lilly B, Nemeth E, Dalzell S (2020) Tracking and disrupting the illicit antiquities trade with open-source data. Rand Corporation

Schøyen M (2016) Acquisition and ownership history: a personal reflection. In: Elgvin T, Davis K, Langlois M (eds) Gleanings from the caves: dead sea scrolls and artefacts from the Schøyen collection. Bloomsbury, pp 27–32

Sijpesteijn P (1968) Griechische Ostraka aus dem "Rijksmuseum van Oudheden" in Leiden, IV. OMRO 49:1–17

Smith E, Thompson E (2023) A case study of academic facilitation of the global illicit trade in cultural objects: Mary Slusser in Nepal. Int J Cult Prop 30(1):22–41

Thompson E, Priest M (2021) Small museums, big problems: failure to comply with the American Alliance of museums' policies on archaeological materials and ancient art. In: Oosterman N, Yates D (eds) Crime and art: sociological and criminological perspectives of crimes in the art world. Springer, pp 191–206

Tomorad M (2014) "Shabtis"—ancient Egyptian funerary figurines: classification (typology), findings and role in ancient Egyptian cults and beliefs during late and Graeco-Roman periods. In: Lekov T, Buzov E (eds) Cult and belief in ancient Egypt: proceedings of the fourth international congress for young Egyptologists, 25–27 September 2012, Sofia (pp. 139–150). Bulgarian Institute of Egyptology

Tomorad M (2017) Shabtis from the museum and private collections in Croatia: dating and typological study. In: Tomorad M, Popielska-Grzybowska J (eds) Egypt 2015: perspectives of research. Proceedings of the seventh European conference of Egyptologists (2nd-7th June, 2015, Zagreb – Croatia). Archaeopress, pp 217–238

Topçuoğlu O, Vorderstrasse T (2019) Small finds, big values: cylinder seals and coins from Iraq and Syria on the online market. Int J Cult Prop 26(3):239–263

Tremain C (2017) Fifty years of collecting: the sale of ancient Maya antiquities at Sotheby's. Int J Cult Prop 24:187–219

Tsirogiannis C (2017) Nekyia: museum ethics and the Toledo museum of art. J Art Crime 17:77–87

Turner H (2016) Critical histories of museum catalogues. Mus Anthropol 39(2):102–110

Turner H (2020) Cataloguing culture: legacies of colonisation in museum documentation. UBC Press

Villa F (2021) Authentically exotic and authentically beautiful: constructing the authenticity of Peruvian antiquities at Sotheby's and eBay. In: Oosterman N, Yates D (eds) Crime and art: sociological and criminological perspectives of crimes in the art world. Springer, pp 135–152

Vleeming S (2011) Demotic and Greek-demotic mummy labels: and other short texts gathered from many publications (Short Texts II 278-1200). Peeters

Wasserman T, Choat M (2020) "The cable guy": Constantine Simonides and codex Mayerianus. Bull Am Soc Papyrologists 57:177–218

Wirth C, Rasmussen JM (2023) The value of forgeries for historical research. In: Brodie N, Kersel M, Rasmussen JM (eds) Variant scholarship: ancient texts in modern contexts. Sidestone Press, pp 169–188

Yates D (2015) Value and doubt: the persuasive power of 'authenticity' in the antiquities market. Parse J 2:71–84

Yates D, Graham S (2024) Reputation laundering and museum collections: patterns, priorities, provenance, and hidden crime. Int J Herit Stud 30(2):145–164

Yates D, Smith E (2022) Museums and the market: passive facilitation of the illicit trade in antiquities. In: Stevenson A (ed) The Oxford handbook of museum archaeology. Oxford University Press, pp 87–97

Richard A. D. Bott is an ECR in the Discipline of History and Archaeology, School of Humanities at Macquarie University and a member of the Forging Antiquity Project. His recently completed dissertation examined the collection of forged papyri during the 20th century by institutional collections to better understand how forgeries, even when of obvious inauthenticity, are able to shift from market to collections. More broadly, his research focuses on the methods used by the market, collections, and academics to evaluate and communicate authenticity; the history of the antiquities market; and the presentation of provenance by collections and the market.

Open Access This chapter is licensed under the terms of the Creative Commons Attribution-NonCommercial-NoDerivatives 4.0 International License (http://creativecommons.org/licenses/by-nc-nd/4.0/), which permits any noncommercial use, sharing, distribution and reproduction in any medium or format, as long as you give appropriate credit to the original author(s) and the source, provide a link to the Creative Commons license and indicate if you modified the licensed material. You do not have permission under this license to share adapted material derived from this chapter or parts of it.

The images or other third party material in this chapter are included in the chapter's Creative Commons license, unless indicated otherwise in a credit line to the material. If material is not included in the chapter's Creative Commons license and your intended use is not permitted by statutory regulation or exceeds the permitted use, you will need to obtain permission directly from the copyright holder.

Filling in the Blanks: The Use of Digitised Historical Newspapers to Contextualise Auction Data

Summer Austin

Abstract While auction data provides an accessible, long-term source of quantifiable market data, recent scholarship has emphasised the need for contextualisation of sales data to gain a more comprehensive understanding of external and internal market dynamics. But how and with what data? This chapter proposes digitised historical newspapers as a viable choice for contextualising both auction data and the market for cultural heritage. An overview of the use of auctions and their records as data is presented alongside some potential blind spots in their analysis. This will be followed by a comprehensive overview of digitised newspapers as a complementary qualitative source of data for auctions, including methodological approaches, tools, resources and technological, ethical and legal considerations. Using my doctoral research, which investigates Tutankhamun blockbuster museum exhibits and the market for Egyptian material as a case study, I will illustrate how a systematic survey of newspaper coverage of both auctions and exhibitions contextualises auction data and the market for Egyptian material.

1 Introduction

Auction catalogues provide an accessible, long-term, open access form of data to analyse the market for cultural heritage. Increasingly, scholarship has employed auction catalogues as their primary qualitative source of data, analysing topics such as the high cost of prestige (Chippindale and Gill 2000), the effectiveness of international legislation (Brodie 2006a, b, 2008), and the extent of looting (Elia 2001). These studies, and many more, provide interesting insights into the market through auction data, attempting to influence policy and further scholarship (Brodie 2014a, b). However, as Brodie (2019) reflects, auction data without contextualisation provides a 'distorted' view of the market.

S. Austin (✉)
Institute of Archaeology, University College London, London, UK
e-mail: summer.austin.20@ucl.ac.uk

© The Author(s) 2026

E. Smith, S. Austin (eds.), *Researching a Rigged Game: Digital Approaches to Tracing the Illicit Trade in Cultural Objects*, Studies in Art, Heritage, Law and the Market 11, https://doi.org/10.1007/978-3-032-02014-7_9

A significant weakness identified in previous studies is that they attribute causation to a demonstrated correlation but do not offer any empirical support for such a causal relation. Both Brodie (2019) and Yates (2022) have argued that auction data may be misconstrued: overstretching correlation with causation while failing to consider external or internal influences on market stakeholders, resulting in an incomplete understanding of market dynamics (Brodie 2019; Yates 2022). For more reliable research, long-term auction data should be contextualised with data available from other sources. While both Brodie and Yates emphasise the need for supplementary and diverse forms of evidence, Brodie only offers a limited option for contextualising data through the use of court documents, of which there are few due to the limited rate of prosecution in this field (see Brodie et al. 2021). So, what is one meant to do with all this auction data? What available sources, if any, can fill in the gaps left by auction catalogue data alone? And perhaps more importantly, how does one go about this?

This chapter provides a case for the use of digitised historic newspapers as a source of complimentary qualitative data to contextualise not only auctions but the market itself. Digital newspapers provide new avenues for investigation and insights and start to fill in some of the blanks that auction data alone leaves (as well as raise a few new questions). News articles reveal supplemental auction data such as buyer and seller names, eyewitness accounts of auctions, internal and external market influences, fashions in collecting, bidding practices, auction house policies and much more. This information helps researchers understand how the market is engaged with by stakeholders and how it is marketed to the public. Newspapers offer unique and invaluable insights into auctions and the market and are potential valuable additions to an auction data study.

Using newspapers as source material is not new or novel: social scientists have used them for decades as primary source to understand past social, cultural, and economic influences and trends (e.g. Fortunati et al. 2015; Franzosi 1987; Taft 1970). The mass-digitisation of newspapers has transformed these traditional analogue objects into digital artefacts (Fortunati et al. 2015; Fyfe 2016). As such, it has been equated to a new ‘El Dorado’ for social scientists (Ehrmann et al. 2022). The use of newspapers within the study of cultural objects is also not new or novel. Newspapers have long been a valuable resource for museum practitioners and provenance researchers. These are the true experts on the use of newspapers as source material for the trade in cultural heritage; yet most of their time-laborious work is hidden within online catalogue lines or in brief comments in publications. There is no established and published methodology for this type of research, which this chapter aims to rectify. Furthermore, this study breaks new ground by expanding the focus from individual items and/or auctions to the broader antiquities market, moving beyond tracing objects and transactions to cultural and economic impacts on the market. The notable absence of published methodologies or critical reflections on using digitised newspapers to research the trade in cultural heritage results in researchers being unaware or un(der)prepared to undertake a large survey of newspaper data. This research addresses that need, offering insights into the systematic use of digital newspaper archives as a tool for contextualising auction data and better understanding market dynamics.

The case for newspapers as complementary data starts with a brief overview of auction catalogue data and its previous use in examining the trade in and demand for cultural heritage. Strengths and weakness of these studies will be offered along with the recent calls questioning the reliability or even usability of catalogues as data. This will be followed by an extensive overview of digitised newspapers as data, explaining the digitisation process, followed by a methodological proposal informed by my own epistemic journey engaging with digitised newspapers. As an institutionally trained archaeologist and not a digital historian, my methodological approach to the digital archive is similar to an archaeological dig, shifting through layers upon layers of digital artefacts (i.e. newspapers), slowly uncovering features and themes within the data with the aim of uncovering the context of a physical (and digital) site. Several questions, reflections and suggestions are offered in this section in the hope of informing readers on methods and considerations when assessing the viability of digitised newspapers as resources. That section continues with an overview of the strengths and potential insights newspaper coverage can offer for the antiquities market, followed by available resources and databases to consult. The section continues with an examination of the challenges of this data source, including levels of access, technological challenges and inherent biases in both the source material and the infrastructures built for us to engage with digitised newspapers. The final section of this chapter comprises of a case study from my doctoral research, to illustrate the treasure trove of insights that digitised newspapers can provide as well as future avenues of inquiry.

When considering what constitutes open access, this chapter builds on Christine Borgman's foundational overview of data, in which they rightly point out that while open access carries "the intent to improve the flow of information, minimize restrictions on the use of intellectual resources, and increase the transparency of research practices", it is not uniform. Rather, openness exists on a spectrum and does not necessarily equate the same "kinds of value for scholarship, the array of stakeholders involved, and their mobility across contexts and over time" (Borgman 2015, p. 39). In this sense, open does not always mean equal; it signals an aspiration toward accessibility, while remaining contingent on disciplinary norms, institutional infrastructures, and socio-technical constraints.

2 Auction Catalogues as Data

The term auction data is being used here to denote data contained within auction catalogues and relating to the auction sale itself. It includes sold and unsold lots and is not restricted to sold lots only. Terms like auction data, sales data or catalogue data are all used interchangeably in this chapter. Likewise for the use of the term 'the market' which within this chapter means the market for cultural heritage (i.e. the antiquities market).

Major auction houses have been compiling and publishing auction catalogues since the late eighteenth century (McLeod 2001), functioning as a marketing campaign and list of upcoming sales. They contain a wide variety of information, dependent on several factors, including the date (age) of the catalogue, the auction house, the prestige of the collection or collector, and the types of items being sold. Very old auction catalogues include little information, usually only a very brief listing of the lot and have limited visual illustrations, comprising of occasional hand-drawn or engraved images, with photography rarely used until the late 1960s to early 1970s (McLeod 2001). Price lists, when included in catalogues, fluctuate in information as well: some include the price realised, the (hypothetical) buyer names and sales totals, while some are simple lists of the price realised. Anyone who has worked with auction data knows that finding price lists is one of the cruellest, most frustrating aspects of catalogue research. However, in the last fifty years, catalogues have become glossy, professionally curated publications that contain professional photography, various levels of provenance, price estimates, and advertisements for other services auction houses provide such as storage, financial services, and educational programs. For art market researchers, these catalogues are oftentimes the only physical record we have of an object's existence, which makes them invaluable sources of information.

By placing cultural objects within a catalogue for sale, this cultural object is transformed into a commodity to be evaluated, estimated, marketed, and sold (Appadurai 1986). Sales catalogues can offer valuable insight into the sale and purchase of cultural heritage at auction (Tremain 2017). The established practice of marketing cultural objects in sales catalogues allows for trends and changes through time to be recognised, not only regarding auction houses and collectors but also regarding the objects themselves (Lobay 2007). Information contained within catalogues can reveal the quantity and quality of cultural objects sold at auction, their minimum and maximum prices, provenance information, and fluctuations in sales and prices over long periods of time. As the antiquities market is grey, opaque, and difficult get a view into (Mackenzie et al. 2019) researchers are already limited in the data they have access to; auction catalogues serve as but one viable resource to examine the market for cultural heritage.

2.1 *Auction Data and the Market in Cultural Heritage*

The first to use auction catalogue data to examine the antiquities market were Chippindale and Gill (Chippindale et al. 2001; Gill and Chippindale 1993; Chippindale and Gill 2000), who focused on Bronze Age Cycladic figures to investigate objects' provenance and the scale of the market. They found that over 90% of lots did not cite a verifiable findspot and determined that most were illicit in nature. They concluded that such a large scale of unprovenanced and illicit funerary objects caused the destruction of the archaeological record of approximately 11,000 graves, resulting in unmeasurable loss of knowledge which they termed the "material and intellectually consequences of esteem" (Gill and Chippindale 1993; Chippindale and Gill 2000; Chippindale et al. 2001). Further studies by the pair analysed the provenance of objects acquired or displayed in museums from private collections. They discovered that over 75% of the antiquities had no ownership history before 1973 and only 2% had a documented findspot, further linking museum displays to illicit objects and demonstrating that the display of artefacts in exhibitions increased their monetary value since it provided them with authenticity and respectability (Gill and Chippindale 1993). Ultimately, Chippindale and Gill determined that further empirical data was paramount to overcome assumptions about and practices within the antiquities market.

Nørskov (2002) focused on the market for decorated Greek pottery and concluded that between 80–90% of the objects had no verifiable provenance before 1996. Nørskov contextualised demand for Greek pottery within the overall collecting history of the west and the cultural significance of these collections, both private and public. Nørskov further identifies the 'invisible market' were private sales take place in auction house, but no public records of the sale exist, making the sale invisible and thus impossible to trace or research.

Similarly, Elia (2001) focused on Apulian red-figure vases and found that only 5% of these vases in museum collections or on the market had come from archaeological excavation and that the other 95% must have been obtained by way of looting. They calculated that approximately tens of thousands of tombs would have had to be looted to result in these quantities. Elia therefore held that the looting of tombs for Apulian red-figured vases was an ongoing criminal enterprise.

Beltrametti and Marrone's (2016) use of longitudinal repeat sales analyses focused on the impact of upheld regulations within market nations. Using United States v. Schultz, 178 F. Supp. 2d 445, 448 [S.D.N.Y. 2002] as a case study, they found that only after an international law was upheld in a U.S. court, was the law taken seriously by the market. They demonstrated that legal standards had to be upheld in a court of law (specifically in a market country like the U.S.) for regulation to be effective.

Focussing on another avenue for research, Gilgan (2001) illustrated how auction catalogue data could be used to measure the effectiveness of regulatory or other policy interventions on the antiquities market. Gilgan focused on Mesoamerican objects offered at Sotheby's New York from 1971–1999 and identified a reduction in lots offered after 1983. They initially attributed this change to the US enactment of the 1983 Convention on Cultural Property Implementation Act. However, Gilgan soon after realised that the data was skewed due to the use of vague geographical assignments: for example, instead of attributing objects to "Sipán", which would be illegal, Sotheby's ambiguously listed the origin as "Lowlands", illustrating a weakness in sales catalogue research and an example of auction houses actively participating in the opaqueness of the market. Gilgan's (2001) research demonstrated the utility of long-term auction data in assessing the direct and indirect effects of regulatory, legal, and ethical control measures on the market as well as auction house tactics of optical due diligence.

Subsequent studies have attempted to use sales data to illustrate direct or indirect influences on the market through regulatory means; Brodie's (2006a, b) study of the effect of the United Nations Security Council Resolution 1483 on the sale of Iraqi material found a measurable decline in unprovenanced cuneiform tablets and cylinder seals sold after 2003. Brodie (2006a, b) concluded that this was in response to public outcry over the looting of the National Museum in Baghdad. Further studies purported to show a direct or indirect impact of the 2003 CPIA Memorandum of Understanding[1] (MOU) on auction sales of Cambodian items (Davis 2011), and of the CPIA MOUs with Guatemala[2] (1997), Honduras[3] (2004), and El Salvador[4] (1995) on sales of Mesoamerican artifacts (Levine and de Luna 2013). However, not all regulations registered an impact, as seen in the case of the 2001 CPIA MOU with Italy[5] on the sales of central Italian artifacts (Lobay 2007). These studies all used time series histograms to visualise changing sales volumes over time.

While the above studies offered innovative and useful insights into the market for cultural heritage, influencing public opinions and national policies, they are not without their blind spots. Brodie has subsequently published two articles questioning their own findings (Brodie and Manivet 2017; Brodie 2019). In their pivotal paper, Brodie (2019) argues that sales catalogue data, without contextualisation, provides a 'distorted' view of the market:

"Long-term sales data might open a window onto the inner workings of the auction market, but it is a dark and distorting glass view, and the inner workings are complex. Care should be taken when interpreting the results of such studies, and, where possible, contextual information should be used to help the move from demonstrating a correlation between market control and sales volumes or prices toward establishing a causal relationship" (Brodie 2019, p. 281).

Brodie's re-examination of their previous findings and others auction studies concludes that the assertions made based on long-term sales data regarding influences on the market were potentially misattributed. A major weakness identified in previous studies was that they attribute causation to a demonstrated correlation, but they do not offer any empirical support for such a causal relation. Furthermore, they failed to consider other structural variables, both external and internal, that impact

[1] Cambodia (03–919)—Memorandum of Understanding Regarding the Imposition of Import Restrictions on Khmer Archaeological Material.

[2] Guatemala (97–929)—Memorandum of Understanding Concerning the Imposition of Import Restrictions on Archaeological Objects and Material from the Pre-Columbian Cultures of Guatemala.

[3] Honduras (04–312)—Memorandum of Understanding Concerning the Imposition of Import Restrictions on Archaeological Material from the Pre-Columbian Cultures of Honduras.

[4] Memorandum Of Understanding Between the Government of The United States of America and The Government of The Republic Of El Salvador Concerning The Imposition Of Import Restrictions On Certain Categories of Archaeological Material From The Pre-Hispanic Cultures of The Republic of El Salvador.

[5] Italy (13141)—Memorandum of Understanding Concerning the Imposition of Import Restrictions on Categories of Archaeological Material Representing the Pre-Classical, Classical and Imperial Roman Periods in Italy.

market demand (Brodie 2019, p. 268). Brodie's research examines a specific case of misattribution involving Sotheby's and Cambodian cultural heritage as example. Previously, declining sales at Sotheby's were attributed to reactions to international policies or changing public opinion, however, subsequent internal communications revealed through court proceedings showed that the reduction in sales volume was actually a deliberate strategy by Sotheby's to improve profits. Brodie emphasises that auction houses are global businesses that react and readjust their market strategies for a wide variety of veiled reasons, and that any examination of auction data must consider the environments that it is constructed within (Brodie 2019, p. 280). This example highlights how market trends can be misinterpreted without access to empirical information, resulting in incomplete insights about the influences of market trends. For more reliable research, long-term auction data should be contextualised with information available from other sources (Brodie 2019, p. 268).

Yates (2022) further criticises the reliance on auction data as a source of accurately understanding the market. They highlight that auctions make up a relatively small and elite part of the market, particularly in the modern digital markets. Yates argue that sales data may be an unsuitable method for understanding the very mechanisms that researchers are attempting to measure. Yates (2022, p. 43) uses a case study of the Sotheby's 2013 Barbier-Mueller Pre-Columbian sale to demonstrate that such analysis may result in misleading or incomplete conclusions. They conclude that it is beyond the scope of auction data to measure market-autoregulation, buyer or seller sentiments, impacts from external or internal actions, or even if an auction is 'successful': "the information that many researchers seek in auction data just is not there. […] in other words, neither the Barbier-Mueller sale, nor, indeed, any auction is a clear window into the market for illicit antiquities" (Yates 2022, p. 57). Harsh reflections from two of the leading researchers in the field. And while I do agree that there is potential for overstretching of the importance and impact of auction data, I argue that Yates' case study of a single major auction is perhaps not a suitable comparison to other larger-scale studies that utilise long-term auction data, since those studies examine a larger portion of the market, allowing for trends to be identified, analysed and contextualised further. While single-auction analysis can only give a distorted snapshot view of the market, more long-term, targeted auction data investigations can still provide useful insights, so long as it is further contextualised within larger market environments.

Auction catalogues have evident blind spots, as demonstrated by some of these studies. Researchers must acknowledge these constraints in their work and actively seek alternative data sources. Given that the market is unlikely to voluntarily provide greater data access or insights in the short term, it is incumbent upon researchers to innovate and uncover new or overlooked sources of information in order to research the antiquities market, and by extension, to effectuate increased legal and moral compliancy. The following section will advocate for the use of digital print media, and digital newspapers specifically, as a complementary qualitative source of context for both auctions and the market for cultural heritage.

3 Newspapers as Data

Print media, and newspapers in particular, are a vital primary and secondary source; they record and publish an array of events, opinions and other information and are a valuable open resource that can offer otherwise invisible insights into the larger social, economic, and political environments (Franzosi 1987; Taft 1970; Wodak and Krzyżanowski 2008). Newspapers can be categorised based on various criteria, including their ownership (public, private, governmental, institutional), geographical scope (national, metropolitan, local), format (broadsheet, tabloid, Berliner, commuter, community, student), target readership, language, publication frequency (daily, weekly, semi-weekly, monthly), content or focus (general, politics, local vs international news, finance, art, etc), medium (print, electronic), and layout characteristics (arrangement, fonts, typology, advertisements, etc), all of which contribute to their distinct roles in informing and shaping public discourse (Fortunati et al. 2015). Most newspapers rely on advertising and subscriptions sales to generate revenue. This business model is important to remember when assessing the viability of newspapers as a possible source of data for auction data (Franzosi 1987).

Previously, the use of newspapers for market (or any) analysis was limited due to time, access, and labour. Any researcher that has sat hunched over a microfilm reader for hours in the vain hope of finding a few relevant articles understands the tedious work, patience and a bit of luck analysing historical newspapers requires. In many ways, archaeologists can relate to the time and tenacity needed for such evidentiary excavations, be it archival or assemblage. However, the realities of utilising newspapers have greatly expanded in the last twenty years. With the rapid rise in digitisation, termed the 'digital turn' (Nicholson 2013), new sources, insights, methods and considerations for these digital artefacts must be explored, expanded and reflected on (Fortunati et al. 2015; Fyfe 2016).

3.1 Digital Artefacts

Two developments that have driven the digital transformation of newspapers into digital artefacts are mass digitisation, which facilitates access to remote holdings and, more recently, improved search capabilities, which alleviate the tedious exploration of vast collections, opens up new prospects and transforms research practices. While open access has increased dramatically in the last twenty years, scholarship considering this type of data and access lags. Thus, it is vital that researchers consider source, purpose, intent and clearly make their choices both transparent and pragmatic (Ehrmann et al. 2022).

Generally, digitised newspaper collections are digital archives of historical newspapers converted from their original analogue format into searchable digital files.

The digitisation process typically involves several key steps and decisions by numerous participants. First, original newspaper pages or microfilm copies are scanned to create high-quality digital images. Nowadays, this is usually done by outside firms which specialise in this technology, but this was not always the case. Next, these images undergo Optical Character Recognition (OCR), which transforms the visual text into machine-readable text. Alongside this, metadata is created to record essential information about each page, issue, and article, including publication dates, page numbers, and article categories. The digitised content is then stored in standardised formats such as METS (Metadata Encoding and Transmission Standard) and ALTO (Analysed Layout and Text Object) (Bunout 2022, p. 285). Following this, the textual content is indexed to enable efficient searching across the collection. Ideally, the structure of digitised newspaper collections is designed to facilitate accessible navigation and searching. The digitised files and associated metadata are usually stored in a database maintained by the institution that commissioned the digitisation. Users can search the collection using keywords, phrases, or other criteria that query the indexed content. When a user selects a result, they typically see a facsimile of the original page alongside the transcribed text. It is important to note that the execution of digitisation processes does vary between projects (Bunout 2022 p. 286). Factors such as the quality and accuracy of OCR can differ based on the condition of the original material and the technology used. Interfaces steer what users can learn from digitised sources, and they influence workflows by offering functions and tools (Ehrmann et al. 2017; Pfanzelter et al. 2021, p. 1) Additionally, projects may focus on specific time periods, regions, or newspaper titles, affecting the comprehensiveness of the digital collection. Access policies also vary; some collections may be freely available online, while others might require subscriptions or be limited to specific institutions (discussed further below). Understanding these aspects of digitised newspaper collections helps researchers better navigate and utilise these valuable historical resources (Bunout et al. 2022).

The digitisation process not only preserves fragile historical documents but also dramatically enhances their accessibility and searchability for a wide range of users. As a result, digital newspapers are increasingly being used to uncover innovative insights (for an extensive overview of various research projects see Beach and Hanlon 2023; Ehrmann et al. 2022). While provenance researchers have historically used newspapers to fill in the gaps in provenance and trace objects through time, market researchers have yet to approach this treasure trove of insights through a systematic survey to uncover what wider market insights and themes newspapers might contain. This makes digital newspapers, and other forms of digital print media, an untapped resource for understanding the market for cultural heritage.

The following sections will outline a methodological approach for the use of newspapers for research followed by an overview of the data's strengths, weaknesses, and resources tips for approaching newspapers.

3.2 *Methodology*

This section outlines a methodological approach primarily informed by my own epistemic journey and reflexivity in approaching newspapers as qualitative data, further informed by methodological approaches found in Ehrmann et al. (2022). In the principal of transparency, my initial approach to newspapers was much less considered, more of a detour that turned into a road trip which resulted in several procedural misadventures. Moreover, some of the reflections presented here come not from my own best practice but from lessons learned and insights shared with colleagues. It is the very lack of a published methodological approach to guide market researchers that motivates this chapter.

3.2.1 Research Question and Plan

A well-defined research question(s) and aim(s) is essential as it provides focus and direction, guiding the entire research process. A clear question ensures the project's relevance by identifying gaps in existing market knowledge and justifying its significance. It also enhances feasibility by allowing researchers to assess what can be realistically accomplished (King and Rico 2024). For researchers looking to contextualising auction and market data, it will be important to consider what type of information is being sought—e.g. gaps in sales data, market stakeholder activities (marketing strategies, market norms, scandals, etc), collecting trends, and so on—and understand if and how those themes may be revealed in newspaper coverage.

Creating a research plan with steps and rationales for decisions made allows the researcher to reflect on work complete, assess preliminary results and plan future actions as well as provides transparency in the employed methodology. This approach is particularly valuable for newspaper searches given the potential extensiveness of a database and the potential daunting feeling of data overload (Gaillard 2022). Maintaining a record of keywords, combinations, alternative spellings, dates, etc., helps prevent duplicate searches and identify potential themes and gaps during the research process. Flexibility and space for reflexivity should be built into any newspaper research plan to address the unpredictable nature of systematic surveys. As will be discussed below, OCR and keyword searches greatly impact results which necessitates that researchers remain adaptable, regularly reassessing their approaches to optimise the use of digital collections. Finally, while some flexibility in the research plan is necessary, it is equally necessary to understand any constraints (time, funding, scope, storage, etc) the research dictates and to adhere to those limitations. Digital newspapers collections can become a rabbit hole, so setting parameters to the research project is useful.

3.2.2 Identify Appropriate and Available Sources

When conducting research using historical newspapers, it is crucial to select publications and databases that are associated with the specific time periods, editorial and geographic focus and languages relevant to the research focus. Researchers should identify newspapers that focus on their target markets, using auction data as initial reference points. For instance, London and New York publications are particularly valuable for studies on classical antiquities markets due to these cities' reputation as centres of this market, while French newspapers would be more appropriate for Paris-based auctions, or if a collector lived in Germany, German newspapers may have covered their collection as some point. Let the auction data and facts serve as a starting point for your queries. For more local or regional auctions, opt for local newspapers instead of major publications, however there will be fewer digitised options which may result in the use of microfilms.

- When evaluating newspaper collections, researchers should consider several key factors:
- What titles and time spans are covered in the collection?
- What is the focus of the publications at the time period selected?
- What are the levels of access to this collection (institutional, free, subscription)?
- Who owns this collection (public/private institutions, cultural heritage institutions, commercial)?
- What is the digitisation status, (completed, ongoing or limited)?
- What is the availability across supplementary portals that have published the title and processed and accessed differently (for example, *The New York Times* is available on both ProQuest vs *The New York Times Archive*, but the interface and tools are different).

Additionally, it is important to assess user interfaces, tools and searchability, data transparency and offline storage options. While custom search features such as date ranges, image searches, and article type filters can be beneficial, researchers should be aware that these may inadvertently over-limit results depending on the database's indexing. Built-in data visualisation tools can be particularly useful in avoiding statistical inaccuracies in word frequency counts (Oberbichler and Pfanzelter 2022). Some interfaces may be limited in language options. User accessibility should also be considered, as most interfaces do not have tools built in for visual impairments or offer colour contrast or alternative text for images. Finally, researchers should consider their desired outputs, due to issues around copyright reuse. Identifying which publications and databases best address the research question(s) is vital. For auction data, I have found newspapers that report in market countries (i.e. North America, Europe, and the United Kingdom) particularly useful for identifying market influences and dynamics. By carefully considering the above factors researchers can optimise their use of historical newspapers.

3.2.3 Targeted Searches

The primary method for searching newspapers is through keyword searches. To begin, identify initial keywords such as auction houses, relevant and time-period auction jargons (e.g. Old Masters, antiquities, Americans, tribal, primitive, etc). After your initial search you may identify further keywords, word combinations, patterns, dates of auctions, authors of auction reviews, etc. to search. It is useful if you can identify relevant themes throughout your search to help you identify further related articles. For example, are auction reviews always published the day after the auction or regularly on a specific date? If so, (for example, every Thursdays after an auction) you can target that day to obtain regular auction reviews that keyword or OCR noise might have excluded (explained below). Who generally writes the reviews? What sections of the newspaper are they generally included in? Society sections, arts, finance, front page? What other information is included in these articles? What other information is surrounding these articles, e.g. advertisements, financial advice, art reviews, etc.? What does the placement of this article tell us about the purpose of the article? Is it meant to inform or influence readers? Are there photos of objects auctioned? Understanding and contextualising not only the auction data but the newspaper data as well is a useful step for clearer understandings of the larger market environments. The challenge here is to know when you have enough data, or have accomplished so-called 'data saturation', which is difficult to identify in the age of digital abundance. This is when your research parameters are particularly useful.

3.2.4 Collecting Data

Data points collected from newspapers can vary wildly, from metadata to basic data including headlines, authors, content, images, etc. While conducting your research, it is imperative that you download and securely store all relevant articles and required data. Current access today is not guaranteed access tomorrow and any researcher that has dealt with digital material will attest to the undying frustration of not being able to find something later that was previously available. By regularly storing and backing up your findings, you safeguard your research materials against potential loss due to changes in database access, subscription status, or technological issues.

3.2.5 Tools, Resources and Databases

How you go about analysing your data will greatly depend on both your research aims and technological fluency. There are several tools and coding packages available that offer advance visualisation tools that can reveal trends, patterns, and insights into past societies, language use, and events. Combining these tools can help you handle various aspects of newspaper research, from OCR and text mining to topic modelling and geographic analysis. Choosing the right tools depends on the specifics of your project, your technical skills, and the level of customisation required. For a thorough overview of several resource and methods of analysing newspaper data, see the footnote below and at the end of the chapter for a list of newspaper databases.[6] While technical driven analysis is useful and can offer insights, a careful reading of articles selected is also vital and should not be replaced with only digital tools.

3.3 Source Strengths

Digitised newspapers offer a potentially immense data set of both primary and secondary sources that can help situate auctions and the market for cultural heritage. There is a large scholarship of source criticism, methodology and case studies to help guide researchers. Newspapers can provide invaluable insights into the market that are often invisible to researchers. The press frequently has exclusive access to market stakeholders, be it auction houses, dealers, collectors or museum staff; these privileged accounts of inner-market workings offer useful details on potential market dynamics; however, such accounts should be further corroborated.

At a basic level, newspapers can inform researchers about when and where an auction took place, its focus, and results; considering how often very old auction catalogues do not survive, even having a listing of an auction can fill in a gap in the record. Beyond this, newspaper coverage can reveal a wide range of market dynamics, including the identification of buyers and sellers (including collector and collection profiles); collecting fashions, trends and shifts in taste; and performance of lots (both sold/unsold), including reasons for lots withdrawn. Newspapers can also provide deeper insight into external and internal influences impacting the market, such as financial (e.g. oil crashes, investment collecting, currency concerns, VAT, etc) or sociocultural (e.g. headlines that promote and shape market perceptions) influences. They can also offer an understanding of bidding wars and other competitive market behaviours; marketing techniques employed by auction houses; negative press or scandals impacting auction houses (price fixing, increase in premiums, etc); and market reports including annual sales. Lastly, newspapers can offer valuable insight into contemporaneous public opinion of and sentiment towards the art market.

Another aspect of art auctions that is usually invisible to researchers, is the social engagement with and at auctions. Auction catalogues serve as the script (Geismar 2001) for the main attraction, the auction; something that is generally hidden from researchers investigating auctions. Catalogues only provide the prelude and the credits (price list) with the main show (the auction) hidden from researchers. That is where newspaper coverage can help bring the show to life for the researcher.

[6] Living with Machines (https://livingwithmachines.ac.uk/); *Impresso* (https://impresso-project.ch/); Accessing and Using Historical Newspaper Data (https://yann-ryan.github.io/newspapers/); The Atlas Project (https://www.digitisednewspapers.net/).

Newspapers both report on the market and serve as marketing for the market, therefore allowing researchers to understand how the market is being presented to and consumed by the public contemporaneously. Newspaper coverage offers contextual information about the broader cultural and economic environment in which the art market operates. This comprehensive view allows researchers to understand not just auction transactions, but also the social, economic, and cultural factors influencing the market.

3.4 Challenges of Digital Newspapers

The digitisation of historical newspapers provides a treasure-trove of research; however, this technological transformation has introduced challenges and considerations for researchers. Newspapers data will not be a suitable resource for all auction research; this can be due to research questions and scope, or due to the availability of appropriate data. Only a small portion of the vast corpus of archival newspapers have been digitised, (e.g. only six percent of the British Library's collection has been digitised) and while an increasing number of institutions are investing in digitisation and infrastructure, the data researchers could be searching for may simple not have been digitised yet.

At the basic level, access to these online collections is not universal or democratic. Varying levels of access (fully open-access, institutional, paid subscriptions) present researchers with funding and accessibility hurdles that perpetuate the 'digital divide' (van Dijk 2006). Digital accessibility remains a critical yet often neglected aspect of collection interfaces, with many platforms lacking essential features for users with visual impairments including the absence of built-in magnification or text-to-speech tools, insufficient colour contrast options, and inadequate alternative text for images. These shortcomings exclude a significant portion of potential users and should be addressed by institutions.

Access to online collections can be jeopardised by changes in database ownership, loss of funding, or outdated technology. These factors may lead to data being placed behind paywalls or becoming outdated. Access today is not guaranteed access tomorrow, as demonstrated by the British Library's 2024 cyberattack. This ransomware incident, described as "one of the worst cyber incidents in British history" (British Library Cyber-Act Report 2024), resulted in months-long disruptions to most library services, including access to digital collections. Just as the physical archive can be threatened, lost or destroyed, these manufactured digital collections can also be at risk.

The transformation of analogue collections into digital artefacts alters not only our access, but also how we fundamentally engage with the material: this transformation potentially compromises the contextual richness inherent in traditional newspaper engagement. The physical act of leafing through a newspaper, with its strategically placed headlines, carefully designed layouts, articles and illustrations, and enticing advertisements provides readers with a holistic experience that digital interfaces do not fully replicate (Gaillard 2022, p. 115). This shift from tactile browsing to targeted digital examination raises concerns about the potential loss of contextual understanding. Gaillard (2022, p. 114) cautions that "it seems to me that the digital tools we have, further distance us from the materiality that we can share with the original users of our sources". The ability to be instantly transported to specific articles, while efficient, may inadvertently lead to the overlooking of surrounding content that could provide valuable insights into the broader economic, cultural, and social influences in which the market operates. To mitigate this, researchers should consider viewing the page in its entirety to better understand where market data is being situated within the publication. This approach allows for a more nuanced view both the article itself and the context in which the market is presented to the public in.

While this treasure trove of possibilities may seem like a researcher's dream, it presents users with an additional challenge: navigating the immense digital corpus that we have access to, which has resulted in a state of information overabundance. Just as traditional newspaper analysis was limited due to its intense time commitment, digital newspapers can suffer from the same issue due to the vastness of available data. The process of sifting through vast amounts of information can be time-consuming and may often result in unproductive queries. Collections of data that span centuries, coupled with machine learning tools, can "allow us to measure the depth of archives, [yet] nothing is easier than getting lost in the excess" (Gaillard 2022, p. 115). Conversely, researchers may experience a false sense of viewing the whole picture due to the amount of data available, resulting in an overinflation of media reporting (Gaillard 2022). When one is submerged in the vastness of the dataset, continuously reading similar accounts of events, it may seem like these accounts are gospel, thus it is important to remember the potential bias and motivations of such reporting, to take a large step back and view the information within the larger picture.

The digitisation of historical newspapers has increased access to information but has also introduced new biases that researchers must navigate. For instance, the selection of articles that are digitised often favours larger publications over local or less prominent ones, skewing the research corpus towards more widely circulated narratives. Inclusion and exclusion from the digital corpus is not random, but a result of a series of choices that are not often known or visible to the researcher. These choices may be influenced by institutional funding and scope of a project, quality of microfilms, or internal policy (Tolfo et al. 2022). Rarely are these internal decisions made public. This lack of transparency results in unacknowledged inequalities in the digital collection (Tolfo et al. 2022). Moreover, the existence or absence of digitisation partially conditions our choices of corpus, resulting in potential missed information and source biases. As both Yates and Brodie (2023) and Brodie (2025) have correctly articulate, misreporting and/or overreporting, particularly on heritage issues, is rampant and has serious consequences, thus it is vital that when performing this type of research, one is mindful of the social, economic and cultural influences that are interwoven within media, museums and the market.

Digitised newspapers suffer from two key technological challenges: OCR noise and keyword search discrepancies. OCR noise refers to the errors and inaccuracies introduced during the digitisation process of historical newspapers. This includes misinterpreted words generated by optical character recognition (OCR) and texts re-edited by auto-segmentation tools, which result in an extreme amount of noise in the digital collection, potentially impacting the integrity and authenticity of the newspaper content (Jarlbrink and Snickars 2017).

When OCR systems scan of an image of the word "the," an effective OCR program should be able to recognise the individual "t" "h" and "e" letters and then save those as "the" in text form. OCR systems generally perform well on modern printed texts with specific fonts, but historical newspaper images present unique challenges. These challenges primarily stem from the quality of microfilmed, which can vary significantly. Older microfilm often lacks grayscale, resulting in poor image quality and subsequently inaccurate OCR results. Additionally, historical newspapers typically used small, ornate fonts in narrow columns, with punctuation throughout, further compounding OCR accuracy issues. OCR rates function particularly poorly with non-Roman fonts (particularly Gothic fonts which most German newspapers were published in) and non-English spelled words. Further OCRs issues arise with poor paper quality. These limitations can introduce errors, such as confusing letters with numerals (e.g., "t" with "1" or "antiq-uity" with "an1iq" "-uity"), significantly impacting research outcomes. For instance, if "auction" is frequently misread as "auc1ion" or "@ution" due to poor OCR, it would substantially affect searches (Torget 2022, pp. 50–51) and statistics such as word frequency. One method to mitigate poor OCR rates is the 'snowball' strategy: after the first query of a word, you may come across a different OCR version of the queried word and search for that.

OCR accuracy rates are the single most important metric in determining the usability of a dataset of digitised historical newspapers for research, yet these rates are often withheld from researchers (Torget 2022, p. 48). The importance of OCR quality transparency in digital newspaper databases cannot be overstated. Researchers require this information to identify the best source material and determine appropriate research methodologies. For instance, if a newspaper had a 90% OCR accuracy, a researcher could confidently search the corpus, while if another had a 52% accuracy rate, this would necessitate manual examination of scanned pages due to unreliable search results. Without readily available OCR accuracy rates, researchers cannot make informed decisions about the most effective approach to their research, potentially compromising the validity of their findings (Burchardt 2023; Torget 2022, p. 63; Van Strien et al. 2020).

Keyword searches remain central to digital queries, despite their limitations, which include language complexities such as "alternative spellings, abbreviations, polysemy, changing word usage, idioms, misspellings or omissions of parts of words as well as sentences" (Oberbichler and Pfanzelter 2022, p. 136). As Deacon (2007) notes, "keyword searching are best suited for identifying tangible 'things' (i.e. people, places, events and policies) rather than 'themes' (i.e. more abstract, subtler and multifaceted concepts)" (Deacon 2007, p. 8). The choice of keywords can significantly influence results, often "on the basis of the researcher's prior knowledge" (Oberbichler and Pfanzelter 2022, p. 138). While keyword searches offer time-saving benefits, they also alter the traditional archival approach, potentially leading to irrelevant results. An example of this would be searching for the term 'Egyptian', resulting in advertisements for Egyptian cotton sheets. Another challenge is term segmentation: searching for two keywords in a single article or an entire issue of a newspaper may give very different results, especially when searching for terms that are less frequently associated with each other. At the same time, less prominent articles are made visible by the keyword searches, this is particularly evident in advertisements of auctions which can be helpful if a researcher is attempting to identify when an auction took place but can skew results if the goal is to analyse term frequency. To mitigate these issues, researchers should employ broader search strategies, such as alternative searches with dates or proper names as well as contextualising their findings. This approach helps balance the efficiency of digital methods with the need for comprehensive market analysis.

No historic sources, newspapers (both analogue and digital) and the interfaces designed to engage with these sources are neutral. When working with historical newspapers, it is necessary to address their inherent biases compounded through the digitisation processes, digital interfaces and search strategies (Oberbichler and Pfanzelter 2022 p. 128) which are inherited from the various commercial stakeholders, political and economic interest groups, and local or national audiences, all of whom influenced the shape and content of the newspaper landscape, but are usually absent in the accompanying metadata (Tolfo et al. 2022, p. 40). The lopsided digitisation of sources can lead to an overrepresentation of certain narratives while marginalising others. As Gaillard (2022, p. 114) notes, "media inflation is part of the history of social imaginaries," indicating that journalistic representations can amplify specific issues at the expense of a balanced view. Newspapers operate on business models reliant on advertising and subscriptions, making them susceptible to internal and external influences such as ownership changes, editorial shifts, corporate partnership, alternative forms of income and so on. These commercial pressures can lead to a prioritisation of sensational stories or popular topics over more nuanced or critical reporting to attract readers and/or advertisers, thus skewing historical narratives and shaping public perceptions in ways that may not accurately reflect broader societal realities. Political, economic, and social events may be underreported or overreported depending on editorial focus. Sensational and perhaps misleading headlines that are meant to grab readers attention have been shown to influence readers' overall comprehension of the article (Ecker et al. 2014). In short, newspapers, like auction houses, are selling a product, thus researchers must be aware of the biases and blind spots in both the source material and the interfaces we use to engage with them. And while the newspapers themselves are not neutral, biases built into the collection infrastructure may also influence search results as Beelen et al. (2023) illustrated in their analysis of the British Library's online collection which demonstrated a conservative bias and failed to capture a significant category of 'neutral' and 'independent' papers, leading to a divergence between the sample and population over time. No data or database is neutral; researchers must be aware of and address inherent biases within the research set.

Digital newspapers have been referred to as the new Eldorado for digital social scientist. Just as the mythical treasure of Eldorado symbolised colonial exploration and exploitation, the digitisation (or lack of) perpetuates historical injustices. While the ever-growing corpus of digitised newspapers allows researchers to easily access this data, it also sustains postcolonial archival and global copyright regimes. "As a historian who works on news media across the Third World in the post-1945 era, it has been difficult to find this Eldorado" (LeBlanc 2024, p. 165). For example, Tworek (2024) found a lack of transparency around pricing schemes and variability in pricing based on institutional affiliation, which restrict scholars' (particularly scholars from the Global South) ability to conduct large-scale analysis and data scraping of these databases. This results in what Tworek (2024) terms the "double politics" of digitised newspapers: the original politics being their production, coupled with the politics of newspapers transformation and commercialisation. Most newspapers currently digitised are disproportionately from and focused on the Global North, thus further amplifying those voices and narratives within research. While the number of digitised twentieth-century newspapers from the Global South has grown exponentially in the last two decades, LeBlanc (2024) argues that there has not been a parallel rise in experimental digital projects using these digitised resources. This disparity is attributed to various factors, including the lack of digital training for historians, unclear reward structures for this type of work, and the continued under-resourcing of scholars and archives in the Global South (Hauswedell et al. 2020; LeBlanc 2024; Manrique-Gómez et al. 2024). As the geographical scope of these digital collections expands, historians must address the colonial foundations of these sources, as newspapers that were previously relegated to the "offline penumbra" (Leary 2005) are now being brought to light. For example, Wilkinson (2024) highlights that while the increasing online presence of colonial-era newspapers from South Asia is exciting, these collections need to be approached with caution and care. The digitisation of early Indian newspapers exemplifies the unique challenges posed by the fragmentary, multilingual remains of colonial newspapers, and demonstrate how and why certain sources, particularly those that do not fit neatly within national narratives, have tended to fall through the cracks of digitisation initiatives. Newspapers from this period emerged in a context of global inequality and form part of a colonial legacy that persists into the present: "Digitisation threatens to reproduce or exacerbate these asymmetries, requiring researchers to reflect on who is served by these initiatives — and upon whose unrecognised labour these resources might rely" (Wilkinson 2024, p. 159). Considering these postcolonial realities, it is imperative for researchers to critically examine the biases and inequalities within their digital data, ensuring that their efforts contribute to a more equitable representation of historical narratives and acknowledging the ongoing legacies of colonialism in the digital age.

Finally, when utilising digitised newspapers, researchers must navigate significant legal constraints, particularly copyright regulations. The procurement of rights to use newspaper data often requires substantial time and resources (Ehrmann et al. 2022; Ahnert et al. 2023). As stated previously, newspapers are businesses that generate a product (the newspaper) which is generally protected by copyright laws.

Most digital collections allow for free use of their material for personal research, however, permission to use newspapers (whole, clippings, images, metadata) for educational or commercial purposes varies wildly. It can become very expensive very quickly to acquire copyrights of newspaper material. Copyright permission generally gets more complex for more recent resources, making work with late twentieth and twenty-first-century digitised collections more challenging.

It is necessary to draw a distinction between the library's rights and ownership of the newspapers on the one hand, and of the digital versions of their collection on the other (Ahnert et al. 2023). For research into the market, clippings of news articles are generally all that is needed, however, publications will still require citations at the minimum with the potential for further copyright fees. Images within newspapers are also often owned under a secondary copyright (usually the photographer or other news outlet) and the use of those may require separate copyright. Given the complexity of this process, researchers are advised to consult their institution's legal team for guidance where possible, and request for assistance in obtaining necessary permissions.

This section has extensively outlined the case for newspapers as a complementary qualitative dataset for auctions and the market. Methodologies and considerations when engaging with the material as well as strengths, resources, tools and tips and technological, ethical and legal considerations for this data have been presented. The following section will demonstrate how newspapers can contextualise both auctions of and market for Egyptian material.

4 Case Studies: Tut on Tour

In this section I will illustrate the use of newspaper data as a complementary empirical source to contextualize the market for Egyptian material. These examples come from my doctoral research, *Tut*[7] *on Tour: 30 years of Demand Creation through Blockbuster Exhibition*.[8] An overview of the project including research questions and aims will be presented, followed by a concise summary of the quantitative results, before providing examples of newspapers as data. Some final reflections on the findings and use of newspapers will conclude this section.

---

[7] The purposely problematic title of this work "Tut on Tour" is a deliberate delineation from Tutankhamun who has been transformed from an individual, into a commodity to be moulded, recast, objectified and commodified repeatedly. This title is a conscious separation of the brand that has been created, from the person whose life, death and after-life has been rebranded. When Tut tours, it is the brand that is on tour.

[8] University College London, Institute of Archaeology, 2025 (supervisor Dr. Alice Stevenson and Dr. Mark Altaweel).

4.1 Tut on Tour

Tut on Tour is a multidisciplinary investigation into historic factors that create, enhance, and normalise demand for collecting cultural heritage. Using the original blockbuster exhibition, Treasures of Tutankhamun (1972–1981) as a case study, this research investigates the correlation of antiquities markets with the Tutankhamun exhibition by gathering, quantifying, and historically contextualising 30 years of exhibition and antiquities market data. The objective of this study is to introduce reliable data to the crucial debate concerning the relationship between museum blockbuster exhibitions, end-market demand, and the illicit antiquities trade. By identifying and contextualising historic trends related to blockbuster exhibitions and collecting, the goal of this research is to proactively implement measures to protect present-day cultural heritage.

Tutankhamun has dominated international headlines for over a century—from the moment Tutankhamun was uncovered in 1922, he has headlined newspapers, exhibitions, and auctions—all generating significant amounts of attention and capital (Bourdieu 1986; Moser 2015; Riggs 2021). These headlines promote the impression that Tut—and ancient Egypt—are for sale, which may motivate individuals to loot Egyptian sites in hopes of obtaining even a small portion of the exorbitant sums broadcasted internationally.

The market for illicit Egyptian antiquities is a demand-driven economic system predicated on collectors and museums acquiring antiquities (Mackenzie et al. 2019); thus, we must understand what creates, influences, enhances, justifies, and normalises demand for these antiquities. This research addresses the broad assumption that blockbuster exhibitions influence demand in the antiquities market. Anecdotal evidence cited in news articles (e.g. Mason 2000) and single-auction evidence in academic journals (e.g. Hardwick 2011); make up the totality of evidence for this assumption thus, this research addresses a pivotal gap concerning causality between museums, the market, and the trade in cultural heritage. Interviews with dealers and museum curators have found that both markets and museums blame the other for influencing demand (Satov 1997). This blind spot in our understanding of the responsibilities and repercussions of museum exhibitions results in museums, governments, and other stakeholders making decisions based on assumptions rather than realities. Accepting that the illicit trade in cultural heritage is a demand-driven crime, it is vital that we better understand influences on demand, in this case, museum exhibitions.

These questions make up the cornerstones of this research:

- Do blockbuster exhibitions influence demand for their subject matters?
- If so, to what extent and for how long?
- How do exhibitions influence demand?
- What are the consequences of demand created through exhibition?

Using a mixed-methodological investigation, this research presents compelling evidence to support the hypothesis that blockbuster museum exhibitions generate demand for their subject matter. Museums host largescale special exhibitions known as blockbusters; Barker (1999, p. 127) defines blockbusters as "a scholarly endeavour which serves to educate and entertain the public, bringing prestige and profit to the host institution". Both Balfe (1987) and Barker (1999) characterise blockbusters as: (1) overtly political (2) targeted to large audiences (3) displaying aesthetical and powerful artwork (4) at multiple locations with sponsorship (5) resulting in substantial media coverage. These types of special exhibits almost always take place at what Frey and Meier (2006) label 'superstar museums' that are defined as: (1) 'a must-see' for tourist (2) with high attendance (3) showcasing world-famous art and artist (4) which are housed in architecturally significant buildings and (5) are highly commercialised. They define this commercialisation aspect as: "a significant part of [the museums] income derives from the revenue of the bookshops and restaurants, and they have a major impact on the local economy" (Frey and Meier 2006, p. 1037). Museums produce monetary values for external economic actors by creating additional jobs and commercial revenue, particularly in the tourism and hospitality industries. If museums can generate revenue for tourism, it is fully conceivable that they can and do, generate revenue for the art market. These overtly political and economically driven exhibitions, housed in the world's premier museums, and seen by millions of people create a frenzied obsession with Tut.

The 1970s Treasures of Tutankhamun tour (1972–1979) is used as a case-study to investigate preceding and subsequent (1960–1989) antiquity market trends relating to the collecting of ancient Egyptian cultural objects. Tutankhamun is a prime case-study due to the numerous tours, first in the 1960s and followed by the much more famous 1970s 'blockbuster' tours. These series of tours offer comparative data regarding what, if any, types of museum exhibits influence the market. Through an extensive survey of auction sales catalogues from Christie's and Sotheby's, in both their London and New York locations from 1960–1989, coupled with a systematic survey of newspaper coverage from *The Times* and *The New York Times* between 1960–1989, this study quantifies and contextualises the series of Tut exhibitions and correlating market reaction.

This study provides a foundation to understand what motivates and inspires demand and collecting with the objective of protecting today's heritage. If blockbuster exhibitions indeed generate demand, then resources, education and international attention can be more effectively applied to regions before looting, trafficking and illicit trade occurs. If we can understand and anticipate demand, more can be done to proactively implement measures to protect cultural heritage.

4.2 Auction as Data

The quantitative portion of this study analysed auction catalogues from Christie's and Sotheby's, in London and New York, between 1960–1989 to derive data on the sale of Egyptian material and how it corresponds to the exhibition. In total, the dataset comprised 7598 lots from 415 antiquities auctions. All monetary values

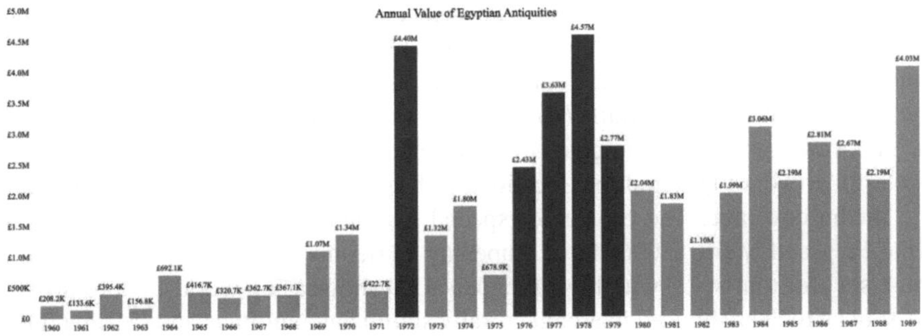

Fig. 1 Annual value of Egyptian antiquities sold at auction, with dark grey denoting the years of Tutankhamun blockbuster tours. Noticeable spikes in total sales value correlate with these highlighted exhibition years (1972, 1976–1979)

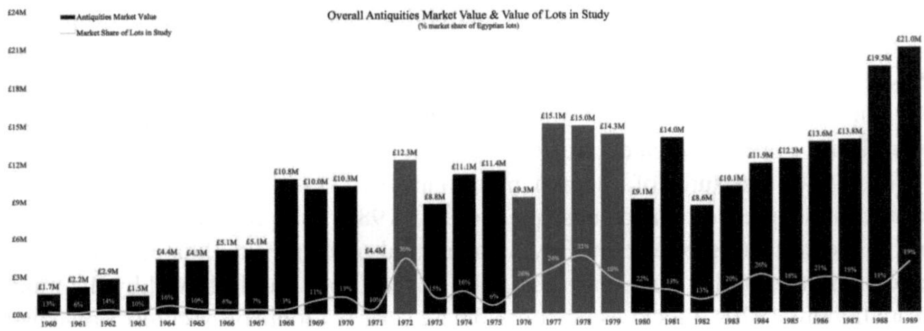

Fig. 2 Annual overall antiquities market values (bars) and percentage share of Egyptian lots in the study (line). Light grey indicate the Tutankhamun tour years. The Egyptian market share peaks align with blockbuster exhibition periods

collected where convert to 2020 GBP for analyses. To analyze the market, I used several forms of analyses including time-series analysis, pattern matching, object type comparisons, repeat sales regression, buyer insights, and provenance analysis. Plausible rival explanations were identified and tested to verify the findings.

Figure 1 illustrates the annual sales of Egyptian material. In the years 1972 and 1978 (the two years that Tut is in London and New York) the annual sales for Egyptian material skyrocket. The market pre-1972 is strikingly lower compared to post-1972. Figure 2 compares Egyptian antiquities' market share against the overall antiquities market, revealing that Egyptian material occupied a substantial proportion of total sales. This suggests that the increase is not merely part of a general market expansion, but rather that Egyptian material was outperforming other collecting categories.

Further analysis compares pre/post-1972 lot volumes, auction frequencies, median and mean prices of Egyptian material, object typology sales trends, object resales, and comparisons between Christie's and Sotheby's and London and New York markets. While space prevents further overview, in summary, these trends reveal a clear causal relationship between Tutankhamun blockbuster museum exhibitions and heightened market demand, with empirical evidence showing that the exhibitions acted as catalysts for both immediate and sustained demand. This market response to the Tutankhamun exhibitions is demonstrated through exponential growth in sales totals, market profit margins and press coverage.

4.3 Newspapers as Data

In this section, I will provide an overview of the qualitative epistemological journey undertaken, outlining decisions made and lessons learned. The initial research plan did not include the use of newspapers, however, due to the pandemic and subsequent lockdowns, the need arose for an accessible form of qualitative data. So, while my research questions and hypothesis informed my approach to digitised newspapers, the journey did not have a roadmap (yet). This is in part due to the dynamic research environment during the pandemic, but mainly due to the lack of published scholarship identifying newspapers as a viable empirical data source for the market, as well as a lack of established methodological steps for newspaper market research. Since I could not predict the richness of the dataset, nor the vastness, I ventured into newspapers with only a cursory approach. This resulted in a series of trial successes and errors of which I expand upon below.

Once the potential for newspaper coverage was clear, I started to record my searches (keywords, word combinations, dates, etc) to focus the process. Initially, the timeframe was limited to the auction data years (1960–1989). However, during the survey, it became evident that market events were occasionally identified and discussed in subsequent years. Therefore, I decided to extend the timeframe by three years (1960–1992). This adjustment proved beneficial, as it allowed for the inclusion of retrospective articles on market events that occurred within the primary study period but were reported outside the initial scope.

The New York Times and *The Times* were appropriate choices as sources for several reasons. Both were industry leading broadsheets with large readerships within the study timeframe, based in market countries that correlated with the marquee stops for the Tutankhamun exhibition. Both publications had dedicated reporters for the art market and regularly reported on auctions and market dynamics. While considering factors such as political leanings, ownership, and editorial changes, it was noted that while not neutral, neither publication held extreme positionalities, making them suitable for providing a balanced overview of the market. Additionally, both newspapers offer accessible online collections through institutional access via ProQuest and Gale or individual subscriptions, with user-friendly interfaces which include keyword searches and search parameters.

However, these two newspapers also came with challenges. Neither report their OCR rate, and there was a noticeable variance in quality witnessed in early 1960s and 1970s searches compared to 1980s and 1990s results. Both have gaps in their coverage during the study timeframe—*The Times* went on strike from Dec 1978-Nov 1979 and *The New York Times* from Dec 1962-Mar 1963, and from Aug-Nov 1978 which resulted in gaps in reporting, particularly in 1978, a key year for the exhibition and the market. Furthermore, *The Times* had corporate partnerships with both Sotheby's and the British Museum during portions of the study timeframe. While the corporate relationship could potentially result in overly positive, biased report, I decided the privileged access and commitment to market reporting ultimately made *The Times* a beneficial resource.

I chose to access both *The Times Digital Archive* and *The New York Times Archive* through my own paid subscription. This was principally done since I already had an online subscription to these publications for my personal use and I found the direct user interfaces more streamline than going through a third-party platform such as Gale or ProQuest. In addition, one major downside of ProQuest is the absences of images on the platform, since this third-party platform did do not have image copyright which resulted in large blocks on the page with "Blocked due to Copyright. See full page image or microfilm" that was avoided by using the publications own digital platform. I conducted data sampling on both Gale and ProQuest to confirm that I was obtaining consistent results across the primary databases and third-party platforms, which verified the initial results.

4.3.1 Targeted Searches

The initial keyword searches included "Christie's" and "Sotheby's" combined with "Egyptian". Searches targeting "Tutankhamun" were more complex due to spelling variations and punctuation, and were more difficult to survey, particularly in the 1960s and 1970. To counter this OCR noise, the use of "Egyptian" became necessary but resulted in less targeted results. Once I started to understand the patterns and limitation of each platform's OCR returns, I was able to make more targeted segmented keyword searches—e.g. "auction" + "Egyptian", "Sotheby's" + "antiquities", etc. (see Fig. 3 for a list of terms and variations searched).

The initial results led me to identify reporters who regularly covered the art market, and I included them in my search terms: for example, "Geraldine Norman" (maiden name Keen), and "Sales Room Correspondent", "Peter Hopkirk", "Bevis Hillier", and "Rita Reif". To contextualise the market comprehensively, I expanded

Market Terms	Egyptian Terms	Newspaper Terms	Other
Christie's/Christies	Egypt	Times-Sotheby's Index	British Museum (BM)
Sotheby's/Sothebys	Egyptian	Sales Room Correspondent	Metropolitan Museum (Met)
(Sotheby's) Parke-Bernet	Tutankhamun	Geraldine Norman (née Keen)	Blockbuster
Auction	Tutankhamon	Collecting	Exhibit(ion)
Auction House	Tutankhamen	Peter Hopkirk	Loot(ing)
Antiquities	Tut	Bevis Hillier	Treasure
Primitive	Boy-King/Pharaoh	Rita Reif	UNESCO

Fig. 3 Keyword and spelling variations used in survey

my search beyond auction data to include general market articles, such as seasonal and annual reviews, and relevant economic dynamics, even when they did not specifically mention Egyptian objects. To explore the relationship between markets and museum exhibitions, I investigated articles discussing the Tutankhamun exhibition, particularly those focusing on public presentation and reception. Additionally, I searched for themes related to heritage issues, including illicit activities, the UNESCO 1970 convention, and restitution. This approach aimed to create a corpus of context encompassing markets, museums, and heritage within the study timeframe, allowing for a more nuanced understanding of both the Tutankhamun exhibition and corresponding market. The search terms and themes largely emerged organically from previous results, rather than being predetermined. While this iterative approach contributed to the epistemological journey, it was time-consuming and did not consistently yield productive queries. During the systematic survey, I evaluated over a thousand articles, ultimately collecting 493 relevant news articles. Standard auction advertisements were excluded as they did not provide the substantive insights for this research. While I did look at frequency of reporting on certain topics and themes, I chose not to perform any word frequency analysis due to the potential for statistical inaccuracies and limited potential insights for this project.

4.3.2 Collecting Data

A comprehensive approach to data collection was implemented, focusing on several key data points, including publication details (date, author, page, headline), auction houses, buyers, sellers, and museums, keywords, photographs of Egyptian material, individual lots identified, and relevant quotes. Articles were systematically downloaded and stored as either PDFs or JPEGs. The collected data was organized into a database that featured a master list of articles as well as segmented lists by publication and decade.

Each interface had its strengths and weaknesses, particularly regarding OCR rates and searchability. *The Times Digital Archive*[9] has an approachable interface that initially allows for keyword searches and timeframes. Search results are displayed in a list by either relevancy or by date, and users can further refine their search by category (classified, arts and entertainment, etc.) or extra words. Once an article is selected, the clipping is instantly isolated and magnified to the article with successfully queried keywords highlighted. The interface does allow for users to zoom out of the clipping to view the page in its entirety.

The Times Digital Archive suffered from lower OCR rates, particularly in older publications, misspellings and punctuation issues resulted in a reliance on date-based searches (±3 days from auction dates) to account for publications delays due to Sundays or public holidays. The platform also exhibited sensitivity to punctuation in queries which required adjustments in searches, for example: the headline "Egyptian cat sales for £20,000", would require "Egyptian cat sales for 20000" due

[9] https://www.thetimes.com/archive

to the consistent OCR issues with commas and currency symbols. Selected articles would have corresponding 'plain text' panels for reference and here is where users could see the OCR return noise. As seen below, this plain text from the headline above has several OCR errors in it from the multiple n's in correspondent, to the issues with punctuation, and converting pound signs into question marks:

> By Geraldine Norman Sale Room Corre.nnnnlnt Antiquities used not to fetch high prices at auction because of lack of knowledge or interest; vast sums could be involved in private deals between knowledgeable dealers and museums but they were not reflected in public auctions. That situation is changing, and Sotheby's yesterday held an outstanding salc totalling ?145,254. The top price of ?31,000 (estimate ?12,000 plus) was paid for a Sumerian baked-clay relief dating from about 2000 BC (Norman 1975a, b, c, d, e, p. 16)

This plain text highlights the poor OCR return for this article. Due to these discrepancies in OCR returns, I relied on auction dates for more accurate search results. Overall, OCR rates were more successful surveying headlines verses the body of the articles, however, by adapting my searches with dates and authors, I was able to mitigate the impact of poor OCR rates. Despite the technical challenges encountered with *The Times* Digital Archive, the extensive dataset collected from the platform proved to be a valuable research resource.

The New York Times Digital Archive[10] platform offered a more detailed and user-friendly interface compared to *The Times*. It provided comprehensive search options, including keywords, date ranges, sections, and article types, with results available in both English and Spanish. Search results are presented as a list, and upon selecting an article, users can access either a digitized original or in more recent publications, a plain text version. The former is viewable through *The New York Times TimeMachine,*[11] which allows for a more immersive experience, simulating the act of browsing through the actual newspaper. TimeMachine also provides additional publication details such as bylines, subjects, and page numbers. Notably, *The New York Times* platform demonstrates superior OCR rates, resulting in fewer spelling and punctuation errors compared to *The Times Digital Archive*. While some older material may be less accurately indexed, the overall user experience of the platform surpassed those of *The Times Digital Archive*. Both platforms provided valuable pathways to market insights. Although *The Times* required more technical adjustments, its extensive reporting made the search process rewarding. Conversely, while *The New York Times* offered less comprehensive market coverage, its user-friendly interface enhanced search efficiency and result reliability.

---

[10] https://www.nytimes.com/search/?srchst=p

[11] https://timesmachine.nytimes.com/browser

4.4 *Corpus of Context*

This section offers representative examples of insights gleaned from newspaper coverage. While space prevent an exhaustive overview of my qualitative findings, I have endeavoured to highlight several insights offered by newspapers. These include essential auction details, contextualisation of objects, auctions, and market dynamics illustrated through a detailed case study, privileged insights from journalists, and revealing both internal and external market influences. Since the aims of the research was to understand both the market and museum exhibitions, I additionally examined the how Tutankhamun exhibition was presented to and consumed by the public, as well as the exhibition's connections to the market. Themes and further avenues for research are presented before concluding with reflections on newspapers as data.

4.4.1 Contextualising Auctions and Artefacts

Newspaper coverage provided valuable necessary information and reflections on auctions, ranging from pre-auction advertisements to regular post-auction reviews, particularly in *The Times*. Not every auction in the study had a review, approximately thirty-six percent of auctions in the data set appeared in a review. Information contained in the reviews varied depending on author, editorial space, and noteworthiness of the sale. Reviews from the 1960s tended to be concise, focusing on notable lots, prices achieved, buyers, and sale totals. For example: "At Christies in a sale of antiquities totaling £6,250, Moss 360gns for a series of 14 small Egyptian bronzes" (Sale Room Correspondent 1960, p. 14).

In contrast, reviews from the 1970s and 1980s tended to provide more insights into various aspects of the auction experience. These include collecting trends and fashions (Keen 1970a, b, c), pre-sale anticipation (Hillier 1972a, b) and descriptions of auction atmospheres (Reif 1981). Some reports highlight competitive bidding, as exemplified by Norman's (1974a) observation: "Yesterday's sale of antiquities was unusually crowded and there was intense competition, especially for the Egyptian pieces." Other articles offer photographs of lots (Norman 1978), highlighted Egyptian auction records (Norman 1972b, 1976a, b, c; Reif 1979a, b, c, d, e, f, 1983a, b, c, d, 1986), discuss the resale of Egyptian objects (Norman 1974a, b, c, d, e, f; Reif 1977b), reasons for lot withdrawals (Norman 1975a; Checkland 1987), as well as annual auction sales totals and frequency of auctions (Norman 1977d). Additionally, these types of reviews provide researchers with valuable insights into the auction experience, including the auction atmosphere, interest in specific lots or fields of collecting—elements that auction data alone fails to convey. Even basic information such as sales totals and buyer names were instrumental. As mentioned previously, auction price lists can be difficult to track down, thus newspaper coverage can offer some basic information to help fill auction data. Some buyers' names were included in reviews; however, these were overwhelmingly names of dealers (e.g. Spink & Sons, Robin Symes, K.J. Hewett, Charles Ede), with a few exceptions for notable collectors (e.g. J. Paul Getty, Seijiro Matsuoka, George Ortiz) and institutions (e.g. The British Museum, The Metropolitan Museum of Art, Boston Museum of Fine Art). Contemporaneously these listings served as free advertisements for dealers, giving readers insight into the types of stock available. For researchers today, these details provide valuable clues for tracking the provenance of objects and understanding collecting behaviours.

Throughout the study period, several notable collections and impressive objects entered the market, and these auctions received extensive pre- and post-auction coverage in the press. Auction houses' strategies become evident through newspapers, offering insights into marketing strategies including the use of expert opinions (Reif 1982), the emphasis in auction catalogue production and design (Reif 1977a, b, c, d, e, f, g), and invoking the association with Tutankhamun (Reif 1978g, 1982). Common market anecdotes are evident, the 'long lost masterpiece' (Reif 1982), 'the garden-art that turned into the genuine article' (Reif 1986) and the 'used as a doorstop' (Norman 1977a, b, c, d). Market participant insights included collectors' motivations (Reif 1986, 1991), reasons for selling collections (Sale Room Correspondent 1961), and potential uses for the proceeds from the sales (Glueck 1972). These market details are absent from auction data alone, yet they affect the market in measurable ways and thus it is vital to capture these details for greater market understanding.

The following case study of an Egyptian pectoral breastplate exemplifies the unique capacity of newspapers to unveil novel market insights that might otherwise remain obscured. The lot which was brought to auction by Sotheby's in New York in 1980 was described as:

> Lot 249 'Property from a Pennsylvania Private Collection'—Silver and Electrum Cloisonné Collar of Nekhebet and Edjo, late 12th Dynasty/early 18th Dynasty, circa 1850-1500 B.C., probably the pectoral inlay from a wood anthropoid coffin, representing the winged vulture and cobra of the goddesses Nekhebet and Edjo, patron deities of the kings of Upper and Lower Egypt. (Sotheby's catalogue, December 1980)

This lot is accompanied by a full page write up and a two-page colour photo foldout, with an estimated price by request only, subtly signaling its presumed value through the listing. The auction takes place on December 11, 1980, and the lot fails to sell as is indicated by the skipped lot number on the auctions price list. Relying solely on auction data, this object is presented as an impressive piece through the catalogue that seems to have failed to sell at auction. However, this case illustrates how newspaper coverage can provide a more comprehensive narrative than auction data alone, revealing complexities in provenance, authenticity, and market dynamics that may not be immediately apparent at the time of sale.

There was substantial press coverage and anticipation surrounding the piece. Under *The New York Times* headline "Antiquities: Two Great Rarities Go to Auction" by Rita Reif, a full article is dedicated to two impressive lots that are coming to onto the market in the coming days, one the Leonardo da Vinci's notebook "Of the Nature, Weight and Movement of Water", and the other, this Egyptian pectoral.

Despite the dual focus of the article, over seventy-five percent of the article discusses the pectoral and includes a photo. The lot is described as:

> The rarest Egyptian antiquity to be auctioned in decades […] Should it reach Sotheby's most optimistic expectations of $300,000, it will establish a new auction high for an Egyptian work of art […] 'This is the first time in memory that Egyptian jewelry of this importance has appeared at auction,' Richard M. Keresey, Sotheby's antiquities specialist recently said. 'It's size and complexity make it unique in the market.' […] He said he was told that an uncle of the current owner had brought the pectoral back from travels in the Middle East in the 1920s or 30s. […] 'One immediately thinks of Tutankhamun or Ramses II for most Egyptian jewelry designs,' […] Although some experts question its [Egyptian] origins, Sotheby Park Bernet regards this cloisonné ornament as the rarest Egyptian antiquity to be auctioned in decades. (Reif 1980e, p. 239)

The concerns alluded to in this article refer to issues raised around the pieces' authenticity as pharaonic Egyptian verses potentially "an example of Egyptianizing possibly done during the Middle Kingdom, by Phoenicians in Byblos, a city about 20 miles from modern-day Beirut" (Reif 1980a, b, c, d, e, f, p. 239). So, while Sotheby's dismisses these claims based on their own "thorough research on the piece" (Reif 1980a, b, c, d, e, f, p. 239), there seems to be little concern about the legality of the piece and great excitement for its sale.

Unlike most star lots, this one is not mentioned in the post-auction reviews printed in the following weeks. This did not fit the pattern of publication, especially for a piece that had garnered so much attention. Thus, I specifically searched out for articles related to this pectoral and found this market review in January 1981 from *The New York Times* under the headline "Not Everything at Auction Sells, Even in a Good Year" by Rita Reif (15 January, 1981). Reif starts with:

> Even in a boom auction year, owners and bidders know that not everything consigned to an auction sells for the prices expected, and many works do not sell at all. At most of the top art-auction houses, 10 to 25 percent of the offerings do not find buyers. The reasons vary from no bids at all to bidding that stops short of the object's reserve price—a level below which the owner will not sell […] At an auction at Sotheby's a piece of jewellery, which had been expected to establish a record of about $300,000 for an Egyptian antiquity, wasn't sold. The reason? The eagle-shaped heraldic decoration was thought by some experts not to be Egyptian. Following the auction, Richard Keresey of Sotheby's said, 'Its obscure provenance may have been a problem'. (p. 54)

Little information is given here as to the auction dynamics, if there was indeed interest in the pectoral but it failed to meet the reserve price or if buyers were generally deterred due to concerns about its pharaonic heritage. This case highlights an intriguing aspect of collector preferences in the Egyptian antiquities market. Buyers appear to prioritize objects with clear pharaonic heritage, even when there are no doubts about the item's general age. This selective approach suggests a targeted collecting discretion within the market, where the specific cultural attribution of an artifact can significantly influence its desirability and value. While these articles provide valuable insights into market conditions, such as the strength of the art market, unsold lot rates, and authenticity concerns, they leave many questions unanswered such as overall interest in the piece as well as its fate after the auction. This case illustrates the benefits of extending the scope of newspaper coverage beyond the initial timeframe. As of 1989, the original end of the study period, the fate of the pectoral after its failure to sell in 1980 remains unknown.

The pectoral surfaces in the press again in 1991, this time under the headline "Who Owns Stolen Artifacts? College Confronts a Museum" (Glueck 1991, p. 1). This frontpage story presents a true-crime murder-mystery involving a stolen Egyptian artefact, a murdered librarian, the art market and the Boston Museum of Fine Arts. Through a series of news articles both in *The New York Times* and local newspapers, the story of how this object arrived in Boston comes to light. In brief, sometime between 1978–1979 (at the hight of Tutmania in the U.S.) (Brier 1992), a librarian at Lafayette College in Easton, Pennsylvania—Robert Gennett, stole the pectoral from storage at Skillman Library at Lafayette College and destroyed all its corresponding documentation. Gennett cosigned it anonymously through John T Granger, a Pennsylvania dealer, to Sotheby's New York in 1980 where it was highly publicised and brought to auction in December 1980, where it failed to sale. In 1981, Sotheby's facilitated a private sale of the breastplate to the MFA in Boston[12] for $160,000 (a far lower price than the anticipated $300,000 at auction). It was not until 1990 that Lafayette College became aware of it was even missing the artefact and brought claim against the MFA Boston for the return of the pectoral. The case concluded in 1992 when an agreement was reached transferring title to the MFA for an undisclosed sum. Robert Gennett, who had been fired from Lafayette College in 1983 for stealing money, admitted to the theft in 1993 and in 1995 was ordered to pay $100,845 to cover Lafayette College's legal fees (Elser 1995; Elwell 1995; Glueck 1991; Vogel 1992). The story gained further intrigue due to the still unsolved 1984 murder of Alice Hall, a cataloguer at the Lafayette library. While never proven, speculation about a connection between her death and the theft featured prominently in press coverage.

Throughout the scandal, Sotheby's maintained their innocence due to lack of knowledge regarding the breastplate's theft. Richard M. Keresey stated: "Our concern at the time was whether it had come illegally out of Egypt. I guess we were aiming in completely the wrong direction" (Vogel 1992, p. 13). This statement reveals that while the auction house had concerns about the piece's legality, they ultimately proceeded with the sale despite its weak provenance. This artifact's journey through the art market illustrates "invisible sales" Nørskov (2002) as reported in the press, "Although the breastplate appeared on the cover of Sotheby's catalogue in December 1980, it was not sold at auction […] The auction house then arranged a private sale to the Museum of Fine Arts in Boston" (Glueck 1991, p. 1). The auction discussed here took place in 1980, yet events surrounding this object only come to light in 1991. Replying solely on auction data would have given only a snapshot of the story, it would have simply shown that an object failed to sell, yet newspaper coverage allowed for the whole story to become apparent. The breastplate at the centre of this story came onto the market in December 1980 at Sotheby's in New York.

[12] MFA accession number 1981.159—https://collections.mfa.org/objects/155959

This example illustrates the significant value of newspapers as data for the market. Newspaper coverage reveals crucial details about market dynamics that auction data alone cannot capture, such as private sales and auction house decision making. The pectorals journey, from its theft at Lafayette College to its eventual acquisition by the Museum of Fine Arts in Boston, reveals complex dynamics within the market that auction data alone fails to capture. The press coverage exposed issues of provenance, cultural collecting tastes, and the auction house's decision-making processes, providing crucial context to market trends and stakeholder behaviours as well as factors affecting sale outcomes (e.g., expert opinions, market conditions). Furthermore, the extended timeframe of newspaper analysis proved essential, as the full story of the pectoral's theft and legal disputes only came to light in the early 1990s, beyond the initial study period. This example underscores the usefulness of systematic newspaper coverage in uncovering legal and ethical issues in the market, including illicit activities and highlights the intricate relationships between museums, auction houses, and the market.

4.4.2 Privileged Market Access

Another benefit of newspaper coverage is the privileged access that some of market journalist enjoy. This is perhaps no more evident than in case of Geraldine Norman (née Keen). Norman (then Keen) was first hired by *The Times* as a statistician before they started to author *The Times*-Sotheby's Index in 1967; a corporate calibration between *The Times* and Sotheby's to present art as a safe investment. *The Times*-Sotheby Index visually presented art as an investment through detailed charts, percentages and sensational headlines. Each feature centred on a single collecting category and was accompanied by charts illustrating sales prices trends. The message was clear, art and selective types of antiquities (never Egyptian), were a hot commodity and should be considered next to stocks and bonds for investment purposes (Morgan 2019). *The Times*-Sotheby's Index and the press, in general, proved to have a measurable influence on the market. Due to this partnership, Norman enjoyed extremely privileged insights into the market, and while that could lead to a presumption of biased reporting: "Norman was the first saleroom journalist to expand beyond reportage, evincing a determination to bring transparency into the auction house" (Stourton 2025, p. 198). Even after the discontinuation of the Index in 1971, Norman continued at *The Times* as the Sales Room Correspondent where they covered auctions, scrutinised, and reported on the culture of secrecy that defines the market. Norman's reviews and access to market insiders offered invaluable insights into the otherwise opaque art market, brought to light by Normans reporting. While their immense contributions to the market are outside the scope of this chapter, it is worth emphasizing: "no one journalist had such an impact on the art market from 1967, whether on auction houses, museums, or members of the fine art trade as Geraldine" (Herbert 1990, p. 144). Thus, due to Norman's privileged access and dedication to reporting on the market, *The Times* becomes an invaluable resource into the inner mechanism of the market and what impacts it.

4.4.3 Market Dynamics

Norman's tenacious reporting forms the foundation for understanding internal and external dynamics on the market, influences that would not be visible through auction data alone. External influences during this study included several oil crisis and stock market crashes, currency and inflation concerns. These external market factors impacted the market in different ways:

> There are essentially two reasons why currency doubts affect the fine art market. The first is quite simply its international character. It is by no means exceptional to find buyers from 20 to 30 different countries at an important sale. Thus, fine art treasures are a truly convertible currency and will maintain their value on the international market. The second and related reason for an interaction between the currency and fine art markets is the advantage of having your money tied up in "things" if currencies go berserk. These arguments apply to any sector of the fine art market and prices in all fields have been extremely buoyant over the past year. (Keen 1968b, p. 13)

While inflation may serve as a buoyance for the art market, it is essential to interpret market trends with caution. Norman (1977a, b, c, d) aptly notes: "In an inflationary year, it is virtually inevitable that each year's figures represent a new record, at least when measured in devalued sterling" (p. 14). This observation underscores the importance of considering the effects of currency devaluation when analysing market performance. External influences that impact the market include shifts in the collector base, particularly the emergence of new participants from oil-rich nations (Reif 1981) and an increased presence of Japanese collectors (Norman 1973). These changes in the composition of buyers provide valuable insights into the market's evolving landscape and its responsiveness to global economic shifts. While external influences offer a broad context for understanding market trends, the internal dynamics of the art market, as reported in newspapers, provide even more nuanced and insightful information.

Internal market influences and decisions are often the least transparent yet arguably have some of the biggest impact on how the market functions. During the studies timeframe, both Sotheby's and Christie's open branches in New York (Sotheby's in 1964, Christie's 1977) and both go public (Sotheby's 1977–1983, Christie's in 1973–1999). The practice of buy-ins is brought to light by Norman in 1970 and the resulting public pushback eventually forces the auction houses to abandon the practice. Various profit-increasing tactics were employed including introducing buyers' premiums and the increase in commissions. *The Times*-Sotheby's Index should be regarded as an internal market dynamic since it was created by Sotheby's as a marketing tool to promote art as an investment. This initiative was notably successful, and in addition to the forty-eight articles that comprised the Index, many other publications emerged to promote and analyse the concept of art as an investment asset. This extensive coverage reinforced the Index's influence on market perceptions and behaviours, highlighting its role in shaping the art market landscape. Headlines and articles were dominated by the theme of art as investment, including headlines such as "Your money is safe in art" (Keen 1968a, b, c) and "Art for money's sake" (Keen 1968a, b, c) and demonstrate how media framing can transform public perception of the art market as an investment opportunity. The latter article noted, "With a successive financial crisis causing distrust of other kinds of investments, many more people put their money into art, and hardly a day passed without some new world record being set up" (Keen 1968a, b, c, p. 12).These sensational headlines, accompanied by graphs, charts, and detailed sales data, generated a culture of commerce around art that was readily comprehensible to the public. The relocation of auction reports and the price index from the social pages to the financial section added legitimacy to the concept. However, it is noteworthy that among all of *the Times*-Sotheby Index articles published, none included Egyptian material as a viable investment. The majority of 'safe investments' focused on traditional art forms such as Impressionist or Old Master paintings, drawings, and prints, while also encompassing Chinese and Japanese ceramics, books, French furniture, and English silver and glass in their assessments of valuable commodities. This extensive coverage reinforced the Index's influence on market perceptions and behaviours, highlighting its role in shaping the art market landscape.

Newspaper coverage serves as a critical lens for illuminating scandals within the art market, particularly how they are presented to and reacted to by the public: "The recent scandals involving Sotheby's and Christie's in New York have underlined the extraordinary extent to which the auction houses can make up the rules as they go along. By hiding their activities behind a cloak of "client confidentiality" they can get away with practices that would not be tolerated in other markets" (Norman 1985, p. 10). The extended coverage allows researchers to trace the trajectory of market trends, expose potential conflicts of interest, and facilitate public discourse about questionable market practices. Moreover, tenacious reporting can prompt regulatory scrutiny and potentially drive changes in industry behaviours such as Keen's reporting on buy-ins in 1974. Through detailed newspaper survey some external and internal market dynamics can be brought to light, offering researchers a more complete understanding of the market.

4.4.4 Linking Markets to Museum

Since the aims of my research were to understand how Tutankhamun blockbusters impact the market for Egyptian material, it was necessary to survey both the market for Egyptian material and the press coverage that the exhibition received, which was substantial. While space does not allow for an overview of the exhibition coverage, it is worth illustrating how the market reacted to Tut in town. Articles surveyed in the decade preceding the blockbuster exhibition were characterised by their promotion of the art market as a 'safe' and lucrative investment opportunity coupled with an overall lack of interest in Egyptian objects as art or an investment. There are limited examples of Egyptian objects mentioned in pre- or post-auction reviews that *The Times* consistently published. The impression that these reviews give is that Egyptian antiquities are a niche market; they only warrant a mention when it is a slow news day, or an exceptional object reaches the market. This further highlight that there is little market for Egyptian material despite Tutankhamun touring in the

1960s: it is only after Tut's blockbuster exhibition in the 1972 that Egyptian cultural objects are considered a viable investment.

The first year of the Tut achieving blockbuster status produces a plethora of newspaper headlines: daily exhibit-attendance, pharaonic dynastic charts, full-page exhibit reviews, stories of Tut's discovery, mummies curses, and full-page photos dominate the media. This demand for Tut extended beyond museum visitors; auction houses anticipated near-instant demand for Egyptian antiquities, as is evident in the auction review on 12 April 1972:

> The opportunity Christie's yesterday offered up following up the enthusiasm generated by the Tutankhamun exhibition by the purchase of Egyptian treasures was not seized by many buyers. […] The top price in the sale of Egyptian and Middle Eastern antiquities, which totalled £19,479, was £1,470 for a New Kingdom life-size black and pink granite head. (Norman 1972a, p. 4)

This review is incredibly insightful because it highlights the assumed demand generated from the exhibition. The exhibition had only been open twelve days when this auction occurs, yet Christie's is anticipating a new collecting trend based solely on the exhibition. What is even more insightful, is that the delay in demand indicates that one must view, in-person, the 'treasures' and experience the exhibit before demand can be generated; thus, it is not just the opening of the exhibition that produces demand, it is the power of seeing, in-person, which influences demand.

However, it does not take long for enough people to see the exhibit and respond. By May 1972, a new record price for an Egyptian antiquity sold at auction is set with headlines reading "Record price for sphinx from Carter collection", with the subheading "Small Egyptian sphinx of faience from the collection of Howard Carter, which also brought $260,000" (Strafford 1972). This small sphinx, now at the Met[13] is one of four record breaking Egyptian antiquities sales in the studies timeframe. Further articles advertise: "for those who are inspired by the Tutankhamun exhibition to begin their own ancient Egyptian collection, there are two shows to help you start" (Hillier 1972a, b, p. 7). Articles like this are written as collecting guides for Egyptian antiquities; art fairs, auctions and galleries are consistently covered to inform readers from which galleries (Hillier 1972a, b) and dealers (Sales Room Correspondent 1972a, b) they can obtain Egyptian antiquities.

Auction houses complement this demand with catalogues containing pharaonic-dynastic charts and educational diagrams to help place their antiquities within the context of Tutankhamun. Almost every auction review after March 1972, when the exhibition opens, mentions Egyptian objects sold at all the major auction houses, building to the pinnacle of the season at the December 5th 'Important Egyptian Antiquities from the Temple of Mut at Asher' auction at Christie's London. This auction receives a half-page preview in *The Times* (Hillier 1972a, b), recounting the riveting story of the British female 'amateur' archaeologist who excavated at the Temple of Mut. Entertaining accounts, interviews, photos and anticipated record sales were included in the review. Frank Herbert characterises this year as: "1972

[13] Accession number 1972.125—https://www.metmuseum.org/art/collection/search/544498

was a year of enthusiasm and imagination. A most unusual and academic sale of Egyptian sculpture discovered between 1895 and 1897 by two English ladies—in the Temple of Mut in Asher, near Luxor" (Herbert 1990, p. 208). This sale, like the exhibition, glorify British Egyptology, adventure and glory. This auction was the main event of the antiquities market that year: "It was clearly a good year for selling Egyptian sculpture, with Tutankhamun lying in state at the British Museum, but Christie's prices yesterday outstripped all hopes or expectations" (Norman 1972a, b, c, d, e, p. 19). Newspapers are clearly indicating that the demand for Egyptian material is influenced by the blockbuster exhibition.

The years between Tut's first blockbuster stop in London in 1972 and his 1979 New York appearance are characterised by economic downturn and a slowing of the art market, yet strong Egyptian art market sales. One of the first headlines of 1973 states: "Antiquities boom goes on as shares fall" (Norman 1973, p. 18), reporting strong antiquities sales within the backdrop of the stock market crash. While Egyptian objects are mentioned in passing in auction reviews, none of them are spectacular sales. Tut is relatively removed from *The Times* this year, only garnering 36 mentions in *The Times*, most of which compare it to the new Chinese exhibition at the British Museum. Overwhelmingly, headlines report on the 1973 Oil Crisis and the secondary stock market crash, resulting in the second banking crisis.

The year 1974 sees the same economic concerns and the lowest point of the stock market crash, resulting in the art market going bust (Norman 1974a, b, c, d, e, f). However, co-mingling among stories of economic concerns are headlines such as: "Egyptian figure, sold for £357 two years ago, fetches £3,675 at Christie's" (Norman 1974a, b, c, d, e, f, p. 20). The article further offers:

> An Egyptian black schist ushabti figure sold for £3,675 to Symes; at a Christie's sale two years ago, the same figure fetched £357. Not all Egyptian antiquities have multiplied 10 times in value in two years but there has been a notable increase in collecting interest. It may be because of the Tutankhamun exhibition [...] Yesterday's sale of antiquities was unusually crowded and there was intense competition, especially for the Egyptian pieces.

This auction review puts 1974 into greater context. Not only are objects increasing in value at astronomical rates, but there is also competition for these objects. The article lists several more Egyptian sales, and their price achieved, mostly by dealers acting on behalf of clients. It references Tut as an influencing factor and describes the robust, long-term market preference for Egyptian antiquities since the exhibition. This article also acts as an advertisement to collectors looking for investment opportunities who will understand resale values and connect Egyptian objects with sound investments. Headlines with eye-catching values and corresponding photo make the point that Egyptian objects are still a sound investment.

Another auction review offers useful insight; in July 1974: "the British Museum paid £4,725 for an Egyptian red quartzite sphinx of Senusret III (1878-1841 BCE) with the head and front paws missing" (Norman 1974c, p. 4). This acquisition by the British Museum[14] is only known in this study because of this article. It is worth

[14] Museum number EA 1849—https://www.britishmuseum.org/collection/object/Y_EA1849

noting that this sphinx did not have any provenance before the British Museum purchased it. Further, the reporting of an authoritative institution such as the BM purchasing Egyptian antiquities during a global recession legitimises the value and thus the desirability for ancient Egypt in the eyes of the market.

In 1977, just as the Tutankhamun exhibition is making its rounds throughout the U.S., record-breaking headlines continue: "Egyptian statue sold for £110,000" (Mallalieu 1977, p. 21) and "Big Demand for works of Ancient Egypt" (Norman 1977a, b, c, d, p. 16) and "£3,700 paid for Egyptian statue used as doorstop" (Norman 1977a, b, c, d, p. 14). These headline illustrate the premium buyers will pay for an entertaining story; the otherwise unremarkable statue was 'discovered being used as a doorstop in a Scottish manor': this entertaining anecdote makes what would otherwise be an ordinary sale memorable. In the March 1977 auction of Christie's London, the £110,000 paid for the one statue was over a third of the £308,585 auction total. At the auction in November: "an ancient Egyptian faience hippopotamus was sold for £26,000 at Christie's yesterday to the McAlpine Gallery [...] That was the highest price in the sale of antiquities, but Egyptian works generally were in strong demand", reiterating the undiminished demand and high prices for Egyptian objects. "Art is an investment at any time, but Egyptian art has proven a better investment than most art" (Reif 1977d, p. 3). Tut-mania has become so endemic by 1977 that it is equated to the plague in one article (Kron 1977, p. 50), with the only cure being the purchase of a Tut trophy:

> There are symptoms. Black around the eyes. A craving for hippos, lion's feet, turquoise and bangs. Egyptian fever is spreading faster than Asian flu, and by the time the Treasures of Tutankhamen exhibit arrives at the Metropolitan Museum in December 1978, the fever will no doubt have reached epidemic proportions. [...] While there is, so far, no known cure, symptomatic relief is available. It's called possession therapy. Instead of taking an aspirin for this fever, you take an amulet, mount it on a pedestal, display it prominently and inhale the aura. Unfortunately for some people, the medicine can be addictive. Purveyors of Egyptian (or Egyptian inspired) artifacts are proliferating faster than aspirin manufacturers and they're offering an assortment of charms to suit every taste and pocketbook [...] Samuel Haddad, a private dealer in Egyptian artifacts, is a good person to know if you're allergic to anything but the real thing.

While this comparison to a virus is troubling and tasteless, it is also telling. That by the time Tut is in New York, the "public infatuation with golden relics from the tomb of the Egyptian boy king Tutankhamen has inspired a wave of commercialism that threatens to become a Tut-Glut" (Chase 1978, p. C1). There are clear connections between the fevered infatuation with everything Egyptian and the markets capitalization on this syndrome. As Reif (1978a, b, c, d, e, f, g, h, i, j) accurately articulates:

> It is anything but a coincidence that during the weeks and months ahead when the "Treasures of Tutankhamen" is on view at the Metropolitan Museum of Art, New Yorkers will have more opportunities than in many years to acquire what art dealers and auctioneers describe as everything from Egyptian temple treasures to tomb debris. Indeed, the opening next week of the long-awaited exhibition has pushed the intensity of Tutmania among certain merchants and collectors to fever pitch. (Reif 1978a, b, c, d, e, f, g, h, i, j, p. D40)

After the blockbuster tours end, there is still interest in Egyptian objects, yet the scale and obsession narrow to notable pieces versus a whole collecting field. These examples illustrate the significant impact of the Tutankhamun exhibition on the market for Egyptian objects. Prior to the exhibition, Egyptian objects were considered a niche market with limited investment potential despite a booming art market. However, the blockbuster exhibition in 1972 dramatically shifted this perception, generating unprecedented public interest and market demand. Newspaper coverage played a crucial role in amplifying and documenting this transformation. Articles transitioned from sporadic mentions of Egyptian antiquities to frequent, detailed reports on record-breaking sales, collecting guides, and market trends. This change in newspaper coverage not only reflected the changing market dynamics but also contributed to them by educating potential buyers and promoting Egyptian objects as viable investments. Newspaper coverage thus serves as a valuable lens through which researchers can observe the immediate and long-term influences of cultural events such as blockbuster exhibitions on market behaviours, demonstrating the complex interplay between museum exhibitions, media representation, and economic trends in the market.

4.4.5 Reflections

While this section may seem exhaustive, it is actually only a sample of the insights gained through newspaper coverage. Further insightful themes that were collected include reporting on heritage issues such as cultural heritage crimes (looting, theft, fakes/forgeries, etc.), the UNESCO 1970 convention and the changing tone of these articles from the 1960s through the end of the 1980s. Another heritage theme identified surrounds museum collecting practices as exemplified in the surprisingly forward-looking headline "The World's Greatest Warehouse Stuffed with Other People's Glories" (Keats 1971), a long article full of insights (restitution claims, museum ownership, display and storage, etc.) which focuses specifically on the British Museums' collection and that: "there is so much here, the legends say, that even the keepers know not what they are keeping" (p. 1); ironic considering the present day scandal the BM finds itself in (Brodie 2025). Concurrently, there is an increase in criticism for the rise of commercialisation in the museum sector, particularly surrounding the Tutankhamun exhibition exemplified through examples such as museums selling authentic Egyptian objects in their gift shops during the tour (Austin 2025a, b). It is not an exaggeration to say that the insights obtained through this systematic survey of newspapers has profoundly impacted and improved the research, contextualising not only auction data and the market for Egyptian material but also the relationship between museums and the market had how they impact one another.

However, it is crucial to acknowledge the inherent limitations of newspaper data in this research. Firstly, this dataset suffers from confirmation biases, as I am looking for data to confirm the hypothesis, which influences my decision making and methodology (Klayman 1995). Secondly, while this data set may seem exhaustive, it can be assured that not all relevant articles were identified and collected due to technical limitation and size of the database. Immersion in such a large corpus of articles can lead to an overwhelming sense of certainty, necessitating periodic critical reflection on both sources and reporting motivations. While newspapers inherently contain biases, to mitigate these issues, the study surveyed multiple themes related to the cultural heritage market, aiming to provide a more comprehensive perspective. Just as auction data only gives a narrow view of the market as a whole, news articles only give a targeted view of both auctions and the market. Both newspapers are positioned in market countries thus their view of the market and its impacts and harms have the potential for bias. There is also a potential conflict of interest for reporters from *The Times* due to their temporary corporate partnership with Sotheby's. Auction houses self-reporting of annual sales totals, lots sold/unsold, and guarantees of authenticity and legality should always be questioned and double checked. Sometimes, news articles leave researchers with more questions than answers, such as reporting on further auctions that seem to have never taken place (Hopkirk 1969) or names of dealers and buyers which may be pseudonyms (Sales Room Correspondent 1962). Newspaper coverage suffers from weakness and challenges that require researchers to be reflective and diligent in their survey and while newspapers may not have all the answers, they can offer a viable complementary data source for auction data.

5 Conclusion

This chapter examines two forms of open-source data available to market researchers: auction catalogue data and digitised newspapers. This chapter acts as a response to recent calls for contextualising auction data and offers both a data source as well as a methodology. While the use of newspapers as source data is not novel, the methodologies and considerations presented here offer expanded opportunities for cultural heritage market research. This chapter has presented the case for the use of digitised newspapers as a complementary, qualitative source for investigating and contextualizing auction data. A summary of auctions as data and the increasing need for situating the quantitative data within larger antiquities market environments is presented before an overview of the transformation of newspapers into digital artefacts and the inherent strengths and challenges of this source has been provided, including technological, ethical and legal considerations. The potential for this type of data is illustrated through a case study from my forthcoming doctoral research which highlights the treasure trove of insights that can be obtained from digital newspapers, leading to new understandings and new avenues for investigation. The analyses of newspaper coverage revealed nuanced market dynamics, such as the assumed demand creation by auction house, the capitalisation of such demand by museums and the explicit link between the Tutankhamun exhibition and increased market demand for Egyptian material. This methodology demonstrates how digital print media can serve as a valuable empirical source for contextualising auction data and understanding the multiple factors influencing the cultural heritage market. While digitised newspapers are by no means a crystal-ball into the inner workings of the market, they can however, be a rich empirical source for investigating and contextualizing auction data and for understanding the multiple dynamics that impact the market for cultural heritage.

Acknowledgments Special thanks to Judith Barr whose insights and practical knowledge on the use of newspapers for provenance research was instrumental to this chapter.

Appendix: Introductory Overview of Available Newspaper Databases

1 British Library—Nineteenth Century Newspapers

- Provider: British Library; Jisc; Gale, A Cengage Company
- Holdings: 47 regional and local newspapers from Britain, 1800–1900, over 2 million pages
- Access: Free access in British Library reading rooms; remote access in the UK for higher education institutions via Jisc; outside UK by institutional purchase
- Re-use: XML, OCR, and image data cannot be republished without permission; limited reuse for small quotations with standard citation

2 Chronicling America

- Provider: Library of Congress and Partner Collection Holders
- Holdings: Covers all 50 states, DC, Puerto Rico, and US Virgin Islands; over 2.6 million pages from 1860–1963
- Access: Freely available for personal research; citations provided for images and text
- Re-use: Believed public domain; items published before 1923 are public domain; post-1922 items may contain copyrighted third-party materials requiring clearance

3 Delpher

- Provider: National Library of the Netherlands
- Holdings: Over 15 million pages, from the fifteenth to twenty-first centuries
- Access: Free personal research use; citation provided in interface
- Re-use: Public domain content is freely usable; copyrighted items clearly labelled

4 Europeana

- Provider: Europeana Foundation
- Holdings: Hundreds of newspaper titles spanning four centuries, 20 countries

- Access: Searchable freely; terms vary per item due to copyright complexities
- Re-use: Most materials in public domain with metadata under CC0 license

5 Gallica

- Provider: Bibliothèque Nationale de France
- Holdings: French newspapers from 1631–1951, over 2000 titles
- Access: Significant portion freely accessible; account registration allows extra features
- Re-use: Public domain for pre-1923 items; post-1923 may have copyright restrictions

6 Hemeroteca Nacional Digital de México

- Provider: Hemeroteca Nacional Digital de México
- Holdings: Nearly 8 million pages from 941 titles, 1722–2006
- Access: 516 titles (1722–1889) are open; 425 (1890–2006) restricted to library/university campus
- Re-use: Personal or educational purposes only; credit to HNDM required

7 Newspapers.com

- Provider: Ancestry.com LLC
- Holdings: Over 1 billion pages from 26,900+ newspapers worldwide, primarily US, 1700s–2000s
- Access: Individual and limited institutional subscriptions
- Re-use: Public domain for pre-1924 US newspapers; post-1924 under copyright, with limited reuse

8 Paper Past

- Provider: National Library of New Zealand
- Holdings: Over 6 million pages from 150+ titles, 1839–1950
- Access: Freely accessible worldwide
- Re-use: Public domain items may be reused with citation; link to source requested for online use

9 ProQuest

- Provider: Clarivate
- Holdings: Over 52 million pages, nearly 200 historical newspapers
- Access: Institutional subscription required
- Re-use: Rights held by original publishers; ProQuest provides no special permissions for reuse

10 Suomen Kansalliskirjaston Digitoidut Sanomalehdet

- Provider: National Library of Finland
- Holdings: Over 21 million pages, Finnish newspapers from 1771–1929

- Access: Basic access without account; some restricted features require authentication
- Re-use: Public domain material freely usable; third-party copyright items are labelled

11 RetroNews

- Provider: Bibliothèque Nationale de France
- Holdings: Over 2000 newspaper titles, 1631–1951
- Access: Partially open; advanced features/subscriptions required for full access
- Re-use: Academic use allowed; broader reuse requires license

12 Times Digital Archive

- Provider: Gale, A Cengage Company
- Holdings: Complete run of The Times & The Sunday Times (London), 1785–2013, over 1.6 million pages
- Access: Institutional subscription or individual purchase
- Re-use: Limited reuse for small quotations; XML, OCR, and image data require permission for republication

13 The New York Times Archive

- Provider: The New York Times Company
- Holdings: Digital articles from 1851 to present
- Access: Older material (1851–1923) limited access; post-1923 available via subscription
- Re-use: Pre-1924 public domain; post-1923 permission for redistribution commercial use

14 Trove

- Provider: National Library of Australia
- Holdings: Over 25 million pages from nearly 1500 Australian newspapers, 1803–1954
- Access: Freely accessible globally
- Re-use: Proper attribution required for use; users must confirm copyright status

15 Zefys

- Provider: State Library of Berlin
- Holdings: 193 newspaper titles, around 7 million pages, 1857–1939
- Access: Requires registration via library card or other accounts
- Re-use: Public domain with specific terms for some sub-collections

References

Ahnert R, Griffin E, Ridge M, Tolfo G (2023) Collaborative historical research in the age of big data: lessons from an interdisciplinary project, 1st edn. Cambridge University Press. https://doi.org/10.1017/9781009175548

Appadurai A (ed) (1986) The social life of things: commodities in cultural perspective. Cambridge University Press. https://doi.org/10.1017/CBO9780511819582

Austin SR (2025a) Genuine souvenir: museum gift shops and the selling of authentic cultural heritage

Austin SR (2025b) Tut on tour: 30 years of demand creation through blockbuster exhibition [Doctoral Thesis]. University College London

Balfe JH (1987) Artworks as symbols in international politics. Int J Polit Cult Soc 1(2):195–217

Barker E (1999) Contemporary cultures of display. Yale University Press

Beach B, Hanlon WW (2023) Historical newspaper data: a researcher's guide. Explor Econ Hist 90:101541. https://doi.org/10.1016/j.eeh.2023.101541

Beelen K, Lawrence J, Wilson DCS, Beavan D (2023) Bias and representativeness in digitized newspaper collections: introducing the environmental scan. Digit Scholarsh Hum 38(1):1–22. https://doi.org/10.1093/llc/fqac037

Beltrametti S, Marrone JV (2016) Market responses to court rulings: evidence from antiquities auctions. J Law Econ 59(4):913–944. https://doi.org/10.1086/691725

Borgman CL (2015) Big data, little data, no data: scholarship in the networked world. The MIT Press. https://doi.org/10.7551/mitpress/9963.001.0001

Bourdieu P (1986) The forms of capital. In: Richardson J (ed) Handbook of theory and research for the sociology of education. Greenwood, pp 241–258

Brier B (1992) Egyptomania, surveying the age-old fascination with ancient Egypt. KMT Mod J Anc Egypt 4(1):40–51

British Library (2024) Learning lessons from the cyber-attack, British Library cyber incident review. https://www.bl.uk/home/british-library-cyber-incident-review-8-march-2024.pdf/

Brodie N (2006a) Iraq 1990–2004 and the London antiquities market. In: Kersel MM, Luke C, Tubb KW, Brodie N (eds) Archaeology, cultural heritage, and the antiquities trade. University of Florida Press, pp 206–226

Brodie N (2006b) The effects of an artefact's provenance on its Saleability. Cult without Context 19:4–6

Brodie N (2008) Illicit Antiquities. In Encyclopedia of Archaeology, edited by Deborah M. Pearsall, 1489–96. NewYork: Academic Press. https://doi.org/10.1016/B978-012373962-9.00162-X http://www.sciencedirect.com/science/article/pii/B978012373962900162X

Brodie N (2014a) Provenance and Price: autoregulation of the antiquities market? Eur J Crim Policy Res 20(4):427–444. https://doi.org/10.1007/s10610-014-9235-9

Brodie N (2014b) The antiquities market: it's all in a price. Herit Soc 7(1):32–46. https://doi.org/10.1179/2159032X14Z.00000000017

Brodie N (2019) Through a glass, darkly: long-term antiquities auction data in context. Int J Cult Prop 26(3):265–283. https://doi.org/10.1017/S094073911900016X

Brodie N, Kersel MM, Mackenzie S, Sabrine I, Smith E, Yates D (2021) Why There Is Still an Illicit Trade in Cultural Objects and What We Can Do About It. *Journal of Field Archaeology 47*(2):117–30. It. https://doi.org/10.1080/00934690.2021.1996979

Brodie N (2025) Beyond the streetlight: what the reporting of the British museum thefts reveal about the antiquities trade—and what it doesn't. In: Smith E, Austin SR (eds) Researching a rigged game: handbook on open-source data & the trade in cultural heritage. Springer Law, pp 245–267

Brodie N, Manivet P (2017) Cylinder seal sales at Sotheby's and Christies (1985-2013). J Art Crime:3–16

Bunout E (2022) Contextualising queries: guidance for research using current collections of digitised newspapers. In: Bunout E, Ehrmann M, Clavert F (eds) Digitised newspapers—a new Eldorado for historians? De Gruyter, pp 275–300. https://doi.org/10.1515/9783110729214-013
Bunout E, Ehrmann M, Clavert F (eds) (2022) Digitised newspapers—a new Eldorado for historians? Reflections on tools, methods and epistemology. De Gruyter Oldenbourg. https://doi.org/10.1515/9783110729214
Burchardt J (2023) Are searches in OCR-generated archives trustworthy?: An analysis of digital newspaper archives. Jahrbuch Für Wirtschaftsgeschichte/Economic History Yearbook 64(1):31–54. https://doi.org/10.1515/jbwg-2023-0003
Chase M (1978) Museum show inspires Tutmania, C1
Checkland SJ (1987) Auction of Fragment Is Off. The Times
Chippindale C, Gill DWJ (2000) Material consequences of contemporary classical collecting. Am J Archaeol 104(3):463. https://doi.org/10.2307/507226
Chippindale C, Gill D, Salter E, Hamilton C (2001) Collecting the classical world: first steps in a quantitative history. Int J Cult Prop 10(1):1–31. https://doi.org/10.1017/S0940739101771184
Davis T (2011) Supply and Demand: Exposing the Illicit Trade in Cambodian Antiquities through a Study of Sotheby's Auction House. *Crime, Law and Social Change 56*(2):155–174.
Deacon D (2007) Yesterday's Papers and Today's Technology: Digital Newspaper Archives and 'Push Button' Content Analysis. European Journal of Communication 22(1):5–25. https://doi.org/10.1177/0267323107073743.
Ecker UKH, Lewandowsky S, Chang EP, Pillai R (2014) The effects of subtle misinformation in news headlines. J Exp Psychol Appl 20(4):323–335. https://doi.org/10.1037/xap0000028
Ehrmann M, Bunout E, Düring M (2017) Historical newspaper user interfaces: a review. International Federation of Library Associations and Institutions (IFLA). https://orbilu.uni.lu/handle/10993/50565
Ehrmann M, Bunout E, Clavert F (2022) Digitised historical newspapers: a changing research landscape. In: Bunout E, Ehrmann M, Clavert F (eds) Digitised newspapers—a new Eldorado for historians? De Gruyter, pp 1–22. https://doi.org/10.1515/9783110729214-001
Elia RJ (2001) Analysis of the looting, selling and collecting of Apulian red-figure vases: a quantitative approach. In: Doole J, Brodie N, Renfrew C (eds) Trade in illicit antiquities. McDonald Institute, pp 145–154
Elser C (1995) Librarian's house to be auctioned to satisfy $100,845 debt. The Morning Call 24
Elwell G (1995) Ex-Lafayette librarian faces more questions. The Morning Call, 32
Fortunati L, Taipale S, Farinosi M (2015) Print and online newspapers as material artefacts. Journalism 16(6):830–846. https://doi.org/10.1177/1464884914545439
Franzosi R (1987) The press as a source of socio-historical data: issues in the methodology of data collection from newspapers. Hist Methods J Quant Interdiscip Hist 20(1):5–16. https://doi.org/10.1080/01615440.1987.10594173
Frey BS, Meier S (2006) The economics of museums. In: Handbook of the economics of art and culture, vol 1. Elsevier, pp 1017–1047. https://doi.org/10.1016/S1574-0676(06)01029-5
Fyfe P (2016) An archaeology of Victorian newspapers. Vic Period Rev 49(4):546–577. https://doi.org/10.1353/vpr.2016.0039
Gaillard C-L (2022) Feuilleter la presse ancienne par gigaoctets (ChatGPT, Trans.). In: Bunout E, Ehrmann M, Clavert F (eds) Digitised newspapers—a new Eldorado for historians? De Gruyter, pp 113–124. https://doi.org/10.1515/9783110729214-006
Geismar H (2001) What's in a Price?: an ethnography of tribal art at auction. J Mater Cult 6(1):25–47. https://doi.org/10.1177/135918350100600102
Gilgan E (2001) Looting and the market for Maya objects: a Belizean perspective. In: Doole J, Brodie N, Renfrew C (eds) Trade in illicit antiquities. McDonald Institute, pp 73–88
Gill DWJ, Chippindale C (1993) Material and intellectual consequences of esteem for cycladic figures. Am J Archaeol 97(4):601. https://doi.org/10.2307/506716
Glueck G (1972) Cranbrook to sell art in fund drive. The New York Times 26
Glueck G (1991) Who owns stolen artifact? College confronts a museum. The New York Times 1:55

Hardwick T (2011) Five months before tut: purchasers and prices at the MacGregor sale, 1922. J Hist Collect 23(1):179–192. https://doi.org/10.1093/jhc/fhq015
Hauswedell T, Nyhan J, Beals MH, Terras M, Bell E (2020) Of global reach yet of situated contexts: an examination of the implicit and explicit selection criteria that shape digital archives of historical newspapers. Arch Sci 20(2):139–165. https://doi.org/10.1007/s10502-020-09332-1
Herbert J (1990) Inside Christie's. St. Martin's Press
Hillier B (1972a) Egyptian sculpture for auction. The Times
Hillier B (1972b) Antiques Egyptian market. The Times
Hopkirk P (1969) Egypt to Auction Surplus Treasures. The Times
Jarlbrink J, Snickars P (2017) Cultural heritage as digital noise: nineteenth century newspapers in the digital archive. J Doc 73(6):1228–1243. https://doi.org/10.1108/JD-09-2016-0106
Keats J (1971) The world's greatest warehouse stuffed with other people's glories. The New York Times 464, 475, 476
Keen G (1968a) Old Master paintings. The Times
Keen G (1968b) Your money is safe in art. The Times
Keen G (1968c) Art for money's sake. The Times
Keen G (1970a) £46,000 record for Chinese bowl. The Times
Keen G (1970b) Meissen sale record. The Times
Keen G (1970c) Rare Schiele sold for £39,500. The Times
King R, Rico T (eds) (2024) Methods and methodologies in heritage studies. UCL Press, University College London
Klayman J (1995) Varieties of confirmation bias. In: Busemeyer J, Hastie R, Medin DL (eds) Psychology of learning and motivation, vol 32. Academic, pp 385–418. https://doi.org/10.1016/S0079-7421(08)60315-1
Kron J (1977) Egyptian fever: a rise of the Nile Style. The New York Times 50
Leary P (2005) Googling the Victorians. J Vic Cult 10(1):72–86. https://doi.org/10.3366/jvc.2005.10.1.72
LeBlanc Z (2024) More than keywords: histories of decolonization and digitized newspapers. Am Hist Rev 129(1):164–168
Levine MN, Luna LMD (2013) Museum Salvage: A Case Study of Mesoamerican Artifacts in Museum Collections and on the Antiquities Market. Journal of Field Archaeology 38(3):264–76. https://doi.org/10.1179/0093469013Z.00000000053.
Lobay GB (2007) Objects and Objectivity: An Archaeology of Auctions. Central Italian Antiquities at Bonhams, Christie's and Sotheby's 1970-2005. Doctoral Thesis, University of Cambridge. https://www.repository.cam.ac.uk/handle/1810/284070.
Mackenzie SRM, Brodie N, Yates D, Tsirogiannis C (2019) Trafficking culture: new directions in researching the global market in illicit antiquities. Routledge
Mallalieu H (1977) Egyptian statue sold for £110,000. The Times
Manrique-Gómez L, Montes T, Rodríguez-Herrera A, Manrique R (2024) Historical ink: 19th century Latin American Spanish newspaper corpus with LLM OCR correction (arXiv:2407.12838). arXiv. http://arxiv.org/abs/2407.12838
Mason B (2000) Unfazed by Protesters. The Art Newspaper. http://www.theartnewspaper.com/archive/the-market-for-antiquities-is-growing-unfazed-by-protesters.
McLeod L (2001) Auction catalogues. In: Ford S (ed) Information sources in art, art history and design, 2nd edn. K. G. Saur, pp 90–102. https://www.degruyter.com/document/doi/10.1515/9783110954500-012/html
Morgan T (2019) "Your money is safe in art": how the times-Sotheby index transformed the art market. Hyperallergic. https://hyperallergic.com/476003/your-money-is-safe-in-art-how-the-times-sotheby-index-transformed-the-art-market/
Moser S (2015) Reconstructing ancient worlds: reception studies, archaeological representation and the interpretation of ancient Egypt. J Archaeol Method Theory 22(4):1263–1308. https://doi.org/10.1007/s10816-014-9221-z

Nicholson B (2013) The digital turn: exploring the methodological possibilities of digital newspaper archives. Media Hist 19(1):59–73. https://doi.org/10.1080/13688804.2012.752963
Norman G (1972a) A Sisley sold for £54,600. The Times
Norman G (1972b) Five new auction records set. The Times
Norman G (1972c) Wedgwood collection fetches £118,136. The Times
Norman G (1972d) Salerooms sigh with relief. The Times
Norman G (1972e) Historic sale of Giulio Romano drawings. The Times
Norman G (1973) Antiques boom goes on as shares fall. The Times
Norman G (1974a) Egyptian figure, sold for £357 two years ago, fetches £3,675 at Christie's. The Times
Norman G (1974b) £150,000 for court protrait of Persian. The Times
Norman G (1974c) High auction prices include £11,000 for a Roman figure. The Times
Norman G (1974d) £11,000 for Roman figure. The Times
Norman G (1974e) Fewer sales and lower prices bring turnover at two big sale rooms down with a bump. The Times
Norman G (1974f) Why British rail may be on the wrong track with its investment in the art market. The Times
Norman G (1975a) Prices rise as more learn about antiquities. The Times
Norman G (1975b) Botanical watercolours sold for seven times estimate. The Times
Norman G (1975c) £26,000 for portrait by Devis. The Times
Norman G (1975d) Art market veers east. The Times
Norman G (1975e) Ancient and modern. The Times
Norman G (1976a) Records tumble in Dutch Old Maters sale. The Times
Norman G (1976b) Carving of Egyptian woman fetches record £77,000. The Times
Norman G (1976c) Record bid of £62,500 for English clock. The Times
Norman G (1977a) Harlech gold torc leaves Mostyn family for £30,000. The Times
Norman G (1977b) Art sales: the puzzle over why London has done so well. The Times
Norman G (1977c) Big demand for works from ancient Egypt. The Times
Norman G (1977d) £3,700 paid for Egyptian statue used as doorstop. The Times
Norman G (1978) Jerusalem Museum Buys 1344 Pentateuch for £204,000. The Times
Norman G (1985). Who Will Put the Auction Houses in Order? The Times.
Nørskov V (2002) Greek vases in new contexts: the collecting and trading of Greek vases: an aspect of the modern reception of antiquity. Aarhus University Press
Oberbichler S, Pfanzelter E (2022) Tracing discourses in digital newspaper collections. In: Bunout E, Ehrmann M, Clavert F (eds) Digitised newspapers—a new Eldorado for historians? De Gruyter, pp 125–152. https://doi.org/10.1515/9783110729214-007
Pfanzelter E, Oberbichler S, Marjanen J, Langlais P-C, Hechl S (2021) Digital interfaces of historical newspapers: opportunities, restrictions and recommendations. J Data Min Digit Human. https://doi.org/10.46298/jdmdh.6121
Reif R (1977a). Investing. The New York Times 222
Reif R (1977b) The energy play in antiquities. The New York Times 3
Reif R (1977c) The London art market arrives. The New York Times 105:106
Reif R (1977d) Art auctions setting sales records. The New York Times 29
Reif R (1977e) Antiques. The New York Times 70
Reif R (1977f) On the block: a big collection. The New York Times 76
Reif R (1977g) Auctions. The New York Times 69
Reif R (1978a) Antiques. The New York Times 75
Reif R (1978b) Auctions. The New York Times 46:66
Reif R (1978c) Auctions. The New York Times 68
Reif R (1978d) Sales at Sotheby top $100 million for the first time. The New York Times 38
Reif R (1978e) Auctions. The New York Times 69
Reif R (1978f) Antiques. The New York Times 248
Reif R (1978g) Antiques: In the Egyptian craze, what is the real thing? The New York Times D40

Reif R (1978h). Auctions. The New York Times 75
Reif R (1978i) Auctions. The New York Times 74
Reif R (1978j) Auctions. The New York Times 54
Reif R (1979a) Auctions. The New York Times 68
Reif R (1979b) Auctions. The New York Times 70
Reif R (1979c) Auction houses say boom continues. The New York Times 30
Reif R (1979d) Sotheby's to advise Citibank. The New York Times 70
Reif R (1979e) Auctions. The New York Times 74
Reif R (1979f) Antiques. The New York Times 106
Reif R (1980a) New York Challenges London in Art Sales. The New York Times 51
Reif R (1980b) How auction sales are transforming the art world. The New York Times 71:96
Reif R (1980c) Antiques. The New York Times 117
Reif R (1980d) Auctions. The New York Times 63
Reif R (1980e) Antiques. The New York Times 239
Reif R (1980f) Auctions. The New York Times 82
Reif R (1981) Antiques. The New York Times 114
Reif R (1982) The Case of the Lost Statue. The New York Times
Reif R (1983a) Auctions. The New York Times 74
Reif R (1983b) Auctions. The New York Times C21
Reif R (1983c) Statue a student found brings $341,000 at Sale. The New York Times 47
Reif R (1983d) Auctions; Diamonds in Hamptons. The New York Times, C22
Reif R (1986). Auction. The New York Times 59
Reif R (1991) A Collection of Treasures. The New York Times
Riggs C (2021) Treasured: how Tutankhamun shaped a century. Atlantic Books
Sales Room Correspondent (1960) Ming dynasty cup sold for £2,600. The Times 14
Sale Room Correspondent (1961) Christie's Sell Lord Pembroke's Marbles. The Times
Sales Room Correspondent (1962) £1,400 paid for 1602 book; £170 for a mummy. The Times 5
Sales Room Correspondent (1972a) £2,800 for Roman satyr. The Times
Sales Room Correspondent. (1972b). £7,000 for a tiny Japanese carving. The Times
Satov M (1997) Catalogues, Collectors, Curators: The Tribal Art Market and Anthropology. In Contesting Art. Art, Politics and Identity in the Modern World, edited by Jeremy MacClancy, 215–239. Oxford: Berg Publishers. https://collections.si.edu/search/record/siris_sil_979041.
Sotheby Park Bernet Inc (1980) Important Egyptian, Greek, Roman, Etruscan and Western Asiatic antiquities: including property from the collection of Leon Pomerance; property from the collection of Marquesa Margaret Rockefeller de Larrain; property of a charitable foundation from the André Meyer Collection … Public auction: Thursday, December 11, 1980
Stourton J (2025) Rogues and scholars: boom and bust in the London art market, 1945–2000, 1st edn. Head of Zeus
Strafford P (1972) Record price for sphinx from Carter collection. The Times
Taft WH (1970) Newspapers as tools for historians. Lucas Bros
Tolfo G, Vane O, Beelen K, Hosseini K, Lawrence J, Beavan D, McDonough K (2022) Hunting for treasure: living with machines and the British Library newspaper collection. In: Bunout E, Ehrmann M, Clavert F (eds) Digitised newspapers—a new Eldorado for historians? De Gruyter, pp 23–46. https://doi.org/10.1515/9783110729214-002
Torget AJ (2022) Mapping texts: examining the effects of OCR noise on historical newspaper collections. In: Bunout E, Ehrmann M, Clavert F (eds) Digitised newspapers—a new Eldorado for historians? De Gruyter, pp 47–66. https://doi.org/10.1515/9783110729214-003
Tremain CG (2017) Fifty years of collecting: the sale of ancient Maya antiquities at Sotheby's. Int J Cult Prop 24(2):187–219. https://doi.org/10.1017/S0940739117000054
Tworek HJS (2024) Digitized newspapers and the hidden transformation of history. Am Hist Rev 129(1):143–147. https://doi.org/10.1093/ahr/rhad496

van Dijk JAGM (2006) Digital divide research, achievements and shortcomings. Poetics 34(4):221–235. https://doi.org/10.1016/j.poetic.2006.05.004

Van Strien D, Beelen K, Ardanuy M, Hosseini K, McGillivray B, Colavizza G (2020) Assessing the impact of OCR quality on downstream NLP tasks. In: Proceedings of the 12th international conference on agents and artificial intelligence, pp 484–496. https://doi.org/10.5220/0009169004840496

Vogel C (1992) A happy ending: museum keeps stolen artifact and college gets cash. The New York Times 13:18

Wilkinson C (2024) Out of the shadowlands: the digitization of early Indian newspapers. Am Hist Rev 129(1):159–163. https://doi.org/10.1093/ahr/rhad497

Wodak R, Krzyżanowski M (eds) (2008) Qualitative Discourse Analysis in the Social Sciences. Houndmills, Basingstoke, Hampshire [England]; New York: Palgrave Macmillan.

Yates D (2022) What auction catalogue analysis cannot tell us about the market. In: Fabiani MD, Burmon KM, Hufnagel S (eds) Global perspectives on cultural property crime, 1st edn. Routledge, pp 43–60. https://doi.org/10.4324/9780367823801-6

Yates D, Brodie N (2023) The illicit trade in antiquities is not the world's third-largest illicit trade: a critical evaluation of a factoid. *Antiquity 97*(394):991–1003. https://doi.org/10.15184/aqy.2023.90

Summer Austin is a PhD candidate at the University College London Institute of Archaeology. Her doctoral research Tut on Tour: 30 years of Demand Creation through Blockbuster Exhibition investigates the role of blockbuster museums exhibitions and how they influence the demand for cultural heritage and the consequences for such demand. Summer holds an Art History MSc in Collecting and Provenance in an International Context from the University of Glasgow, and MSc in Archaeology from the University of Edinburgh. Her research interests include the art and antiquities market, looting and trafficking of cultural and natural resources, museums and the market, ethics of ownership, art crime and cultural heritage law.

Open Access This chapter is licensed under the terms of the Creative Commons Attribution-NonCommercial-NoDerivatives 4.0 International License (http://creativecommons.org/licenses/by-nc-nd/4.0/), which permits any noncommercial use, sharing, distribution and reproduction in any medium or format, as long as you give appropriate credit to the original author(s) and the source, provide a link to the Creative Commons license and indicate if you modified the licensed material. You do not have permission under this license to share adapted material derived from this chapter or parts of it.

The images or other third party material in this chapter are included in the chapter's Creative Commons license, unless indicated otherwise in a credit line to the material. If material is not included in the chapter's Creative Commons license and your intended use is not permitted by statutory regulation or exceeds the permitted use, you will need to obtain permission directly from the copyright holder.

A Discipline that Sat on Its Treasures, but Didn't See Them: Leveraging Online Auction Data for Design Historical Research

Petra Seitz

Abstract This chapter details the Chandigarh Chairs project's collection and analysis of online auction data during the COVID-19 pandemic. Collection and analysis of online auction data is presented as a successful method to remotely study items of modernist furniture from the Indian city of Chandigarh in lieu of more traditional design historical techniques. The method utilized by the project research team is presented, alongside research insights related to the objects of furniture themselves, as well as the broader market within which these objects are bought and sold. The chapter concludes by advocating further utilization of online auction data within the design historical field as both a tool for the generation of greater object knowledge and greater understanding of markets for objects of design.

1 Introduction

The Chandigarh Chairs project is an independent, interdisciplinary research endeavour seeking to address gaps in the internationally and popularly known story and history of Chandigarh's modernist furniture. The project aims to critically interrogate how the history of this furniture has been written, by whom, to what ends, and how this narrative creation process has impacted not only our shared understanding of these pieces of modernist design but also the physical trajectory and use of the pieces themselves. Built around principles of regenerative and redistributive research, from its start, the Chandigarh Chairs project has sought to make its findings and resources openly available to any individuals wishing to further explore Chandigarh's modernist furniture on their own terms. All the project's outputs, including the project database discussed in this chapter, are made available on the project's website, chandigarhchairs.com.

P. Seitz (✉)
Bartlett School of Architecture, University College London, London, UK
e-mail: petra.seitz.20@ucl.ac.uk

© The Author(s) 2026

E. Smith, S. Austin (eds.), *Researching a Rigged Game: Digital Approaches to Tracing the Illicit Trade in Cultural Objects*, Studies in Art, Heritage, Law and the Market 11, https://doi.org/10.1007/978-3-032-02014-7_10

The simultaneous start of the project with the outbreak of the COVID-19 pandemic prevented the implementation and utilization of traditional design-historical research methods, particularly object and place-based analyses. These constraints led the project team to undertake a new-to-us methodology: the collection, collation, and analysis of information from publicly available online auction listings. This research practice yielded significant fruits for the Chandigarh Chairs project, providing empirical information about the physical objects themselves, alongside suggestions of the broader circumstances and processes of the pieces journey from administrative offices in Chandigarh's governmental buildings to museum and private collections in Europe and North America.

Detailing the methods utilized in the Chandigarh Chairs project, this chapter demonstrates how online auction data can help the field of design history, providing key foundational information about objects of study, as well as enriching knowledge of the actors, institutions, and processes involved in the sale, resale, and knowledge creation related to designed objects. Further, the chapter argues that collection and analysis of online auction data pertaining to designed objects indicates the presence of unethical and potentially illegal practices occurring within the trade in designed objects. While such practices have been increasingly documented and discussed within other markets for cultural heritage and property, their occurrence within design markets has until now largely evaded scholarly inquiry. Further collection and examination of auction data is proposed as one way to align design historical research with related fields, and begin to investigate and combat undesirable, unethical, and potentially illegal practices and actions.

This chapter begins with an introduction to Chandigarh's modernist furniture, including what is known about its design and initial location within the city of Chandigarh, as well as its subsequent relocation and resale across the world. After discussion of what is known, attention is paid to the areas where information remains outstanding on these pieces. The data collection project undertaken to fill these gaps is outlined, and initial findings of this research are presented. Finally, findings are analysed and conclusions related to the Chandigarh Chairs project are drawn and presented and potential uses and impacts of similar data collection processes within the field of design history are discussed.

1.1 Note on Definitions

While the fields of design history and design studies infrequently provide definite definitions of 'design' itself, this chapter defines an object of design as a tangible entity whose physical shape is based both on functional and aesthetic considerations (Fallan 2010; Kaufmann Jr. 1969). Designed objects are contrasted with objects of fine art such as paintings, sculptures, and art photographs, which contain predominantly aesthetic value and are not generally used for particular tasks outside of aesthetic appreciation (Fallan 2010; Lindemann 2010; Walker 1989). Within the category of design, reference is made to the sub-category of objects of mass-manufactured design, understood to be objects of design made on a large and standardized scale, frequently by machinery.

2 Chandigarh's Chairs

Chandigarh's modernist furniture was created to furnish the newly built city of Chandigarh, India. Developed in 1947 following the partition of India and annexation of Lahore, Chandigarh was to serve as the Indian Punjab's new capital and administrative centre. After initial project architect Matthew Nowicki's untimely death, Swiss-French architect Charles-Édouard Jeanneret–better known as Le Corbusier–was tapped to design the architecture and plan of the city (Evenson 1966). While Le Corbusier worked from his Paris atelier, making trips to India as needed, Le Corbusier's cousin and frequent collaborator, Pierre Jeanneret, alongside British architects Jane Drew and Maxwell Fry, relocated to the nascent city of Chandigarh for the duration of the project (Joshi 1999; Ruegg 2015). Jeanneret, Fry, and Drew became a part of a larger team of Indian architects and planners, including Aditya Prakash, Urmila Eulie Chowdhury and Jeet Malhotra (Evenson 1966). Throughout their tenure, the Chandigarh architectural team designed everything from cinemas and private homes to day-care centres and hospitals, as well as much of the furniture which would be placed within these buildings (Evenson 1966).

This furniture would largely remain in situ within the city until roughly 1999, when two French antique dealers, Eric Touchaleaume and Gérald Moreau, undertook a prospecting trip to Chandigarh (Touchaleaume and Moreau 2010, pp. 10–11). This was their first of what became over 30 trips to the city in the following seven years (Touchaleaume and Moreau 2010). During this time the dealers purchased an unspecified amount of the city's furniture, removed it to France, had the pieces professionally refurbished, exhibited them, began writing a book on the furniture, and finally put the pieces up for sale at auction (Touchaleaume and Moreau 2010, pp. 14–15). In 2011 an export ban was implemented by the Indian government, preventing further objects from legally leaving the country (Gandhi 2021). As of the time of writing, numerous pieces of the furniture remain in use within Chandigarh's governmental buildings, with further examples in local museums or warehoused under lock and key to prevent theft (Prashar 2020b).

Chandigarh's modernist furniture has proliferated within the cultural and popular zeitgeist, including frequent mentions within mainstream and design publications such as *The New York Times* and inclusion in interior design spreads of some of Hollywood's most famous stars (Gentleman 2008; Martin 2017; Medford 2019). The research team has observed items of furniture with significantly similar designs being sold at several big-name stores, including IKEA, Primark, Oliver Bonas, and Anthropologie. Items sharing the design of Chandigarh's modernist furniture have been used for the creation of ambiance in the French department store Galleries

Fig. 1 Several designs of Chandigarh's modernist furniture in the Studio CHD showroom. Photo courtesy Gregor Wittrick, 2022

Lafayette and within The European Fine Art Foundation (TEFAF) Fair in Maastricht.[1] Chandigarh Chairs were utilized in a central role in the Victoria and Albert Museum's 2024 'Tropical Modernism' show, and iterations continue to be produced by a number of companies around the world including high-end furniture manufacturer Cassina,[2] Bangalore, India-based company Phantom Hands, Chandigarh, India-based Studio CHD, and the Chandigarh Model Jail (Cassina n.d.; Phantom Hands n.d.; Chandigarh Model Jail n.d.; Studio CHD n.d.; Victoria and Albert Museum n.d.). While not yet as famous or as recognizable as many of the heaviest hitters in modernist design, such as the Charles and Ray Eames leather and plywood lounge chair or the Mies van Der Rohe Barcelona chair, the Chandigarh Chair's angular wood and cane frame appears to be a rapidly growing presence and influence within the world of design, and beyond.

As previously indicated, and in contrast to the growing fame of Chandigarh's modernist furniture (see Fig. 1), much information about the design, production, and initial use of these items remains unknown. While much of the popular literature attributes their general design to Pierre Jeanneret, specifics of the creation process for particular pieces, including preparatory or iterative drawings and plans, do not appear to be publicly available. Less information still appears to exist regarding

[1] The former observed in situ by the author, the latter brought to the project team's attention by a colleague at the University of Maastricht.

[2] Cassina currently produces a line of modernist chairs the company has titled a 'hommage' to Pierre Jeanneret, which 'reinterpret' original designs for the furniture (Cassina n.d.).

the physical manufacture of Chandigarh's furniture: no factories, locations,[3] individuals, production methods, materials sources or specific manufacture dates have been identified. Stories of the use of these pieces during their initial introduction to Chandigarh, and throughout their continued use, remain few and far between. Limited information regarding initial sales of pieces within India, from local government authorities to European and/or North American furniture dealers, including details and dates of export from India, has been disclosed. Further, scant information regarding specific furniture pieces, individual chairs, tables, daybeds, and lighting, including individual wear and tear, construction, repair, and reconstruction, could be found by the project team. This lack of information on Chandigarh's modernist furniture presented an initial hurdle to the Chandigarh Chairs research team.

Research difficulties presented by limited sources were compounded by the timing of the start of the Chandigarh Chairs project. In-depth project research began in the winter of 2020, coinciding with the emergence of the COVID-19 pandemic. The closure of archives, issuance of stay-at-home orders, and shutting of international borders further limited research avenues for the project, particularly many of the cornerstone methodologies of design historical research such as first-hand, object-based analysis (Hannan and Longair 2017). The Chandigarh Chairs project team could neither access, handle, and observe iterations of Chandigarh's modernist furniture held in nearby museum collections, such as the Victoria and Albert Museum, nor could we travel to the Indian Punjab to document iterations within Chandigarh and converse with users, manufacturers, and repairers of the pieces.

Although traditional design historical sources appeared temporarily unavailable, the project team had noted continuing listings of objects purported to be items of Chandigarh's modernist furniture on auction house websites, particularly in Europe and North America. Internet searches for 'Chandigarh Chair' alerted the research team to a series of recent sales; Chandigarh chairs had featured in many sales in the final months of 2019 including three October sales of 'Design', and one of 'Classic + Contemporary' items (Aguttes 2019; Phillips 2019; Rago 2019; Wright 2019). The team hypothesized that information collected from these and similar auction listings might be utilized in lieu of both in person object observation, collecting primary information about the objects themselves, and also potentially as a secondary source, potentially providing insights into how these objects were being sold, by whom, and to what end.

[3] Aside vague references to the Indian Punjab or the area surrounding Chandigarh, such as the assertion by the Victoria and Albert Museum that the pieces were 'manufactured from local materials in workshops surrounding Chandigarh' (Victoria and Albert Museum n.d.).

3 Methodology

Collection and analysis of auction house data pertaining to Chandigarh's modernist furniture was undertaken to develop a source by which increased understanding of these items and their sale could be developed. While this online data-based method entailed the collection of a sizeable amount of information, the intention behind this collection was not to be comprehensive, collating data from every sale of Chandigarh's modernist furniture with available information. Rather, this data collection was aimed at establishing a 'lay of the land' regarding Chandigarh's modernist furniture, collecting enough data to generate broader understandings of the furniture itself and gathering sufficient information to enable hypotheses to be made regarding these pieces. The methodology described subsequently in this section reflects this goal.

Collection of auction data began in January 2020 and continued through December of the same year. In total, 1769 individual lots were identified and included in the collected data. Many of these lots included the sale of multiple items, such as sets of dining or lounge chairs, or combinations of desks and purportedly matching desk chairs. A variety of items were included in the listings, including chairs, desks, tables, lights, metal shutters, storage furniture and manhole covers. Lots ranged in sales price from $0, for unsold objects, to $301,000 USD.

Initial internet searches led to the identification of nine auction houses as being the primary public auction house listers of objects purporting to be pieces of Chandigarh's modernist furniture. The websites of these eight auction houses provided the starting location for research. These included two large international houses (Sotheby's and Christies), one mid-sized international house (Aguttes), five specialist houses focused on design and/or modernist art and design (Wright, Phillips, Rago, Toomey & Co. and Artcurial), and one upscale Indian auction house (SaffronArt).

Searches were conducted on the websites of auction houses, using key terms such as 'Chandigarh', 'Jeanneret', and 'Corbusier'. These terms were selected as they encompassed high-level descriptors of the furniture most likely of interest to the buying public, particularly those related to the furniture's designers and its location of origin. More specific search terms, including materials (i.e. 'Teak' or 'Cane'), and type of furniture (i.e. 'Chair' or 'Daybed') were not utilized due to both the breadth of items included within the category of Chandigarh's modernist furniture, and the scope of other lots likely including such terms.

A comprehensive review of relevant sale catalogues within each auction house was conducted to identify objects potentially missed through the keyword search. The title of each auction held from the start of available online records was read, and complete listings for auctions whose titles indicated some relevance to Chandigarh, India, Modernist Furniture, Le Corbusier, or Pierre Jeanneret were manually scrutinized for missed objects, which had perhaps been mislabelled, labelled with differing language, or labelled in a language other than English. This secondary search helped to ensure that most, if not all, items sold as Chandigarh's modernist furniture within the target auction houses were identified and included in the resulting dataset.

A range of data was collected from each relevant lot's webpage including the auction house, sale date, auction name, item title, item dimensions, description, provenance, estimated sale price, final sale price, a link to the auction webpage, the 'model number' and specific reference information if included, and one image.[4] Because of the volatile and ever-changing nature of web data, images were downloaded or screen-captured and saved to ensure future access, before being inserted into the database spreadsheet.

After data was collected, dimensions were standardized to centimetres and prices converted to US Dollars following the prevalent exchange rate of 1.2189 US dollars to one Euro and 1.311 US dollars to one Great British Pound.[5] Prices in original currencies for both estimations and actual sales price were kept within the database for future reference and/or conversion.

After the information collection phase was completed, an initial consultation of data collected revealed that some auction item titles, descriptions, or provenance information contained reference to item codes.[6] Originating from the 2010 Eric Touchaleaume and Gerard Moreau volume *The Indian Adventure* (2010), these codes appeared to be used to identify and separate different 'designs' of Chandigarh's modernist furniture. An office desk sold within a Phillips December 12, 2012, auction, for example, was titled '" Office table" desk, model no. PJ-BU-02-A' (Seitz et al. 2021).[7] Here, the utilized code appeared to differentiate the design of desk being sold from other desk designs within the oeuvre of Chandigarh's modernist furniture.

To create informational parity across surveyed auction lots, project researchers Gregor Wittrick and Petra Seitz undertook a process of initial visual analysis, comparing images of items included in the database against those utilized to categorize and label objects within *The Indian Adventure*. Physical characteristics, including angle and positioning of item limbs, apparent materials utilized, and relative dimensions, were used to make these comparisons. Resulting educated guesses regarding potential object codes were added to the primary tracking document, alongside corresponding page references for the object's code within *The Indian Adventure*.[8]

---

[4] While inclusion of additional images may have been beneficial for data analysis, the time required to capture, label, and store additional images, in addition to file size needed to contain additional images led the research team to limit collection to one representative example per auction lot. This decision to limit number of images collected in the name of efficiency falls in line with the larger motivation behind data collection to enable creation of a broad overview, rather than comprehensive documentation, of Chandigarh chairs sold at auction.

[5] The Indian auction house surveyed, Saffron Art, posts prices in both Indian Rupees and US dollars in all listings, so no external conversion rate was needed between these two currencies.

[6] These codes are discussed in more detail within subsequent sections of this chapter.

[7] As of publication, this auction listing is no longer available online. The contents of the listing can be viewed within the Chandigarh Chairs Project's freely available auction spreadsheet.

[8] *The Indian Adventure* does not provide the methodology, nor the sources utilized to produce the object codes and classifications contained within its inventory listing. Given this, and sparse avail-

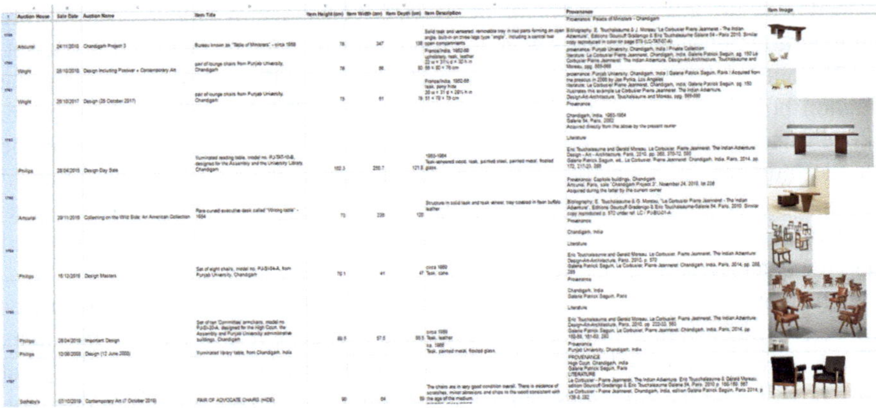

Fig. 2 Screenshot of Master Chandigarh Chairs auction listing database

	Mean	Median	Mode	Variance
Depth	122.9647059	123.2	122	3.2
Width	245.1764706	244.3	244	7.7
Height	104.5941176	112	112	49.9

Fig. 3 Dimensional calculations and variance for object PJ-TAT-10-B, a Library table from Punjab University

As the initial research period concluded, the spreadsheet containing the collected information included 16 columns, 1770 rows and covered sales from 2007 to 2020. The size of the sheet, while impressive, proved too unwieldy for streamlined analysis.

To facilitate use of the collected information, additional sheets were added to the primary tracking document, isolating data both by selling auction house and by type of item sold, following the previously determined object codes (see Fig. 2). Within sheets dedicated to specific designs, average dimensions (mean, median, and mode), were calculated for each dimension (height, width, and depth), alongside variance within each dimension (See Fig. 3).

able primary materials on Chandigarh's modernist furniture, the authors believe *Indian Adventure* authors Eric Touchaleaume and Gerard Moreau may have utilized a similarly visual-based technique in their own categorization.

3.1 Auction Data Collection and Design History

Collection and utilization of auction data, while not an unfamiliar technique in art historical, archaeological, or criminological research (Brodie 2019), represents a relatively novel approach for the discipline of design history. The novel nature of the aforementioned methodology to the field of design history manifests on two fronts. It is novel both because the practice of utilizing auction data for object study is distanced and abstracted from the discipline's traditional object-based methods, and because use of auction data inescapably involves documenting and analysing secondary markets for objects of design, an until now limited practice within design historical scholarship. These disciplinal limits within the field of design history make the utilization of online auction data detailed above a significant departure from design historical methods and techniques, as it involves physical distance from the objects of study and an explicit acknowledgement, if not analysis, of the operations and behaviours of auction houses and the sellers of objects.

3.2 Limitations

While the auction dataset of Chandigarh's modernist furniture is of a substantial size and, as is detailed subsequently in this chapter, provides considerable insights, the data collected is not without its limitations. Although efforts were made during data collection to be as thorough as possible, the data likely does not encompass every item of Chandigarh furniture put up for auction during the research period. Pieces may have been listed within major auction houses without identifiable keywords, and further items may have been listed and sold by smaller auction houses not yet known to the researchers, and therefore not included in the study. Listings placed online after the research phase concluded in the winter of 2020 have likewise not yet been included within the data set. Collection of data was additionally limited by the available working hours of the research team, particularly given that as of the time of writing, the Chandigarh Chairs project remains an unaffiliated, independent research endeavour carried out in the primary researchers' spare time.

Further, the collected data only represents objects sold at public-facing auctions and does not encompass objects sold within private transactions, including gallery and direct sales (sales referred to as 'invisible' by Nørskov 2002). Recognizing that re-sale and re-auction of individual pieces within the same auction house, and at different auction houses is not always made public, it is difficult to use the data collected to determine how many total pieces of furniture and how numerous pieces of each specific design have been sold. As the number of private transactions is definitionally private, it remains unclear what relative proportion of the overall market is covered by the collected auction data (Yates 2022). Such issues are not unique to the market for Chandigarh chairs, or, in fact, the market for design; market opacity obstructing comprehensive research has been noted as an issue within all fields addressing trade in cultural property (Brodie 2019; Davis 2011; Yates 2022).

4 Findings

Several key themes emerge from the collected auction data: knowledge of techniques used in initial construction and subsequent reconstruction of the furniture, aestheticization of objects listed for auction, inconsistent dimensions of items sold as being the 'same' design, and a cyclical and self-referential ecosystem of background and provenance information regarding the furniture.

4.1 Construction and Repair

Collection and collation of over 1700 photographs of Chandigarh's furniture allowed for a comprehensive analysis of the materials and techniques used both in the initial construction of the furniture and subsequent repairs made to pieces. The variety of images collected from auction listings meant objects could be examined from several angles under a variety of lighting, exposing and highlighting different elements of the furniture. Images of design details such as joints, wear, upholstery, and markings facilitated an understanding of the type of workmanship (fast, by hand) and the range of woodwork techniques used to manufacture the furniture; namely that the pieces were constructed rapidly and exclusively by hand. Images allowed for the identification of common areas of heavy use, and subsequent repair, providing information on how pieces were used, as well as the techniques utilized within their repair.

A variety of materials and techniques were highlighted by this visual analysis process. The colour and texture (grain) of wood materials used for various chairs and tables appeared to be different, with some objects displaying a dark red colour, others in warm pale wood tones, and yet further examples in dark, almost chocolate browns. Such variations suggested that items, even those sharing other physical design similarities, may have either been constructed from different wood materials or treated with different varnishes.

Caning techniques, too, appeared to vary within and between object types. Some specimens appeared to have caned seats and chair backs comprised of natural, fibre-based materials, while other objects' caning appeared to have been done in a synthetic plastic material. Caning on some objects appeared technically complicated, involving circular or diamond shaped patterns (such as those utilized in Marcel Breuer's Cesca dining chairs), while other iterations utilized more utilitarian perpendicular weaving techniques (Illustrated in Fig. 4).

Hand painted or stencilled letters and numbers were observed on several pieces, perhaps serving as identification codes for Chandigarh's municipal administration responsible for furniture maintenance (See Fig. 4).

Fig. 4 A close photograph of a wood, metal, and cane chair observed in an antique store in Bangalore, featuring white painted letters and numbers on the rear. Image taken by the author, 2022

4.2 Aestheticization

Review of collected images brought into focus what appeared to be a process of aestheticization in the visual display and presentation of pieces of Chandigarh's furniture. Numerous auction images seemed to depict Chandigarh chairs as pieces of fine art, set atop white plinths and backdrops. This process is well represented by a December 16, 2014, Phillips listing for a set of 'armchairs, model no. PJ-AH-09-A'. In images for this listing six armchairs are positioned, haphazardly, on a raised white platform set against a stark white wall, with an additional two chairs positioned in the foreground (Phillips 2014). A December 15, 2017, Wright Sale additionally illustrates such a setup. Within the images in this listing a 'set of ten' 'committee armchairs from the high court' are arranged in a semi-circle, floating within an otherwise non-demarcated white space (Wright 2017).

Alongside images styled after art galleries, other auction photos depicted Chandigarh's furniture within various nature settings, like a May 20, 2019, Aguttes auction, where a pair of library chairs are photographed within a forest, and a stool is set amongst a sandy beach (Aguttes 2019b). In infrequent situations, such as a May 23, 2018, Sotheby's sale and a November 20, 2018, Artcurial auction, the items listed for auction are staged as functional furniture, with reading material placed upon an illuminated library desk (Seitz et al. 2021),[9] or positioned within a household setting, again with material resting upon them (Sotheby's 2018). Auction images depicting Chandigarh's furniture on plinths and in nature settings seemed to present the chairs, desks, lamps, and daybeds being sold at auction not as functional furniture, but as objects of decorative or fine art—to be seen, but not used.

4.3 Dimensional Irregularities

Collection and analysis of a broad array of data regarding auction sales of Chandigarh furniture allowed for cross-comparison between objects sold as being of the same design and origin, bringing to light significant size discrepancies between objects sharing the same object identification code, and thus nominally sharing the same design.[10]

The object labelled PJ-TAT-10-B, a library table from the University of Punjab, served as a striking example of an object with irregular dimensions. As of the end of the research period, ten versions of this piece were sold, with most objects adhering to roughly the same dimensions: a depth of approximately 122 cm, a width of 244 cm and a height of 112 cm (Seitz et al. 2021). Dimension variances were minimal (Dimensions are illustrated in Fig. 3). The variance in depth was 3.2 cm between the smallest and largest PJ-TAT-10-B library table, while the variance in width was 7.7 cm (Seitz et al. 2021). However, one item appearing to be a PJ-TAT-10-B library table was listed in a December 2, 2012, Artcurial auction with a height of 79 cm, a significant 49.9 cm difference from the largest PJ-TAT-10-B library table iteration (Seitz et al. 2021).

As illustrated in Fig. 5, the dimensions, as well as occasionally the images, within the auction data collected suggested that objects sold as being of the 'same design' more than occasionally had differing measurements. Nominally same objects both within multiple-object auction lots and between auction lots were of different heights, widths, and depths.

4.4 Provenance

Beyond insights into the physicality of Chandigarh's modernist furniture, data collected also provided information regarding how these pieces were presented to the world. Data from 'Provenance' and 'Literature' sections of auction listings

[9] As of publication, this auction listing is no longer available online. The contents of the listing can be viewed within the Chandigarh Chairs Project's freely accessible auction spreadsheet.

[10] Dimensional fluctuations and irregularities are of particular note when they occur in objects of design, as opposed to other categories of cultural heritage. This is because designed objects nominally and definitionally share the same design, the same blueprint from which the objects have been created, often, as is the case with Chandigarh's modernist furniture, in multiples (Cardoso 2010).

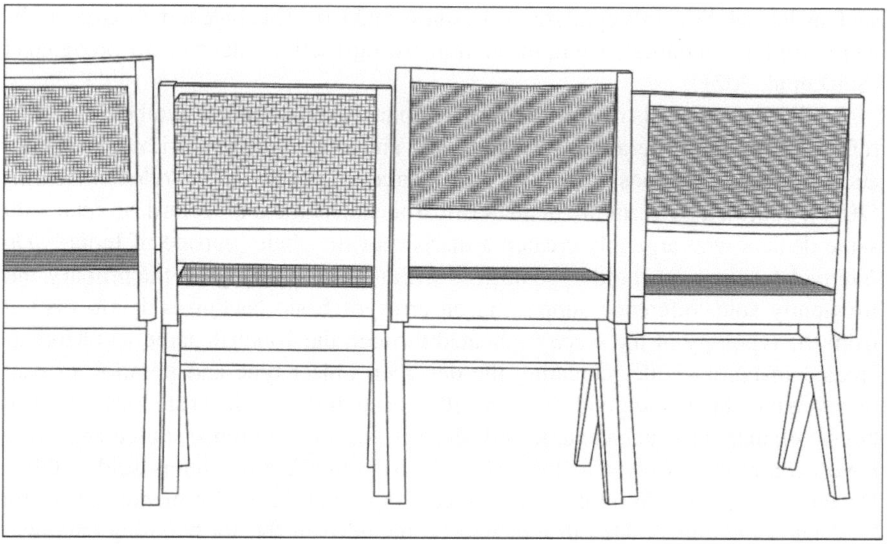

Fig. 5 Artistic rendition of a line of nominally 'same' chairs from an auction house listing, illustrating varying dimensions. Illustration by Nia Thandapani, 2024

contoured a sales environment providing limited information regarding the movement of individual pieces, and a narrow set of sources mobilized to support factual claims.

Specific information regarding initial location, purchase, and removal of items from Chandigarh[11] was found to be consistently absent from auction listings and promotional material. No listings in the dataset included information on which sale within Chandigarh the relevant piece was purchased from. While many listings included information on which building within Chandigarh an item was from, locations within the buildings (i.e. rooms, departments, etc.) were absent (Seitz et al. 2021). Information regarding dates of export from India and details of object restoration or refurbishment were likewise not found within any collected data (Seitz et al. 2021).

While details regarding the movement and sales histories of individual pieces, particularly within and out of India, were largely missing from collected data, information regarding object exhibition and ownership history, particularly within North America and Europe, *was* sporadically included. Prior inclusion within frequently unnamed private collections in Ahmedabad, Chandigarh, Paris, and New York was observed to have been noted within 'Provenance' sections of auction listings (Seitz et al. 2021). Presence in a select number of gallery shows was also found to be highlighted within information sections of auction listings, including a 2006 show at the Sonnabend Gallery put on by Patrick Seguin, and a 2009 show at the University of Westminster's P 3 Gallery (Seitz et al. 2021). Sales made at prestigious galleries,

[11] Or other locations within India.

such as Patrick Seguin's eponymous business and Eric Touchaleaume's *Galerie 54*, were similarly mentioned within auction listing sections devoted to provenance (Seitz et al. 2021).

Review and analysis of collected data emphasized the limited number of sources referred to within 'Literature', 'Provenance', and related sections within the studied auction listings. The most frequently used source was the book *The Indian Adventure* (2010), authored by furniture dealers Eric Touchaleaume and Gerard Moreau—the same dealers who arguably created a market for the chairs outside of India.[12] *The Indian Adventure* appeared to be utilized within auction listings as the primary, and frequently sole, reference supporting an array of basic background information, from the typology of the piece (indicated through the Touchaleaume and Moreau-created inventory code indicating the designer, object type and iteration of each piece) to the object's original location within Chandigarh (Seitz et al. 2021). Auction house reliance on Touchaleaume and Moreau as a sole reference source appears to have occurred even prior to the volume's 2010 publication. Items sold within a December 11, 2008, Wright auction titled 'Important Design' remarked under the heading 'Literature': 'This design will be included in the forthcoming catalogue raisonné' (Wright 2008).[13]

Additional published sources used to prove authenticity and value within auction listings include furniture dealer Patrick Seguin's 2014 volume *Le Corbusier Pierre Jeanneret: Chandigarh India 1951–66*, the seventh volume of Willy Boesiger's 1995 *Le Corbusier Oeuvre complete* ('Le Corbusier Complete Works'), Kiran Joshi's *Documenting Chandigarh* (1999), and Norma Evenson's *Chandigarh* (1966) (Seitz et al. 2021). Despite an initial appearance of scholarly work by auction houses in assembling these citations, upon closer inspection many of the references provided, including those to *The Indian Adventure*, do not appear to provide the concrete factual support of the claims made within auction listings that a reader might expect.

Auction house Artcurial refers to Boesiger in the writeup for an April 15, 2008 listing of 'suite of four armchairs, model called "Senate Chair"' (Seitz et al. 2021).[14] Boseiger, however, neither makes specific mention of Chandigarh's furniture, nor depicts or illustrates the furniture itself, within his volume *Le Corbusier Oeuvre complete* (Boesiger 1995). Auction house Wright's reference to page 225 of Kiran Joshi's *Documenting Chandigarh* to support a listing for a pair of 'library chairs' appears similarly perplexing (Wright 2007). While page 225 in *Documenting Chandigarh* includes discussion of the Chandigarh library building, it *does not*

[12] See Seitz et al. (2020, 2022) for additional discussion of market and narrative creation regarding Chandigarh's modernist furniture.

[13] While this mention could also refer to Jacques Dworczak's *Catalogue Raisonné du Moblier Jeanneret Chandigarh*, Dworczak's volume was not published until 2019, making its reference in 2008 unlikely. *The Indian Adventure*, in contrast, was published just over a year after the 2008 Wright auction, in 2010.

[14] As of publication, this auction listing is no longer available online. The contents of the listing can be viewed within the Chandigarh Chairs Project's freely accessible auction spreadsheet.

contain images or significant discussion of the chair pictured in the listing (Joshi 1999). Reference to Evenson's work appears equally confusing, as *Chandigarh* contains no substantial discussion or illustration of Chandigarh's furniture (Evenson 1966).

Beyond references which do not appear to illustrate or discuss the design being sold, auction listings also appear to use references depicting similar objects, or objects of the same design—not necessarily the particular iterations being sold—sometimes without sign that this practice is occurring. A June 9, 2010 Phillips listing for a 'Low "visitor" sofa from High Court, Chandigarh, India', for example, listed pages 93 and 94 of Boesiger's *Le Corbusier Oeuvre complete* as the sole item under the headline 'Literature' (Seitz et al. 2021).[15] While pages 93 and 94 of Le Corbusier Oeuvre complete, depict Chandigarh's High Court and its furniture, there is no indication that the particular seating furniture included in these images are the same pieces up for auction in the Phillips listing (Boesiger 1995).[16] Absence of indication that the items being sold are not, themselves, depicted in the referenced sources is of particular note, as some auction listings make clear that cited literature depicts a 'similar model' (Seitz et al. 2021).

Overall, collected auction data presents a picture of provenance information provided by auction houses as being dominated by historical gallery display, vague previous ownership details, and factual references stemming from a limited number of sources, particularly a core group of actors within and related to many of these elements, particularly French antique dealers Eric Touchaleaume and Patrick Seguin. Both Touchaleaume and Seguin coordinated early gallery shows of modernist furniture from Chandigarh and continue to sell these and similar pieces within their French gallery spaces. Additionally, Touchaleaume and Seguin authored the most often referenced volumes in auction listings for pieces of Chandigarh's modernist furniture and appear to have been early consigners of such pieces to initial auctions focused on Chandigarh's furniture. Here, the data suggests that the same actors removing, restoring, and selling this furniture also appear to be, through their gallery shows and publications, relied upon for factual information regarding the pieces. Such a closed network or loop of provenance and information generation is not discussed or mentioned in auction listings.

[15] As of publication, this auction listing is no longer available online. The contents of the listing can be viewed within the Chandigarh Chairs Project's freely accessible auction spreadsheet.

[16] This practice appears to suggest that the particular objects being sold have, as occurs with many antiquities, paintings, and sculptures, themselves been previously published and known to the world. However, unlike many paintings, sculptures and antique vases, many objects of design are produced in runs of multiple objects, frequently indistinguishable from each other, even to trained professionals. Therefore, the practice of providing reference to previous publications provides much less solid provenance information for objects of design.

5 Analysis

Research findings from collected and analysed auction data highlight three primary conclusions; a clarification of the physical reality of the objects of study themselves, a questioning of assumptions and claims made in the current predominant narrative of Chandigarh's modernist furniture, and the emergence of issues of morality and ethicality regarding the trade in these pieces.

5.1 Object Clarity

Collected auction data most clearly provided the Chandigarh Chairs project with factual information regarding the physical features of both individual pieces of Chandigarh's modernist furniture, and the broader category of designed objects within which the individual pieces sit. Beyond filling in gaps in basic information regarding the physical makeup of Chandigarh's furniture, such as the frequent and average dimensions of pieces and materials utilized in their construction and or restoration, the data suggested how pieces of Chandigarh's furniture were manufactured (quickly, by hand, using simple techniques), by whom (likely a sizeable pool of craftspeople working in disparate workshops), and where (within the North of India and beyond). The data, particularly measurement data, highlighted the difficulty in simple or neat categorization of 'designs' within the larger suite of Chandigarh's modernist furniture. Further research undertaken after the conclusion of auction data gathering, including more traditional object-based observation conducted in Chandigarh on furniture specimens, has subsequently supported many of the object-related conclusions drawn from auction data analysis.

5.2 Questioning the Narrative

Collected data also called into question several elements of the core 'narrative' of Chandigarh's modernist furniture. Often repeated by sellers of these pieces, as well as the popular press, this 'narrative' asserts that Chandigarh's modernist furniture is largely European in origin, was designed by Pierre Jeanneret, was underappreciated and mistreated within Chandigarh, and was 'saved' from destruction by European dealers and collectors.[17]

Variations in dimension between objects previously categorized as being of the 'same' design suggest a high level of involvement and agency of the many Indian craftspeople responsible for physically creating Chandigarh's chairs, tables, desks,

[17] See Seitz et al. (2020, 2022) for additional discussion of market and narrative creation regarding Chandigarh's modernist furniture.

and storage furniture. The data suggests these makers could, and did, alter designs according to their own wishes, thus making individual and unique marks on the final pieces produced. This reality, suggested by the collected research data, contrasts with the popular, and auction house driven narrative that the pieces are French in nationality, that they were designed primarily or exclusively by architect Pierre Jeanneret (Seitz et al. 2020).

The extensive signs of wear and tear visible within images collected from auction listings counters the tale that Chandigarh's residents did not appreciate the modernist furniture until it was 'rediscovered' by European dealers. These signs of wear indicate that the furniture was, instead, very well used within the city. Broken or rewoven cane demonstrates that chairs had been repeatedly sat in. Weathered and chipped leather on the seams of chair arms prove countless individuals used these arms to propel themselves out of the seat, and scratches on the feet of furniture items illustrate their movement across many floor surfaces. These elements are not signs of unappreciation. They are signs of use. And as Chandigarh's modernist furniture is, and was intended to be, functional furniture, they are signs that the pieces were used, appreciated, and valued for what they are—pieces of functional furniture.

Further, the variance between objects previously considered to be of the same design calls into question both the coding system established by Eric Touchaleaume and Gerard Moreau.[18] While these object codes are presented within *The Indian Adventure* as factually based categorizations of reality, the sometimes dramatic differences in size and shape between objects which share what appear to be the characteristics used to classify and code types suggest a more complicated reality. Can objects truly be labelled and considered of the same type if they do not share dimensions?

5.3 *Ethical and Moral Issues*

Perhaps most importantly, auction data shed a light on potential ethical and moral issues within the trade in Chandigarh's modernist furniture. To start, several elements of the trade appear to be immersed in Eurocentric assumptions, positions, and framings, which systematically minimize or erase the Indian history and origins of Chandigarh's modernist furniture. This erasure begins with the assignation of Pierre Jeanneret as the sole designer of the large majority of Chandigarh's modernist furniture. Jeanneret has been given sole attribution despite a dearth of clear information directly tying him to specific designs (such as plans drawings and studio notes), and contradictory accounts that many designs were collaborative efforts between Jeanneret and the project's larger team of Indian architects, designers, and planners (Prakash 2018). Little, if any, mention is made in auction house listings regarding the Indian craftspeople responsible for producing Chandigarh's furniture, and, by

[18] As well, potentially, as the possibility of any meaningfully accurate coding or categorization for the overarching category of Chandigarh's modernist furniture.

neglecting to discuss or acknowledge varying dimensions and elements within otherwise similar pieces, the role of these individuals within the larger process of creation is minimized. This fits within a wider trend of erasing the very real Indian origins of Chandigarh's modernist furniture, presenting the furniture as European, and through this furthering a narrative of Modernism as an exclusively European construction.

Minimization of the Indian origins of Chandigarh's modernist furniture additionally bolsters the problematic narrative that the pieces were not appropriately appreciated within Chandigarh, and the related conclusion that they would be better appreciated and cared for within the collections of wealthy individuals and institutions within the West. This problematic and neocolonial narrative is illustrated in part by the aestheticization of Chandigarh's furniture within auction imagery. Continued representation of Chandigarh Chairs as pieces as objects of fine art, meant only to be looked at, reinforces the implication that their physical use, including wear and tear, within Chandigarh was wrong or inappropriate. This conception may support or embolden the continued movement of pieces out of their original location and use within India.

Ethical, moral, and potential legal issues regarding both the authentication and movement of Chandigarh chairs are also visible through the collected data. It is possible that forgeries, recently created pieces, or related similar works may be more easily passed off as 'authentic original' Chandigarh chairs because of the lack of information regarding chain of object custody within India within auction listings (Tompkins 2020). Without proof linking a specific piece back to its creation, seemingly any item could be passed off by an unscrupulous actor as an 'original authentic' Chandigarh chair (Tompkins 2020). This item would only have to share *some* of the visual characteristics of other pieces: distressed wood, angular forms, approximate dimensions, and caned or upholstered seats. Considering the significant disparities of object dimensions, a deliberate forgery need not even share the same size as other objects (Seitz et al. 2022).

Absence of import or export paperwork, including a lack of information regarding export dates, in auction listings may open the door to sales and purchases, unintentionally or intentionally, of furniture removed after the 2011 export ban (Tompkins 2020). Given the volume of Chandigarh's modernist furniture on the market, the volume produced, the volume still in use within the city of Chandigarh, and the difficulty previously described in telling one piece from another, certainty of the legal export of any individual item can likely only be proven through the provision of export paperwork. Without this paperwork, or indeed any mention of the export date of objects within auction listings, it is possible that some or many of the pieces included in the data collected during this study were removed from India after 2011 and are therefore illegally held.[19]

[19] The potential illegal export of objects is supported by firsthand observation of the continued export both of 'original authentic' pieces and deliberately aged forgeries from the city has been mentioned in anonymous conversations with the research team on several occasions. The research team has not been able to independently verify or refute these claims.

5.4 *Analysis Summary*

Together, these three key findings suggest that questionably moral, ethical, and perhaps even illegal behaviours and activities are occurring in relation to the trade in and sale of pieces of Chandigarh's modernist furniture. Questions regarding legality, morality, or ethicality aside, it is undeniable that a flow of Chandigarh's modernist furniture from India to collections in Europe and North America is ongoing. Citing potential for theft, local Chandigarh government has felt compelled to move many remaining items of furniture to guarded, locked warehouses, limiting public view and use of these furniture items (Prashar 2020b). The problem of extraction and removal even extends to the city's manhole covers, which have been the subject of ongoing discussions regarding geo-tagging to prevent their removal (Rohtaki 2017a, b; Yadav 2022). Local heritage officials have made a consistent stream of requests to stop auctions of Chandigarh's modernist furniture, or to receive more information regarding object histories for objects under the hammer (Hindustan Times 2023; Indian Express 2022; Kaur 2021), and local media have continually reported the listing and sale of pieces at international auctions (Prashar 2020a; Rohtaki 2017a, b, 2023, 2024; The Tribune 2021). Regardless of the perspective of furniture dealers, auction houses, and Western owners, it is clear that the status quo regarding the market for and trade in Chandigarh's modernist furniture is seen as unacceptable to many individuals within Chandigarh.

6 Conclusion

Issues regarding seller behaviour, construction of narratives, establishment of provenance, legality of export, and authenticity were noticed by the Chandigarh Chairs project because these elements were so well indicated by the data collected. It is possible, and perhaps even likely that, had, the project begun as initially planned, and more traditional object-based design historical methodologies been relied upon, these threads in the history and story of this furniture would not have been explored, or may not have been explored in the depth in which they have.

Conclusions drawn from the collection of auction data related to Chandigarh's modernist furniture thus highlight the relevance of collection and analysis of publicly available auction data both for the Chandigarh Chairs project and for the broader field of design history. Further, the results suggest that use of auction data is a powerful tool to combat undesirable, yet to date relatively unaddressed, practices and trends in secondary markets for designed objects.

Questionably moral, ethical, and legal practices within the trade in cultural heritage have been increasingly documented and discussed within relevant literatures and fields. Immoral, unethical, and illegal practices have been examined and discussed as occurring the trades in and sales of many categories of cultural heritage, from rare and exotic plants and animals (Mackenzie and Yates 2016), and

Greco-Roman vases and statuary (Tsirogiannis et al. 2022; Tsirogiannis 2015; Watson and Todeschini 2006) to Nepalese statuary (Smith 2022), and European paintings (Watson 1997). Questionable practices noted within these, and other fields include the proliferation of forged/faked objects, illegal excavations of antiquities, illegal export and international transit of objects, support of questionable provenance histories given by academics and museums, continued movement of cultural heritage objects from the developing to the (over)developed world and erasure of original object histories and uses (Bichler et al. 2013; Brodie 2011, 2019; Brodie et al. 2021; Prescott and Rasmussen 2020; Smith and Thompson 2023; Yates and Smith 2022).

The data presented and discussed in this chapter suggests that many similar actions may have been, and may continue to be, undertaken regarding Chandigarh's modernist furniture. Widespread lack of provenance information in listings for Chandigarh's modernist furniture, particularly regarding its purchase in, and removal from, India means clarification or proof of legal purchase and export is difficult to find out (Tompkins 2020). A lack of clarity from sellers and auction houses regarding authentication processes, and a reliance on feelings of trust in sellers and auction houses, makes the authenticity of individual pieces largely unknowable for potential buyers (Tompkins 2020).[20] Furthermore, utilization of racist, colonial language, tropes, and images in materials published by dealers in this furniture,[21] and heavily referenced and relied upon by auction houses suggests the existence of a selling environment characterized by lopsided power dynamics and potential exploitation (Tompkins 2020; Seitz et al. 2020).

The combined impact of the prevalence of similar questionable practices across markets in other categories of cultural heritage and the potential appearance of these behaviours within markets for Chandigarh's modernist furniture is the suggestion that such practices may also be present in markets for, and sales of, other designed objects. While there are unquestionably many unique elements, both in terms of design and history, regarding Chandigarh's modernist chairs, the overall auction house sales environment within which they have been sold and is not unique. The same auction houses, same milieu of dealers and gallerists, and likely similar buyers, are also involved in the trade in other designed objects—particularly the works of other high-profile, high-price European mid-century modernists.[22] However,

[20] Questions of authentication and authenticity of items of Chandigarh's modernist furniture sold at auction are discussed by the author in greater depth in 'Design Crime in Context' (Seitz et al. 2022).

[21] This includes statements that the furniture was not properly cared for within Chandigarh, inclusion of images of the dealers problematically posing with piles of discarded furniture and unnamed, uncredited Chandigarh residents, and the titling of the book '*The Indian Adventure*', an explicit exotification of Chandigarh and India, evocative of the period of British and French colonial forays into and follies within the Indian subcontinent.

[22] Galerie Patrick Seguin trades in pieces by Jean Prouvé, Charlotte Perriand, Le Corbusier, and Jean Royère in addition to pieces of Chandigarh's modernist furniture (Galerie Patrick Seguin n.d.). Likewise, Eric Touchaleaume's Galerie 54 offers a variety of modernist furniture and architecture including works by Jean Prouvé, Charlotte Perriand, Le Corbusier, Alvar Aalto and Gio Ponti (Galerie 54 n.d.). More often than not sales covered in the Chandigarh Chairs auction data-

despite evidence that the market for designed objects may operate along similarly nebulous lines as markets for other items of cultural heritage, exploration of this topic appears to have so far evaded significant scholarly and journalistic scrutiny.

The relatively young age and mass, frequently machine-made, nature of many objects of design appear to exclude these pieces from definitional, legal, and scholarly inclusion with many other objects of cultural significance. For example, the 1970 UNESCO *Convention on the Means of Prohibiting and Preventing the Illicit Import, Export and Transfer of Ownership of Cultural Property*, explicitly *excludes* items of more recent cultural heritage from its remit. The Convention specifies that only articles of furniture *over* 100 years old are covered by the Convention's protections (UNESCO 1970 Art 1 §K). This definition means that objects of modern design, even those as well-known as Chandigarh's modernist furniture, will not legally be considered objects of cultural heritage until the late 2050's or early 2060's. Further, while 'property of artistic interest' younger than 100 years old *may* be covered by the Convention, the document clarifies that 'property of artistic interest' does *not* include 'industrial designs and manufactured articles decorated by hand' (UNESCO 1970). Exclusion of machine-made objects, while not a problem for Chandigarh's hand-constructed furniture, would exclude many of the most well-appreciated and well-known objects of modern design. Such choices in terminology, phrasing, and in/exclusion therefore result in a document which, while providing at least nominal protection to paintings, lithographs, sculptures, coins, statuary, books, and even postage stamps, does not provide legal protection for the extraction of objects of modern design, regardless of their financial or cultural value.

Further, consistent use of the term 'cultural heritage' (rather than 'cultural property' or 'cultural objects') within national and international legal frameworks adds to the temporal definition of objects of importance (Forrest 2009), suggesting important items are, at least in part, defined by their age—an age which objects of modern design simply do not possess.[23] Similarly, utilization of identifying terms such as 'unique' within national cultural heritage statues of counties such as Germany and Switzerland would seem to exclude many items of design, particularly items of modern or mass-manufactured design which are produced on a large scale and thus cannot be unique (Kono and Wrbka 2010). As legal frameworks appear to be constructed in a way which definitionally excludes objects of design, particularly objects of modern design, within their remit or protection, it logically

base also included works of other prominent mid-century modernist designers. The October 2019 auctions referred to in Sect. 2 of this chapter included works by Le Corbusier, Charlotte Perriand, Jean Prouvé, Mies van der Rohe, Charles and Ray Eames, Hans Wegner, Arne Jacobsen, Frank Lloyd Wright, Marcel Breuer, Eero Saarinen, and Florence Knoll (Aguttes 2019; Phillips 2019; Rago 2019; Wright 2019).

[23] It is, for example, notable that Craig Forrest's (2009) in-depth analysis of the definitions of cultural heritage includes significant discussion of the relevancy of such statues to intangible or immoveable objects but excludes discussion of the temporally limiting effects the discussed definition imposes.

follows that scholars and authors using legality as their initial framework would not examine such objects.

Exclusion of recent and mass-manufactured objects from definitions of cultural heritage means many objects of design, including Chandigarh's modernist furniture, are not afforded similar international levels of protection as given to other items. This means non-covered design items can be moved, sold, traded, refurbished and/or altered without even the nominal international legal scrutiny afforded to other objects. The exclusion of recent and mass-manufactured items from international definitions of cultural heritage may hamper or discourage academics with experience and knowledge in logistics, morality, ethicality and legality in the sale and movement of cultural heritage, such as archaeologists, criminologists, and art historians, from extending their research into designed objects.

When designed objects *do* make an appearance in literature exploring the trade in cultural heritage and property, these objects are discussed in ways which separate them from the broader field of cultural heritage, both in terms of definitional inclusion and market dynamics at play. Colin Renfrew's seminal *Loot, Legitimacy and Ownership* (2000), for example, appears to both echo the exclusion of designed objects within the broader category of cultural heritage discussed in the volume, while simultaneously exempting trade in these objects from the potentially nefarious behaviour Renfrew identifies within other, more established cultural heritage markets. While Renfrew uses *Loot, Legitimacy and Ownership* to implicate museums, collectors and dealers of antiquities in a cycle of immoral and potentially illegal behaviours, he takes pains to clarify that no similar criticism or scrutiny is 'intended of collectors of…furniture, objects de vertu, cigarette cards, Dinky Toys etc.' (Renfrew 2000, pp. 16–7). Sellers and buyers of these design historical objects, Renfrew insists, warrant 'respectability', unlike their compatriots involved in the trade of antiquities (Renfrew 2000, pp. 35–6). Such treatment of the market for designed objects at best minimizes, if not erases, any questionably moral, ethical and legal practices within the trade, potentially allowing these actions to continue without academic or journalistic scrutiny.

Examination of second-hand markets and trade are also noticeably absent from design historical writings, which tend to focus scholarly attention within the discipline's signature design-production-consumption paradigm. Following initial examples set by art historian Nikolaus Pevsner, early design historical works made individual Western designers, their practices, influences, and products the central focus of study (Fallan 2010; Walker 1989). This focus shifted over time, in line with larger cultural and sociological trends, to a wider variety of designers and objects in terms of geography, temporality, and type (Fallan 2010). While there has been continual updating of the design-production-consumption paradigm as the design historical discipline has matured, including recent efforts to explore the re-use and re-purposing of objects (Kalantidou et al. 2023), this expansion has largely excluded movement towards analysis of markets for resale, particularly analysis involving highly priced objects of design. This means the designed object, the designer, the design process, and the user remain the centre of many investigations, rather than more nebulous sociological, legal and political frameworks which may, or may not, be influencing the aforementioned elements of design.

Donna Loveday's *Curating Design* (2022), for example, links "rising consumer demand for design" and authorship of design-related scholarship and monographs to "a developing antiquities trade" in the 1960s (Loveday 2022, p. 53). However, Loveday's analysis stops with this connection between rising popularity of design and the developing antiquities trade. No further work is done to unpick *how* and *why* the trade in historical designed objects may have led to a generally increased awareness of and interest in objects of design. The nature and content of the scholarship inspired by a booming antiquities trade, nor the impact of an increased trade on broader understandings of design and designed objects are explored or addressed. Here Loveday's investigation is typical of design history's broader disinterest in the physical and procedural operations of secondary markets, and resistance to analysis of how markets shape understandings of design and design history, including how these spaces may influence where objects are located, how they are treated, and who has access to them and for what purposes (Seitz et al. 2022).

There are many potential reasons for the absence of design historical investigations of secondary markets. The close relationships between scholars, curators, and market agents, to begin, may disincentive scholars and curators from investigating markets, for fear of reprisal and limited future access to objects and career opportunities (Brodie 2011). Design historians, already proficient in a number of disciplinal research methods (Walker 1989), may lack the theoretical knowledge to feel confident undertaking the economic methodologies market analysis requires. Or, more simply, in a field with an almost overwhelming and continually expanding number and type of subjects within the scholar's purview, criminological, legal, and economic topics may not yet be of pressing interest (Walker 1989).

Definitions placing objects of design outside the sphere of cultural heritage, exclusion of designed objects within literature addressing market forces, alongside historic disinterest in the operations of second-hand markets by design historians creates a sizeable research gap regarding potentially illegal, immoral, or unethical trade practices vis-à-vis these objects. A lack of scholarly coverage may, in turn, allow potentially harmful practices to go undiscovered and/or unchallenged (Brodie 2011; Brodie et al. 2021; Prescott and Rasmussen 2020; Smith and Thompson 2023).

Collection and analysis of online data provides an easily accessible, yet still impactful way for design historians to explore the effects of markets on design history, and through this, taking steps needed to address the research gap. The low-cost nature of auction data provides a small financial barrier to scholars and journalists exploring market relations and impacts for the first time. Collection, storage, and analysis of auction data can generally be undertaken without specialist software or training, allowing a wide variety of scholars and researchers to implement the methodology—a useful feature for a field composed of individuals with diverse, and frequently practice-led professional backgrounds. Further, many auction houses around the world now host listings and sale information online, providing design historians and researchers with a potentially international scope for their research, both in terms of the locations of sales and in the types and nationalities of designed items for which information is available.

Large-scale collection of auction data provides opportunities for design historians to extend the scope of their research in several ways. Collection of images from auction listings can allow the design historian to visually analyse a significantly larger pool of objects than is typically studied. When analysed as a set, auction images of the same design can allow the design historian to determine overarching trends for the object of inquiry; how it was constructed, how it was used, and what repairs have been made. Collating item measurements from auction listings can function in many of the same ways, allowing the design historian to compare physical features of many more discrete objects than are typically accessible during in-person, physical, object analysis.

In addition to bolstering approaches already widely accepted and undertaken by design historians, analysis of auction data opens doors to new and critically important avenues of design-related research, particularly regarding the influence of market actors and forces upon understandings of designed objects, as well as the physical trajectories of specific objects. Overarching analysis of the sale of objects can illustrate from where the objects are coming, what sort of clientele is purchasing them, and what tools and techniques are used to make the pieces more enticing, as well as how each of these elements have evolved. Online auction data research thus provides the design historian with a powerful and relatively accessible new method, capable of expanding lines of design historical research already underway, as well as opening new avenues of exploration for the discipline.

By beginning to explore market dynamics and the ways sales trends and procedures influence both our understandings of objects and the physical trajectories and locations of objects through methods such as the use of online auction data, design historians can heed the calls of area experts to understand the trade in cultural heritage as an important first step toward ridding these spaces of illegal, immoral, and unethical behaviour (Brodie 2011; Brodie et al. 2021; Smith and Thompson 2023). Given design history's flexibility and resilience over the discipline's relatively short fifty-plus year history (Fallan 2010; Walker 1989), future adaptation along these lines seems a wholly possible challenge to next conquer.

Acknowledgements This chapter is based on work done by the Chandigarh Chairs research team, which consists of Petra Seitz (the author), Nia Thandapani, and Gregor Wittrick. As an independent, unaffiliated research project, outputs from time to time are written, designed, or otherwise conceived by individual project members, according to availability. This chapter has been written by the author alone. Full outputs of the project's work, including the data upon which this chapter is based, can be viewed on the Chandigarh Chairs project website, chandigarhchairs.com.

References

Aguttes (2019). DESIGN lundi 07 octobre 2019 17:00. https://www.aguttes.com/catalogue/99637? Accessed 14 October 2024

Aguttes (2019b) Pierre Jeanneret (1896-1967): Chaise dite Library chair. https://www.aguttes.com/lot/96060/10211431?refurl=Chaise+dite+Library+chair%3Cbr%2F%3ETeck%2C+moelle+de+rotin%3Cbr%2F%3E76+x+46+x+42+cm.%3Cbr%2F%3ECirca+1959%3Cbr%2F%3EProvenan. Accessed 1 May 2024

Bichler G, Bush S, Malm A (2013) Bad actors and faulty props: unlocking legal and illicit art trade. Global Crime 14(4):359–385. https://doi.org/10.1080/17440572.2013.828999

Boesiger W (1995) Le Corbusier - Ouvre complète, Volume 7: 1957-1965. Birkhäuser https://doi.org/10.1515/9783035602975

Brodie N (2011) Congenial bedfellows? The academy and the antiquities trade. J Contemp Crim Justice 27(4):408–437. https://doi.org/10.1177/1043986211418885

Brodie N (2019) Through a glass, darkly: long-term antiquities auction data in context. Int J Cult Prop 26(3):265–283. https://doi.org/10.1017/S094073911900016X

Brodie N, Morag K, Mackenzie S, Sabrine I, Smith E, Yates D (2021) Why there is still an illicit trade in cultural objects and what we can do about it. J Field Archaeol 47(2):117–130. https://doi.org/10.1080/00934690.2021.1996979

Cardoso R (2010) Craft versus design. In: Adamson G (ed) The craft reader. Berg, pp 321–332

Cassina (n.d.) Capital complex armchair. https://www.cassina.com/gb/en/products/capitol-complex-armchair.html?cas_rivestimento=X-X201#053-capitol-complex-armchair_38151. Accessed 14 October 2024

Chandigarh Model Jail (n.d.) Factory articles. https://chdmodeljail.gov.in/products/factoryproduct. Accessed 14 October 2024

Davis T (2011) Supply and demand: exposing the illicit trade in Cambodian antiquities through a study of Sotheby's auction house. Crime Law Soc Chang 56(2):155–174. https://doi.org/10.1007/s10611-011-9321-6

Evenson N (1966) Chandigarh. University of California Press

Fallan K (2010) Design history: understanding theory and method. Bloomsbury

Forrest C (2009) Defining cultural heritage in international law. In: Forrest C (ed) International law and the protection of cultural heritage. Routledge

Galerie 54 (n.d.) Design—available. https://galerie54.com/en/design. Accessed 14 October 2024

Galerie Patrick Seguin (n.d.) Galerie Patrick Seguin. https://www.patrickseguin.com/en/. Accessed 14 October 2024

Gandhi T (2021) Authorities fail to stop rampant smuggling of heritage items in Chandigarh. The Daily Guardian, July 27. https://thedailyguardian.com/authorities-fail-to-stop-rampant-smuggling-of-heritage-items-in-chandigarh/. Accessed 14 October 2024

Gentleman A (2008) A city that sat on its treasures, but didn't see them. The New York Times, March 19. https://www.nytimes.com/2008/03/19/world/asia/19chandigarh.html. Accessed 14 October 2024

Hannan L, Longair S (2017) History through material culture. Manchester University Press. https://doi.org/10.7765/9781526153418

Hindustan Times (2023) French auction of Chandigarh's heritage furniture cancelled. Hindustan Times, January 29. https://www.hindustantimes.com/cities/chandigarh-news/french-auction-of-chandigarh-s-heritage-furniture-cancelled-101674945327801.html. Accessed 14 October 2024

Indian Express (2022). Three Chandigarh heritage items auctioned off in Paris, Rajya Sabha intervention sought. Indian Express, December 2 https://indianexpress.com/article/cities/chandigarh/three-chandigarh-heritage-items-auctioned-paris-rajya-sabha-intervention-sought-8301857/. Accessed 14 October 2024

Joshi K (1999) Documenting Chandigarh: the Indian architecture of Pierre Jeanneret, Edwin Maxwell Fry, Jane Beverly Drew. Mapin

Kalantidou E, Keulemans G, Mellick Lopes A, Rubenis N, Gill A (eds) (2023) Design/repair: place, practice & community. Springer. https://doi.org/10.1007/978-3-031-46862-9

Kaufmann E Jr (1969) Introductions to modern design. Museum of Modern Art and Arno Press

Kaur A (2021) Heritage cell member seeks return of 6 items of Chandigarh. The Tribune, September 14. https://www.tribuneindia.com/news/chandigarh/heritage-cell-member-seeks-return-of-6-items-of-chandigarh-310810. Accessed 14 October 2024

Kono T, Wrbka S (2010) National and legal frameworks. In: Kono T (ed) The impact of uniform laws on the protection of cultural heritage and the preservation of cultural heritage in the 21st century. Brill, pp 111–231

Lindemann A (2010) Collecting design. Taschen

Loveday D (2022) Curating design: context, culture and reflective practice. Bloomsbury

Mackenzie S, Yates D (2016) Collectors on illicit collecting: higher loyalties and other techniques of neutralization in the unlawful collecting of rare and precious orchids and antiquities. Theor Criminol 20(3):340–357. https://doi.org/10.1177/1362480615607625

Martin H (2017) How the famous Chandigarh chair landed in Kourtney Kardashian's dining room. Architectural digest, August 16. https://www.architecturaldigest.com/story/pierre-jeanneret-chandigarh-chair. Accessed 14 October 2024

Medford S (2019) Is your Jeanneret a fake? WSJ Magazine, August 14. https://www.wsj.com/articles/is-your-jeanneret-a-fake-11565785593. Accessed 14 October 2024

Nørskov V (2002) Greek vases for sale: some statistical evidence. In: Brodie N, Walker Tubb K (eds) Illicit antiquities: the theft of culture and the extinction of archaeology. Routledge, pp 23–37. https://doi.org/10.4324/9780203165461

Phantom Hands (n.d.) Project Chandigarh. https://phantomhands.in/collection/project-chandigarh. Accessed 14 October 2024

Phillips (2014) Pierre Jeanneret: set of eight armchairs, model no. PJ-AH-09-A, from the mill owner's association building, Ahmedabad, India. https://www.phillips.com/detail/pierre-jeanneret/NY050414/29?fromSearch=pierre%20jeanneret&searchPage=2. Accessed 1 May 2024

Phillips (2019) Design London auction 17 October 2019. https://www.phillips.com/auctions/auction/UK050219. Accessed 14 October 2024

Prakash, V. (2018). Life and work of Pierre Jeanneret with Maristella Casciato. Architecture Talk, January 3. https://www.architecturetalk.org/home/11. Accessed 2 November 2021

Prashar S (2020a) 10 Chandigarh heritage items designed by Jeanneret & Corbusier sold for RS 2.11 cr. The Indian Express, October 16. https://indianexpress.com/article/cities/chandigarh/10-chandigarh-heritage-items-jeanneret-corbusier-sold-rs-2-11-cr-6754650/. Accessed 14 October 2024

Prashar S (2020b) Mumbai link: the challenge for Chandigarh police in every case. The Indian Express, November 23. https://indianexpress.com/article/cities/chandigarh/mumbai-link-the-challenge-for-chandigarh-police-in-every-case-7061915/. Accessed 10 March 2022

Prescott C, Rasmussen JM (2020) Exploring the "cozy cabal of academics, dealers and collectors" through the Schøyen collection. Heritage 3(1):68–97. https://doi.org/10.3390/heritage3010005

Rago (2019) 10.19.19 Remix: Classic+ Contemporary. https://archive.ragoarts.com/auctions/2019/10/19/remix-classic-contemporary. Accessed 14 October 2024

Renfrew C (2000) Loot, legitimacy and ownership: the ethical crisis in archaeology. Bristol Classical Press

Rohtaki H (2017a) Heritage furniture: two lounge chairs from PU sold for RS 1.14 crore at Chicago auction. The Indian Express, November 3. https://indianexpress.com/article/cities/chandigarh/heritage-furniture-two-lounge-chairs-from-pu-sold-for-rs-1-14-crore-at-chicago-auction-4920464/. Accessed 14 October 2024

Rohtaki H (2017b) UT heritage panel wants GPS chips on Corbusier's manhole covers. The Indian Express, November 2. https://indianexpress.com/article/chandigarh/ut-heritage-panel-wants-gps-chips-on-corbusiers-manhole-covers-4918357/. Accessed 26 September 2021

Rohtaki H (2023) Chandigarh's heritage chair auctioned for Rs 5.4 lakh in Barcelona. The Indian Express, September 9. https://indianexpress.com/article/cities/chandigarh/chandigarhs-heritage-chair-auctioned-rs-5-4-lakh-barcelona-8931303/. Accessed 14 October 2024

Rohtaki H (2024) Chandigarh's heritage armchairs auctioned for Rs 8.35 lakh in California, book rack goes for Rs. 4.70 lakh. The Indian Express, March 4. https://indianexpress.com/

article/cities/chandigarh/chandigarh-heritage-armchairs-california-punjab-engineering-college-9193590/. Accessed 14 October 2024
Ruegg A (2015) Le Corbusier. Furniture and interiors 1905–1965: the complete catalogue Raisonné. University of Chicago Press
Seitz P, Thandapani N, Wittrick G (2020) Chandigarh chairs: missing histories. Bangalore International Centre, September 24. https://bangaloreinternationalcentre.org/video/chandigarh-chairs-missing-histories/
Seitz P, Thandapani N, Wittrick G (2021) Chandigarh furniture auction tracking database, November 21. https://docs.google.com/spreadsheets/d/e/2PACX-1vQ5fPeMkyM_c2Vb-YF4eOfy95Xub0QVMS61-SJ8C2Cj8xKePPzvKoOiduC_hdSgXvswaO_XEfjbhLyB/pubhtml?gid=0&single=true
Seitz P, Thandapani N, Wittrick G (2022) Design crime in context: mass-manufactured design, design-as-art, and Chandigarh's modernist furniture. In: Oosterman N, Yates D (eds) Art crime in context. Springer, pp 25–44. https://doi.org/10.1007/978-3-031-14084-6_3
Smith E (2022) The ongoing quest to return Nepal's looted cultural heritage. Georget J Int Aff 23(2):264–271. https://doi.org/10.1353/gia.2022.0039
Smith E, Thompson EL (2023) A case study of academic facilitation of the global illicit trade in cultural objects: Mary Slusser in Nepal. Int J Cult Prop 30(1):22–41. https://doi.org/10.1017/s0940739123000048
Sotheby's (2018) Pierre Jeanneret: student desk from the College of Architecture, University of Punjab, Chandigarh, India. https://www.sothebys.com/en/auctions/ecatalogue/2018/art-and-design-from-the-homes-of-delphine-and-reed-krakoff-n09881/lot.165.html. Accessed 1 May 2024
Studio CHD. (n.d.) Studio CHD. https://studiochd.in/. Accessed 14 October 2024
The Tribune (2021) Chandigarh heritage goes for RS92 lakh in France. The Tribune, June 8. https://www.tribuneindia.com/news/chandigarh/chandigarh-heritage-goes-for-rs92-lakh-in-france-264993. Accessed 14 October 2024
Tompkins A (ed) (2020) Provenance research today: principles, practice, problems. Lund Humphries
Touchaleaume E, Moreau G (2010) Le Corbusier Pierre Jeanneret: L'aventure Indienne: design - art - architecture. Gourcuff Gradenigo
Tsirogiannis C (2015) Something is confidential in the state of Christie's. In: Charney N (ed) Art crime: terrorists, tomb raiders, forgers and thieves. Palgrave Macmillan UK, pp 200–228
Tsirogiannis C, Gill DWJ, Chippindale C (2022) The forger's tale: an insider's account of corrupting the corpus of Cycladic figures. Int J Cult Prop 29(3):369–385. https://doi.org/10.1017/S0940739122000352
UNESCO (1970) Convention on the means of prohibiting and preventing the illicit import, export and transfer of ownership of cultural property. https://www.unesco.org/en/legal-affairs/convention-means-prohibiting-and-preventing-illicit-import-export-and-transfer-ownership-cultural
Victoria and Albert Museum (n.d.) The Chandigarh Chair. https://www.vam.ac.uk/articles/the-chandigarh-chair?srsltid=AfmBOooWgDD0yxnJ6j9fV8K8jlKUk8BXHW6XLFdPYcyyVbLNBPSSTGer. Accessed 14 October 2024
Walker J (1989) Design history and the history of design. Pluto Press
Watson P (1997) Sotheby's: inside story. Bloomsbury
Watson P, Todeschini C (2006) The Medici conspiracy. PublicAffairs
Wright. (2007) Pierre Jeanneret, pair of library chairs from TS Central Library, Chandigarh. https://www.wright20.com/auctions/2007/12/important-design-session-2/537?search=pierre+Jeanneret. Accessed 1 May 2024
Wright (2008) Pierre Jeanneret: set of three lounge chairs from Punjab University, Chandigarh. https://www.wright20.com/auctions/2008/12/important-design-day-2/577?search=pierre+Jeanneret. Accessed 2 May 2024

Wright (2017) Pierre Jeanneret: Committee armchairs from the High Court, Chandigarh, set of ten. https://www.wright20.com/auctions/2017/12/design/142?search=Pierre+Jeanneret. Accessed 1 May 2024

Wright. (2019) Design 24 October 2019 11am ct. https://www.wright20.com/auctions/2019/10/design. Accessed 14 October 2024

Yadav D (2022) MC weighs geo-tagging heritage manhole covers. The Times of India, March 8. https://timesofindia.indiatimes.com/city/chandigarh/mc-weighs-geo-tagging-heritage-manhole-covers/articleshow/90064041.cms. Accessed 10 March 2022

Yates D (2022) What auction catalogue analysis cannot tell us about the market. In: Fabiani D, Burmon K, Hufnagel S (eds) Global perspectives on cultural property crime. Routledge, pp 43–60. https://doi.org/10.4324/9780367823801

Yates D, Smith E (2022) Museums and the market: passive facilitation of the illicit trade in antiquities. In: Stevenson A (ed) The Oxford handbook of museum archaeology. Oxford University Press, pp 97–97. https://doi.org/10.1093/oxfordhb/9780198847526.001.0001

Petra Seitz is a PhD candidate at the Bartlett School of Architecture, UCL. Her dissertation explores and re-theorises the history of commercial office through the application of Marxian labour process theory. Alongside this work, Petra serves as principal investigator on the Chandigarh Chairs project, an independent research endeavour which seeks to critically re-evaluate the history of modernist furniture from the northern Indian city of Chandigarh. Categorising herself as a Design Historian, Petra's primary research interests lie within the field of mid-century interiors and furniture, and the relationship between politics, particularly political economy, and design. Petra holds a BA in Politics from Oberlin College (Ohio, USA) and an MA in History of Design from the Victoria & Albert Museum and Royal College of Art. She has lectured Architectural History and Theory at the University of Greenwich, alongside Postgraduate Teaching Assistant work for the BSc Architecture at the Bartlett.

Open Access This chapter is licensed under the terms of the Creative Commons Attribution-NonCommercial-NoDerivatives 4.0 International License (http://creativecommons.org/licenses/by-nc-nd/4.0/), which permits any noncommercial use, sharing, distribution and reproduction in any medium or format, as long as you give appropriate credit to the original author(s) and the source, provide a link to the Creative Commons license and indicate if you modified the licensed material. You do not have permission under this license to share adapted material derived from this chapter or parts of it.

The images or other third party material in this chapter are included in the chapter's Creative Commons license, unless indicated otherwise in a credit line to the material. If material is not included in the chapter's Creative Commons license and your intended use is not permitted by statutory regulation or exceeds the permitted use, you will need to obtain permission directly from the copyright holder.

Beyond the Streetlight: What the Reporting of the British Museum Thefts Reveals About the Antiquities Trade—And What It Doesn't

Neil Brodie

Abstract Investigative journalism has been and continues to be an important open source of information about the antiquities trade. It should be borne in mind, however, that the aims of the investigative journalist are not necessarily concordant with those of the academic researcher or policymaker. To date, there has been no examination of any inherent weaknesses, deficiencies or biases embodied within those aims. With reference to the reporting of thefts during the 2010s of ancient gems from the British Museum, this chapter explores some possible shortcomings of investigative journalism but also demonstrates how it constitutes a valuable resource for academic research and policymaking.

1 Introduction

One key open source of information for research into the trade in ancient cultural objects or "antiquities"[1] has been and continues to be the work of investigative journalists, which dates back at least to Nicholas Gage's (1973) dogged pursuit of the Metropolitan Museum of Art over its acquisition of the so-called Euphronios Krater. Books such as those written by Peter Watson (1997, Watson and Todeschini 2006), Jason Felch and Ralph Frammolino (2011), and Ariel Sabar (2020), to name only a few of the more obvious English-language examples, have followed in Gage's footsteps and shed light onto the inner-workings of the antiquities trade. They have released into the public domain a wealth of otherwise inaccessible information that might be used by researchers and policymakers. But while the information made available by journalism is of undoubted importance for supporting both research

[1] I use the term "antiquities" as a shorthand to describe ancient artifacts, coins and manuscripts (Brodie and Yates 2022, pp. 87–88).

N. Brodie (✉)
Brighton, UK

© The Author(s) 2026

E. Smith, S. Austin (eds.), *Researching a Rigged Game: Digital Approaches to Tracing the Illicit Trade in Cultural Objects*, Studies in Art, Heritage, Law and the Market 11, https://doi.org/10.1007/978-3-032-02014-7_11

and policymaking, it is not without problems and until now it has not been systematically evaluated.

As I hope to show in this chapter, investigative reporting is indeed invaluable. Journalists are perhaps in an advantageous position in that they can conduct undercover or unsolicited interviews and other research of a type that would be considered problematical in an academic context due to the strict risk-related ethical constraints of many disciplines and institutions that prioritize the safety and security of "research subjects" over the material requirements of the research itself. Journalists are also adept at acquiring what would otherwise be considered confidential documentation, which again would raise ethical questions in academia. Once published, their work is both accessible and, with proper attribution, reproduceable. But at the same time, the journalistic and academic research agenda are not seamlessly concordant, they diverge in at least one important way: very broadly speaking, journalism prioritises the story over the objective analysis. This divergence holds within it the possibility of misleading academic research and misdirecting policy aimed at regulating the antiquities trade and reducing its harmful consequences.

When using published journalism as an information source for research or policymaking, there is a potential problem of incomplete reporting. I have in the past sometimes been frustrated by what I consider to be the inept attempts of a journalist to report upon some documents in their possession when the documents themselves, which might comprise an invaluable source of information, remain out of sight (and a guarded resource for the journalist concerned). I do not consider any of the works I have referenced here to fall into that incompetent category. They are uniformly excellent. Nevertheless, it is a shame that usually the basic documentation is not made publicly available. Researchers or policymakers are forced to use what information has been chosen for publication, which may well be an unrepresentative sample of what information is actually available, selected to support the particular story that is of journalistic interest.

A related issue, and the one that I will be discussing in this chapter, is that of biased reporting. Often, investigative journalism is scandal driven, aimed at exposing the shameful deviance of what might otherwise be considered a reputable actor or institution. So, the blurb on the front cover of Watson's (1997) exposé of Sotheby's auction house in London, *Sotheby's: Inside Story*, reads "The explosive truth about the world's most famous auction house". Felch and Frammolino's (2011) *Chasing Aphrodite*, a deep dive into the questionable acquisition practices of the J. Paul Getty Museum, is subtitled *The Hunt for Looted Antiquities at the World's Richest Museum*. Sabar's (2020) *Veritas*, a study of the so-called Gospel of Jesus's wife, manages to avoid any claims of world-beating wrongdoing but its associated blurb is still keen to advertise the book as exploring the "scandal that engulfed Harvard University". Sotheby's auction house, the J. Paul Getty Museum and Harvard University are (or were) all internationally respected institutions and considered paragons of cultural propriety. The revelatory exposure of their involvement in unethical or even illegal practice is an irresistible source of voyeuristic delight for the interested reader. Scandals sell books.

On the face of it, there is nothing wrong with scandals. Many years (decades) ago a senior UNESCO official confided in me that policy moves along one scandal at a time. But journalists are likely to prioritise information and develop a narrative that is directly relevant to their particular investigation—to their story. So, while an investigation might illuminate a particularly unsavoury episode or example of wrongdoing—a scandal—there is no guarantee that the scandal in question is an instantiation of a more general pattern of malfeasance and not simply a singular, atypical example of deviant practice or action. This point is not a trivial one. Traders and trade organisations are wont to dismiss publicly documented examples of malpractice as the work of "rotten apples" (Mackenzie et al. 2020, pp. 122–123). They argue instead for a generally honest trade where reputation and trust are better guarantors of market propriety than external regulation or oversight (Mackenzie 2005, pp. 25–32).

Thus, it can be argued that investigative journalism is more likely to prioritise the particular over the general, the subjectively human over the contextually systemic, the agency over the structure, the individual over the institution, the local over the global, and so on. This biased reporting can even create what can be characterised as a "Streetlight Effect":

> The fundamental error here is summed up in an old joke scientists love to tell. Late at night, a police officer finds a drunk man crawling around on his hands and knees under a streetlight. The drunk man tells the officer he's looking for his wallet. When the officer asks if he's sure this is where he dropped the wallet, the man replies that he thinks he more likely dropped it across the street. Then why are you looking over here? the befuddled officer asks. Because the light's better here, explains the drunk man. (Freedman 2010)

So, while the investigative reporting of a scandal might shed light onto the inner workings of the antiquities trade, it is important to know whether that light is illuminating a practice or action that is unrepresentative of the antiquities trade more generally, or alternatively, centrally constitutive of its organisation and operation. It needs to be established if what is lit up in the streetlight of investigative journalism is a sufficient foundation in itself for productive academic research and constructive policymaking or whether further complementary research is needed.

In this chapter, I will explore a possible manifestation of the Streetlight Effect with reference to the reporting of thefts from the British Museum (BM) of nearly 2000 ancient gems and pieces of ancient jewellery, allegedly by senior curator Peter Higgs.[2] I am not concerned to establish the veracity of the reporting, which I don't think is in question, but I do want to discuss the policy responses to the reporting and consider any important information that has been overlooked or not followed up. I believe this overlooked information is more illuminating of the organisation and operation of the antiquities trade, particularly in the United Kingdom, and thus more relevant for policymaking than the specific circumstances of the BM thefts,

[2] As a disclaimer, I should state that I know Peter Higgs as our times as undergraduate and postgraduate students at the University of Liverpool overlapped.

which on present evidence can be attributed to the actions of a "rogue" curator working within a negligent institution.

2 Overview of the Thefts from the British Museum

This first part of this section which outlines the chronology of events related to the BM thefts follows Katie Razzall's report of the BM thefts and their discovery in a series of BBC podcasts (BBC 2024a, b, c, d, e, f, g, h, i, j; Razzall et al. 2024a, b, c) and a television documentary (BBC 2024k). These outputs were produced with the cooperation of Ittai Gradel, who is an antiquities dealer based in Denmark specialising in ancient jewellery and gemstones and who was centrally involved in discovering and exposing the thefts.[3] Razall's reporting is corroborated by accounts published by Max Colchester (2023) in the *Wall Street Journal* and by Kate Fitz Gibbon (2024) for the Cultural Property News blog. Razzall and Fitz Gibbon had personal access to court documents prepared by the BM. Quotes and specific facts are referenced individually. The second part of this section continues to rely upon these sources, together with BM press releases.

The reported investigation starts with Gradel, who first heard of what he would ultimately establish was stolen material in 2010 when he received an email from UK-based antiquities dealer Rolf von Kiaer. Von Kiaer was hoping to sell him some ancient gems he had bought from one "Paul Higgins" who claimed to have inherited them from his grandfather. Then, in 2014, Gradel started buying under-priced pieces of ancient jewellery from the seller "sultan1966" on the Internet platform eBay. The seller was listed as "Paul Higgs", later "Paul Higgins", located in England, who claimed the material he was selling derived from the collection of his grandfather who had owned a junk shop in York and who had died in 1953. Gradel established that someone with that name had indeed existed and had died in 1952, so assumed that the provenance was most likely correct. Von Kiaer had been buying material from "Paul Higgins" since July 2009 and continued to do so until 2013, when he received an email communication from someone professing to be "Paul Higgins's" son that his father had died. He continued to buy on eBay from "sultan1966".

In 2016, "sultan1966" posted on eBay a grey and white agate Roman cameo fragment that he subsequently withdrew from sale, though not before Gradel had taken a screenshot of the image. Upon enquiry, "sultan1966" told Gradel that the cameo fragment belonged to his sister and that she had decided not to sell. Gradel kept the screenshot for his records. In 2020, he was able to match his screenshot of the cameo fragment with a photograph that had appeared on the BM's website, depicting the same fragment in its collection. The fact that the fragment was part of the BM's collection undermined the familial account of provenance being offered by "sultan1966". That same year, Gradel separately established that an olive-green

[3] He is also an expert at TimeLine Auctions of the United Kingdom.

gemstone sold by "sultan1966" in December 2015 was recorded in the 1926 *Catalogue of the Engraved Gems and Cameos, Greek, Etruscan, and Roman in the British Museum.* This gemstone had been bought by von Kiaer, who had then sold it in June 2019 to UK-based dealer Malcolm Hay.[4] These two identifications of what appeared to be objects belonging to the BM prompted Gradel to investigate more closely the identity of "sultan1966"/"Paul Higgs"/"Paul Higgins". He had by that time bought hundreds of gems from "sultan1966" and, checking back through his documentation, discovered that the PayPal account for "Paul Higgins" was in the name of one Peter Higgs. He shared his news with von Kiaer who informed him that there was a Peter Higgs working as a curator in the BM's Department of Greece and Rome.

After receiving notice from Gradel in 2020 that the gemstone he had bought from von Kiaer was most likely stolen, Hay visited the BM in May 2021 to arrange for its return. He met with Deputy Director Jonathan Williams, who made some perfunctory enquiries about the gem's sales history but thought the loss had most likely occurred during World War II. It was later discovered that someone, said though not proven to be Higgs, had inserted a handwritten note into the museum's records, which reported the loss and was falsely dated to 1963. In February 2021, Gradel had already emailed Williams, notifying him of the two gems (and one other) appearing on eBay that he suspected were the property of the BM and alerting him to his suspicions about Higgs. Unfortunately, Gradel had previously shared his concerns with author and classicist Dorothy Lobel King, who had warned Higgs on February 26, 2021 that someone was "trying to 'set him up'" (Fitz Gibbon 2024, quoting a BM court document). Higgs had forwarded King's email to Williams, who was thus forewarned and prejudiced against Gradel's allegations. After being warned about Gradel's investigation by King, Higgs is reported to have closed down his eBay and PayPal accounts (Fitz Gibbon 2024), though a causative connection between the King email and Higgs' actions has not been established.[5] Then, after a lapse of several months, in July 2021 Williams replied that Gradel was mistaken and that the "the objects concerned are all accounted for and with no suggestion of any wrongdoing on behalf of any member of museum staff" (quoted in Marshall 2023a).

Without informing Gradel, however, after an internal audit had revealed missing objects in the Greece and Rome collection, in April 2022 the BM initiated an internal assessment of the collection, with Aurelia Masson-Berghoff as project curator. Masson-Berghoff was not informed of Gradel's warning about Higgs, who since

[4] The BM website reports that from 1972 onwards the museum acquired a number of coins and other small antiquities from Hay (retrieved July 7, 2024, from https://www.britishmuseum.org/collection/term/BIOG144665). It is amusing to imagine that Hay might inadvertently have bought an object stolen from the BM and then sold it back to the museum for a profit.

[5] On July 10, 2024, there was a seller with the ID "sultan1966" active on eBay, offering coloured inks and paints for sale. The seller was said to have joined eBay in February 2014 and be located in Spain. Feedback comments suggest the seller has in the past been buying coins. It seems unlikely that this seller has any relationship with Peter Higgs, but it does raise questions about the uniqueness or transferability of eBay IDs.

January 2021 had been acting head of the Department of Greece and Rome and was in a position to obstruct her investigation. Nevertheless, she was able to report in December 2022 that more than 1000 objects were missing.

Frustrated at the BM's intransigence, and unaware of its internal audit, in October 2022, Gradel contacted a trustee of the BM, who passed on his information to George Osborne, who was at the time Chair of the BM. Osborne consulted with the BM's Director Hartwig Fischer, who dismissed the allegations. But in December 2022, Fischer contacted Osborne about the results of Masson-Berghoff's report. They recognised the likely connection with Gradel's information and decided that the police should be informed.

The BM made the thefts public on August 16, 2023, announcing in a press release that material from its collection had been discovered to be missing, stolen or damaged, that it was initiating legal action against a member of staff who had been dismissed, and that it had launched an independent review of museum security. The Metropolitan Police had also commenced investigating the thefts, presumably several months earlier. The press release described the material as follows:

> The majority of the items in question were small pieces kept in a storeroom belonging to one of the Museum's collections. They include gold jewellery and gems of semiprecious stones and glass dating from the 15th century BC to the 19th century AD. None had recently been on public display, and they were kept primarily for academic and research purposes. (BM 2023a)

Gradel was aggrieved that the BM press release failed to mention that he had already warned about the possible thefts two years earlier but had been ignored. He was also angry that Fischer accused him publicly of withholding information (Slow 2023). Consequently, he decided to go public himself, providing media interviews that highlighted what he perceived to be the inaction of Williams and Fischer (Rayner et al. 2023a, b, c). Higgs was named publicly as the member of staff dismissed by the BM (Rayner et al. 2023c; Seymour 2023). The Metropolitan Police had searched Higgs' home earlier in August, seizing ancient coins and medals and other material (Razzall et al. 2024a). Following on from this flurry of media activity, on August 25, 2023 Fischer announced his resignation as Director, accepting responsibility for the BM's failure to react appropriately to Gradel's warnings in 2021 (BM 2023b). Williams' resignation as Deputy Director was revealed on December 13, 2023 (Razzall 2023). In the following months, the BM established a website reporting on the thefts,[6] which describes with images the general types of objects stolen. It also provides images of some recovered objects.

The independent review announced in the BM's August 16, 2023 press release delivered its report and recommendations in December 2023. It estimated that approximately 2000 mainly unregistered objects were damaged or missing from the collection and recommended improvements in documentation and registration, risk

[6] Retrieved October 28, 2024 from https://www.britishmuseum.org/our-work/departments/recovery-missing-items#:~:text=We%20have%20registered%20missing%20items,and%20retrieving%20the%20lost%20items

preparedness, internal auditing, governance, and management (BM 2023c). The review also noted that the thefts had been discovered due to an internal audit started at the BM in April 2022 and acknowledged that the BM had wrongfully dismissed Gradel's warnings in 2021. Pre-empting the review's report, already in October 2023, the BM had embarked on a five-year project to digitise and make available online records of every object in the museum's collections (BM 2023d), at a projected cost of £10 million, which the museum hoped to raise privately (Marshall 2023b).

In March 2024, the BM initiated civil proceedings against Higgs, claiming to have evidence that he had been selling objects since 2009 using false names and documents (Razzall et al. 2024a; Fitz Gibbon 2024). He is alleged to have stolen at least 1800 small pieces of jewellery, sometimes damaging metal mounts while removing gemstones. By May 2024, the BM had recovered 626 missing and stolen objects (BM 2024). The number reported had not changed by March 2025 when this chapter was going to press. Similarly, despite the widespread media allegations reported in this chapter, no criminal charges had been made against Higgs. There had been no further update on the BM's recovery operation.

It is believed that 45 dealers in the United Kingdom and abroad bought gems on eBay from seller "sultan1966" (BBC 2024k). In the late 2000s, before "sultan1966" had started selling on eBay, Peter Szuhay, a dealer at Grays Antique Market in London, had bought a gem for £400 from a man he thinks might have been Higgs. Although his recollection hardly constitutes proof, BM court documents reveal that at least one stolen gem did pass through his hands (BBC 2024j; Fitz Gibbon 2024). Gradel himself had sold gems from "sultan1966" to dealers around the world before realising their illicit source (BBC 2024h). Once he realised their true nature, he set out to recover them.

3 Moving Beyond the Streetlight: The Transit and Destination Markets of the Antiquities Trade

In the previous section, I have tried to present a faithful account of the BM thefts as they have been reported in the media. The tale that has been told, with Gradel appearing as a central protagonist, is a good example of how investigative journalism (made possible here only through Gradel's cooperation) might uncover a scandal. It is a fascinating story for casual and professional readers alike: the hubris and ultimately the nemesis of a powerful cultural institution; the story of Gradel's David confronting and bravely dispatching the BM's Goliath. There are political overtones too, with countries such as Greece using the evidence of the BM's lax security to further their claims for the repatriation of contested objects (Mathers 2023). Commentary has followed suit, highlighting the problems posed to museums by deficient documentation, poor security, and perhaps below-standard staff wages (Cobham and Dalton 2023; Felch 2003; Jones 2023), or questioning the BM's role as a capable custodian of objects misappropriated during periods of imperial/colonial domination (Bossoh 2024; Hicks 2023; Smith 2023). The story has been nourished by the BM itself, which has reacted publicly and contritely to accept responsibility for the thefts through a series of press releases, a dedicated website, and a physical display of recovered antiquities.

But although the BM thefts have been caught fairly and squarely inside the journalistic streetlight, there is more to be discerned in the streetlight's crepuscular penumbra of incomplete reporting and insufficient investigation. The reporting and associated commentary have examined the thefts in their own terms and not surprisingly have focused on museum security or lack thereof. Museum security is obviously important. While the BM thefts were ongoing, 83 km to the west ancient papyrus fragments belonging to the Egypt Exploration Society were being stolen from the University of Oxford's Art, Archaeology and Ancient World Library. Oxford professor Dirk Obbink faced allegations of theft and was reportedly under police investigation (Brodie et al. 2023, pp. 13–14). Poor security is not an issue that affects only the BM. But in what follows, I want to move away from the illuminated subject of museum security and discuss what might be learned from the reporting of the BM thefts about the organisation and operation of the antiquities trade more generally.

Since at least the work of Patrick O'Keefe and Lyndel Prott (1989), it has been recognised that the global antiquities trade can usefully be conceptualised as comprising three stages or markets: source, transit and destination (Kersel 2007; Mackenzie et al. 2020). Often these markets are geographically separated, but not always. This tripartite structure can be seen quite clearly in the public account of the BM thefts. The BM was the source of the stolen material, eBay comprised the transit market, and Gradel, von Kiaer, Hay and other dealers and customers were located in the destination market. In fact, the BM thefts present an almost exemplary case study of the structure and operation of the antiquities trade. It is surprising, then, that most published appraisal and criticism of the thefts has focused on the BM as source and very little attention has been paid to the actors and agencies of the transit and destination markets that enabled the ongoing trade of the stolen gems. The following sections will explore these market stages in more detail.

3.1 The Transit Market: eBay

The transit market is important for laundering stolen or looted material by disguising its true nature and origin through fictitious accounts of provenance, sometimes backed up by counterfeit documentation. This is exactly what happened on eBay when Higgs adopted a fake identity ("Paul Higgins") and provided a fictitious provenance (the grandfather's shop in York). Since its launch in 1995, eBay has attracted its fair share of academic attention, albeit in a sporadic and unsustained fashion (Altaweel 2019; Altaweel and Hadjitofi 2020; Barker 2000; Bland 2009, pp. 88–96; Brodie 2015a, b, 2017a, b; Bruhns 2000; Chippindale and Gill 2001; Dundler 2021;

Fay 2011; Lidington 2002; Mazza 2024, pp. 107–124; Stanish 2009; Takla 2014). It is now well-established that it is not difficult to buy and sell unprovenanced antiquities on eBay that are likely fake or illegally traded, with no notice to customers of the potential risks involved of buying such material. On July 9, 2024, for example, the simple search "Roman intaglio gem" revealed 655 objects for sale on eBay's UK platform. The two highest priced objects were listed at £7403.66 (or best offer) each. One was located with a seller in the United States, dating to the second or third century AD and without any provenance. The other was with a seller in Bulgaria, with no specific date of manufacture but with a provenance "Formerly acquired at the ancient art market in Munich, Germany in 1995". At the other end of the price range, there were five Roman brass rings located with a seller in the United Kingdom open for bidding with a starting price of 99p each described as "ancient authentic artefacts" and with a provenance "All Items are Acquired from Legitimate Sources Such as International Coin Fairs, European Auction Houses and Old 1970s European Collections. Authenticity certificate is available at an additional cost upon request before shipment of your item". The cheapest fixed price object was selling for £28.27 (or best offer) located in Morocco with no specific dating or provenance.[7] The 655 offered objects no doubt included stolen and illegally traded antiquities, historical and modern reproductions, fakes, and genuine antiquities legitimately on the market. For the inexpert buyer, this mix is a hazardous mess. But for experts such as Gradel, it is a convenient source of under-priced antiquities. That is exactly what "sultan1966" was selling and Gradel and others were buying—bargains.

eBay offers an online platform functioning as a marketplace but does not in itself own or trade antiquities (or any other material). It does have policies that ostensibly regulate the use of the platform for trading stolen and illegally traded antiquities, but they are not immediately obvious and it requires some effort to find them. For example, in July 2024, I had to click "Help & Contact" at the top of the eBay UK home page, which took me to the Customer Service page, then click "Policies" in the small print footer, before scrolling down the list of policies to "Artifacts" (eBay 2024). None of this was intuitive. In fact, while searching for this policy statement, an image popped up offering "NEW BATCH—Job Lots of 20 Roman Bronze Coins for Study and Research Most as Dug" with no indication of country of origin, provenance or legality. Thus, in my experience, any cautious buyer would be more likely to be offered dubious antiquities for purchase than to discover and read the policy that is intended to regulate the sale of such material. Even when I did manage to discover the appropriate policy, there was no clear statement of selling conditions. The policy was primarily concerned with UK and Native American artifacts. It did state:

---

[7] Interestingly, there were 15 sellers listed as located in Morocco, which is a disproportionally high number. Morocco ranked ninth in Altaweel's (2019, p. 15, Fig. 6) listing of eBay's "top ten selling countries of antiquities", though strangely with Viking artifacts comprising its top selling culture. These observations might be pointing towards Morocco's previously unremarked status as a transit country.

> The following items can't be sold on eBay: Tainted cultural goods illegally excavated or removed after 30 December 2003 (UK's Dealing in Cultural Object (Offences) Act 2003). Looted or stolen goods. See the INTERPOL Stolen Works of Art Database as well as the International Council of Museums Red Lists Database, which identifies categories of cultural goods most vulnerable to illicit traffic. (eBay 2024)

Ironically, this policy was developed in collaboration with the BM (Bland 2009, pp. 88–96). Writing for the *Financial Times* in 2006, Peter Aspden reported that:

> The British Museum is joining forces with the online auctioneer eBay to prevent valuable antiquities being sold illegally on the internet. The London-based museum, one of the world's pre-eminent cultural institutions, has set up a team to monitor all antiquities sold on eBay, and to make sure their sellers have a right to trade them. If it finds a listing to be illegal, it will report it to the Metropolitan Police art and antiques unit. (Aspden 2006)

David Lammy, who was at the time the UK's Minister for Culture, was quoted as describing eBay as "one of this century's greatest success stories" (Aspden 2006). The collaboration had a limited focus on recent metal-detecting finds from England and Wales, and not, for example, on antiquities stolen from major museums. The BM shouldered the responsibility of monitoring eBay listings, but the impact on sales was minimal and writing retrospectively a few years later, BM curator Roger Bland suggested that:

> On the face of it, therefore, the memorandum would seem not to be worth the paper it is written on and it is certainly weaker than the British Museum would have liked: not only is the bar set very high by eBay before it will take finds down from the website—the British Museum more or less has to prove that a find will be treasure before eBay will act, whereas the Museum feels that eBay should take down finds if there is suspicion about them—but also eBay itself puts no resources into this checking, which is very time consuming. (Bland 2009, p. 91)

So, although eBay advertises that tainted or stolen antiquities "can't be sold on eBay" (eBay 2024), it disclaims any responsibility and provides no resources for monitoring the legitimacy of material being offered on its platform. Presumably, sellers are expected to adhere voluntarily to the offered guidance. The BM staff charged with monitoring eBay were also responsible for recording private metal-detecting finds in England and Wales, so of necessity their time spent monitoring eBay could only be limited. In 2013, it was reported that the BM "has been monitoring eBay as time allows" and that "More resources are needed in order to pursue this work; arguably these should come from eBay and similar sites which profit from the sale of antiquities" (Bland et al. 2017, p. 116). Unfortunately, support from eBay has not been forthcoming and the present status of the BM monitoring scheme is unknown.

So, there is a prohibition against selling stolen and illegally traded antiquities buried deep within the eBay platform, though as the BM thefts show, it is easily ignored and little more than performative. All this has been well known for years. Yet in the reporting of the BM thefts, very little attention has been paid to the role of eBay, even though it offered a platform allowing the sale of hundreds of stolen antiquities. The BBC investigation, for example, did not approach eBay for comment. Tara Cobham and Jane Dalton (2023) writing for the *Independent* were unusual in reproducing a statement from eBay: "eBay does not tolerate the sale of stolen property. If we identify that a listing on our site is stolen, we immediately remove it and work with law enforcement to support investigations and keep our site safe". Mark Wilding (2024) writing for the *Observer* also contacted eBay, reporting that: "... a spokesperson declined to answer specific questions, but said the sale of illicit antiques is prohibited on the platform and encouraged users to contact law enforcement about any suspicious listings".

Its reply to Wilding confirms that although eBay does ostensibly regulate the sale of antiquities, it does not self-police and is dependent upon outside observers to report stolen or otherwise illicit material. It is not obvious from the reporting that Gradel notified eBay of his suspicions. But if he had, at first, without hard evidence, he would most likely have been ignored, as Bland (2009, p. 91) had already complained. Even when he had secured his two firm identifications of stolen gems, he still does not appear to have notified eBay. Nor did he contact any competent law enforcement agency. But, as he himself has said, while the BM rejected his allegations, he had no crime to report: "I asked friends of mine, and they advised me, 'You can't do anything, because the victim of the crime you claim is the British Museum, and the injured party denies that a crime has even taken place'" (quoted in Mead 2024). This quote highlights another harmful consequence of the BM's failure to engage constructively with Gradel in 2021: a couple of years had passed before the police were finally alerted. In April 2024, when contacted by Wilding, eBay stated that: "With regards to the theft of items from the British Museum, our dedicated law enforcement liaison team has been in close contact with the Met for several months, and is supporting the investigation into this case" (quoted in Wilding 2024).

It is regrettable that the police investigation did not start sooner, when the evidence trail was fresher. A few years after "sultan1966" had (unbeknownst to me) set up shop, in a policy paper written at the request of the Antiquities Coalition (Brodie 2017a), I suggested that eBay should have a strong corporate interest in regulating and policing the sale of antiquities because they account for only a very small part of its overall turnover but carry a disproportionate risk of generating bad publicity. The avoidance of reputational harm would outweigh any financial loss incurred through diminished sales volume (Brodie 2017a, p. 9). To that end, I recommended that eBay should adopt strong requirements for the sellers' description and provision of valid provenance, and clear statements alerting buyers to the legal requirements and damaging consequences of purchasing unprovenanced antiquities, preferably in a pop-up window that has to be checked in acknowledgement by a potential buyer before proceeding to the sales pages (Brodie 2017a, pp. 9–12). But these suggestions and recommendations for a safer and more secure trading environment, which might have deterred or at least hindered "sultan1966", were not acted upon. Their implementation now would be very much dependent upon negative publicity exerting pressure upon the company to take action. Unfortunately, with the focus of this scandal fixed fairly and squarely on the BM, eBay seems to have escaped any opprobrium and, as I have shown, it is continuing business as usual: most eBay shoppers can search for and purchase an antiquity without any guarantee of its authenticity or legitimacy and without any notice of the potential risks involved.

3.2 The Destination Market: Antiquities Dealers

One and perhaps the most prominent reason for the absence of eBay from the story of the BM thefts is that it has been constructed very firmly around the sympathetic and even romantic figure of Gradel and the account of his struggle with the BM. Gradel is the hero of the story. He recognised the stolen antiquities for what they were and has been active in securing their recovery. He was instrumental in exposing the thefts and lax security at the BM and arguably responsible in part at least for the 2023 independent review and implemented recommendations. But the reporting named other dealers around the world who had acquired stolen gems and who had not recognised them for what they were. Three at least were based in the United Kingdom. All told, it is believed that 45 dealers bought material directly from Higgs. Presumably they could also have been buying and selling unprovenanced gems of other uncertain or unknown origins that could not be identified definitively as stolen or illegally traded. After all, buying and selling antiquities is their business. But the reporting has had nothing to say about the poor due diligence of the other dealers or the impossibility for even a diligent dealer like Gradel to identify antiquities that have been clandestinely excavated and illegally traded and entered the market with a fictitious provenance: a daily reality on eBay with the tens-of-thousands or more objects being offered annually (Altaweel and Hadjitofi 2020). If, hypothetically for example, "sultan1966" had been selling gems that had been dug out of the ground in Italy and marketed illegally, it seems unlikely that anyone would have noticed.

The antiquities market is characterised by the absence of reliable information with regards to provenance. Higgs was able to pass off his stolen antiquities as the property of a deceased family member, and it was a lie that remained unquestioned until Gradel's recognition of the BM gems. But in this market of unreliable information, personal relations are important for establishing trust in material being traded. The importance of personal relations was highlighted when Gradel said that he had sold gems to other dealers and collectors already known to him around the world (BBC 2024h). The reporting showcased the communications between Gradel, Hay and von Kiaer and noted that antiquities dealers maintain communication among themselves through the use of messaging groups (BBC 2024i). There are clearly open channels of communication within the market that allow the easy circulation of news and information, which in an environment of scarce information is crucial for effective market participation (Velthuis 2005, p. 40). But these communication networks also allow for the propagation of a discourse constructing moral justifications for participation in what can be characterised as a noxious market (Brodie 2023a; Mackenzie et al. 2020, pp. 60–61). This discourse can be used publicly to normalise the trade in unprovenanced antiquities while at the same time discounting or trivialising imputations of harmful practice. One dealer based in France interviewed by the BBC did not want his name made public because of possible problems with law enforcement and border control. When asked about the nature of these problems, Gradel dismissed them as "aspersions, suspicions, rumours" and the interviewer did not press further (BBC 2024h).

It is noticeable that while Gradel has been vocal in his criticism and condemnation of the BM, he has maintained what might be characterised as a diplomatic silence about his market colleagues who unknowingly and unquestioningly participated in the trade of the stolen material. Indeed, Gradel wanted to keep the issue away from the press and only went public in 2023 when the BM failed to acknowledge his work (BBC 2024g). It is hard to avoid the impression that Gradel was keen to keep the whole episode secret, away from public curiosity. Perhaps he had the reputation of the BM in mind, but secrecy is the leitmotif of the antiquities trade more generally. Speaking on the BBC podcast (BBC 2024i), US academic Erin Thompson suggested that no dealer would want it to be known that they had been buying stolen gems on eBay as it would be damaging to their reputation. In fact, with no critical interrogation of their trade practices, interviewed dealers have been able to direct scrutiny and blame towards the BM and, in the beneficent glow of Gradel's actions, cast themselves as public-spirited members of a "niche profession" (BBC 2024k) holding the incompetent and even conspiratorial BM to account.

4 Outside the Streetlight: The BM Thefts and Policymaking

The hard facts of the BM thefts cannot easily be dismissed as aspersions, suspicions or rumours, particularly when placing them within their broader historical and commercial contexts, and it is time now to look outside the streetlight of the reporting. To start with, I want to look back to the years immediately following 2014 when "sultan1966" was active on eBay and dealers were buying his stolen gems without recognising them for what they were. In 2014, Da'esh (ISIS, Islamic State of Syria and Iraq) established its Caliphate across large parts of Syria and Iraq and was shown to be deriving finance from the antiquities trade (Brodie 2022; Sabrine et al. 2022). Ancient gemstones and rings were being sold inside Syria for about $10 each, with precious metal jewellery selling for more (Sabrine et al. 2022, pp. 124–125). Electronic images of jewellery were recovered by US special forces in 2015 during a raid on the Syrian compound of Abu Sayyaf, who was head of the Da'esh antiquities division (Keller 2015; USA 2016). If the evidence of looted coins is anything to go by (Brodie 2022, p. 33, 2023b, in press), which are also small, portable antiquities, large quantities of gems and other pieces of jewellery could have entered the European market—the market of untraceable antiquities and secretive transactions so graphically exposed (though not explored) by the reporting of the BM thefts, where stolen gemstones were able to circulate almost (with the glaring exception of Gradel) without question.

To my knowledge, no gems or jewellery looted and illegally traded from Syria have been publicly identified on the European antiquities market. That is not surprising, as it would be difficult if not impossible to ascertain the county of origin of an object from the object alone, just as it was, with two exceptions, impossible to identify the museum of origin of the stolen BM gems. It does not take a Holmesian leap of deduction to argue that during the late 2010s, when they were buying stolen gems from "sultan1966", unknown to the traders involved some if not many of the other unprovenanced gems they were buying on eBay or acquiring through other channels had originated in Syria, and that they were unwitting participants in a trickle-up economy whose ultimate beneficiary was Da'esh or some other militia or criminal group in Syria. I say unwitting, but that might be a generous assessment of their likely level of awareness bearing in mind the prominent reporting of this issue (Brodie 2022, pp. 41–43). They should have known. Although it would have been impossible to know with any certainty that a particular gemstone or piece of jewellery had been illegally traded from Syria, there should certainly have been a strong suspicion and perhaps even presumption among dealers with relevant expertise that any gem without verifiable provenance was from Syria, or if not from Syria, from some other questionable source. Nevertheless, whatever the dealers' suspicions, as the purchases of the BM gems go to show, they were not enough to deter their market participation.

Not surprisingly, given they are both following the media (Mackenzie et al. 2020, pp. 128–129), the scandal-driven approach to policymaking bears many similarities to the crisis-driven approach (when conflict or other human or natural disasters exacerbate the illicit trade in antiquities) and shares its weaknesses (Brodie 2015c, 2015d, 2017c; Brodie et al. 2022; Mackenzie et al. 2020, pp. 127–131). First, it focuses reactively and usually too late on developing solutions to an emergent problem in a particular location (provided the problem captures public and political attention through media intervention). This reactive one-at-a-time approach is the policymaking equivalent of "whack-a-mole" and does nothing to engage more proactively and unremittingly with the antiquities trade as a long-term, systemic threat to cultural heritage. Second, as with the case of the BM thefts, when the problem is portrayed as a singular departure from normality it encourages it to be understood as one of source vulnerability. The policy solutions can then be characterised as aiming at "supply reduction", with various improvements to physical and human "capacity" aimed at deterring theft through reducing opportunities and motivations. In this case, going forward, improved documentation and security at the BM will make it harder in future for any member of staff to steal from its collections. Again, though, supply reduction of this type is a one-at-a-time solution. Improved security at the BM will do nothing to prevent theft at all the other museums around the world. It will not, for example, offer enhanced protection to ancient papyri fragments housed at the University of Oxford's Art, Archaeology and Ancient World Library.

The implemented BM reactions to the thefts constitute a textbook example of what I term a "protection and recovery" strategy, aiming to protect what is left and recover what has been lost. But the strategy does nothing to prevent future episodes of theft or looting at other sites or locations that are left unprotected. It is prevention, not protection, that should be key (Brodie 2017c). What is needed is a mixed strategy of market governance aimed at "demand reduction", achieved through moral persuasion as much as legal compulsion—the so-called ethical consumption market (Mackenzie et al. 2020, pp. 115–126). One instrument of persuasion, as I have already described, would be to encourage eBay to raise customer awareness and improve standards of provenance provision. It is regrettable that the reporting of the BM thefts has treated eBay almost as an innocent bystander and an opportunity to pressurise eBay into change has surely been lost.

Not only is the policy of protection and recovery ineffective, but it is also wasteful. Resources committed to one scandal or crisis are not available for the next one. I have noted the intention to raise £10 million to improve security at the BM, which might deter or stop any future thefts from the museum of small antiquities. But it will do nothing to stop the international trade of unprovenanced and often stolen or looted antiquities nor interrupt funding to criminal and militia groups, which, internationally, would be considered a more serious problem. The BM stated that it hoped the money would be raised privately, though to date has not named a benefactor. The BM will also compensate people who purchased stolen gems and who have agreed to return them. But again, a BM spokesperson stated that "None of the money will come from public funds—the Museum has specifically raised funds for this purpose" (quoted in Alberge and Parker 2024).

If the money the BM is raising is taken out of a notional "cultural heritage protection pot" made available by charitable donors, it will diminish the amounts available for other and perhaps more worthwhile projects. I would argue that the sum of £10 million might be better spent endowing a monitoring system for eBay, which might deter the sale of stolen or otherwise illegally-traded antiquities and perhaps, through attendant negative publicity, encourage eBay itself to take a more proactive stance against the use of its platform for laundering and illegally trading antiquities, as previously advocated by the BM (Bland et al. 2017, p. 116). By discouraging or preventing the trade of stolen or trafficked antiquities, this would extend some level of enhanced protection to archaeological and cultural heritage sites around the world, not just to one museum in London. Not surprisingly, though, given the focus on the BM as the scandalous villain, there has been no public questioning or even discussion of the decision to spend more than £10 million of privately sourced money to make good the failings of a publicly-funded institution. It might be good publicity for the BM, heading off any damaging criticism that it is wasting taxpayers' money, but going forward it is not good use of funding for cultural heritage protection.

5 Conclusion

It might be true that policy as regards the antiquities trade advances one scandal at a time, but as I have tried to demonstrate in this chapter, the scandal might not comprise the entirety nor even the substance of the problem and any policy or implemented actions based on the reporting of the scandal might be misdirected at best or comprise a costly mistake at worst. The investigative reporting of the BM thefts has constructed a compelling narrative that has directed attention towards the failings of the BM. But away from the direct streetlight of this narrative it has also provided some insights into the antiquities trade that would not normally be readily accessible. As I have tried to show, this information can be used to construct a competing narrative that directs attention away from the BM as a problem of source vulnerability and towards the antiquities trade as a problem of unhindered demand. This competing narrative with its own alternative implications for policy development is one that I would argue is more deserving of attention (and financial support). The conclusion is clear. For academic research and policy development, it always necessary to look beyond the immediate narrative streetlight of investigative reporting and examine how published information can be differently interpreted. There is a well-established, multi-disciplinary academic literature relating to the organisation and operation of the antiquities trade and its potentially harmful consequences and it is with reference to this literature that any novel evidence or insights should be interpreted. Situating a story within its broader research context enhances the undoubted value of investigative journalism for understanding the antiquities trade and sharpens its relevance for further research or policymaking.

Acknowledgments I would like to thank the editors for inviting me to write this chapter, for kindly allowing me the time to finish it, and for their critical and insightful commentary.

References

Alberge D, Parker F (2024) British museum to compensate buyers of gems stolen from its collection. Telegraph, May 27

Altaweel M (2019) The market for heritage: evidence from eBay using natural language processing. Soc Sci Comput Rev 39(3):391–415

Altaweel M, Hadjitofi TG (2020) The sale of heritage on eBay: market trends and cultural value. Big Data Soc 7(2):1–17

Aspden P (2006) British museum in eBay alliance. Financial Times, October 2

Barker A (2000) Ethics, e-commerce, and the future of the past. SAA Bull 18(1):26–27. https://documents.saa.org/container/docs/default-source/doc-publications/publications/saa-bulletin/2000/saa-bulletin-18(1)-final.pdf?sfvrsn=aef182b8_2. Accessed 22 July 2024

BBC (2024a) Introducing thief at the British museum. BBC Radio 4, Shadow World. https://www.bbc.co.uk/programmes/m001zspz/episodes/player. Accessed 6 July 2024

BBC (2024b) Thief at the British museum: 1. The man with the cardboard box. https://www.bbc.co.uk/programmes/m001zspz/episodes/player. Accessed 6 July 2024

BBC (2024c) Thief at the British museum: 2. White paper dots. https://www.bbc.co.uk/programmes/m001zspz/episodes/player. Accessed 6 July 2024

BBC (2024d) Thief at the British museum: 3. lightbulb moment. https://www.bbc.co.uk/programmes/m001zspz/episodes/player. Accessed 6 July 2024

BBC (2024e) Thief at the British museum: 4. Seeds of doubt. https://www.bbc.co.uk/programmes/m001zspz/episodes/player. Accessed 6 July 2024

BBC (2024f) Thief at the British museum: 5. Secret missions. https://www.bbc.co.uk/programmes/m001zspz/episodes/player. Accessed 6 July 2024

BBC (2024g) Thief at the British museum: 6. Lone wolf or scapegoat. https://www.bbc.co.uk/programmes/m001zspz/episodes/player. Accessed 6 July 2024

BBC (2024h) Thief at the British museum: 7. Treasure hunt. https://www.bbc.co.uk/programmes/m001zspz/episodes/player. Accessed 6 July 2024

BBC (2024i) Thief at the British museum: 8. Stateside. https://www.bbc.co.uk/programmes/m001zspz/episodes/player. Accessed 6 July 2024

BBC (2024j) Thief at the British museum: 9. An ending, a beginning. https://www.bbc.co.uk/programmes/m001zspz/episodes/player. Accessed 6 July 2024

BBC (2024k) Scams and scandals: thief at the British museum. BBC iPlayer, May 27. https://www.bbc.co.uk/iplayer/episode/m001zrbs/scams-scandals-thief-at-the-british-museum. Accessed 29 July 2024

Bland R (2009) The United Kingdom as a source country. In: Mackenzie S, Green P (eds) Criminology and archaeology. Hart, pp 83–102

Bland R, Lewis M, Pett D, Richardson I, Robbins K, Webley R (2017) The treasure act and portable antiquities scheme in England and Wales. In: Moshenska G (ed) Key concepts in public archaeology. UCL, pp 107–121

BM (2023a) Announcement regarding missing, stolen and damaged items. British Museum, August 16. https://www.britishmuseum.org/about-us/press/press-releases. Accessed 6 July 2024

BM (2023b) Announcement from Hartwig Fischer. British Museum, August 25. https://www.britishmuseum.org/about-us/press/press-releases. Accessed 6 July 2024

BM (2023c) British museum announces completion of independent review. British Museum, December 12. https://www.britishmuseum.org/about-us/press/press-releases. Accessed 6 July 2024

BM (2023d) British museum sets out plans to digitise fully the collection. British Museum, October 18. https://www.britishmuseum.org/about-us/press/press-releases. Accessed 6 July 2024

BM (2024) Update on the recovery of missing or stolen objects. British Museum, May 17. https://www.britishmuseum.org/about-us/press/press-releases. Accessed 6 July 2024

Bossoh N (2024) Rediscovering gems: British museum exhibition exposes hypocrisy of new loan agreements for looted objects. Conversation, March 12. https://theconversation.com/rediscovering-gems-british-museum-exhibition-exposes-hypocrisy-of-new-loan-agreements-for-looted-objects-224422. Accessed 6 July 2024

Brodie N (2015a) The internet market in pre-Columbian antiquities. In: Kila J, Balcells M (eds) Cultural property crime: an overview and analysis on contemporary perspectives and trends. Brill, pp 237–262

Brodie N (2015b) The internet market in antiquities. In: Desmarais F (ed) Countering illicit traffic in cultural goods. ICOM, pp 11–20

Brodie N (2015c) Why is no one talking about Libya's cultural destruction? Near Eastern Archaeol 78(3):212–217

Brodie N (2015d) Syria and its regional neighbors: a case of cultural property protection policy failure? Int J Cult Prop 22:317–335

Brodie N (2017a) How to control the internet market in antiquities? The need for regulation and monitoring. Antiquities Coalition Policy Brief, no. 3. Antiquities Coalition. https://think-tank.theantiquitiescoalition.org/how-to-control-the-internet-market-in-antiquities-the-need-for-regulation-and-monitoring/#:~:text=Author%20Biography,one%20is%20watching%20and%20acting. Accessed 22 July 2024

Brodie N (2017b) Virtually gone! The internet market in antiquities. In: Proceedings of the 6th international conference of experts on the return of cultural property. Overseas Korean Cultural Heritage Foundation, pp 190–204

Brodie N (2017c) Protection not prevention: the failure of public policy to prevent the plunder and traffic of cultural property from the MENA region (1990-2015). In: Anderson J, Geismar H (eds) The Routledge companion to cultural property. Routledge, pp 89–107

Brodie N (2022) The looting and trafficking of Syrian antiquities since 2011. In: Hashemi L, Shelley L (eds) Antiquities smuggling: in the real and the virtual world. Routledge, pp 21–58

Brodie N (2023a) Noxious scholarship? Publishing unprovenanced cuneiform tablets from Iraq. In: Brodie N, Kersel MM, Rasmussen JM (eds) Variant scholarship: ancient texts in modern contexts. Sidestone, pp 95–112

Brodie N (2023b) 'Standing caliph' coins from Syria: probably looted and on the market. In: Finkel I, Fraser JA, Simpson SJ (eds) 'To Aleppo gone …' Essays in honour of Jonathan N. Tubb. Archaeopress, pp 175–180

Brodie N (in press) EU regulation 2019/880 on the import of cultural goods: the pernicious effect of poor evidence upon legislative regulation. In Ulph, J. & Vigneron, S. (Eds.), Research handbook on art, culture and heritage. Edward Elgar

Brodie N, Yates D (2022) Antiquities and money laundering. Transfer J Provenance Res Hist Collect 1:97–109. https://doi.org/10.48640/tf.2022.1.91516. Accessed 29 October 2024

Brodie N, Kersel MM, Mackenzie S, Sabrine I, Smith E, Yates D (2022) Fifty years on. Why is there still a global illicit trade in cultural objects (and what can we do about it)? J Field Archaeol 47(2):117–130

Brodie N, Kersel MM, Rasmussen JM (2023) Variant scholarship: ancient texts in modern contexts. In: Brodie N, Kersel MM, Rasmussen JM (eds) Variant scholarship: ancient texts in modern contexts. Sidestone, pp 95–112

Bruhns K (2000). www.plunderedpast.com. SAA Bull 18(2), 22–25. https://documents.saa.org/container/docs/default-source/doc-publications/publications/saa-bulletin/2000/saa-bulletin-18(2)-final.pdf?sfvrsn=256db1cf_2. Accessed 22 July 2024

Chippindale C, Gill D (2001) On-line auctions: a new venue for the antiquities market. Cult Without Context 9:4–12. https://traffickingculture.org/publications/culture-without-context-2001-issue-9-cambridge-mcdonald-institute-for-archaeological-research/. Accessed 22 July 2024

Cobham T, Dalton J (2023) 'Incredibly poor' British Museum security let thief take valuables over years, ex-curator claims Independent, August 27. https://www.independent.co.uk/news/uk/crime/british-museum-theft-security-items-higgs-b2397362.html. Accessed 25 July 2024

Colchester M (2023) How an academic uncovered one of the biggest museum heists of all time. Wall Street J October 24. https://www.wsj.com/style/british-museum-ittai-gradel-heist-efec0847. Accessed 25 July 2024

Dundler L (2021) #antiquitiesdealers. In: Oosterman N, Yates D (eds) Crime and art: sociological and criminological perspectives of crimes in the art world. Springer, pp 45–62

eBay (2024). Artefacts and cave formations policy. https://www.ebay.co.uk/help/policies/prohibited-restricted-items/artefacts-cultural-heritage-graverelated-items-policy?id=4282. Accessed 28 October 2024

Fay E (2011) Virtual artifacts: eBay, antiquities, and authenticity. J Contemp Crim Justice 27:449–464

Felch J (2003) What a scandal at the British museum reveals. New York Times, September 17

Felch J, Frammolino R (2011) Chasing Aphrodite. Houghton Mifflin Harcourt

Fitz Gibbon K (2024) Dirty details: British museum presses case against former curator Peter Higgs. Cultural Property News, April 30. https://culturalpropertynews.org/dirty-details-british-museum-presses-case-against-former-curator-peter-higg/. Accessed 25 July 2024

Freedman D (2010) Why scientific studies are so often wrong: the streetlight effect. Discover, December 10. https://www.discovermagazine.com/the-sciences/why-scientific-studies-are-so-often-wrong-the-streetlight-effect. Accessed 7 July 2024

Gage N (1973) How the metropolitan acquired the 'the finest Greek vase there is'. New York Times, February 18

Hicks D (2023) 'The last remaining argument against restitution has now been lost'. Art Newspaper, August 29

Jones J (2023) Get your own art detective! My simple solution for the British Museum fiasco. Guardian, August 30

Keller A (2015) Documenting ISIL'S antiquities trafficking: the looting and destruction of Iraqi and Syrian cultural heritage: what we know and what can be done. US Department of State, September 29. https://2009-2017.state.gov/e/eb/rls/rm/2015/247610.htm. Accessed 7 July 2024

Kersel MM (2007) Transcending borders: objects on the move. Archaeologies 3:81–98

Lidington H (2002) The role of the internet in removing the 'shackles of the saleroom': anytime, anyplace, anything, anywhere. Public Archaeol 2:67–84

Mackenzie S (2005) Going, going, gone. Regulating the market in illicit antiquities. Institute of Art and Law

Mackenzie S, Brodie N, Yates D, Tsirogiannis C (2020) Trafficking culture. Routledge

Marshall A (2023a) British museum was warned gems were being sold on eBay, emails show. New York Times, August 22

Marshall A (2023b) British museum announces plan to stop thefts. New York Times, October 18

Mathers M (2023) Greece accused of 'blatant opportunism' for suggesting British museum is not safe. Independent, August 23

Mazza R (2024) Stolen fragments. Stanford University Press, Redwood

Mead R (2024) The British museum's blockbuster scandals. New Yorker, May 6. https://www.newyorker.com/magazine/2024/05/13/the-british-museums-blockbuster-scandals. Accessed 7 July 2024

O'Keefe P, Prott L (1989) Law and the cultural heritage. Volume 3: Movement. Butterworths

Rayner G, Alberge D, Corless B (2023a) Stolen British museum items worth up to £50k offered on eBay for as little as £40. Daily Telegraph, August 17

Rayner G, Alberge D, Corless B (2023b) British museum told three years ago that its stolen artefacts were being sold on eBay. Daily Telegraph, August 17

Rayner G, Corless B, Alberge D (2023c) Revealed: British museum curator of 30 years accused of stealing artefacts. Daily Telegraph, August 17

Razzall K (2023) British museum deputy director to leave after thefts inquiry. BBC News, December 13. https://www.bbc.co.uk/news/entertainment-arts-67710217. Accessed 7 July 2024

Razzall K, Kennelly L, Graham D, Saunders E (2024a) Thief sold stolen gems to at least 45 buyers on eBay, British Museum says *BBC News*, March 26. https://www.bbc.co.uk/news/entertainment-arts-68665773. Accessed 7 July 2024

Razzall K, Kennelly L, Graham D (2024b) British museum gems for sale on eBay - how a theft was exposed. BBC News, May 27. https://www.bbc.co.uk/news/articles/cpegg27g74do. Accessed 7 July 2024

Razzall K, Graham D, Kennelly L (2024c) FBI investigating missing ancient treasures from British museum. BBC News, May 27. https://www.bbc.co.uk/news/articles/c3gqq7xy5xdo. Accessed 7 July 2024

Sabar A (2020) Veritas: a Harvard professor, a con man, and the gospel of Jesus's wife. Doubleday

Sabrine I, Abdo R, Brodie N (2022) Some new evidence documenting the involvement of Da'esh in Syria with the illicit trade in antiquities. J East Mediterr Archaeol Herit 10(2):115–136

Seymour T (2023) British museum antiquities thief alleged to be veteran curator Peter Higgs. Art Newspaper, August 17

Slow O (2023) British museum boss Hartwig Fischer defends 2021 theft investigation. BBC News, August 23. https://www.bbc.co.uk/news/uk-66596432. Accessed 29 October 2024

Smith E (2023) The sun is setting on the British museum. Hyperallergic, September 6. https://hyperallergic.com/843150/the-sun-is-setting-on-the-british-museum/. Accessed 7 July 2024

Stanish C (2009) Forging ahead: or, how I learned to stop worrying and love eBay. Archaeology 62(3):18, 58–60, 65–66. http://archive.archaeology.org/0905/etc/insider.html. Accessed 7 July 2024

Takla H (2014) The massacre in San Jose - the sale of dismembered manuscripts of Christian Egypt on eBay. Synaxis Katholike 6(2):705–716

USA (2016) United States of America v. one gold ring with carved gemstone, an asset of ISIL, discovered on electronic media of Abu Sayyaf, president of ISIL antiquities department; one gold coin featuring Antoninus Pius, an asset of ISIL, discovered on electronic media of Abu Sayyaf, president of ISIL antiquities department; one gold coin featuring emperor Hadrian Augustus Caesar, an asset of ISIL, discovered on electronic media of Abu Sayyaf, president of ISIL antiquities department; one carved Neo-Assyrian stone stela, an asset of ISIL, discovered on electronic media of Abu Sayyaf, president of ISIL antiquities department. Civil Action Complaint, December 15. https://www.justice.gov/usao-dc/press-release/file/918536/download. Accessed 7 July 2024

Velthuis O (2005) Talking prices. Princeton University

Watson P (1997) Sotheby's: inside story. Bloomsbury

Watson P, Todeschini C (2006) The Medici conspiracy. PublicAffairs

Wilding M (2024) The big steal: how do ancient treasures from museums end up for sale on the internet? Observer, April 14

Neil Brodie graduated from the University of Liverpool with a PhD Archaeology in 1991 and has held positions at the British School at Athens, the McDonald Institute for Archaeological Research at the University of Cambridge, where he was Research Director of the Illicit Antiquities Research Centre, Stanford University's Archaeology Center, and the Scottish Centre for Crime and Justice Research at the University of Glasgow. Most recently he was Senior Research Fellow on the Endangered Archaeology in the Middle East and North Africa project at the University of Oxford's School of Archaeology and is a member of the Trafficking Culture project. He has published widely on issues concerning the market in cultural objects, with more than fifty papers and book chapters devoted to the subject.

Open Access This chapter is licensed under the terms of the Creative Commons Attribution-NonCommercial-NoDerivatives 4.0 International License (http://creativecommons.org/licenses/by-nc-nd/4.0/), which permits any noncommercial use, sharing, distribution and reproduction in any medium or format, as long as you give appropriate credit to the original author(s) and the source, provide a link to the Creative Commons license and indicate if you modified the licensed material. You do not have permission under this license to share adapted material derived from this chapter or parts of it.

The images or other third party material in this chapter are included in the chapter's Creative Commons license, unless indicated otherwise in a credit line to the material. If material is not included in the chapter's Creative Commons license and your intended use is not permitted by statutory regulation or exceeds the permitted use, you will need to obtain permission directly from the copyright holder.

BY NC ND

From Policy to Practice: Analyzing the Impact of Cultural Property Policies in Combating Antiquities Trafficking in the United States

Melissa Metzgar

Abstract Over the past century, the United States has implemented five cultural property policies and currently maintains over thirty bilateral agreements with individual foreign powers aiming to fight the illicit antiquities trade. Despite these initiatives to combat the issue, the illegal trade of cultural antiquities remains a veiled, multi-million-dollar market predominantly driven by United States collectors and institutions. In a discipline ridden with ethical concerns and research restrictions, this chapter presents one way of researching the illicit trade and explores potential methods of quantification and prevention. By examining prosecuted cases of antiquities trafficked from the Middle East and North Africa into the U.S. since the Gulf War, this chapter outlines a database framework for examining the impact cultural property policies have on combating the illicit trade from the demand side of the market. By utilizing publicly available sources to gather case documents, the database categorically and statistically analyzes prosecutions alongside object provenience, provenance, and related stakeholders. Adaptable across different jurisdictions, the methodology examined here presents a quantifiable, non-financial means of measuring the impact of the illicit trade in cultural objects alongside an assessment of the application and effectiveness of a country's cultural property policies, which could contribute to more effective prevention measures.

M. Metzgar (✉)
American University of Rome, Rome, Italy
e-mail: m.metzgar@aur.edu

© The Author(s) 2026

E. Smith, S. Austin (eds.), *Researching a Rigged Game: Digital Approaches to Tracing the Illicit Trade in Cultural Objects*, Studies in Art, Heritage, Law and the Market 11, https://doi.org/10.1007/978-3-032-02014-7_12

1 Introduction

The primary objective of this study is to more clearly identify how effective current United States ("U.S.") cultural property policies are at countering the trafficking of antiquities from the Middle East and North Africa ("MENA region") since the Gulf War. Measured primarily based upon the percentage of objects trafficked after the implementation of policies protecting cultural heritage, this research more broadly aims to better quantify the relationship between armed conflict, humanitarian crises, and the art market to uncover more effective means of deterring the illicit trade in cultural heritage. Utilizing a widely adaptable database framework, this research model will specifically examine the benefits and limitations of employing legal policies as a tool to combat the illicit trade. To more broadly address gaps in available research, such as a limited understanding of the precise role legal policies play in combatting the illicit trade, (Brodie et al. 2021; Mackenzie et al. 2019), this chapter additionally serves to disseminate an accessible investigative and reflective tool for constructing better preservation and prevention methods.

There are an increasing number of analyses exploring the tight-knit relationship between armed conflict, economics, terrorism, and the illicit antiquities trade, especially in the Middle East (Bogdanos and Patrick 2006; van Lit 2016; Greenland et al. 2019). The evolution and adaptation of technology in archaeology over recent decades has allowed new remote techniques of monitoring these conflict zones and humanitarian crises, providing additional insight into the physical damage that results from looting, climate disasters, and armed conflict (Brodie and Contreras 2012; Parcak et al. 2016; Casana and Laugier 2017; Al-Azm and Paul 2019). Delicately interwoven, monitoring these complex issues reveals ongoing connections to a thriving illicit trade, particularly in market countries like the U.S. (Brodie et al. 2021).

One of the significant ways in which individual jurisdictions have reacted to the illicit trade is by implementing policies against illegal excavation, smuggling, and ownership of cultural property in hopes of reducing the trade's size and the demand for antiquities. However, there is currently no measure of how effective today's cultural property policies are, nor a central center of academic research on the trade, which limits the ability of policymakers to draft effective legal measures (Brodie et al. 2021). As this study will show, examining the intricacies of legal frameworks alongside statistical analysis of illicit antiquities trade prosecutions provides an accessible means for identifying gaps in policy supported by quantitative assessment, of which is adaptable in further research.

Gauging the effectiveness of legal policy, especially concerning those related to cultural heritage, is crucial to ensure said policies are achieving the goals and intentions outlined within them. Moreover, the continuous evaluation and re-consideration of policies aids in establishing accountability on behalf of implementors and creates a foundation for informed decision making. When bearing in mind the continued evolution of threats towards cultural heritage, particularly due to armed conflict and climate change, a reflective analysis of policies seeking to protect said heritage is an essential step towards improving preestablished preventative measures and future means of enforcement (U.N. Environment 2019).

Writing from the perspective of an American-born, European-educated art historian and cultural anthropologist, this research would be remiss without acknowledging the inherent white, cisgender privileges I hold as a woman in academia. I seek to utilize these privileges to advocate for and raise awareness of the irreversible cultural destruction resulting from the illicit antiquities trade and related heritage crimes—which have occurred/occur most often to the eventual benefit of American and European collectors, museums, and institutions. In this same vein, the armed conflicts and humanitarian crises occurring in the many source countries within and beyond this data set cannot go without mention. While a thorough discussion of the relationship between the illicit antiquities trade and conflict would require a more exhaustive word count, this research would be remiss without recognizing the multifaceted connections and parallels armed conflict and other crises have with the continuation of the illicit market. It is from these perspectives and considerations that this research aims to catalyze change and broaden understanding by encouraging critical self-reflection and accountability from the impacts of the market's ongoing demand.

The primary objective of the methodology outlined below is to more clearly identify the role cultural property policies play in the cessation of cultural property trafficking. While this chapter takes antiquities trafficked from the MENA region into the U.S. since the Gulf War as example, the framework proposed supports comparison of multiple policies, source countries, and destination countries over any range of time. It is important to note the use of official legal texts within this study, as investigations and cases do not reflect an all-encompassing view of collections and trade operations, there is the possibility of unseized objects and unidentified data going unstudied and unaccounted for. Section 2 below outlines relevant literature and prior research. Section 3 subsequently details the proposed methodology and exemplifies its application through case study review. Section 3.2 discusses the difficulties and limitations of conducting this research, after which Sect. 4 presents final conclusions alongside potential avenues for further study and application.

1.1 A Note on Terminology

The following discussion is constructed with terms which are imbued with both social and political subtexts, and often used interchangeably, leaving readers without widely accepted definitions that are contextually harmonious across disciplines. Terms such as 'cultural heritage,' 'provenance,' 'cultural property,' 'heritage crime,' 'cultural property policy,' 'illicit antiquities,' 'repatriation,' 'provenience,' and 'restitution,' represent a complicated set of vocabulary that is ever present in global contemporary legal and academic discussions, yet maintains vastly different implications, intentions, and translations across disciplines, jurisdictions, and languages. Moreover, concepts of cultural ownership vary from culture to culture, introducing potential challenges between nations, especially in the attempt to utilize legal frameworks to protect and return cultural heritage.

Differentiating between the terms 'cultural heritage' and 'cultural property' presents multifaceted questions of ownership alongside evaluations of legal values and cultural principles (e.g. Hoffman 2006), impacting the ethics, effectiveness, and sustainability of cultural protection policies and the vocabulary used within them. Keeping these intricacies in mind, the terms 'cultural heritage', 'heritage', 'cultural property', and 'antiquities' are all used within this discussion in reference to tangible, material culture, unless otherwise noted as intangible. Readers should consider the potential implications and power dynamics presented with the use of "cultural property," and understand that the term is used here to indicate a tangible form that is the direct result of a cultural process, albeit artistic, natural, etc., as opposed to legally demonstrating any kind of inherent or assumed possession. Throughout legal contexts however, 'property' is a term used to demonstrate "the legal relations among people in regard to a thing" (Hoffman 2006, p. 9). 'Illicit' is used here to describe cultural objects obtained/discovered/possessed through uncertain, and likely unsanctioned, methods such as looting, theft, and conflict plunder, which often constitute a 'heritage crime.' This term 'heritage crime' is utilized throughout this discussion to summarize multifaceted harmful and illegal acts against tangible or intangible culture which are punishable by law (Hoffman 2006; Mackenzie 2019). It is essential to note that while 'antiquities' is a term defined by varying parameters across jurisdictions and disciplines, it always constitutes tangible heritage that dates back a certain age (Mackenzie 2019).

2 Background

The market for art and antiquities exists in legal and illegal forms, often with blurry boundaries between the two, making it notoriously challenging to quantify and effectively prevent or intercept (Kersel 2007; Mackenzie and Yates 2016; Adams 2019). This section provides an introductory discussion of relevant literature surrounding the illicit antiquities market, its existence in the U.S., and the policies under review with the intent of outlining pertinent gaps and points for consideration while conducting this research.

Much has been written about the legal framework of antiquities trafficking and associated crimes, including examiniations of different national and international policies and laws in place (e.g. Gerstenblith 2013; Vlasic and DeSousa 2018; Burroughs 2019). Many sources evaluate current cultural property laws and international agreements through the analysis of specific cases of illicit antiquities trafficking to describe policy failures (Pearlstein 2014; Kuzma 2019; Brodie et al. 2021; de Jesus Hoiça et al. 2021). Other scholarship focuses on academic analyses of illegal international trade and its material demographics: "what is traded, what it is worth, and what physical damage is caused by its movement" (Brodie et al. 2021, p. 122). Furthermore, some scholars have highlighted remaining gaps in existing scholarship, criticizing the lack of funding for and enforcement by both domestic and international legal agencies (Bogdanos 2016; Brodie 2017; Brodie et al. 2021). Sources widely agree, however, that current policies are not enough to single-handedly combat the illicit trade (Burroughs 2019; Mackenzie et al. 2019; Brodie et al. 2021).

This lack of effectiveness is in part due to the multifaceted connections between the illicit trade and armed conflict, especially in the MENA region. There have been significant disagreements between scholars, law enforcement, and international professionals regarding the financial values and profits from the illicit antiquities trade, especially concerning the earnings of extremist groups. These instances have become known primarily through the market's pre-existing ties to the drug trade and extremist groups like ISIS and their regional affiliate, Daesh (Vlasic and DeSousa 2018; Muñoz 2018; Holmes 2022). Daesh is more commonly lumped together with ISIS by foreign governments, which in recent decades has tapped into the looting, smuggling, and sale of black-market antiquities to fund its violent operations throughout the Middle East (Vlasic and DeSousa 2018; Lehr 2019). In 2018, Vlasic and DeSousa more closely examined the connections between the illicit antiquities market and terrorism financing, emphasizing that this relationship indicates that the illicit trade is not purely a low-level criminal business anymore. This relationship shows that the international community must take more significant, more immediate action to combat the trade (Vlasic and DeSousa 2018, p. 1182).

Countermeasures against the illicit trade often rely on international and national policies rooted in the 1970 UNESCO Convention on the Means of Prohibiting and Preventing the Illicit Import, Export, and Transfer of Ownership of Cultural Property ("the 1970 UNESCO Convention"), which currently has 147 States party to it (UNESCO 2022a, b). As the 1970 UNESCO Convention carries no legal weight unless countries sign its protocols and legally implement its prescribed measures, variations in interpretation have arisen, of which have led to international discrepancies in application and a wide array of enforcement methods across State Parties (Brodie et al. 2021; Gerstenblith 2013). For example, multiple institutions and professional associations in the U.S. have implemented ethical standards and acquisition policies rooted in the 1970 UNESCO Convention, all with varying success. As a result, the 1970 UNESCO Convention, therefore, "does not pose a realistic deterrent because of the jurisdictional gaps and fractures that impede international action" and the lack of imposing consequences (Brodie et al. 2021, p. 122; Snyder 2019). Mackenzie et al. (2019) highlight further challenges, such as long-term sustainability, armed conflict, the failure to effectively deter looting, and increasing pressures on local resources. In response to these limitations and difficulties, Mackenzie et al. (2019, pp. 129–130) argue that "we should look to [implement] controls that regulate the destination market for antiquities" and focus less on implementing source country policies. By implementing more policies limiting the illicit trade in market countries such as the U.S. and therefore decreasing demand, Mackenzie et al. (2019) reason that there will be a more significant reduction in the trafficking of antiquities. Similarly, Felch and Frammolino (2011, p. 227) assert that "like the drug trade, the illicit antiquities trade [has] to be attacked from both the supply and demand sides. [For,] prosecuting a few dealers or middlemen [will] not stop the trade for long". However, without an accurate estimate of the size of the trade, its illicit components, and the physical damage caused by ongoing market demand, it is difficult to assess the effectiveness of existing regulatory responses and the potential for future interventions (Brodie et al. 2021). The scarcity of such assessments allows for a wide range of incorrect valuations and hypotheses regarding the actual size of the market, which subsequently skews public understanding and opinion regarding illicit trade and allows it to continue unabated (Brodie et al. 2021). This research therefore seeks to contribute to an enhanced understanding of the effectiveness of current legal initiatives in the U.S. as market country, in order to develop more effective, targeted countermeasures.

3 Methodology

Based on a quantitative data collection model, this chapter evaluates the effectiveness of current policies related to the import and trade of cultural objects from the MENA region into the U.S. The following section outlines how the database statistics were compared against the physical/tangible objectives and overall intentions outlined in relevant international and domestic cultural property policies. Within this study, the effectiveness of a legal policy refers to the extent to which a policy meets its proposed regulations and intentions in combatting antiquities trafficking. Introducing a policy framework detailing what is legally permitted and what is not permitted, in any area of study, indicates that there is an issue at hand that seeks legal aid in resolving. Routinely exploring how said policy meets the goals described within it and the motivation(s) behind its creation is an essential step in wholly and ethically addressing the issue at hand (such as the trafficking of cultural heritage).

This research builds on data accessed from international databases and the Manhattan District Attorney's Office, of which provide tangible insight into how cultural property trafficking is most effectively prosecuted in the U.S. The primary source material includes prosecution documents and related case materials obtained through the International Foundation for Art Research ("IFAR") and the Manhattan District Attorney's Office. Subsequent open-access sources were selected based upon their ability to provide information relevant to the artifacts and cases concerned within the database, such as news media and academic journals. The generation of statistics on the basis of these data allows users to more tangibly identify the interplay between antiquities trafficking and cultural property policy in the U.S. and beyond.

3.1 Research Approach & Structure

Designed by the author, the database structure seeks to utilize essential "demographic" data about each trafficked object and its related legal proceedings in the United States. This demographic data, as identified by the author, was sourced from prosecution documents initially retrieved from art crime databases and legal offices. Organized across 22 categories based on cultural, legal, art historical, and mobility information, this demographic data was initially pinpointed through its direct relevance to the object's provenance and provenience (Table 1). Utilizing categories to cross-reference this detailed information allows for central, precise organization and fluid analysis of data.

Gathered over a six-month period in 2022 and funded by the author, the thirteen cases analyzed here yielded a high volume of data that required the development of acronym-based codes to maintain the clarity of the database. Content analysis is commonly utilized in social science research and can be particularly helpful to empirically contextualize legal scholarship (Salehijam 2018; Williams et al. 2022). Within this database, categories were established based upon the information yielded from content analysis performed of relevant court documents. For example, in determining the type of object(s) within each case, materials were identified and abbreviated based upon two letters in their names (e.g. 'Manuscript' becomes 'MS;' 'Sculpture' becomes 'SC;' Coin becomes 'CO'). Alternatively, the country abbreviations used throughout the database are drawn from the standard international abbreviations established by the Central Intelligence Agency (Central Intelligence Agency n.d.) due to their wide application and accessibility, such as AFG, BHR, IRN, FRA, etc. Coding is an ongoing process throughout the evaluation and gathering of data here, and building the database successfully requires vigilant data scraping of each legal case. Reviewing the prosecutions comes with ethical considerations as they present a heavily legal perspective, and it is essential to conduct multiple

Table 1 Database categories organized by type of information the data reflected most closely

Demographic information	Provenance information	Legal information
Case title	Means of illegal discovery	Law(s) utilized in prosecution
Object name/collection number	Date of object seizure	Prosecuting agency
Source country	Earliest provenance date	Legal consequences
Type of object	Stakeholders involved	Means of law enforcement discovery
Date of object	Length of time on the market	Date of object discovery by law enforcement
Date of case	Known transit countries involved	Duration between illicit discovery and repatriation
Date of investigation initiation	Repatriation status	Value of object at the time of prosecution
Stakeholder socio-economic profile		Duration between illicit discovery and legal prosecution

reviews of the court documents and relevant discovery to ensure the inclusion of all relevant data.

As court documents and their accessible discoveries were analyzed here individually by case, all relevant information was underscored and noted for consideration and evaluation before being transcribed directly into the appropriate category within the database. It is important to review cases individually as to not confuse data input and also actively reflect on any additional research that might be needed to confirm or fill any informational gaps (such as verifying trade transactions, dates, etc.). This intricate data scraping, while a time-intensive methodology, allows for careful review and verification of presented information, which is essential to conduct as there is the potential for falsifications and misnomers in presented evidence. Moreover, it establishes clearer identification of informational gaps and how to address them.

For data triangulation and output design, it is important to consider the research parameters and intentions. In seeking to identify the legal and social impact of cultural property policies in the U.S. it was essential to prioritize analyzing data related to object acquisition, import, and provenience. For example, an essential question in identifying these impacts concerns establishing the percentage of objects illegally imported after the implementation of legal restrictions and protective policies. When triangulating this, it is essential to compare acquisition and purchase records, as well as import documentation, to the timeline of relevant legal frameworks (Fig. 2; Table 3). Given the large number of categories, this framework allows for such a selective, conditional processing of data as a singular reflection on individual cases as well as broader cross-comparison between prosecutions.

When identifying the current relevant legal policies for analysis, it is important to consider the current government regulations at national, international and regional levels applicable to the parameters of the study at hand. Concerning the U.S., legal resources on the current cultural policies are available on the website of the Department of State (United States Department of State n.d.). As of July 2024, the U.S. maintained bilateral cultural property agreements with 32 countries, ten of which are relevant to this case study: Afghanistan, Algeria, Egypt, Iraq, Jordan, Libya, Morocco, Syria, Turkey, and Yemen (U.S. Department of State n.d.). Internationally, the U.S. is party to the 1954 Hague Convention and the 1970 Convention. Domestically, the U.S. has implemented the Convention on Cultural Property Implementation Act (19 U.S.C. §§ 2601-2613); the 1983/1987 National Stolen Property Act; and the 2016 Protect and Preserve International Cultural Property Act (Public Law No. 141-151).

Given the illicit and opaque nature of the antiquities trade, consulting a diversity of records from museums, private collections and organizations, as well as legal offices and the media is essential to evaluate the validity of data. This type of triangulation is essential for maintaining data accuracy (Brodie et al. 2021). Furthermore, the discussion presented here would be remiss without acknowledging how essential transparency and ethics are in the success of this research. The material culture implicated in the legal cases and cultural property policies analyzed here possess cultural value far greater than any financial attribution, and researching it often involves vulnerable, underrepresented populations (see Campbell 2013; Al-Azm and Paul 2019). As recent literature has been exploring (van Duyne et al. 2015; Mercadier et al. 2020), tangible heritage is more likely to originate in vulnerable areas experiencing climate disaster, armed conflict, and economic crises. Financial quantifications of the trade, therefore, skew the perspective of tangible damage that results from the operations of supply chain actors, presenting biases and limitations in their interpretations. Aiming to more objectively quantify the trade, the success of this database and its application is reliant upon obtaining as precise and transparent information as possible, which is not always explicitly available in open access, formal sources.

3.2 *Difficulties and Limitations*

Acquiring documents and contacting individuals relevant to this research design proved challenging; international databases, art crime organizations, and U.S. government offices were consulted for their holdings and experience relevant to the scope of research outlined in Sect. 3. While often useful in their own ways, the functionality, accessibility, and transparency of many art and legal databases can prove to be limiting and difficult to navigate, especially for those outside the relevant field. For example, the first avenue for obtaining data for this study entailed filing a request through the Freedom of Information Act (FOIA), an initiative to provide citizens with access to U.S. government documents on a wide range of topics, including legal prosecutions. Depending on the number of documents requested and the type of individual requesting, document requests are often free, making them widely accessible to the public. Given their direct coverage of legal proceedings, official court documents can supply more specific information about the prosecutions of offenders as opposed to press releases and news stories. The author's 2022 FOIA request for documents related to the research scope yielded a 'Burdensome Request' notice in 2024, explaining that it would take FOIA six years of manpower to process the documents found relevant to this request and therefore a narrower scope would need to be identified, or the request would be closed.

Untangling the implications of these resource limitations within the U.S. legal system can constitute another discussion entirely; however, these difficulties speak to previously established and widely observed obstructions to our understanding of the illicit antiquities market (Mackenzie et al. 2019; Brodie et al. 2021). Limited access to information is a well-known dilemma in researching art crime (Campbell 2013), however, in recent years, this limited access to information has spurred the development of research organizations who are dedicated to combating cultural heritage crime and establishing centers for information (websites, projects, databases, etc.), a key element in establishing an effective, multifaceted approach to countering the issue. These have raised further challenges of data accuracy and bias. For example, the International Foundation for Art Research (IFAR) hosts a database of international cases of art crime, which yielded documents for twelve different legal cases pertinent to this study, although accessing this database initially required a payment and designated time slot. In Fall 2024, IFAR announced that it would be closing its doors as an organization and rehoming its database, echoing concerns of sustainability and accessibility found elsewhere in the field. In another example, the Art Loss Register (Art Loss Register n.d.) is privately run and offers packages for prospective users to conduct searches (starting at $100 per item, or $750 for 10 in one year). When analyzing policy application and effectiveness within prosecuted cases, this type of database-user methodology is not conducive or financially accessible in the broader processes of gathering and analyzing large data sets such as the one introduced here. These types of cost-based databases introduce additional challenges to researching data that is already lacking transparency and verifiable information. For example, it was difficult to gauge the amount of time it took for objects to be seized by law enforcement after their owners were initially suspected of trafficking due to a lack of information provided in the court documents found.

The inconsistency of data availability, transparency, and harmonization experienced here, and previously by Mackenzie et al. (2019) and Brodie et al. (2021), reveals greater need for further quantitative research in this niche area supported by qualitative investigation. Moreover, the data reflect how the illicit antiquities market persists in the U.S. despite decades of international policies and domestic restrictions on the ownership and trade of cultural objects, particularly highlighting inconsistencies within the current policies and their enforcement. This research has revealed many potential areas for improving the fight against the illicit antiquities trade and increasing the effectiveness of these current policies and means of regulation. However, it is essential to note that even with these policy changes, the trade will continue on some level, as this multifaceted issue requires a multifaceted approach to wholly reduce and prevent. Academics, law enforcement officials, and international representatives agree that while a single solution to end the market for illicit cultural antiquities does not exist, implementing effective, deterring policy is an essential legal step toward combating the trade (Brodie et al. 2021).

3.3 *Information Categories*

The following table contains 22 data categories that form the core of the database, identified through examining relevant case documents. As is the case with investigating any illicit trade (Campbell 2013; Mackenzie et al. 2019), gaps in data are expected (see Sect. 2) and the design of this database allows for these to be accounted for in final analysis with labeling the indeterminable or unidentifiable information as a separate statistic (e.g. the percentage of objects with no provenance, compared to the number of objects with provenance, see Sect. 3.5). While these gaps may remain unfilled, they highlight the informational complexity and erasure that results from the activities involved in looting, the illicit trade, and other heritage crimes.

Individually, each trafficking case can yield data regarding the court case and date; the prosecuting and investigating agencies involved; the date of the investigation initiation; and the laws used to prosecute the offenders. For the object(s) concerned, further identifiable information was recorded such as its materials, creation date, provenance, and source country where known. Together, this data can reveal where these objects originate in relation to how they are taken, as well as how the crime is detected, investigated, and prosecuted in the U.S. Analysis of this data yields potentially instrumental insight into both the geographical coverage and effectiveness of legal policies seeking to stop the illicit trade and provide protections for cultural property.

Furthermore, to more thoroughly understand the illicit trade and its relationship with cultural property policy, it is vital to trace the physical and digital networks that objects move within. This includes earliest provenance date; related stakeholders; all known previous physical locations; any and all transfers of ownership; all financial valuations of object; date of legal discovery and seizure; and length of time on the market. This information was recorded from the prosecution discovery evidence, and when analyzing this data together, it is possible to more clearly identify a timeline of legal action in relation to object movements and stakeholder actions. Additionally, identifying and recording the prosecution results is essential for later assessment of policy effectiveness and impact. Information such as the object's repatriation status, any consequences administered to convicted perpetrators, and their demographic data carries vital reflections for the efficacy and application of cultural property policies. Additional key information sought in this study are durations of time on the illicit market, and the amount/type of stakeholders involved in the process of protection, detection, prosecution, and restitution to piece together object provenance and provenience.

3.4 Data Analysis

To better identify patterns and variability among the analysed cases, database content was exported from Microsoft Excel, extracted respectively within each category, and processed through data visualization software Microsoft PowerBI. This platform specifically, alongside Google Sheets, allows for an easily accessible generation of descriptive statistics from various data sets and a fluid translation into visualizations such as pie graphs and column charts, which increases the accessibility and understanding of the results. Rooted in quantitative analysis, this methodological approach seeks to provide a detailed study of the relationship between legal policy and its impact in protecting cultural heritage and the cessation of the illicit antiquities market.

Many trafficking cases involve a myriad of objects, and not one single item, which therefore made many of the results presented here duplicative and overlapping. While these results skew the visualization and calculation of data in their repetition, they also show a greater need to legally address the multifaceted ways that stakeholders are obtaining illicit antiquities. For example, within a single case against a defendant, multiple objects often were obtained in various illegal ways, such as organized archaeological looting, theft, and subsistence looting. Similarly, cases utilized various methods in the legal detection of artifacts, and often several legal agencies appeared within a single investigation (e.g. New York District Attorney's Office ("NYDA"), HSI and ICE). To account for these discrepancies, the cases within the database were organized based upon individual object(s) concerned within them, rather than case title or individual ruling, allowing for deeper analysis of the diversity of information that exists within each case. This breakdown of cases allows for a closer examination of the diverse means in which supply chain actors and stakeholders encounter antiquities and permits greater focus on identifying information gaps across the collection of cases.

Processed through *Microsoft PowerBI*, the statistics within the following section provide a tangible analysis of 13 prosecuted cases of antiquities trafficking (Table 2), encompassing a total of 6522 cultural objects. A detailed analysis of the results and their implications is beyond the scope of this chapter, and thus the data included here serves merely to demonstrate the potential usability of the methodology presented in this chapter. The following sections will discuss the results of this study while reflecting on the challenges and opportunities of utilizing this methodology.

3.5 Overview of Results

The data indicates a notable increase in prosecutions since the turn of the twenty-first century (Fig. 1), with 11 cases (84.62%) having court dates after 2001, as opposed to only two cases (15.38%) between 1990 and 2001. Between 2011 and 2021, there were five cases (38.46%), two of which (15.38%) included Hobby Lobby.[1] Of note, Turkey initiated three claims to recover roughly 1912 objects (29.32%), of which 100% were repatriated.[2] The court proceedings for these 13 cases revealed an overlapping pattern of distribution when analyzing which party initiated the related investigation (Table 2). In two court cases, only one party initiated and participated in the relevant cultural property investigation: the United States Customs and Border Patrol (n = 1) and the United States Fish and Wildlife Service (n = 1). The remaining 11 cases resulted from the collaboration of two or more parties: private claimants (n = 10); Homeland Security Investigations (n = 4); and/or the Manhattan District Attorney's Office (n = 4) (Fig. 2).

While these claims and court cases all started in the period between 1991 and 2021, there were some whose investigations began before 1991. For example, all three of Turkey's investigations into artifacts began before 1991; however, their

[1] The first case against Hobby Lobby was brought in 2017, and the second occurred in 2021 (*U.S. v. Four Hundred Fifty Ancient Cuneiform Tablets (Hobby Lobby)*, 2017; *U.S. v. Cuneiform Tablet - Hobby Lobby*, 2021).

[2] This number is so high due to one of these cases involving a collection of 1661 coins, also known as the Emali Hoard. The case was initially brought in 1989 and was eventually settled out of court after ten years of legal disputes (the *Republic of Turkey v. OKS Partners*, 1992).

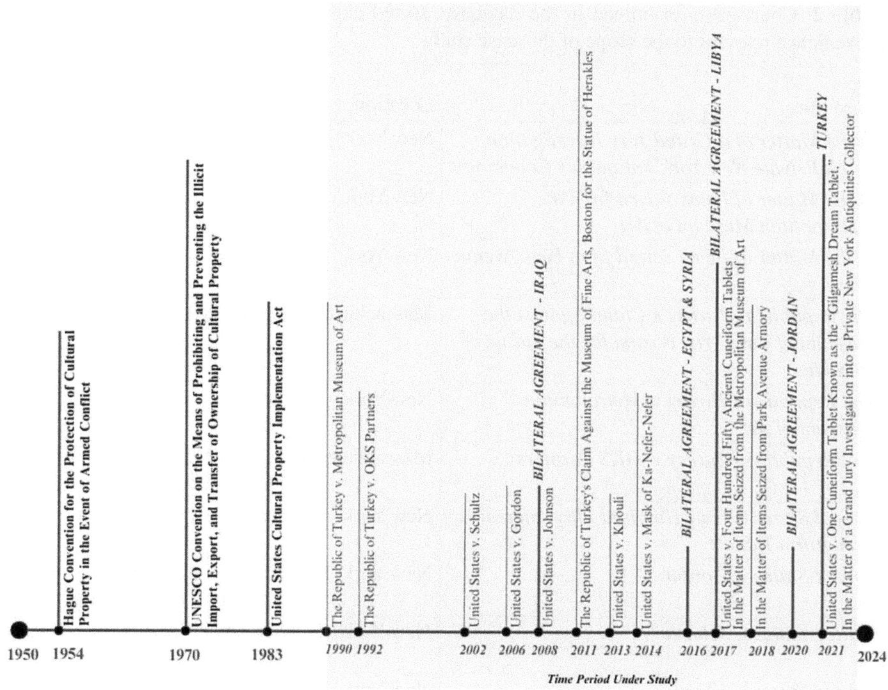

Fig. 1 Timeline of discovered prosecutions overlaid with international and regional cultural policies, including bilateral import restrictions

related legal claims and court cases were not brought until years later.[3] Overall, the average time between the initiation of an investigation and its subsequent court case was four years, with the most extended period being 21 years and the shortest duration being one year. The 6522 objects included in the database illicitly originated from nine countries within the MENA region (Figure 3). As per the scope of this research, the U.S. was the only destination country in all cases; however, seven known transit countries were uncovered in the corresponding investigations, namely Canada, China, France, Germany, Switzerland, the United Arab Emirates (UAE), and the United Kingdom (UK). Overall, 3944 artifacts (60.47%) came without any known provenance, and the remaining 2578 objects (39.53%) had, on average, no known provenance before 1997.

Across the database, 2530 artifacts (38.79%) contained the provenance information necessary to compute the average duration of time between their illicit

[3] The claim against the MFA Boston regarding the Statue of Herakles was brought in 2011, whereas the investigation initially began in 1990. In the case of Turkey v. MET, the investigation began in 1987, only three years before the first court case in 1990, and six years before the case was eventually settled in 1993 (the *Republic of Turkey v. Metropolitan Museum of Art,* 1990, 1993). The last case involving Turkey was against OKS Partners, where the investigation began in 1989 and led to the issue being brought before a court in July 1992 (the *Republic of Turkey v. OKS Partners,* 1992).

Table 2 Court cases examined in the database, sorted chronologically. [a]With provenance and provenience relevant to the scope of this case study

Case title	Location	Date	Number of objects[a]
In the Matter of a Grand Jury Investigation into a Private New York Antiquities Collector	New York	December 6, 2021	180
In the Matter of Items Seized from the Metropolitan Museum of Art	New York	September 22, 2017	1
In the Matter of Items Seized from Park Avenue Armory	New York	May 2018	1
The Republic of Turkey's Claim Against the Museum of Fine Arts, Boston for the Statue of Herakles	Massachusetts	Settled 2011	1
The Republic of Turkey v. Metropolitan Museum of Art	New York	1990	250
The Republic of Turkey v. OKS Partners	Massachusetts	1992–1999 January 23, 1998	1900
United States v. Four Hundred Fifty Ancient Cuneiform Tablets	New York	July 6, 2017	3450
United States v. Gordon	New York	2006, 2011, June 12, 2014	492
United States v. Johnson	New York	September 22, 2008	90
United States v. Khouli	New York	January 9, 2013	141
United States v. Mask of Ka-Nefer-Nefer	Missouri	June 12, 2014	1
United States v. One Cuneiform Tablet Known as the "Gilgamesh Dream Tablet,"	New York	July 26, 2021	1
United States v. Schultz	New York	2002–2004	3

discovery and related legal prosecution, resulting in an average of 24 years. In other words, 24 years typically elapsed after an artifact was illicitly removed from its place of origin before the crime was legally addressed. The average length of time an object spent on the market, measured by the duration between looting and purchase, was typically ten years and nine months for those objects that included any provenance information (38.79%). Unfortunately, there were 3992 objects (60.13%) that did not include verifiable records about their movements.

The lack of provenance and market records not only affects our knowledge of an object's length of time on the market, but also directly infringes upon our knowledge and understanding of the object itself. There are 4434 objects (67.99%) in the database with no creation date, and another 3,947 objects (60.52%) lacking information about their means of illicit discovery (Fig. 4). Of the remaining 2088 objects (32.01%), their assumed date of creation ranged from 7000 BCE to 500 CE. In six cases, the trafficked artifacts were detected through related investigations into other objects. Customs seizures as a method of detection were a crucial part of only one case. One case was initiated after an item was stolen from a museum, and during that investigation, officials uncovered the object's illicit origins. Seven cases were

Table 3 Trafficking cases organized by country of origin. [a]Before Import Restrictions, After 1983; [b]After Import Restrictions; [c]Before Import Restrictions and 1970 UNESCO Convention

Origin country	Number of artifacts	Percentage of total artifacts	Import restriction implementation	Case(s)	Date of artifact USA purchase/import (quantity)
Iraq	3835	58.80%	2008	4	2003(1)[a]; 2004(1)[a]; 2008–09(32);[b] 2010(3800);[b] 2019(1)[b]
Egypt	110	1.69%	2016	6	1974(1);[c] 1989(1)[a]; 1998(1)[a]; 1992(3)[a]; 1999(5)[a]; 2002(90)[a]; 2008–09(8)[a]; n.d.(1)
Syria	4	0.06%	2016	1	1989(1)[a]; 1992(2)[a]; 2003(1)[a]
Libya	1	0.02%	2017	1	2000(1)[a]
Jordan	9	0.14%	2020	1	1991(4)[a]; 1995(1)[a]; 1999(3)[a]; 2001(1)[a]
Turkey	1926	29.53%	2021	4	1966–68(250);[c] 1975(1);[c] 1981(1);[c] 1984(1661)[a]; 1991(4)[a]; 2002(1)[a]; 2005(8)[a]
Unknown	557	8.54%	–	2	2006(492); 2008–09(65)
Israel	40	0.61%	None	1	1991(6); 1993(3); 2001(2); 2002(1); 2003(5); 2005(1); 2006(21); 2009(1)
Lebanon	2	0.03%	None	1	1996(2)
Iran	38	0.58%	None	2	1950(1); 2008(37)

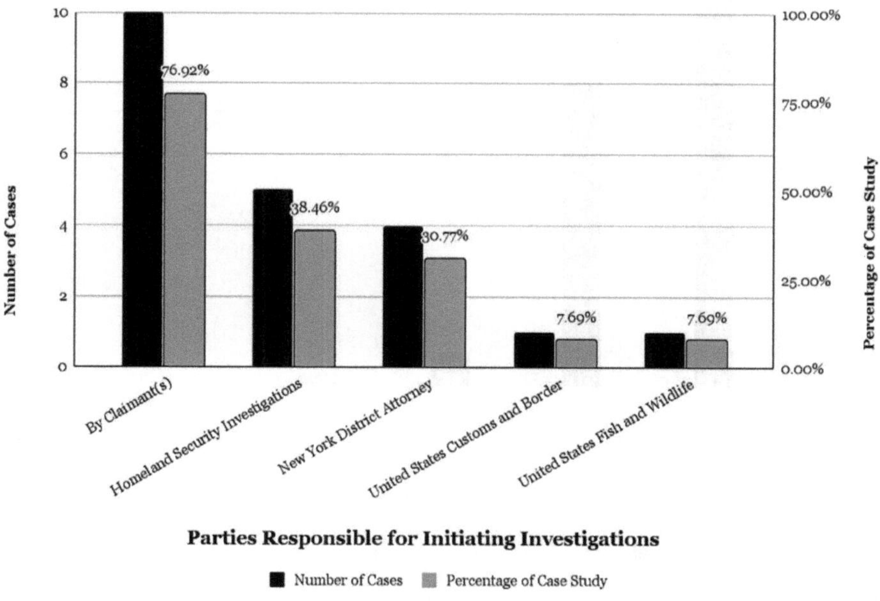

Fig. 2 Parties utilized to initiate investigations

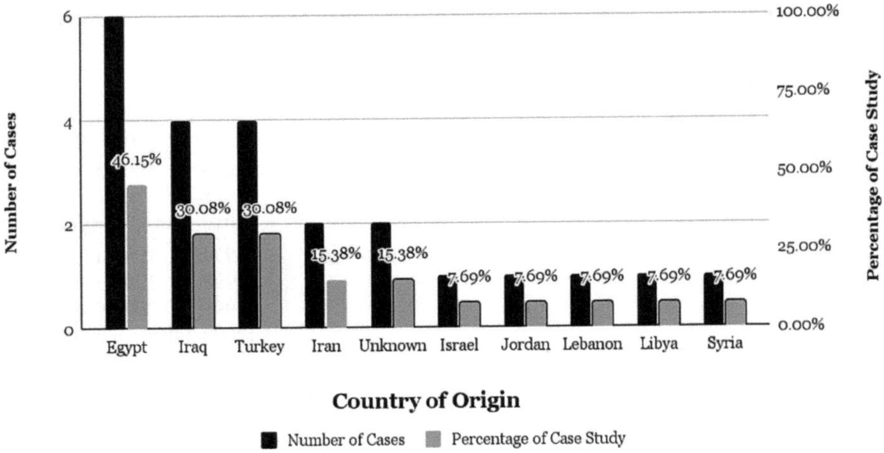

Fig. 3 Data organized by object country of origin

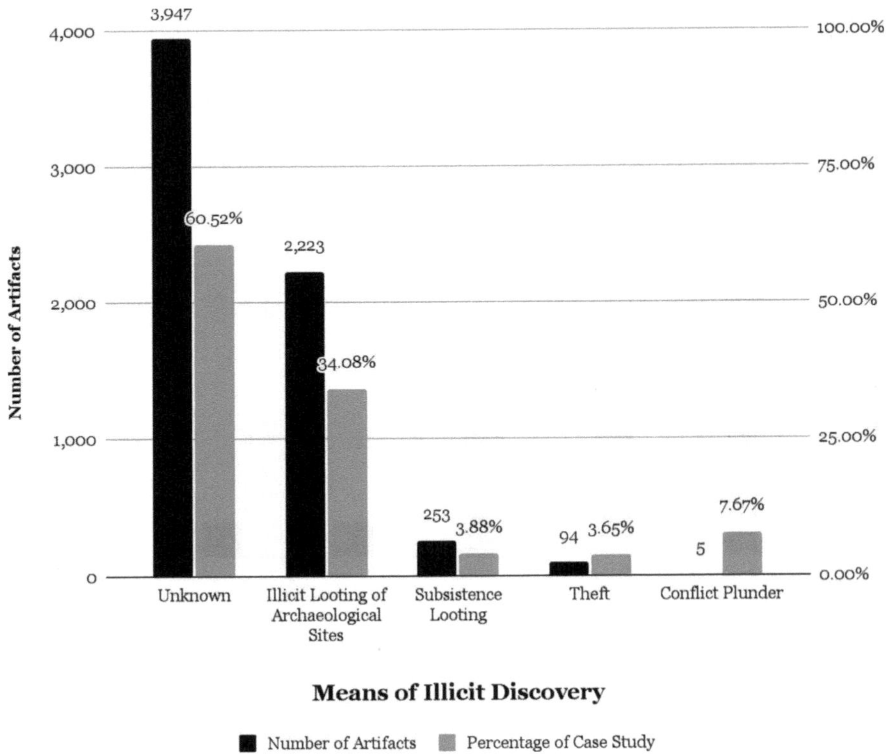

Fig. 4 Case data organized by the means in which objects were discovered

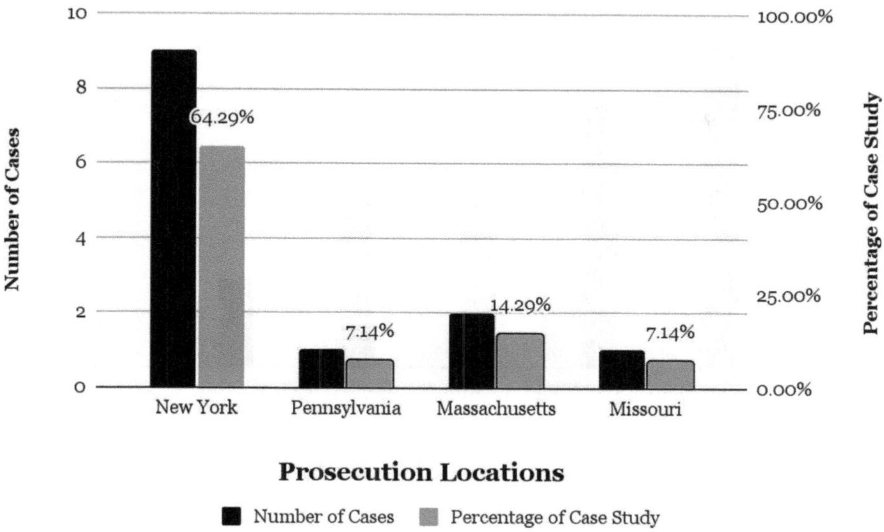

Fig. 5 Cases organized by distribution of location

brought after professionals (e.g., academics, journalists, and legal officials) suspected an object's illicit origins upon evaluating the artifacts in museums, private collections, or at auctions (see Brodie 2011, 2017). Prosecutions were identified in four states, with over half of the cases (64.29%) occurring in New York (Fig. 5).

Regarding the legal proceedings (Table 2), there was little to no mention of international conventions in the court documents of these 13 trafficking cases. The laws that were used in the court proceedings include the 1983 Cultural Property Implementation Act, sections of New York State Laws (New York Penal Law §155.00; New York Penal Law §450.10; New York Criminal Procedure Law §690.10); Title 16 (16 U.S. Code §1538; 16 U.S.C. §3371; 16 U.S.C. §4223), Title 18 (18 U.S. Code §542; 18 U.S. Code §545; 18 U.S. Code §662; 18 U.S.C. §981(a)(1)(C); 18 U.S.C. §982(b); 18 U.S.C. §982(a)(2)(B); 18 U.S.C. §983; 18 U.S.C. §1001(a)(2); 18 U.S.C. § 2314 - 2315), Title 19 (19 US Code Sec. 1595a(c)(1)(A)), and Title 28 (28 U.S.C. §2461(a)).

In terms of the stakeholders involved with these prosecutions, there were museums and museum staff, galleries, and related employees, private collectors, supply chain actors, antiquities dealers, institutions and companies in the private and public sectors, governments, auction houses, and political groups connected to these cases. Many of these stakeholders were involved with multiple cases, and the methods and implications of their involvement has been discussed elsewhere (see e.g. Gerstenblith 2013; Campbell 2013; Brodie 2017). While they committed harmful acts against tangible, moveable cultural heritage that are similar in nature, the stakeholders found to be illicitly involved in these cases did not face equitable legal consequences, and patterns of preference emerged in the distribution of penalties by the United States justice system in relation to perpetrator's socio-economic status (see Sect. 3.6). This trend exemplifies previous findings and the need

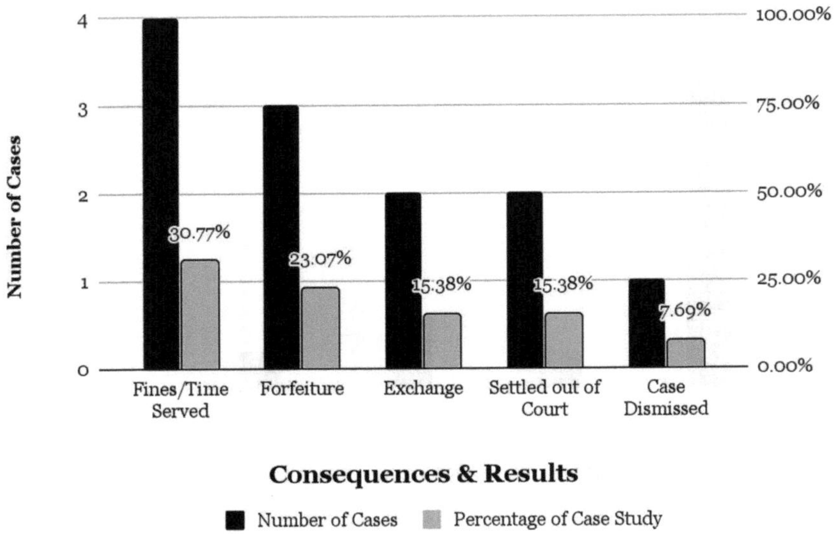

Fig. 6 Cases organized distribution of consequences and results

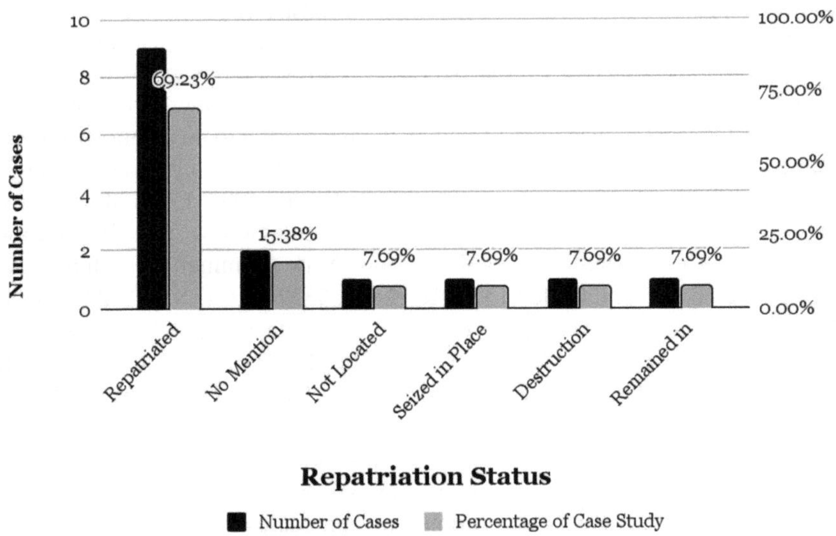

Fig. 7 Cases organized by repatriation of objects involved

for more focused empirical research into application of legal consequences (Brodie et al. 2021) (Fig. 6).

All 13 cases in this study (total = 6522 cultural artifacts) occurred since the signing of the 1970 Convention and implementation of the CPIA in 1983. In all, 5874 artifacts (90.06%) objects saw repatriation to their source countries (Fig. 7), and 557 artifacts (8.54%) had no listed country of origin (Fig. 3). There were 5885 objects (90.33%) which originated in countries that currently have bilateral import restrictions with the U.S. For 253 (4.30%) of these 5885 objects, their movement and transfer of ownership occurred before the signing of the 1970 UNESCO Convention and CPIA implementation in 1983. In comparison 80 objects (1.23%) came from countries which have no import restriction agreements with the U.S. (Israel, Lebanon, and Iran). 1798 objects (30.55%) were purchased or imported after 1983, when the U.S. signed the 1970 UNESCO Convention and implemented the CPIA, but before relevant bilateral restrictions were enacted. One object (0.017%) had no known date of its movements into the U.S., and 3833 artifacts (65.13%) were trafficked after the U.S. implemented relevant import restrictions. Of these 3833 objects, 100% were sourced from Iraq.

3.6 *Policy Observations*

The data here glimpse into the logistics of and legal consequences presented to perpetrators found guilty of operating within the illicit market. While they committed similar violations, the various stakeholders found to be involved in the thirteen cases upon which this research is based did not face the same legal consequences, and patterns of preference emerged in the distribution of penalties by the U.S. justice system in relation to a perpetrator's socio-economic status. Notably, the data show that there is a low rate of dissuading legal consequences administered to white-collar offenders, with a clear preference for exchanging or forfeiting objects and issuing fines. This issue is explored more in-depth elsewhere by Mackenzie (2011, 2019) and presents vital ethical considerations concerning the applicability and administration of legal policy. In one example from this study, *In the Matter of a Grand Jury Investigation into a Private New York Antiquities Collector*, 2021, consequences for the collector entailed relinquishing ownership of the artifacts in exchange for no fines or jail time. Here, collector Michael Steinhardt was found to have 180 antiquities within his collection whose provenance, or lack thereof, warranted search and seizure by the NYDA's Office. Furthermore, part of his legal agreement stipulates that he cannot collect antiquities dating before 1500 CE and was granted conditional immunity from prosecution by the NYDA's Office regarding future purchases and his remaining antiquities (*In the Matter of a Grand Jury Investigation into a Private New York Antiquities Collector*, 2021).

When considering the amount of illegal activity that the NYDA identified Steinhardt to be involved with, and compared to cases of similar nature, these penalties are light. In *United States v. Johnson*, Edward Johnson also acquired and sold antiquities from the MENA region, which amounted to half of Steinhardt's total collection seized in 2021, yet the U.S. courts ordered Johnson to pay over $20,000 in restitution fees and two years' time-served of probation and house arrest. Both individuals illegally owned artifacts from Egypt, a country with strong national patrimony laws in place and which has ratified the 1970 UNESCO Convention (UNESCO 2021). A striking difference in the cases is that of the socio-economic status of the perpetrators, with Johnson being a 44-year-old U.S. Army pilot, and Steinhardt being an 83-year-old hedge-fund manager (International Foundation for Art Research-Case Law n.d.). While there were thirteen years between the prosecutions and different judges in the two cases, the difference in quantity of illicit goods compared to legal enforcement reveals unmistakable disparities here when comparing the socio-economic power of the offenders.

Another example of this enforcement discrepancy is in the 2017 and 2021 cases against Steve Green (the owner of a U.S. chain store, Hobby Lobby) and the 2013 case against antiquities dealer Mousa Khouli. Despite Hobby Lobby having purchased nearly 4000 illicit Iraqi artifacts across ten years, the company received a fine based on the profits they made from the antiquities, were required to implement acquisition policies, and mandated to submit their purchases to the government for a short period afterwards. Their second case does not detail any legal repercussions. At the same time Hobby Lobby made their first known illicit purchase, Khouli was found responsible for smuggling 140 Iraqi antiquities into the U.S. and sentenced to $80,000 in funds being frozen; six months house arrest; one year of probation; 200 hours of community service, along with fines (International Foundation for Art Research-Case Law n.d.; St. Hilaire 2013). In this comparison, Khouli illicitly introduced 3400 fewer objects to the USA. and received one-fifth of the profit from their trade than Hobby Lobby did—yet Khouli's consequences were far more imposing than the owners of Hobby Lobby. Steven Green, his father David, and their families are owners of a nation-wide department store (Gerstenblith 2022). Khouli, on the other hand, is a 49-year-old immigrant from Syria who came to the U.S. in 1992 from Damascus. On one of his business web pages, he refers to himself as a third-generation gallery owner that learned about the business from his father and grandfather (Eko 2011). There are apparent differences in the socio-economic power of Khouli and the owners of Hobby Lobby despite the unmistakable variance in the tangible impact of their crimes. This trend is not a new idea but exemplifies previous stereotypes and the need for more significant equity in enforcement of legal consequences for violators (Mackenzie 2019; Mackenzie et al. 2019; Brodie et al. 2021).

In the same vein, the prosecution of antiquities trafficking occurs more often through state laws and extraneous U.S. legal codes rather than with legal policies implemented to protect foreign cultural property, such as the 1970 UNESCO Convention and the 1954 Hague Convention. Furthermore, while fewer cases concerned antiquities trafficked after the implementation of bilateral import restrictions, a sizable portion of antiquities are being trafficked from areas with no bilateral import restrictions, such as Israel, Lebanon, and Iran (*In the Matter of a Grand Jury Investigation into a Private New York Antiquities Collector* 2021). Given the average 24-year period between illicit discovery and prosecution identified here, it is too early to gauge how impactful the recent enactments of import restrictions are; however, there are noticeable weak areas for further consideration. A notable element missing from the CPIA, and 1970 UNESCO Convention is that of legal consequences. Together, the CPIA enforces Articles 7b and 9 from the 1970 Convention (Public Law 97-446 § 310(a)) (Prott 2012; Gerstenblith 2013). While it establishes that "all provisions of law" related to customs violations are applicable, it fails to identify cultural property crimes as distinct from crimes involving general goods and merchandise. Outside of "seizure, forfeiture, and condemnation" of the cultural property concerned, there is no outline of legal consequences for violators. Additionally, both the CPIA and 1970 UNESCO Convention describe no legal consequences for violations committed before enactment. The National Stolen Property Act, however, stipulates that perpetrators should be fined or sentenced to a maximum of ten years in prison (18 U.S.C. § 2314-2315), directly providing judges and prosecutors with a baseline of consequence to assign perpetrators. The data gathered and quantified in this database framework overwhelmingly suggests that the international conventions, bilateral restrictions, and domestic laws the U.S. is a party to are not combating the illicit trade in cultural property effectively. As explored above, the current enforcement of U.S. policies shows a pattern of legal leniency with upper-class citizens and their corporations, with middle- and lower-class individuals receiving heavier, more dissuading punishments. The motivations behind this lack of prosecutor action need further exploration, however changes in legislation in recent years have undoubtedly helped to facilitate prosecuting the crime of prior antiquities trafficking, such as New York Criminal Laws and the statute of limitations. However, as a whole, the current policies and application of their legal consequences reveal patterns suggesting that in their current form and enforcement they are not enough to adequately deter actors from future involvement with the illicit trade.

4 Conclusion

Even with the drafting of multiple international conventions against the antiquities trade in the last 100 years, this study illustrates the illicit market for antiquities is still a socially acceptable and financially lucrative business in the U.S. In this research, key themes repeatedly appeared, including multifaceted limitations; the increased vulnerability of artifacts in conflict zones; gaps in international and domestic policies; linguistic challenges; inconsistent enforcement of legal consequences; and a severe lack of provenance. Foremost, these data revealed that broader application is needed to investigate alternative case study parameters outside of the U.S. and the MENA region.

An initial policy suggestion derived from the findings outlined above is greater attention to and application of the 1954 Hague Convention, which would require legal amendments sanctioning the damage and looting by civilians brought on by armed conflict (UNESCO, 1954; S. Rep. No 110-26 (2008)). This would look similar to the 1970 UNESCO Convention, which requires similar alterations. However, as previously discussed, in the U.S. the 1970 UNESCO Convention has manifested into bilateral restrictions, which outline no legal consequences to violators, are cherry-picked by the government, and are a patch on the issue at best. Resolving these problems would entail drafting new legislation to not only include legal repercussions but also expand the import restrictions to not solely sanction the import of specific antiquities from individual countries that have demonstrated their continued loss of cultural heritage.

Similar to the 1970 UNESCO Convention, the 1954 Hague Convention and its Protocols fail to recognize and legally sanction "the harm that comes [to cultural heritage] from the breakdown in law and order and the concomitant surge in market-driven looting" that accompany armed conflict, civil unrest, and political and economic instability (Rothfield 2008; Mercadier et al. 2020). If the 1954 Hague Convention issued protections on targeted, looted, or damaged cultural heritage in conflict areas by non-military personnel during the civil unrest that is a direct result of armed conflict, numerous cases researched here would likely qualify as violations of the 1954 Hague Convention. There is one case that, had the U.S. ratified the 1954 Convention sooner, the offender would have potentially been able to be prosecuted as a violator of the Hague Convention. Based on the research conducted, the enforcement of the 1954 Hague Convention in the U.S. has been limited since its recent ratification in 2009. More legal research is needed to identify the sanctions and consequences associated with violating the 1954 Hague Convention as a member of the U.S. military, as well as its application in other countries.

There are other areas for improvement, such as legally mandating accessible inventories and databases, as well as frequent, routine synchronization by governments, museums, academics, and collectors. This step would enhance provenance research transparency and help to avoid future cases like that of *United States v. Mask of Ka-Nefer-Nefer*, 2012, where authorities were unable to detect the Mask's loss or subsequent movements for several years. Similarly, implementing a type of 'Blacklist' that outlines dealers and collectors who have irrefutably worked with known or convicted smugglers would change the social acceptance of the trade's actors and their future participation in infiltrating the legal market. Moreover, it would aid in the due diligence of museums, auction houses, and other institutions pursuing legal antiquities. Both suggestions would fall under the stipulations in Article 5 (a)–(g) and Article 10 of the 1970 Convention for States Parties about the functions and measures States Parties should implement to safeguard cultural heritage.

Moving forward, this database methodology presents and accessible framework for more closely investigating the multifaceted impacts cultural policies have on the continuation of the illicit antiquities market. The statistics gathered here tangibly reinforce many pre-existing and presumed notions expressed amongst academics, such as Brodie et al. (2021) and Mackenzie et al. (2019), highlighting that the trade is not adequately deterred by current cultural property policies. As current policies are ineffective and given that conflict is on the rise in the Middle East and North Africa, it is clear that more significant resources and education need to be dedicated to publicly and legally condoning illicit antiquities collection to help stop the trade from the demand side.

References

Adams G (2019) Dark side of the boom: the excesses of the art market in the 21st century. Lund Humphries, London

Al-Azm A, Paul K (2019) Facebook's black market in antiquities: trafficking, terrorism, and war crimes. ATHAR Project. https://atharproject.org/wp-content/uploads/2019/06/ATHAR-FB-Report-June-2019-final.pdf

Art Loss Register (n.d.) The world's largest private database of stolen art. Art Loss Register. https://www.artloss.com/

Bogdanos M (2016) Thieves of Baghdad: and the terrorists they finance. In: Charney N (ed) Art crime. Palgrave Macmillan, London. https://doi.org/10.1007/978-1-137-40757-3_10

Bogdanos M, Patrick W (2006) Thieves of Baghdad: one marine's passion to recover the world's greatest stolen treasures (reprint). Bloomsbury USA

Brodie N (2011) Congenial bedfellows? The academy and the antiquities trade. J Contemp Crim Justice 27:408–437

Brodie N (2017) The role of conservators in facilitating the theft and trafficking of cultural objects: the case of a seized Libyan statue. Libyan Stud 48:117–123

Brodie N, Contreras DA (2012) The economics of the looted archaeological site of Bâb edh-Dhrâ': a view from Google earth. In: Lazrus PK, Barker AW (eds) All the King's horses: looting, antiquities trafficking and the integrity of the archaeological record. Society for American Archaeology, Washington, DC, pp 9–24

Brodie N, Kersel MM, Mackenzie S, Sabrine I, Smith E, Yates D (2021) Why there is still an illicit trade in cultural objects and what we can do about it. J Field Archaeol 47(2):117–130. https://doi.org/10.1080/00934690.2021.1996979

Burroughs T (2019) US and EU efforts to combat international money laundering in the art market are no masterpiece. Vand J Transnatl Law 52:1061–1096

Campbell PB (2013) The illicit antiquities trade as a transnational criminal network: characterizing and anticipating trafficking of cultural heritage. Int J Cult Prop 20:113–153

Casana J, Laugier EJ (2017) Satellite imagery-based monitoring of archaeological site damage in the Syrian civil war. PloS one, 12(11), e0188589.

Central Intelligence Agency (n.d.) Country data codes [Review of country data codes]. The World Factbook; Central Intelligence Agency. Country Data Codes - The World Factbook. (n.d.). https://www.cia.gov/the-world-factbook/references/country-data-codes/. Accessed 19 October 2024

de Jesus Hoiça J, de Camargo Guedes SPL, de Oliveira Areas P (2021) Armed conflicts and the repatriation of cultural property: global democratic challenges. Revista Confluências Culturais 10(2):83–94

Eko (2011). A closer look at the case against Mousa "Morris" Khouli and the Greco-Roman coffin. Lawyer Future. https://lawyerfuture.blogspot.com/2011/07/closer-look-at-case-against-mousa.html

Felch J, Frammolino R (2011) Chasing aphrodite. Houghton Mifflin Harcourt

Gerstenblith P (2013) The meaning of 1970 for the acquisition of archaeological objects. J Field Archaeol 38(4):364–373

Gerstenblith P (2022) Hobby Lobby, the Museum of the Bible and the law: a case study of the looting of archaeological artifacts from Iraq. In: Antiquities smuggling in the real and virtual world. Routledge, pp 59–95

Greenland F, Marrone JV, Topçuoğlu O, Vorderstrasse T (2019) A site-level market model of the antiquities trade. Int J Cult Prop 26(1):21–47

Hoffman BT (2006) Introduction: exploring and establishing links for a balanced art and cultural heritage policy. In: Art and cultural heritage - law, policy, and practice. Cambridge University Press, pp 1–18

Holmes, H (2022) The louvre Abu Dhabi is rocked by antiquities trafficking scandal. The Daily Beast. https://www.thedailybeast.com/the-louvre-abu-dhabi-is-rockedby-antiquities-trafficking-scandal

In the Matter of a Grand Jury Investigation into a Private New York Antiquities Collector, Statement of Facts. (N.Y. Sup. Ct. December 06, 2021)
In the Matter of Items Seized from the Metropolitan Museum of Art (N.Y. Sup. Ct. Sept. 22, 2017) Am. Compl. Beierwaltes v. Director General of Antiquities of the Lebanese Republic, No. 1:17-cv-04755 (S.D.N.Y. 2017)
In the Matter of Items Seized from the Park Avenue Armory (N.Y. Sup. Ct. July 23, 2018)
International Foundation for Art Research-Case Law (n.d.) International Foundation for Art Research. https://ifar.org/case_law.php?ID=12. Accessed 14 August 2022
Kersel MM (2007) Transcending borders: objects on the move. Archaeologies 3(2):81–98
Kuzma W (2019) Potentiating loopholes: how erratic and piecemeal implementation of the 1970 UNESCO convention has failed to protect cultural antiquities. Colum J Law Arts 501:501–518. https://journals.library.columbia.edu/index.php/lawandarts/article/view/1986/952
Lehr D (2019) Art and antiquities: conduits for money laundering and terrorist financing. ACAMS Today. https://www.acamstoday.org/art-and-antiquities-conduits-for-money-laundering-and-terrorist-financing/. Accessed 28 August 2022
Mackenzie S (2011) The market as criminal and criminals in the market: reducing opportunities for organised crime in the international antiquities market. In: Crime in the art and antiquities world. Springer, New York, pp 69–85
Mackenzie, S. (2019). White-collar crime, organised crime and the challenges of doing research on art crime. The Palgrave handbook on art crime, 839–853, Palgrave Macmillan UK
Mackenzie S, Yates D (2016) What is grey about the 'Grey market' in antiquities. In: Beckert J, Dewey M (eds) The architecture of illegal markets: towards an economic sociology of illegality in the economy. Oxford University Press, pp 70–86
Mackenzie S, Brodie N, Yates D, Tsirogiannis C (2019) Trafficking culture: new directions in researching the global market in illicit antiquities, 1st edn. Routledge
Mercadier, S., Shiaa, M., and Koli, A. (2020). Coronavirus: Iraq's heritage sites suffer renewed wave of looting amid pandemic. Middle East Eye. https://www.middleeasteye.net/news/iraq-looting-heritage-culture-coronavirus
Muñoz, P. (2018). El «niño prodigio» del arte antiguo que financió a Daesh.abc.https://www.abc.es/espana/abci-nino-prodigio-arte-antiguo-financio-daesh201804010202_noticia.html
Parcak S, Gathings D, Childs C, Mumford G, Cline E (2016) Satellite evidence of archaeological site looting in Egypt: 2002–2013. Antiquity 90(349):188–205. https://doi.org/10.15184/aqy.2016.1
Pearlstein WG (2014) White paper: a proposal to reform U.S. law and policy relating to the international exchange of cultural property. Cardozo Arts Ent Law J 32(2):561–650
Prott LV (2012) Strengths and weaknesses of the 1970 convention: an evaluation 40 years after its adoption. UNESCO
Rothfield L (2008) Hague ratification: fighting the last war? The punching bag: thoughts on cultural heritage, cultural economics, and cultural politics. http://larryrothfield.blogspot.com/2008/
S. Rep. No 110-26 (2008) https://www.congress.gov/110/crpt/erpt26/CRPT-110erpt26.pdf
Salehijam M (2018) The value of systematic content analysis in legal research. Tilburg Law Rev 23(1–2):34–42. https://doi.org/10.5334/tilr.5
Snyder C (2019) Out of context: examining the role of context in active enforcement foreign patrimony law disputes. Columbia Law Rev 119(1):205–248
St. Hilaire R (2013) Jail or no jail? Sentencing arguments filed in US v. Khouli. Cultural Heritage Lawyer Rick St. Hilaire. https://culturalheritagelawyer.blogspot.com/2012/11/jail-or-no-jail-sentencing-arguments.html
The Republic of Turkey's Claim Against the Museum of Fine Arts, Boston for the Statue of Herakles, Settled in 2011
The Republic of Turkey v. Metropolitan Museum of Art, 762 F. Supp. 44 (S.D.N.Y. 1990)
The Republic of Turkey v. OKS Partners, 797 F. Supp. 64 (D. Mass. 1992) (denying motion to dismiss), discovery motion granted in part and denied in part, 146 F.R.D. 24 (D. Mass. 1993), summary judgment denied, No. 89-CV-2061, 1994 U.S. Dist. LEXIS 17032 (D. Mass. June 8,

1994), summary judgment on different claims denied, No. 89-CV-3061- RGS, 1998 U.S. Dist. LEXIS 23526 (D. Mass. Jan. 23, 1998). Settled in 1999
UNESCO (1954) 1954 Convention. https://www.unesco.org/en/node/66328
UNESCO (2021) Convention on the means of prohibiting and preventing the illicit import, export, and transfer of ownership of cultural property. https://en.unesco.org/about-us/legal-affairs/convention-means-prohibiting-and-preventing-illicit-import-export-and. Accessed 16 June 2022
UNESCO (2022a). States parties. https://en.unesco.org/protecting-heritage/convention-and-protocols/states-parties
UNESCO (2022b) Legal texts on illicit trafficking. https://en.unesco.org/fighttrafficking/legal-texts. Accessed 23 July 2022
U.S. Department of State (n.d.) Current agreements and import restrictions. Bureau of Educational and Cultural Affairs. https://eca.state.gov/cultural-heritage-center/cultural-property/current-agreements-and-import-restrictions. Accessed 16 June 2022
UN Environment (2019) Approach to assessment of policy effectiveness [online]. In: Global environment Outlook 6. Cambridge University Press, pp 273–281.https://doi.org/10.1017/9781108627146
United States v. Four Hundred Fifty Ancient Cuneiform Tablets, No. 1:17-cv-03980 (E.D.N.Y. July 6, 2017)
United States v. Gordon, No. 1:11-cr-00517 (E.D.N.Y. June 12, 2014)
United States v. Johnson, No. 08-CR-00491, (S.D.N.Y. Sept. 22, 2008)
United States v. Khouli, CR-11-340, (E.D.N.Y. Jan. 9, 2013)
United States v. Mask of Ka-Nefer-Nefer, No. 11-cv-504 (HEA) (E.D. Mo. March 31, 2012), aff'd, Civ. No. 12-2578 (8th Cir., Jun. 12, 2014)
United States v. One Cuneiform Tablet Known as the "Gilgamesh Dream Tablet," No. 1:20-cv-02222 (E.D.N.Y. July 26, 2021)
United States v. Schultz, 178 F. Supp 2d 445 (S.D.N.Y. 2002), aff'd, 333 F.3d (2d Cir.2003), cert. denied, 540 U.S. 1106 (2004)
van Duyne PC, Louwe L, Soudijn M (2015) Money, art, and laundering: coming to grips with the risks. In: Balcells M, Kila J (eds) Cultural property crime: an overview and analysis on contemporary perspectives and trends. Brill, pp 79–95
Van Lit T (2016) Destruction, plunder, and trafficking of cultural property and heritage by Islamic state in Syria and Iraq—a war crimes perspective. Dutch National Police, Driebergen
Vlasic MV, DeSousa JP (2018) The illicit antiquities trade and terrorism financing: from the Khmer Rouge to Daesh. In: King C et al (eds) The Palgrave handbook of criminal and terrorism financing law. Palgrave Macmillan, pp 1167–1191
Williams M, Wiggins RD, Vogt WP (2022) Beginning quantitative research. Sage

Melissa N. Metzgar is a provenance researcher with Odyssey Global Consulting, LLC. Beginning with a dual Bachelor of Arts in Art History and Anthropology from Kutztown University of Pennsylvania, she also holds a Master of Arts in Art History from John Cabot University and a Master of Arts in Cultural Heritage from the American University of Rome. Since 2019, she has worked with the Alliance for Restoration of Cultural Heritage; the Qatar National Library; the Association for Research into Crimes Against Art; and the United Nations Interregional Crime and Justice Research Institute, where her research has primarily focused on heritage in the MENA region, trafficking networks, and the impacts of legal policy. Melissa's research aims to contribute towards fostering the expansion of public resources and education on the trade in art and cultural heritage.

Open Access This chapter is licensed under the terms of the Creative Commons Attribution-NonCommercial-NoDerivatives 4.0 International License (http://creativecommons.org/licenses/by-nc-nd/4.0/), which permits any noncommercial use, sharing, distribution and reproduction in any medium or format, as long as you give appropriate credit to the original author(s) and the source, provide a link to the Creative Commons license and indicate if you modified the licensed material. You do not have permission under this license to share adapted material derived from this chapter or parts of it.

The images or other third party material in this chapter are included in the chapter's Creative Commons license, unless indicated otherwise in a credit line to the material. If material is not included in the chapter's Creative Commons license and your intended use is not permitted by statutory regulation or exceeds the permitted use, you will need to obtain permission directly from the copyright holder.

MIX
Papier aus verantwortungsvollen Quellen
Paper from responsible sources
FSC® C105338

If you have any concerns about our products,
you can contact us on
ProductSafety@springernature.com

In case Publisher is established outside the EU,
the EU authorized representative is:
Springer Nature Customer Service Center GmbH
Europaplatz 3, 69115 Heidelberg, Germany

Printed by Libri Plureos GmbH
in Hamburg, Germany